Portraits of Old Russia

Dedication

M.P. To the memory of Richard Hellie.

D.O.: To my father Anthony Ostrowski, who inspired me to become a historian.

PORTRAITS OF OLD RUSSIA

IMAGINED LIVES OF ORDINARY PEOPLE, 1300—1725

DONALD OSTROWSKI AND MARSHALL T. POE

M.E.Sharpe
Armonk, New York
London, England

Copyright © 2011 by M.E. Sharpe, Inc.

All rights reserved. No part of this book may be reproduced in any form without written permission from the publisher, M.E. Sharpe, Inc., 80 Business Park Drive, Armonk, New York 10504.

Library of Congress Cataloging-in-Publication Data

Portraits of old Russia : imagined lives of ordinary people, 1300-1725 / edited by Donald Ostrowski and Marshall T. Poe.
   p. cm.
Includes bibliographical references and index.
   ISBN 978-0-7656-2728-5 (cloth : alk. paper) — ISBN 978-0-7656-2729-2 (pbk. : alk. paper)
   1. Russia—Social life and customs. 2. Russia—History—To 1533—Biography. 3. Russia—History—1533-1613—Biography. 4. Russia—History—1613-1917—Biography. 5. Imaginary biography. 6. Social classes—Russia—History. I. Ostrowski, Donald G. II. Poe, Marshall T.
DK32.P67 2011
947—dc22   2010044379

Printed in the United States of America

The paper used in this publication meets the minimum requirements of
American National Standard for Information Sciences
Permanence of Paper for Printed Library Materials,
ANSI Z 39.48-1984.

∞

IBT (c)   10   9   8   7   6   5   4   3   2   1
SP (p)   10   9   8   7   6   5   4   3

Contents

Chronology of Old Russia from 1304 to 1725	vii
Map of Muscovy	xxii
Introduction	
Donald Ostrowski	xxiii

I. Members of Ruling Families

1. Anna Koltovskaia: A Russian Tsaritsa
 Russell E. Martin — 3
2. Memoir of a Tatar Prince: Ismail ibn Ahmed
 Donald Ostrowski — 14
3. Gleb Vasilievich: A Prince in Fourteenth-Century Yaroslavl
 Lawrence N. Langer — 24

II. Government Servitors

4. A Dialogue Between Two Seventeenth-Century Boyars
 Marshall T. Poe — 37
5. The Power of Knowledge: *Vita* of the Secretary Andrei Putilov
 Sergei Bogatyrev — 44
6. Larka the Clerk
 Peter B. Brown — 56

III. Military Personnel

7. "My Brilliant Career": Autobiography of a Career Army Officer
 Carol B. Stevens — 71
8. The Life of a Foreign Mercenary Officer
 W.M. Reger IV — 81
9. Vasilii Zotov: A Military Colonist on the Southern Frontier
 Brian Davies — 92

IV. Church Prelates

10. A Seventeenth-Century Prelate: Metropolitan Pavel of Sarai and the Don
 Cathy J. Potter — 105
11. Vasilii Kalika, Archbishop of Novgorod (r. 1330–52)
 Michael C. Paul — 116

V. Monks

12. Holy Images for the Grand Prince
    Michael S. Flier — 129
13. Three Scholars at the Kirillo-Belozersk Monastery: A Teacher, a Student, and a Librarian
    Robert Romanchuk — 139
14. Greeks in Seventeenth-Century Russia
    Nikolaos A. Chrissidis — 154
15. Akakii Balandin of Novgorod-Volotovo and Solovki Monasteries (1526–95)
    David M. Goldfrank — 165

VI. Provincial Landowners, Artisans, and Townspeople

16. Provincial Landowners as Litigants
    Nancy S. Kollmann — 179
17. Artisans: The Prokofiev Family
    J.T. Kotilaine — 188
18. A Poor Townswoman Accused of Witchcraft
    Valerie Kivelson — 198

VII. Siberian Explorer and Trader

19. S.U. Remezov, Cossack Adventurer, and the Opening of Siberia
    Christoph Witzenrath — 209
20. A Siberian Trader: Urasko Kaibulin
    Erika Monahan — 222

VIII. Peasants, Slaves, Serfs, and Holy Fools

21. The Parfiev Family: Northern Free Peasants
    Jennifer B. Spock — 233
22. Muscovite Lives: A Slave and a Serf
    Richard Hellie — 243
23. Dunia, a Fool for Christ
    Hugh M. Olmsted — 252

Glossary
    Hugh M. Olmsted — 271

On the Use and History of Personal Names in Muscovy
    Hugh M. Olmsted — 279

Transcription and Pronunciation Guide for Russian Names
    Hugh M. Olmsted — 291

About the Editors and the Contributors — 301
Index — 307

Chronology of Old Russia from 1304 to 1725

Early modern Russians adopted the Byzantine calendar and counted years from the Creation, 5508 years before Christ's birth. They regarded September 1 as their New Year. Therefore, to convert an Old Russian year into a Julian or Gregorian calendar year, 5508 years, for the period between January 1 and August 31, would be subtracted from, say, 7134 (or 134 since the Muscovites frequently eliminated the initial thousandth's column) and 5509 years would be subtracted for the portion of the Old Russian year between September 1 and December 31.

Events related specifically to individuals in *Portraits* are given in **bold typeface**.

1304	Grand Prince Andrei Aleksandrovich dies; Mikhail Iaroslavich of Tver becomes grand prince; Iurii Daniilovich becomes prince of Moscow.
1315	Iurii Daniilovich summoned to Sarai, remains there two years, marries Konchaka (Agrafa), sister of Khan Özbeg; Novgorod sends 50,000 grivnas of silver to Grand Prince Mikhail.
1317	Iurii marches against Tver; Mikhail of Tver defeats Iurii; Agrafa captured, dies a prisoner in Tver.
1318	Grand Prince Mikhail Iaroslavich executed by Khan Özbeg; Iurii Daniilovich of Moscow made grand prince.
1320–22	Rostov and Yaroslavl uprisings.
1322	Khan Özbeg deprives Iurii Daniilovich of grand princely patent and makes Dmitrii Mikhailovich of Tver grand prince.
1325	Grand Prince Dmitrii kills Prince Iurii of Moscow; Ivan Daniilovich becomes prince of Moscow.
1326	Aleksandr Mikhailovich becomes grand prince of Vladimir; Khan Özbeg orders the execution of Grand Prince Dmitrii Mikhailovich in Sarai for murder of Iurii; Cathedral of the Assumption founded in Moscow; Metropolitan Peter dies.

1327	Aleksandr Mikhailovich relieved of grand princely patent; uprising in Tver and again in Rostov; grand prince takes over duties of baskaks in certain areas of Rus.
1328	Ivan Daniilovich of Moscow becomes grand prince of Vladimir; Feognost becomes metropolitan of Rus.
1330	**Archbishop of Novgorod Moisei steps down and retires to a monastery; Vasilii Kalika becomes archbishop of Novgorod** (chap. 11); Savior of the Forest Church constructed in Moscow.
1332	Stone Church of the Archangel Michael replaces wooden one in Moscow kremlin; stone Church of St. John Climacus built in the Moscow kremlin; Grand Prince Ivan travels to Sarai.
1333	Vychegod and Pechora begin paying tribute to Moscow.
1337	**In Novgorod, a mob attacks Archimandrite Efim, who has taken refuge in the Church of St. Nicholas on the Market** (chap. 11).
1338	**Great Bridge in Novgorod over the Volkhov River swept away in a flood** (chap. 11).
1339	Aleksandr Mikhailovich, prince of Tver, executed in Sarai.
ca. 1340	**Birth of Theophanes (Feofan Grek)** (chap. 12).
1341	Grand Prince Ivan I (Kalita) dies; Semen Ivanovich becomes grand prince; **death of Evdokia Ivanovna, daughter of Ivan I and mother of Gleb Vasilievich** (chap. 3).
1342	**Fire in Novgorod followed by widespread looting; the archbishop and the hegumens of the monasteries call a fast and hold processions and prayer services at various monasteries around the city** (chap. 11).
1345	**Death of Vasilii Davidovich, prince of Yaroslavl and father of Gleb Vasilievich** (chap. 3).
1347	Grand Prince Semen pays cost of repairing St. Sophia Cathedral in Constantinople.
1351	Grand Prince Semen's sons die of the plague.
1352	Grand Prince Semen (the Proud) dies of the plague; **Vasilii Kalika, archbishop of Novgorod, dies** (chap. 11).
1353	Ivan Ivanovich, the younger brother of Semen, becomes grand prince; Metropolitan Feognost dies.
1359	Grand Prince Ivan II (the Meek) dies; Dmitrii Konstantinovich of Suzdal appointed grand prince; Metropolitan Aleksei becomes regent for Dmitrii of Moscow; death of Janibeg, khan of the Ulus of Jochi.
1363	Khan Mürid appoints Dmitrii of Moscow as grand prince, then changes mind, because the emir Mamai supports Dmitrii; Mürid reappoints Dmitrii of Suzdal instead.
1364	Rostov, Ustiug, and Ustiug's possessions in Velikaia Perm begin paying tribute to Moscow; plague in Nizhnii Novgorod.
1365	Riazan defeats Tatar raiding force; plague kills Konstantin, prince of Rostov.

1366	Fire destroys much of Moscow.
1367	Palad driven off from Nizhnii Novgorod; stone replaces wood in fortification of the Moscow kremlin; Velikaia Perm, Mezen, and Kegrola begin paying tribute to Moscow.
1368	Algirdas (Olgerd), grand duke of Lithuania, besieges Moscow.
1370	Algirdas besieges Moscow again.
1372	Tver–Moscow war begins; **Yaroslavl is plundered by** *ushkuinniki* (chap. 3).
1373	Mamai lays waste Riazan.
1374	Mamai's envoys and 1,500 Tatars killed at Nizhnii Novgorod; Vasilii Veliaminov, the last *tysiatskii*, dies in Moscow; Urus becomes khan of the Ulus of Jochi.
1375	Nizhnii Novgorod devastated; treaty between Dmitrii of Moscow and Mikhail of Tver.
1376	Dmitrii compels Kazan to pay him to raise the siege; first Toqtaqyia, then Temur Melik becomes khan of the Ulus of Jochi.
1377	Rus force routed on the Piana; Grand Duke of Lithuania Algirdas dies; Jagiełło (Jagailo) becomes grand duke of Lithuania.
1378	Tatars burn Nizhnii Novgorod; Dmitrii wins on the Vozha; Metropolitan Aleksei dies; **Feofan Grek paints the frescoes in Novgorod's Church of the Savior on Elijah Street** (chap. 12).
1379	Pimen becomes metropolitan of Rus.
1380	Battle of Kulikovo Field. **Gleb Vasilievich may have participated and even been killed there** (chap. 3); Dmitrii imprisons Metropolitan Pimen.
1381	Toqtamysh defeats Mamai at the Kalka River; Kiprian becomes metropolitan of Moscow.
1382	Toqtamysh sacks Moscow.
1385	Metropolitan Kiprian travels to Sarai.
1386	Novgorod placed under tribute by Dmitrii of Moscow; Jagiełło marries Jadwiga, uniting Lithuania with Poland.
1388	Metropolitan Theognostus of Trebizond travels to Moscow seeking donations.
1389	Grand Prince Dmitrii (Donskoi) dies; Vasilii I becomes grand prince; Metropolitan Pimen dies; Kiprian (Cyprian) becomes metropolitan of all Rus'.
1390	Vasilii I marries Sofia, daughter of Vytautus (Vitovt) of Lithuania.
1391	Sergei of Radonezh dies.
1393	Vytautus becomes grand duke of Lithuania; Patriarch of Constantinople Antonios writes letter upbraiding Vasilii I.
1395	Timur invades Ulus of Jochi.
1397	**Kirillo-Belozersk Monastery founded** (chap. 13).

1398	Vasilii I sends money to Constantinople to help in the defense against the Ottoman Turks.
1399	Battle on River Vorskla; Vytautas defeated by Timur Qutlug; **Feofan Grek heads team that decorates Moscow's kremlin Cathedral of the Archangel Michael** (chap. 12).
1401	Sadi Beg becomes khan of the Ulus of Jochi.
1405	**Feofan Grek heads team that decorates Moscow's Assumption Cathedral** (chap. 12).
1406	Metropolitan Kiprian dies.
1408	Treaty between Moscow and Lithuania; Edigei's expedition against Moscow; Fotii (Photius) becomes metropolitan of Rus.
1410	Battle of Tannenberg; Teutonic knights defeat Vytautas; Temur becomes khan of the Ulus of Jochi.
1415	**Letter by the hagiographer Epifanii the Most Wise to Kirill, the archimandrite of the Savior-Afanasii Monastery in the city of Tver** (chap. 12).
1417	Jeremferden becomes khan of the Ulus of Jochi.
1425	Vasilii I dies; Vasilii II becomes grand prince.
1427	Kirill of Belozero, founder of the Kirillo-Belozersk Monastery, dies; **St. Aleksandr Oshevenskii is born in the village of Vazheozerskaia and named Aleksei** (chap. 13).
1430	Vytautas, grand duke of Lithuania, dies.
1431	Iurii, brother of Vasilii I, claims throne from Vasilii II; Metropolitan Fotii dies; Iurii and Vasilii travel to Sarai to have Khan Ulug Mehmed decide the succession.
1432	Ulug Mehmed decides in favor of Vasilii, who is installed in Moscow as grand prince by a Jochid.
1433	Iurii gives up claim but reconsiders; Sajjid Ahmed claims to be khan (until 1465).
1434	Iurii dies after defeating Vasilii II in battle; **Khristofor, hegumen of the Kirillo-Belozersk Monastery, dies; Trifon becomes hegumen** (chap. 13).
1436	Vasilii II orders the blinding of Vasilii Kosoi, his cousin; Isidor becomes metropolitan; Josef Barbaro visits Riazan and Kolomna.
1437	Council of Florence begins; Ulug Mehmed defeats Rus at Belev.
1439	Council of Florence ends; Ulug Mehmed besieges Moscow.
1440	Casimir becomes grand duke of Lithuania; **sometime in the 1440s Oleshka Palkin heads a secondary school at the Kirillo-Belozersk Monastery and composes colophon to a codex of the *Grammatica* of Serbian monks and *Dialectica* of John Damascene** (chap. 13).
1441	Metropolitan Isidor returns to Moscow; after conducting church service in Catholic manner, he is forced to flee from Moscow.

1445	Ulug Mehmed captures Vasilii II at Battle of Suzdal; Mahmeduk, Ulug Mehmed's son, captures Kazan from Ulus of Jochi; Crimean khanate breaks away from Ulus of Jochi; Moscow fire; **Aleksei from Vashe-ozerskaia (the future St. Aleksandr Oshevenskii) begins secondary-school education under the Kirillo-Belozersk *d'iak* Oleshka Palkin** (chap. 13).
1446	Ulug Mehmed allows Vasilii II to return to Rus after taking a ransom of 20,000 rubles; Dmitrii Iurievich Shemiaka seizes throne, and blinds Vasilii II.
1447	Vasilii II ousts Shemiaka from Moscow, resumes rule; Mahmeduk driven off from Moscow; Casimir IV becomes king of Poland.
1448	Council of bishops elects Iona as Metropolitan; **Trifon expelled as hegumen of Kirillo-Belozersk Monastery; Kassian becomes hegumen** (chap. 13).
1449	Vasilii II declares his son Ivan coruler; Casimir IV signs treaties with Vasilii II and Boris Aleksandrovich of Tver. Vasilii II concludes treaty with Ivan Vasilievich of Suzdal.
1450	Shemiaka driven off from attack on Moscow, seeks refuge in Novgorod.
1451	Sajjid Ahmed driven off from attack on Moscow.
1452	Khanate of Kasimov established; Tatars accept Rus suzerainty at Kasimov; Vasilii II writes to Byzantine Emperor Constantine XI.
1453	April 9: Moscow and the entire kremlin burn; May 29: Constantinople falls to Ottoman Turks; Dmitrii Shemiaka dies in Novgorod.
1456	Vasilii II imposes fine and treaty on Novgorod limiting *veche*.
1459	Vasilii II conquers Viatka, but Viatka reasserts independence.
1461	Metropolitan Iona writes letter to Khan Mahmud of Kazan; Metropolitan Iona dies; Feodosii becomes metropolitan.
1462	Vasilii II dies; Ivan III becomes grand prince.
1463	Ivan III obtains submission of Yaroslavl.
1464	Ivan's daughter Anna marries prince of Riazan; Metropolitan Feodosii resigns; Filipp becomes metropolitan.
1465	Tatar punitive expedition stopped in border area; Ahmed becomes khan of the Ulus of Jochi.
1466	Halil chosen khan of Kazan.
1467	Ivan III sends army to help friendly khan at Kasimov, but fails; Halil, khan of Kazan, dies; Ibrahim chosen khan of Kazan.
1468	Ivan III refuses Pskov a separate bishop; Ivan III presents Great Zion to Assumption Cathedral.
1469	Ivan III sends army against Kazan; fails twice to take Kazan.
1470	Novgorod turns to Casimir IV for help.
1471	Ivan III advances on Novgorod; Battle on Shelon River; treaty between Moscow and Novgorod.

1472	Ivan III captures Perm; Ivan marries Zoe (Sophia); Ivan inherits Dmitrov.
1473	Metropolitan Filipp dies; Gerontii becomes metropolitan.
1474	Muscovy obtains Rostov.
1475	Ivan III comes to Novgorod; Aristotle Fioroventi arrives in Moscow; Crimean khan recognizes suzerainty of Ottoman sultan.
1476	Ambrogio Contarini, Venetian ambassador, visits Moscow; Ivan III enters Novgorod to take action against plague.
1478	Great bell of Novgorod taken to Moscow.
1479	Ibrahim, khan of Kazan, dies; Ilham chosen khan of Kazan.
1480	Ivan III encounters Khan Ahmed at Ugra River; Andrei and Boris, brothers of Ivan III, threaten to go over to the grand duke of Lithuania, but eventually come to terms with Ivan; **monks of Kirillo-Belozersk Monastery, including the hieromonk and elder Efrosin, compile a catalog of the monastery's liturgical books in the 1480s** (chap. 13).
1481	Andrei of Vologda bequeaths estate to Ivan III; Khan Ahmed is killed; Murteza and his brother Sajjid Ahmed II, and their half-brother Šaih Ahmed all claim to be khans of the Ulus of Jochi.
1482	**Ismail ibn Ahmed born** (chap. 2).
1483	Mikhail of Tver declares himself "younger brother" of Ivan III; Ivan begins confiscations of lands in Novgorod.
1485	Ivan III captures Tver; Prince Mikhail flees to Lithuania; Ilham deposed as khan of Kazan and Mehmed Emin chosen as khan of Kazan.
1486	Mehmed Emin deposed as khan of Kazan and Ilham chosen khan of Kazan again.
1487	Ivan III sends army against Kazan; Ilham deposed as khan again and Mehmed Emin chosen as khan of Kazan again; Kudai Kul becomes hostage of Ivan III.
1489	Viatka submits to Moscow; Metropolitan Gerontii dies; Nicholaus Poppel meets with Ivan III; Cathedral of Annunciation in the Moscow kremlin is completed.
1490	Ivan III makes agreement with Holy Roman Emperor against Poland; Ivan Molodoi, son of Ivan III, dies; Zosima becomes metropolitan; church council investigates charges of heresy.
1491	Ivan III and Crimean Tatars crush Sarai Tatars.
1492	Casimir IV dies; Muscovite–Lithuanian hostilities Metropolitan Zosima begins to refer to Ivan III as autocrat (*samoderzhets*).
1493	Uglich absorbed; Ivan assumes title Sovereign (*gosudar*) over Novgorod; Russo-Danish alliance;
1494	Muscovite campaign against Lithuania; Zosima resigns as metropolitan; Ivan III closes off Novgorod to Hansa.
1495	Grand Duke of Lithuania Alexander marries Ivan's daughter Elena; Simon becomes metropolitan.

CHRONOLOGY xiii

1496	War with Swedes; Muscovy sends ambassador to Ottoman empire; Mehmed Emin, khan of Kazan, flees to Moscow when Kazan attacked by Khan Mamuk of the Siberian khanate.
1497	*Sudebnik* (Law Code) issued; Truce with Swedes; Abdullatif chosen khan of Kazan.
1498	Dmitrii, grandson of Ivan III, installed as coruler.
1499	Ahmed becomes khan of the Ulus of Jochi; Ivan III ends Novgorod's connection with Hanseatic League.
1500	Muscovite campaign against Lithuania; Battle of Vedrosha River.
1501	Rus forces subdue Livonians at Helmed; **the monk German Podolnyi departs and lives beyond the Kirillo-Belozersk Monastery for two years, four months, and three weeks** (chap. 13).
1502	The uluses and *ordu* of the Ulus of Jochi (Great Horde) submit to the Crimean Tatar Khan Mengli Girey in 1502; Ivan III arrests his grandson and co-ruler Dmitrii; Abdullatif, khan of Kazan, is deposed; Mehmed Emin chosen khan of Kazan a third time.
1503	Treaties with Lithuania and Livonia; church council concerning widower priests and simony.
1504	Leaders of Novgorod–Moscow heretics punished.
1505	Ivan III dies; Vasilii III becomes grand prince; Vasilii III marries Solomonia Saburova; new stone Church of the Archangel Michael constructed in Moscow kremlin; Mehmed Emin withdraws safe-conduct decree for Muscovite merchants and has them attacked in Kazan; Tsarevich Kudai Kul converts to Christianity, adopting the name Peter; **Efrosin's colophon written** (chap. 13).
1506	Kudai Kul/Peter marries Evdokia Ivanovna, sister of Vasilii III.
1508	Nil Sorskii dies.
1510	Vasilii III takes over Pskov.
1511	Metropolitan Simon resigns; Varlaam becomes metropolitan.
1512	War with Lithuania resumes.
1514	Vasilii III captures Smolensk. **Building of the St. Barbara Church (Tserkov' sviatoi Varvary) in Kitai-Gorod by the Italian architect Aloisio Lamberti da Montagna (Aleviz Friazin)** (chap. 23).
1515	Iosif of Volokolamsk dies; **construction of a new minster in the Savior's Transfiguration Monastery in Yaroslav** (chap. 5).
1517	Vasilii III acquires Riazan; Abdullatif, former khan of Kazan, dies.
1518	Maksim Grek arrives in Moscow; Patriarch Theoleptos of Constantinople refers to Vasilii III as tsar; Mehmed Emin, khan of Kazan, dies; Shah Ali chosen khan of Kazan. **Prince I. I. Kubenskii begins serving at court of Vasilii III** (chap. 5)
1521	Varlaam resigns as metropolitan; Muscovy incorporates Riazan; Shah Ali, khan of Kazan, is deposed; Sahib Girey chosen khan of Kazan;

	Ismail ibn Ahmed enters service of Muscovite grand prince (chap. 2); c rimean Tatars under Mehmed g irey attack Moscow.
1522	Daniil becomes metropolitan.
1523	Treaty with l ithuania conőrming Muscovite gains in 1514.
1524	Sahib g irey, khan of Kazan, goes to c onstantinople to gain support of the o ttoman sultan for making him khan of the c rimea. **Prince I.I. Kubenskii becomes head of Great Household Office** (chap. 5).
1525	Trial of Maksim g rek for heresy; marriage of Vasilii III and Solomonia annulled; Sefa g irey chosen khan of Kazan.
1526	Vasilii III marries Elena g linskaia; **birth of Andrei Putilov in Yaroslavl** (chap. 5).
1532	Sefa g irey, khan of Kazan, is deposed; c an Ali is chosen khan of Kazan.
1533	Vasilii III dies; his three-year-old son Ivan becomes grand prince under the regency of Elena g linskaia and the Boyar c ouncil.
1534	Beginning of war between Muscovy and l ithuania (July); brick wall built around Moscow's Kitai-gorod (őnished in 1538).
1535	**Andrei Putilov's father, Mikhail, wounded near Orsha** (chap. 5); c an Ali, khan of Kazan, dies; Sefa g irey chosen khan of Kazan a second time.
1537	End of war between Muscovy and l ithuania (January).
1538	Elena g linskaia dies; Vasilii Shuiskii becomes regent.
1539	Metropolitan Daniil is deposed; Ioasaf becomes metropolitan; Ivan Belskii becomes regent.
1541	**Andrei Putilov made a clerk in the Great Household Office** (chap. 5).
1542	Metropolitan Ioasaf is deposed; Makarii becomes metropolitan.
1545	**Andrei Putilov takes part in campaign against Kazan and as a reward is made a secretary in the Military Office** (chap. 5).
1546	Sefa g irey deposed as khan of Kazan; Shah Ali chosen khan of Kazan, then deposed; Sefa g irey chosen khan of Kazan a third time.
1547	Ivan IV marries Anastasia r omanovna after a bride show; Ivan crowned tsar; great őre in Moscow; Iurii g linskii killed by mob.
1549	Zemskii sobor meets; **Andrei Putilov marries Anastasia Pushechnikova (chap. 5)**; Sefa g irey, khan of Kazan, dies; o temish g irey chosen khan of Kazan with his mother Suyun Bike as regent.
1550	*Sudebnik* (l aw c ode) issued; **Dementii Parőev born** (chap. 21).
1551	Stoglav (100 c hapter) c hurch c ouncil meets; n ogai prince Belek Bulat sends letter in which he refers to Ivan IV as a c hinggisid; o temish g irey deposed as khan of Kazan; Shah Ali chosen khan of Kazan a third time.
1552	Shah Ali deposed as khan of Kazan; y adigar Mehmed chosen khan of Kazan; **Ismail ibn Ahmed writes memoirs** (chap. 2); Muscovy takes over Kazan.

	chronology xv
1553	English explorer richard chancellor reaches Moscow; Ivan gains oath from boyars.
1555	richard chancellor returns as ambassador of Queen Mary; Service land chancellery (*Pomestnyi prikaz*) established.
1555–61	**Construction of Pokrovskii Cathedral (later known as St. Basil's Cathedral) on what later became known as Red Square.**
1556	regulations for military service of gentry; Astrakhan taken; Embassy from Ivan IV to Sigismund II justiões Ivan's adoption of the title *tsar*.
1557	Vasilii Blazhennyi dies.
1558	Beginning of livonian War.
1560	**Dementii Parfiev's Uncle Konan dies; his cousin Ivan sent to Solovki Monastery** (chap. 21).
1561	Ivan IV marries Maria (Kochenei) Temriukovna.
1563	Polotsk captured; embassy of Afanasii n agoi to the crimean khan; Metropolitan Makarii dies.
1564	Afanasii (Andrei Protopopov) becomes metropolitan; Ivan leaves Moscow for Aleksandrova Sloboda; Prince Andrei Kurbskii defects; Ivan Fedorov prints ørst book in Moscow.
1565	Ivan IV establishes *Oprichnina*.
1566	Zemskii sobor meets; Metropolitan Afanasii resigns; german becomes metropolitan for two days before being ousted; Filipp becomes metropolitan.
1568	Synod deposes Metropolitan Filipp; Kirill becomes metropolitan.
1569	Union of lublin; Filipp, former metropolitan, murdered; ottoman empire attempts to capture Astrakhan; death of Maria Temriukovna, second wife of Ivan IV.
1570	oprichnina ravages novgorod; Ivan's proposition to Elizabeth of England; **death of Andrei Putilov** (chap. 5); **Father Aleksandr, priest of St. Nikita's Church in Moscow, tells Dunia about Vasilii Blazhennyi** (chap. 23).
1571	**Bride show in which Anna Koltovskaia** (chap. 1) **takes part**; Ivan IV marries Marfa Sobakina, his third wife, who dies a few weeks later; crimean Tatars under Devlet girei sack Moscow; **Daria Parfiev's husband Konstiantin dies** (chap. 21).
1572	church council decides Ivan IV can marry a fourth time but imposes a penance on him; Ivan IV abolishes *Oprichnina*; Ivan appoints Mikhail Kaibulich to head a recombined Boyar council; Sigismund Augustus dies; Metropoitan Kirill dies (February); Antonii becomes metropolitan; **Ivan IV marries Anna Koltovskaia, his fourth wife** (chap. 1); **Matrena and Okat Parfiev, the parents of Dementii, die of the plague** (chap. 21).

1573	c rimean Tatars stopped at l opasnia r iver; **the monk Akakii Balandin arrives at the Solovki Monastery from Novgorod (chap. 12). Dunia's birth** (chap. 23).
1574	**Anna Koltovskaia ordered to take the veil becomes the nun Daria of the Tikhvin Convent** (chap. 1).
1575	War with Swedes over Estonia; Stephan Batory elected to Polish throne; Ivan IV "appoints" Simeon Bekbulatovich as grand prince of all r us; Daniel Prinz visits Moscow as ambassador of h oly r oman Emperor.
1576	Ivan IV "takes back" his position and makes Simeon Bekbulatovich g rand Prince of Tver.
1578	Swedes defeat Muscovite forces at Wenden.
1579	Poles take Polotsk and Velikie l uki.
1580	Monasteries agree at a church council to register all new land acquisitions with the government in return for being allowed to keep all the lands they had at that point.
1581	Poles under Stefan Bathory take o strov and march as far as Pskov; Swedes take n arva; Ivan kills his son Ivan, the heir to the throne; Metropolitan Antonii dies; Dionisii becomes metropolitan.
1582	Truce with Poland; Antonio Possevino visits Moscow as ambassador of Pope g regory XIII; Ermak defeats khan of Sibir.
1583	Truce with the Swedes; Ermak presents western Siberia to Ivan IV; l ivonian War ends; **Nikon Dementiev *syn* born** (chap. 21).
1584	Ivan IV dies; Fedor begins rule.
1585	Arkhangelsk founded.
1586	Stephan Batory dies; Fedor's unsuccessful bid to become king of Poland; Metropolitan Dionisii deposed; Iov becomes metropolitan.
1588	Boris g odunov becomes effective ruler. **Vasilii Blazhennyi's glorification as Saint and reburial in Pokrovskii Cathedral** (chap. 23).
1589	Patriarchate of Moscow established; Iov becomes ȧrst patriarch of Moscow and all r us.
1590s	**Foma Karpov *syn* registered as a hereditary slave by his owner Bogdan Posnikovich Sheremetev in the great registration of all slaves required by the Muscovite government** (chap. 22).
1592	**Decree removes right of peasants to move on St. George's Day and sets statute of limitations on recovery of fugitive serfs at five years** (chap. 22).
1595	**Akakii Balandin dies** (chap. 15).
1598	Fedor dies; Boris g odunov chosen tsar by zemskii sobor. **Repose of St. Antonii Chernoezerskii** (chap. 23).
1605	Boris g odunov dies.
1606	Vasilii Shuiskii chosen tsar by zemskii sobor.

CHRONOLOGY xvii

1609	Swedes invade Russian North.
1610	Vasilii Shuiskii deposed by zemskii sobor; Polish Prince Władysław considered for Russian throne.
1611	Moscow fire; **Dementii Parfiev dies having been tonsured as the monk Dionisii** (chap. 16).
1613	Mikhail Romanov chosen tsar by zemskii sobor.
1619	Mikhail's father returns to Moscow from Polish imprisonment, becomes Patriarch Filaret and corules Muscovy with his son.
1623	**First evidence of Larka Lvitskii in the Service Land Chancellery** (chap. 6).
1624	**The *stol'nik* D.G. Gagarin goes to Tikhvin Convent bringing gifts for the nun Daria** (chap. 1).
1626	Moscow fire.
1627	**Larka Lvitskii marries the daughter of a fellow Service Land Chancellery clerk** (chap. 6).
1632	Beginning of Muscovite war with the Poles over Smolensk; Peter Mohyla establishes a school in Kiev based on the Jesuit model; Service Land Chancellery clerks petition the tsar for back pay.
1633	Patriarch Filaret dies.
1635	Military Chancellery decides to build garrison town, Kozlov.
1636	**Vasilii Zotov enters the tsar's service as a military colonist in Kozlov** (chap. 9).
1637	**Miachkov and fellow servicemen initiate a petition campaign for the repeal of the statute of limitations on runaway peasants** (chap. 22).
1639	Russian expedition of 20 men led by Ivan Moskvitin reaches Pacific at Sea of Okhotsk.
1640	Mohyla and Kozlovskyj publish the *Pravoslavnoe ispovedanie*; decree limits recruitment base of state secretaries and clerks.
1641	**Vaska, the husband of Osanka, dies of the plague** (chap. 15); **Miachkov and fellow servicemen renew their petition campaign for repeal of the statute of limitations on runaway peasants** (chap. 22).
1642	**Semen Ulianovich Remezov born** (chap. 19).
1642–44	Completion of iconography of the Dormition (Uspenskii) Cahedral in the Moscow kremlin; complaint of townspeople at zemskii sobor about state secretaries and clerks who are enriching themselves.
1643	**Tobolsk reduced to ashes by fire** (chap. 19).
1645	Mikhail dies; his son Aleksei chosen tsar; Mohyla publishes his *Short Catechism (Sbraniie korotkoi nauky. O artykulakh viry. Pravoslavnokafolycheskoi Khristiianskoi)* in Kiev; **Miachkov and his fellow servicemen renew their petition campaign for the repeal of the statute of limitations on runaway peasants** (chap. 22).

xviii   CHRONOLOGY

1646–47	General census.
1648	Riots in Moscow June 1–3; rebellion of Zaporozhian Cossacks begins under leadership of Bohdan Khmel′nyts′kyj; **Zemskii sobor begins work on formulating law code (*Ulozhenie*)** (chap. 22).
1649	**Zemskii sobor finishes formulating law code (*Ulozhenie*)** (chap. 22); Mohyla's *Short Catechism* reissued in Moscow; Monastery Chancellery (Monastyrskii prikaz) established in Moscow; Peter Mohyla dies; Nikon chosen metropolitan of Novgorod.
1650	Publication of a Russian Nomocanon (*Kormchaia kniga*).
1651	**Larka Lvitskii makes circuit journey around Moscow (last evidence)** (chap. 6); **Pavel appointed archpriest of the Church of the Reception in Moscow** (chap. 10).
1652	Patriarch Iosif dies; Nikon chosen patriarch; the Foreign Quarter (*nemetskaia sloboda*) is established; relics of former metropolitan Filipp brought to Moscow.
1653	Statute on Court Duties issued; Church council institutes reforms; Ivan Neronov and Avvakum exiled; revised edition of the Russian Nomocanon published; Printing Office publishes a Psalter (February); Tsar Aleksei places Patriarkh Nikon in charge of Printing Office (December).
1654	Beginning of Thirteen Years War between Poland and Muscovy; church council (March) takes up correction of texts and revision of church manuals; cholera breaks out in Moscow and surrounding regions; Pereiaslav Agreement signed; Arsenii Sukhanov makes trip to Mt. Athos to buy books and manuscripts.
1655	Church council takes up issue of book correction again; Makarios, the patriarch of Antioch, arrives in Moscow; **Archdeacon Meletios comes to Moscow** (chap. 11); plague hits Moscow.
1656	Beginning of war between Sweden and Muscovy; church council (May) supports Nikon; Ivan Neronov tried and condemned; **Vasilii Prokofiev born on March 15** (chap. 14).
1657	Bohdan Khmelnytsky dies.
1658	Nikon leaves the patriarchical see (July 10); decree limits recruitment base of state secretaries and clerks.
1659	**Pavel named archimandrite of Chudov Monastery in Moscow** (chap. 10).
1660	Church council reaches inconclusive results concerning Patriarch Nikon; Avvakum recalled from exile; **Ulian Remezov's mission to Devlet-Kirei, Lauzan-taisha, and the Oirat Ablai-taisha** (chap. 19).
1661	End of war between Sweden and Muscovy; **Iurii Ivanov, a Dutchman, comes to Afanasii Prokofiev's tanning shop** (chap. 14).
1662	"Copper Coin Riot."
1664	Avvakum returns to Moscow from exile; **Pavel becomes metropolitan of Sarai and the Don (chap. 10); death of Vasilii Zotov** (chap. 9).

CHRONOLOGY xix

1666	**Conversation among Colonel William Allen, Captain Boldvin Edvart, and the merchant Andrew Wiggins** (chap. 8).
1666–67	Council deposes Nikon (December 12, 1666) but accepts his reforms.
1667	Treaty of Andrussovo with Poland; New Trading Regulation (*Novotorgovyi ustav*) issued; Ioasaf chosen patriarch.
1667–69	**First Stenka Razin rebellion** (chap. 19).
1668	Beginning of rebellion at Solovki Monastery against reforms; Felony Statute (Criminal Articles) issued.
1669	Maria Miloslavskaia, first wife of Tsar Aleksei, dies.
1670	**Bukharans in Tobolsk collectively petition the tsar to build a guesthouse so that they will not be burdened with quartering merchants from Bukhara** (chap. 20).
1670–71	**Second Stenka Razin rebellion** (chap. 19).
1671	Tsar Aleksei Mikhailovich marries Natalia Naryshkina.
1672	Patriarkh Ioasaf dies; Pitirim chosen patriarch; Peter Alekseevich (the future Peter I) born.
1673	Patriarch Pitirim dies.
1674	Ioakim chosen patriarch.
1675	**Pavel, metropolitan of Sarai and the Don, dies** (chap. 10); **Remezov meets Nikolae Spafarii Milescu in Tobolsk on way to China as ambassador** (chap. 19).
1676	Aleksei dies; Fedor III chosen tsar; beginning of war between Muscovy and the Ottoman empire; end of siege of Solovki Monastery.
1677	Monastery chancellery ended.
1678	**People of Tobolsk petition Moscow for stone construction (chap. 19)**.
1679	**Young girl from Vakulin's household is among a group professing allegiance to the True Orthodox Faith that burn themselves alive protesting changes to the liturgy** (chap. 20).
1680	Simeon Polotskii dies; **conversation between the boyars Vasilii Ivanovich and Iurii Borisovich** (chap. 4); **Andrei Beklenshev born** (chap. 7).
1681	End of war between Muscovy and the Ottoman empire; former Patriarch Nikon dies; Avvakum burned at the stake.
1682	*Mestnichestvo* abolished; Fedor III dies; Ivan and Peter, sons of Aleksei by different mothers chosen co-tsars by zemskii sobor; Ivan's sister Sophia made regent.
1686	**Archdeacon Meletios dies** (chap. 11).
1687	V.V. Golitsyn leads campaign against Crimean Tatars; Slaviano-Greek-Latin Academy founded in Moscow with the Likhudi brothers, Ioannikii and Sofronii, in charge.
1689	V.V. Golitsyn leads campaign against Crimean Tatars; Peter marries Evdokia Lopukhina; Sophia overthrown as regent; Treaty of Nerchinsk with China.

1690	Patriarch Ioakim dies; Adrian chosen patriarch; Tsarevich Aleksei Petrovich born.
1692	**Embassy of Tobolsk *syn boiarskii* Andrei Nepripasov to the Turkmen Tevki-khan (chap. 19).**
1694	Natalia Naryshkina dies.
1695	**Andrei Beklenshev assigned to an infantry regiment (chap. 7).**
1695–96	Campaigns against Azov.
1696	**Remezov returns from campaign in the steppe against the Kazakhs.**
1697–98	Peter I travels to Western Europe.
1698	Disobedience of the *strel'tsy* (musketeers); Peter divorces Evdokia; **Remezov invited to Moscow has audience with Peter, who appoints him head of architectural and building works for the new kremlin in Tobolsk** (chap. 19).
1700	Patriarch Adrian dies; beginning of Northern War; Swedish victory at Narva.
1701	Monasteries are obliged to give their revenues to the state; **Remezov draws an ethnographic map of Siberia** (chap. 19).
1702	Peter decides to build St. Petersburg; **Andrei Vinius arrives in Tobolsk to expedite restoration of the artillery lost in the battle of Narva** (chap. 19).
1703	Foundation of St. Petersburg laid; *Vedomosti* founded to report Russia's military and trade achievements; **Vinius oversees melting ores at Kungur** (chap. 19).
1705	Decree taxing beards; **Remezov captures Cossacks who robbed the *iasak* people** (chap. 19).
1709	Swedish army defeated at Poltava; **Andrei Beklenshev becomes a major (chap. 7)**; construction of St. Petersburg begins.
1710	Peter's army takes Baltic countries; **Remezov buys new homestead in lower town of Tobolsk** (chap. 19).
1711	Senate replaces Boyar Duma; Peter's army surrounded by Ottoman Turks at Pruth River.
1712	Capital moved to St. Petersburg; Peter marries Catherine.
1714	Battle of Hangö.
1716	Tsarevich Aleksei Petrovich flees to Vienna.
1716–17	Peter I's second trip to Western Europe.
1718	Census taken; colleges replace prikaz bureaus; Tsarevich Aleksei Petrovich returns, is tried, and dies in prison.
1719	**Remezov's son Peter marries in Tobolsk** (chap. 19).
1720	Service Land Chancellery abolished; **Andrei Beklenshev retires** (chap. 7).

1721	Peter declares Russia to be an empire and himself the emperor; patriarchate replaced by Holy Synod; Treaty of Nystad ends the Northern War; **foreigners visit Remezov in Tobolsk** (chap. 19).
1722	Peter establishes Table of Ranks.
1722–23	Campaigns against Persia.
1724	Soul tax established.
1725	Academy of Sciences founded; Peter dies.

Map of Muscovy drawn by Gerard de Jode based on an earlier map by Anthony Jenkinson, representative of the Muscovy Company. Jenkinson made four trips to Muscovy between 1558 and 1572. This map was published by de Jode's son Cornelius in his atlas *Speculum Orbis Terrae* (1593).

Introduction

Donald Ostrowski

Imaginative historical re-creation is more than a source of entertainment; it is a time-honored way of presenting interpretive accounts of distant historical figures and events. Robert Graves's *I, Claudius* may be the most famous example of a well-researched, historically accurate creative effort. But other noteworthy works, such as Howard Fast's *Spartacus,* Edison Marshall's *The Viking,* Umberto Eco's *Name of the Rose,* Samuel Shellabarger's *Captain from Castile,* Ernest Gebler's *Plymouth Adventure,* Julie Irwin's *The Young Elizabeth,* and many more, are not far behind. Likewise, the *You Are There* television series from the 1950s, in which Walter Cronkite conducted onsite "interviews" with historical figures, such as George Washington at Valley Forge during the winter of 1777–78, combined journalism with historical accuracy and interpretation.

The present collection is intended to introduce readers to a little-known place and time in world history—early modern Russia, from its beginnings as Muscovy, in the fourteenth century, through the reign of Peter I (1689–1725)—by portraying the lives of representative individuals from the major levels of the society of that era. In that respect, the collection bears some resemblance to *Imaginary Portraits,* a collection of imagined lives of Renaissance art figures, published by the late-nineteenth-century British essayist and historian Walter Pater.

Of necessity, these portraits, like Pater's, are imaginative reconstructions or composites of individual lives, rather than biographies. The authors of these pieces are professional historians, whose training requires them to have the highest regard for primary sources and respect for the limits they impose. The portraits in this collection scrupulously observe the confines of the available historical record. But source testimony for early modern Russia takes us only so far in providing evidence for the actions, thoughts, beliefs, customs, and outlook of the people who lived and worked, fought, and loved during that time. We fill the large gaps in our evidence base with informed speculation.

In this endeavor, we build on a long scholarly tradition. Historians often use imagination in their thinking about a particular time period and their consideration (empathy) for what it must have been like to have lived then. A number of history books use this device openly, such as Philip Matyszak's *Ancient Rome on 5 Denarii a Day* and Ian Mortimer's *The Time Traveler's Guide to Medieval England: A Handbook for Visitors to the Fourteenth Century*. Imagination plays an important role in trying to understand historical sources and how they came to be the way they are. Attempting to put oneself in the place of a historical personage, while divesting oneself of one's own present-mindedness, helps the historian comprehend past societies and their values. But to do these things, one must have as accurate and comprehensive an understanding of the available source testimony as possible.

Maintaining a high regard for the historical record is crucial if the historical imagination is to work well. Often, for example, feature films misrepresent historical evidence for reasons of "artistic creativity," and the filmmakers justify their violation of the historical record on the basis that they are not making a documentary but are trying only to entertain us so as to make money (for an insider's lampooning of this process, see Alan Alda's 1986 film *Sweet Liberty*). Such "artistic creativity" usually turns out to be less interesting than the historical evidence that is being distorted, violated, and suppressed. In the finest historical fiction, artistic creativity and respect for the historical record work hand in hand to produce narratives that are engaging, entertaining, and informative without being misleading.

In the present collection we have arranged the lives of our subjects into sociopolitical categories, from members of ruling families to peasants, serfs, and slaves. Within each category, too, lives are arranged in a roughly "top-down" sociopolitical progression. Another way to have arranged the portraits was chronologically, but the present arrangement is better suited for classroom use. For those who prefer the other approach, we have provided a Chronology of Old Russia from 1304 to 1725, in which events associated with particular individuals described in the narrative portraits are indicated in bold.

The collection begins with members of ruling families. The first portrait in this category is a description by Russell E. Martin (Westminster College) of Anna Koltovskaia, who participated in a bride show to become the fourth wife of Ivan IV the Terrible (1533–1584). In reading this portrait, we catch a glimpse of court intrigue during the time of Ivan the Terrible as well as the importance of marriage politics for ruling the country. Next to the tsar and his family in sociopolitical status were Tatar Chinggisid princes who entered the service of the Muscovite ruler. I imagine a memoir written by a sixteenth-century Tatar prince from Kazan in Muscovite service. This fictional memoir provides insight into the complexity of political relations within the Kazan khanate and between that khanate and Muscovy. It also indicates the personal feelings and motivations of a prince who switches political allegiance, although in this case not his religion.

The Muscovite grand prince also expanded his power by subordinating independent Rus princes and incorporating previously independent Rus principalities. Lawrence N. Langer (University of Connecticut) elucidates the life of Gleb Vasilievich, a fourteenth-century prince of Yaroslavl, in the context of the events that led subsequently to the assimilation of his principality into a larger Muscovite state.

The second sociopolitical category—government servitors—includes those who ran the government. At the top of this category were boyars, who were not of the ruling family but headed prominent clans. Marshall Poe (University of Iowa) imagines a dialogue between two fictional boyars about the political situation in the latter part of the seventeenth century. In that dialogue we encounter an earthy depiction of the uncertainties the Muscovite state faced in their day.

Boyars in turn relied on administrative personnel to manage the day-to-day activities. Sergei Bogatyrev (University College London) tells us about sixteenth-century court intrigues involving a powerful secretary of the Military Chancellery, Andrei Putilov—a composite portrait based on historical personages of the period. Putilov becomes relatively wealthy and is a prominent member of an embassy to the Crimea, but is accused of rape when he returns and has his career ruined.

Lower on the administrative scale we find assistants, such as clerks, who carried out the secretaries' directives and copied documents. Through his depiction of a historical personage, Larka Lvitskii, Peter B. Brown (Rhode Island College) reveals the hard work and difficult conditions endured by clerks in Muscovite chancelleries.

In the third category we have placed military personnel. Carol B. Stevens (Colgate University) imagines a fictional autobiography by an army officer, Andrei Beklenshev, written in the early eighteenth century. She intersperses excerpts of letters to him from his wife, Nadia, while he is away on duty. W.M. Reger IV (Illinois State University) provides information about different types of foreign mercenary officers by imagining a conversation between two of them and a local merchant. This conversation occurs near the end of the so-called Thirteen Years War (1654–67) between Muscovy and Poland. In those years, Muscovy was transitioning to a European-type army under Tsar Aleksei Mikhailovich (1645–76) and depended on European mercenaries to officer the ranks. Brian Davies (University of Texas, San Antonio) tells us about a military colonist named Vasilii Zotov, active on Muscovy's southern frontier. In the 1630s, Zotov joins a group to establish a garrison town, Kozlov, to help protect the southern frontier against Tatar raids.

The fourth category—church prelates—includes portraits of two religious hierarchs. Cathy J. Potter (independent scholar) depicts a historical church prelate from the late seventeenth century, Metropolitan Pavel of Sarai and the Don. From his story we learn about the difficulties churchmen faced in the wake of the tumultuous reign of Patriarch Nikon and the subsequent split within the Church. Michael C. Paul (independent scholar) describes the career and achievements of Vasilii Kalika, a fourteenth-century archbishop of Novgorod, through the eyes of Vasilii's nephew Matvei, a historical personage.

Less exalted churchmen make up the fifth category—monks. Michael S. Flier (Harvard University) depicts the training of a fifteenth-century icon painter. We explore the techniques and theology associated with icon painting through the discussions of a team of fictional Russian painters awaiting the arrival of the master icon painter Theophanes the Greek, a historical personage. Robert Romanchuk

xxvi INTRODUCTION

(Florida State University) provides three fictional texts as they might have been written by three monks—a secondary-school teacher, a secondary-school student, and an academic librarian—of the Kirillo-Belozersk Monastery. That monastery was a paragon of intellectual activity during the mid-fifteenth to early sixteenth centuries, as these imaginative texts well illustrate. Nikolaos A. Chrissidis (University of Southern Connecticut) supplies us with evidence about Greeks in seventeenth-century Muscovy through portraits based on two historical individuals—the hierodeacon Meletios and the merchant Chatzekyriakes Vourliotes. The accounts of foreign travelers to Russia are excellent sources of details about Russians and their church practices that people raised in Russia and in the Orthodox Church would not consider unusual enough to record. David M. Goldfrank (Georgetown University) tells us about a fictional sixteenth-century monk, Akakii Balandin, and his life in the Solovki Monastery. This account provides insight into the hopes and fears of a Russian Orthodox monk who is sincerely concerned about the salvation of his soul.

In the sixth category are provincial landowners, townspeople, and artisans. The account of Nancy S. Kollmann (Stanford University) involves a court case in which a landowner, Vasilii Vasilievich Glebov, seeks recompense for the loss of one of his serfs from his neighbor, another landowner, Aleksei Petrovich Shubalov. The imaginative retelling of this story is based on a trial record of the time. J.T. Kotilaine (independent scholar) shows the vicissitudes endured by some pre-Petrine artisans—in this case, a family of tanners (the Prokofievs). Their story offers insights into the impact of changing economic policies on artisans in the second half of the seventeenth century. Valerie Kivelson (University of Michigan) relates the problems of a poor townswoman, Oksanka, when she is accused of witchcraft. This narrative, too, is based on contemporary trial records.

The seventh category is devoted to Siberian explorers and traders. Christoph Witzenrath (independent scholar) provides a portrait of the cartographer and explorer of Siberia, S.U. Remezov, much of it as Remezov might have narrated it. Erika Monahan (University of New Mexico) tells us about a seventeenth-century Siberian merchant and customs officer, Urasko Kaibulin. As a Muslim whose family originated in Bukhara, Urasko had the requisite language skills and knowledge of commerce to benefit Russian trade in the area.

The eighth and last category is free peasants, serfs, slaves, and holy fools. Jennifer B. Spock (University of Eastern Kentucky) describes several generations of a northern peasant family, the Parfievs, who lived on the shores of the White Sea during the sixteenth and seventeenth centuries. She shows, among other things, that those classified as peasants were sometimes not always or even primarily engaged in agricultural pursuits. The late Richard Hellie (University of Chicago) supplies detailed information about an imaginary slave, Foma the son of Karp, from the 1590s and an imaginary serf, Ignatii the son of Ivan, in the mid-seventeenth century, the time when serfdom was established by law. This account enlightens us about the plight of the vast majority of the population of Muscovy. Hugh M. Olmsted

(Harvard University) provides a portrait of a sixteenth-century "holy fool," Avdotia (Dunia), the daughter of Makar. Although a female "fool for Christ" was rare, there were some, and Olmsted sheds light on what it must have been like for Dunia and her family as they tried to come to grips with her bizarre behavior.

Four of the characters in this collection live to an advanced age: Anna Koltovskaia (chap. 1) into her seventies; the monk Akakii Balandin (chap. 12) to the age of sixty-nine; the Tatar prince Ismail ibn Ahmed (chap. 2) seventy; and S. U. Remezov (chap. 19) to at least the age of seventy-eight. Although average age expectancy at birth for Muscovy was around thirty years, that number can be misleading, since so many deaths occurred within the first years of life. Indeed, the evidence from that time indicates a number of individuals lived into their eighties (for example, Maksim Grek, Metropolitan Makarii, and Vassian Toporkov).

***

The progenitor of this project was Marshall T. Poe, who conceived of the concept and solicited the initial contributions. In March 2003 we held a workshop at Harvard University to discuss them and suggest improvements. Our thanks to the Davis Center for Russian and Eurasian Studies for financial support to hold the workshop and to the Harvard University Extension School for hosting it. Enormous gratitude must go to Patricia Kolb of M.E. Sharpe, who, when editors of other presses hesitated to take on such an innovative and unusual project, saw the value in it and has been an unstinting supporter of this endeavor. Finally, but not least, we were fortunate to have as our copyeditor a historian, one of us early Slavists, Carolyn Pouncy, who understood our professional idiosyncrasies.

Cognizant from the beginning that our "target audience is undergraduates and readers of history everywhere" (e-mail of Marshall Poe, May 9, 2002), and that we are writing for a nonspecialist audience, the contributors to this collection have attempted to use English equivalents for the Russian terms that constitute the patois of specialist discourse. Thus we use "chancellery" for *prikaz,* "yeoman" for *odnodvorets,* "governor" for *voevoda,* and "service" for *sluzhba.* In some cases, the closest English equivalent may not be immediately recognizable to many English speakers, such as "boyar" for *boiar,* "hegumen" for *igumen,* "kasha" for *kasha,* "metropolitan" for *mitropolit,* and "podzol" for *podzol',* but a quick check of a dictionary will confirm that these are, indeed, considered to be words in English usage. When we judged that the English equivalent was likely to be misleading or exceedingly convoluted, however, we maintained the Russian term in transliteration. For example, *deti boiarskie* (literally "boyars' sons") were lower-ranked servitors; *okol'nichie* (persons "around" the ruler) ranked immediately below the boyars in status; and *stol'niki* ("tablemen") served the tsar in various civil, diplomatic, and military capacities. A *pominok* was a gift given after a deal was made; *iasak* was a fur tax paid by non-Christians. Except in these transliterated Russian words, we have eliminated soft signs, hard signs, and most diacritical marks from the text. We have also removed the second "i" from transliterated women's names ending in –iia (Maria, not Mariia). All Russian terms used in the text, even those placed parenthetically following the English equivalent, are listed and defined in the glossary in the back of the book. There the reader will also find notes on the history and use of personal names in Muscovy as well as a pronunciation guide for Russian names. These materials were generously compiled and contributed by Hugh M. Olmsted.

The problem of terminology extends to the name applied to Russia itself. The entire area of East Slavic speakers is generally referred to as Rus beginning in the ninth century. During the late fifteenth and sixteenth centuries, the grand prince, later tsar, of Moscow united under his sway most of the northern Rus principalities and began extending Muscovite influence into Siberia. In the seventeenth century, the tsar of Moscow began incorporating eastern parts of southern Rus into his domains and ordered the establishment of a string of outposts across Siberia to the Pacific Ocean. In 1721, Peter I renamed his domains the "Russian empire" and himself the "emperor" of it. Scholars tend to maintain the distinction between "Muscovy" (the pre-Petrine domains under the sovereignty of the grand prince/tsar of Moscow) and "Russia" (the Petrine and post-Petrine designation).

Then there is the issue of dates. As in the Byzantine empire, years in Muscovy were counted from the presumed date of creation, 5508 years before the birth of Christ. The Muscovite year began September 1 rather than January 1. Thus the year 7134 ran from September 1, 1625, to August 31, 1626. All dates are given according to the Julian calendar, because Russia did not accept the Gregorian calendar reform of 1583 until 1917.

We tried to provide as broad a spectrum of types of Muscovites as possible. Some of the portraits are about imaginary people of a certain historical type. Other portraits are imaginative accounts of a historical person or a composite of two or more people. These accounts present Muscovy with some complexity, both in terms of social relations and within social groups. Although none of us claims to have the literary skills of a Graves, Fast, Marshall, Eco, Shellabarger, Gebler, or Irwin, we do presume to hope the reader will find our individual efforts well researched, historically accurate, and not entirely without creative merit. Although we could not present a narrative portrait for every social type that existed at the time, we feel confident that this collection of imaginative retellings of the lives of fictional and historical personages will bring readers a better understanding of early modern Russia.

I

Members of Ruling Families

1

Anna Koltovskaia
A Russian Tsaritsa

Russell E. Martin

This fictionalized account of the life of Anna Koltovskaia, fourth wife of Ivan the Terrible, is based on scattered bits of historical evidence that survive of her brief time in the Kremlin, her subsequent life as a nun living for many years in several convents, and a variety of sources about the lives of Muscovite royal women in the sixteenth and seventeenth centuries. The narrative details of this biography are gathered from historical documents (many unpublished) that survive from Muscovite bride shows and from official royal wedding descriptions. These materials are preserved in the Treasure Room of the Russian State Archive of Ancient Acts in Moscow. Other sources for this account come from chronicles describing events of Ivan's reign during his brief marriage to Anna; from materials about the history of the Koltovskii family, including various court registers that tell us about the status and station of the family at court; and from documents about the Tikhvin Convent of the Presentation of the Virgin in the Temple, where Anna spent most of her adult life. Anna Koltovskaia (1554–56–April 5, 1626) was born into a fairly undistinguished provincial noble family, but both she and her kinsmen were vaulted to the heights of power in Muscovy after her selection as Ivan's bride in 1572, probably in a bride show. Spurned just a few months later, she spent the remainder of her life (she evidently lived into her seventies) at convents as the nun Daria—a form of political exile. Encapsulated in this fictional biography are some of the triumphs and tragedies that many Russian royal women lived through. In considering her life, even if in fictionalized form, we catch a glimpse of the lives of other Muscovite royal women as well.

The nun Daria sat in silence on a bench in the refectory of the Tikhvin Convent of the Presentation of the Virgin in the Temple, meticulously adjusting the folds of her mantle (*mantiia*).[1] A visitor was coming from Moscow to see her, and the

---

[1] A long, sleeveless black robe or cloak that is worn by monks and nuns as an outer garment.

Ivan the Terrible Chooses a Bride (Ivan Groznyi vybiraet nevestu). Painting by Tatiana Gorokhovskaia. On the far left of the painting are two boyars wearing tall fox-fur hats. The seated man to their left is playing a *gusli* (a stringed instrument similar to a zither), and the boy is playing a flute. We have no contemporary image of a bride show or of Anna Koltovskaia. This artist seems to be indicating that the women being reviewed had to dance before the tsar. The dancing woman and those lined up in the background would have gone through a careful selection process before ever being seen by the tsar.

refectory had been chosen as the most appropriate place for Daria to receive the guest. A spacious room with frescos covering the walls, icons and vigil lamps, and long benches and thick wooden tables, the refectory was the usual point of contact between the cloistered nuns and the outside world—a throne room of sorts for the abbess, where she presided over the assembled nuns each day as they took their meals while listening to the vita for the saint of the day.

It was not unusual for Daria to receive visitors from outside the convent. In her more than fifty years at this and other convents, she had had many visitors from the outside. But the visitor on this gray and chilly October morning in 1624 was very different. The *stol'nik* Prince Daniil Grigorievich Gagarin had made the arduous trek to see her at the remote Tikhvin Convent, situated some 300 miles northwest of Moscow, to present to Daria gifts from the tsar. The entire convent was in a flurry as a result. The issue was not so much that prominent visitors from Moscow were unheard of: the convent got a steady, if not heavy stream of important and high-ranking visitors, most coming to pray or to commission prayers for their dead ancestors. But there was something unusual about this visit, and everyone at the convent knew it. The tsar had married just three weeks before—the young first tsar of a new dynasty, Mikhail Fedorovich Romanov. And Daria was no ordinary nun. She was royalty. Everyone knew that, too.

Prince Daniil arrived, making the sign of the cross as he entered the refectory. He was followed by two men, each holding a large, round silver platter. Prince Daniil made straight for an *analoi*[2] in the middle of the room holding a copy of the Icon of the Tikhvin Mother of God, made the sign of the cross again, three times, and kissed the image. Only then did he turn to Daria, still seated, and recite his scripted speech: "Tsaritsa Daria, consort of our Sovereign, Tsar and Grand Prince Ivan Vasilievich, of blessed memory! I have been sent to you, Tsaritsa Daria, by the Sovereign Tsar and Grand Prince Mikhail Fedorovich and by his consort, Tsaritsa and Grand Princess Maria Vladimirovna, coming directly from their royal wedding, to present you, Tsaritsa Daria, with these gifts, and to beseech you, Tsaritsa Daria, to pray for our Sovereigns, Tsar and Grand Prince Mikhail Fedorovich and his Tsaritsa and Grand Princess, Maria Vladimirovna." Prince Daniil motioned to the two attendants, who stepped forward with the platters, and presented the gifts with a bow—an oblong towel (*ubrusets*), about a meter in length, made of crimson taffeta with pearls sewn into the fabric; and a square cloth (*shirinka*), also of taffeta, with rich gold embroidery and gold tassels running along its edges.

Daria accepted the gifts. Two nuns glided forward and, with a bow, took the silver platters from the two attendants and exited the refectory through a side doorway. With a faint groan, Daria rose to her feet. The chilly weather, the short legs of her bench, her age—all conspired to make changing from a sitting to a standing position something of a chore. She took an icon from under the folds of her mantle and used it to bless Prince Daniil, making the sign of the cross with

---

[2] *Analoi:* a raised and angled pedestal used to hold icons in churches.

great motions of the hand in the air over his head. She thanked him with words more formulaic than heartfelt and invited the prince and his two attendants to sit. Food was brought to the tables, and the nuns rushed about serving the three men without uttering a word. The three men did not observe the usual silence of the refectory but talked with their mouths full the entire time, clanking their cups and dishes carelessly and scraping the wood benches against the floor as they got up to refill their plates and goblets.

Daria disappeared and returned three-quarters of an hour later with a folded and sealed piece of paper addressed to the tsar and his new bride. She handed the letter to Prince Daniil and walked over to the *analoi* holding the icon of the Tikhvin Virgin. "Prince Daniil!" she said. "Give this icon of the Most Pure and Holy Mother of God to our sovereign masters, Tsar and Grand Prince Mikhail Fedorovich and his consort, Tsaritsa and Grand Princess Maria Vladimirovna. May our Lord and Savior Jesus Christ, through the prayers of His Most Pure Mother, bless them and grant them many years."

With a final bow, the audience ended. Daria withdrew to her cell, and the visitors, bellies filled, left for the nearby village to prepare themselves over the next few days for the journey back to Moscow.

Back in her cell, Daria sat next to a small table on which the two gifts had been neatly placed. She examined them closely and was struck by their beauty and exquisite workmanship. These were surely her finest and most valuable possessions. These royal gifts, the visitors from the tsar's court, being called "tsaritsa" again—all of this day's events sent her thoughts reeling back to another royal wedding with other sumptuous gifts just like these. A wedding some fifty-five years before, when she was the bride, and the tsar—a very different tsar—was the groom.

She was the seventeen-year-old daughter of a provincial nobleman living in the town of Kolomna, and her name was Anna Alekseevna Koltovskaia. Her father, Aleksei, served the tsar—that is, he went wherever he was sent and did whatever he was told. Mostly, this meant that he and his kinsmen were away during the summers—sometimes on campaigns with the tsar's armies, at other times assisting in the business of running the town and environs of Kolomna. In winter he was less mobile but no less busy. It was in the long and cold winter months that Aleksei tended to his family's business: their modest landholdings (*pomest'ia*), their religious affairs, and the lives of his wife, children, and kin. Of course, even in the winter Aleksei served the tsar. He was expected to help the regional military governor (*voevoda*) in his duties, which often meant merely being present at his side, or, at most, serving as a glorified errand boy. It was honorable work—a better lot than most Muscovites enjoyed. But "elite" would be too strong a word to describe the Koltovskiis' station and status when Anna was a young girl.

The tsar that Anna's father served was Ivan IV, called the Terrible. And in November 1571, the tsar found himself in a fix. Ivan's third wife, Marfa Sobakina, had died just a few weeks after their wedding. She had been ill even before the wedding, but Ivan had insisted on going through with it. Now he found himself to be a three-time widower. More to the point, Ivan had, so to speak, run out of marriages. The Orthodox Church, as Ivan himself well knew, permits a person to marry only three times (it hopes that only one spouse will suffice!). Undeterred by this canonical inconvenience, Ivan almost immediately began seeking the Church's blessing for a fourth union. He convened his bishops in a council in early 1572 and made his case: his marriage with Marfa Sobakina had never been consummated and therefore was not legitimate; he was the victim of treacherous boyars who had poisoned his bride (he may have been right about that), and their treason ought not be rewarded by the Church; the Muscovite state needed him to remarry for the sake of the royal succession regardless of canon law; and, the argument that probably worked best with the clergymen, Ivan required the fourth marriage for the sake of the salvation of his soul, it being "better to marry than burn with passion" (1 Cor 7:9). All the tsar's arguments notwithstanding, the bishops under the leadership of Metropolitan Kirill, first hierarch of the Russian Church, resolutely resisted all these pleas.

And it was no small thing to resist Ivan. Starting about five years before these events, Ivan had perpetrated successive waves of mass executions, property seizures, and the exiling of his real or imagined enemies. Ivan had divided his realm into two parts, keeping for himself a "widow's mite" (*oprich'*) which gave its name to this bloody period in Russian history—the Oprichnina. Swarms of black-robed horsemen, with severed dogs' heads dangling from their saddles and carrying small symbolic brooms, rode about the towns and countryside sweeping out traitors and terrorizing the people in Ivan's name. Saying "no" to Ivan obviously could involve great risk. Even still, it was not until Metropolitan Kirill died in February 1572 that the Church council's resistance began to wither, and in April a formal blessing was finally given the tsar to find a fourth bride for himself—but not without cost. Ivan would be under penance for years—unable to take communion or even to enter the nave of a church because of his "weakness for the passions." But the price, though high, was worth paying.

Finding a bride for the Muscovite ruler in Ivan's time was accomplished by means of a bride show—a parade of young women in front of the tsar, maidens who had been drawn from the provincial and town gentry from all over the tsardom. Muscovy's tsaritsas were rarely from the great Muscovite boyar families and even more rarely from foreign royalty. Royal brides came from the middle ranks of the Russian gentry—right where the Koltovskiis found themselves in the 1570s.

Ivan IV, like his father before him, used bride shows to find most of his wives (Ivan would eventually collect seven of them). He picked his first, Anastasia Iurieva, out of a bride show in 1547. Because his second wife, Maria Temriukovna, was a foreigner, that wedding was arranged without the help of a bride show. When, in 1569, Ivan found himself again a widower after Maria's death, he almost immediately began to look for a bride at home in the usual fashion. He dispatched his servitors—representatives of the great families—to the far corners of the tsardom to locate young maidens who were beautiful, pious, healthy, and—as best the folksy means available could determine it—fertile.

The tsar's servitors also investigated the family backgrounds of bridal candidates—compiling medical histories of relatives and charting a candidate's genealogical connections with other gentry families. The servitors traveled to designated towns, where they circulated Ivan's edict ordering members of the local gentry to present their young unmarried daughters in the provincial capital. There the interviews and preliminary physical examinations took place. Reports on each candidate and her family were sent to Moscow, describing in detail the physical appearance, health history, and genealogical ties of each prospective royal bride.

Okol'nichii[3] Ivan Ivanovich Bezzubtsov and a crew of four scribes arrived in Kolomna in midsummer 1571 as part of this kingdomwide effort. They circulated the tsar's edict and waited. And waited. In the next two weeks, no gentry appeared with their daughters. Convinced that there simply had to be women of eligible age and agreeable looks in the province, Bezzubtsov re-sent the edict throughout the towns and countryside, but still no one responded. Frustrated, and not a little fearful of the tsar's wrath, Bezzubtsov wrote to Ivan: "You sent us, sire, to Kolomna; and we, sire, having arrived, did circulate your royal edict to the princes and gentry of the province, into the settlements and districts. And we, sire, have been residing in Kolomna for two weeks, but not one prince or gentryman has come to us and brought his daughter to us. And among the gentry in the town of Kolomna, sire, we have found no suitable daughters. They are all too young and skinny."

The tsar, predictably, flew into a rage. He issued a new edict for Bezzubtsov to circulate: "Ivan Ivanovich Bezzubtsov has written to me that he, in accordance with my instructions, circulated our edicts to you that you go to him with your daughters; and we commanded him to examine your daughters as possible brides for us. But you have not gone to him and you have not brought your daughters, and our edicts you have disobeyed. And it is wrong not to obey our edicts! You are to go immediately and without fail with your daughters to Ivan Ivanovich Bezzubtsov. And any that disobey will be in disgrace and be punished."

With this threat looming, Aleksei Koltovskii finally agreed to bring his daughter, Anna, to Bezzubtsov. Until then, Anna had lived in the separate quarters in the family house set aside for the Koltovskii women. Her mother (and later her stepmother), her brother's wife and her uncle's wife, and two of her widowed and aged aunts lived there with her. Anna grew up in a world where women (at least, women of her station) were secluded from men and rarely left the family home. On the few occasions when they did go out—to attend church, for example—they went veiled and covered in layers of clothes from head to toe. It is not surprising, then, that Anna's father had a limited acquaintance with his daughter, but he did know one thing about her: that Anna would attract Bezzubtsov's attention. Anna, everyone agreed, was a stunningly beautiful young woman.

Anna's father also knew that his daughter's participation in a bride show could spell ruin for his family, which is why he initially resisted the tsar's summons. It

---

[3] *Okol'nichii:* the second highest court rank in Muscovy, below the rank of boyar.

was not that Aleksei did not grasp the enormous rewards that could come to him and his kith and kin were Anna to be the tsar's bride. To become royal in-laws was to be vaulted to the heights of power and status at the tsar's court. But Aleksei Koltovskii (and probably the fathers of most of the provincial and town gentry who had eligible daughters) understood what their daughters would have to endure as participants in the bride show: their families' medical histories revealed to strangers; their ancestry scrutinized; their friends and allies investigated; and physical examinations of their daughters to assure their "virtue." Yanking his daughter out of the women's quarters of his home and thrusting her into so public a spectacle as a bride show horrified Aleksei. The investigation might sully the honor of his daughter, which would in turn compromise his and of his family's honor. Would Anna find a good husband—a husband "good" for the local interests of the family out in Kolomna—after she had been subjected to these indecent inspections only to be rejected by the tsar?

Ivan's new edict, however, left Aleksei no choice. He presented his daughter, and, as he feared, her looks were enough to launch a full investigation of her and her family. One of Bezzubtsov's scribes took her parents away and interviewed them. Other scribes focused on Anna, asking questions that were later corroborated with her parents' testimonies. Her father was ordered to produce the family's genealogical records and quizzed about the identities of his in-laws and about Anna's stepmother's family. In the end, the investigation of Anna Koltovskaia alone took more than a week to complete. Bezzubtsov's official report on Anna said:

> Anna is seventeen years old, has a well-proportioned figure and a very appealing face, is not too thin and not too fat, has black eyes, a nose that is not too long for her face, and dark brown hair. Concerning illnesses, her father said that his daughter, Anna, had been ill with a fever when a young child, but now, thank God, is without any ailments.
>
> Her mother was Fetinia, the daughter of Vasilii Ivanovich Kolychev. Her brother Grigorii is married to Evdokia, the daughter of Dmitrii Vasilievich Tulupov. Her uncle Afonasii is married to Agafia, the daughter of Prince Boris Ivanovich Lykov. Her cousin is Konstantin Fedorovich, who is married to Evfimia, the daughter of Roman Dmitreevich Glebov. Her stepmother is Iulia, the daughter of Ivan Ivanovich Saburov. Her stepmother's brothers are Boris, Ivan, Dmitrii, and Aleksander.
>
> Her father, Aleksei, has had a sore foot since the Feast of St. Nicholas. The father and mother have had no other ailments or illnesses to report.[4]

On the basis of Bezzubtsov's positive report, Anna's father was ordered to present his daughter in Moscow the following month. There Anna underwent a second round of physical examinations—these performed by the wives of boyars—and the genealogical investigations continued. Anna was hardly alone. The court was

---

[4] The genealogy is fictitious. The family relations of the Koltovskii clan are not fully known, though this imaginary report does include elements from the actual genealogy of the Koltovskii and Tulupov families.

consumed by this activity, and some reports put the number of women appearing in Moscow for the second round of inspections at near two thousand. Anna spent long hours with strangers: with boyars' wives and other women attendants who interviewed her and examined her body—a new and frightening experience for a young girl who had never ventured far beyond the rooms of her house on her family's Kolomna estate, except to the local parish church. Almost nothing about these inspections was explained to her. No one asked her opinion or her preference about anything she was undergoing. She was treated as if she were an emotionless object.

One day about a week after her arrival in Moscow, Anna was taken to the Terem, the apartments inside the Kremlin where the tsaritsas and boyars' wives lived, secluded from the compound of buildings and churches occupied by the tsar and his servitors. She was taken to a room with six other young women, each standing apart and motionless, as if paralyzed by fright and anticipation. The tsar himself, she was told, was in the next room, and each young woman would shortly be presented to him, one at a time, in this last stage of the bride show, the only stage in which the tsar himself actually participated.

Anna awaited her turn. An elderly boyar's wife was moving about the room, occasionally peeping her head through the doorway to get the signal when she should send the next candidate in to see the tsar. Anna was not the first to go in, and she found herself lost in thought, trying to imagine what lay behind the door. Suddenly, she felt the old boyar's wife tug on her elbow and nudge her in the direction of the door. She entered hesitantly. Ivan sat in a chair off to one side of the room. Boyars and other courtiers, all men, stood around and behind the tsar. One of them waved his hand to direct Anna to the center of the room. She walked over, stood for a bit before the tsar, was told to turn around, then was asked to recite the prayer "O, Heavenly King" (not to see if she knew it by heart, but rather to get some sense of the quality of her voice). The boyars huddled around the tsar and exchanged a few hushed words. Then it was over. A courtier stepped out from behind the tsar and led Anna to the door on the opposite side of the room from where she had entered. The tsar had not uttered a single word to her the entire time, had not given any indication one way or the other of his impression of her. It was over in less than five minutes.

Within an hour of her audience with the tsar, Anna knew she was not the tsar's choice. She was given a small, ornate silk towel—a consolation prize of sorts—and was back in Kolomna within a fortnight. By the end of the month, the tsar had married Marfa Sobakina, one of the other candidates. But Marfa's death just weeks after the wedding changed everything, including the direction Anna's life would take. When Ivan finally received the blessing of a church council to marry for a fourth time, he immediately recalled all the finalists in the earlier bride show, Anna included. This time, Anna was not escorted to the exit door, but the tsar stood up (with some pain in his back, Anna noticed) and handed her a ring and kerchief. With that gesture, the choice was made.

Anna was immediately installed in the apartments reserved for the tsaritsa. Her stepmother and sister-in-law were also given rooms. Anna was introduced to the boyars' wives already living in the Terem—the women who had given her the physical examinations but, despite the intimacy of that affair, had never bothered to tell her their names. She heard that her father and brother and uncle and cousin had moved into the Kremlin, too, but she never saw them. In fact, she did not even see the tsar again until the day she married him. The wedding was an enormous and spectacular affair: banquets, processions, speeches, ritual baths, more soldiers and priests and courtiers than she could count or had ever seen in one place at the same time. Ivan, her groom, seemed like a god at the center of the universe—and just as distant.

There were many obstacles to intimacy with the tsar. Ivan naturally lived in a different part of the Kremlin. Still, Anna saw him quite a lot: at various court happenings such as a banquet for a visiting emissary, at church, and on a lengthy trip together to Novgorod. But she was never close to him physically, and certainly not emotionally. He would come to her bedroom, but he often suffered such excruciating back pain that a physical relationship was difficult, often quite impossible.[5]

Expectations about marriage also impinged on their relationship. Royal marriage was about heirs and successors, not love. Anna felt the enormous burden of Muscovite queenship: the fate of herself and her relatives, now comfortably settled into their new lodgings in the Kremlin, depended on Anna's fulfilling her responsibility: to give her husband sons. She turned to God for help. She prayed incessantly. She gave donations to monasteries and churches asking the prayers of the monks and holy fathers. Once, during her trip to Novgorod with her husband, she spent an entire night in prayerful vigil before the miraculous relics of the saints, beseeching them to open her womb and grant her a strong, healthy, worthy son.

The saints seemed not to be listening, however. Two, three, four months passed; and Anna was not pregnant. Even so, she had no inkling of any problem. There was time, after all. She had been married to the tsar for only a few months, and as far as she was concerned, the tsar's lack of interest in sex probably explained why she was not pregnant. "All things are in God's hands," she used to quip when asked by her stepmother or by the boyars' wives about her physical relations with the tsar.

But it was really in the tsar's hands, not God's. The tsar quickly—too quickly, really—convinced himself that Anna was infertile. Protestations from his boyars and Anna's relatives that not enough time had elapsed would not dissuade Ivan from his view that the situation with Anna was hopeless. No one but Ivan—and perhaps Anna—knew that Ivan's constant and crippling back pain was as much to blame for the lack of a pregnancy as anything else. As much to conceal his disability as to rid himself of a presumedly barren wife, Ivan decided that Anna must go.

---

[5] Forensic examinations of Ivan IV's remains have shown that he likely suffered from ankylosing spondylitis, a debilitating and degenerative disease that fuses vertebrae and is extremely painful for those suffering from it.

On an unseasonably cold September night, just four months and a few days after her wedding, Anna returned from vespers and was met on the portico of the Terem by one of Ivan's boyars. Without greeting her with the deep bow one typically makes before a tsaritsa, the boyar unraveled a roll of paper and in a neutral tone read the message it contained. The tsar ordered Anna, because of her barrenness, to accept monastic vows and to retire to the Convent of the Intercession of the Mother of God in Suzdal, 130 miles northeast of Moscow. Her stepmother and sister-in-law had already been removed from the Terem. She had until the morning to get herself ready for the trip.

Anna did not sleep that night. She did not cry; she felt only shock. She sat and stared at the icon-covered wall, unnerved at the thought of how icons would consume her life from now on. They were always everywhere, of course, but now they would surround her and seclude her, as the walls of her Koltovskii home had, as the Terem had. She felt bewildered. She felt cold. She felt the absence of God.

Before dawn, a caravan of carriages and horsemen arrived in Cathedral Square inside the Kremlin with soldiers and nuns and a lone archpriest. They entered the chapel in the Terem in an orderly, almost rehearsed procession. Anna watched from her anteroom but did not move. Nuns arrived in the anteroom and bowed deeply before Anna. They undressed her—the predawn air chilling her to the bone—and put on her the black robes of the novice. The nuns then led her to the chapel where the archpriest was waiting, the incense from the lit censers already hanging thick in the air. Prayers were chanted, but Anna didn't hear them. No one in the past eight hours had asked her what she wanted. In all her life, no one ever had. The divorce was made final with the kissing of the cross and the Gospels. Shortly after her arrival in Suzdal, she would be shorn. Tsaritsa Anna no longer existed. From now on, she was the nun Daria.

Fifty-five years in a convent—a new sort of Terem. Events had gone by, tumultuous events: the executions of her brother Grigorii and other kin not long after her dismissal from the Terem; Ivan's three other, unrecognized marriages; Ivan's death; fifteen years of civil war over the succession to the throne; the invasion of the Swedes and the Poles; the coming of a new dynasty and a new tsar. She had moved from Suzdal to other convents, most recently Tikhvin. Over the years, she had kept contact with the court: with Ivan's son and successor, Tsar Fedor Ivanovich; with his successor, Boris Godunov; and with the other rulers who had come and gone during the "Troubles." She continually reminded them of her existence, of the promises of land and financial support Ivan and his heirs had made to her, and of the fact that she was once a tsaritsa.

In her cell, Daria looked at the oblong towel and square cloth that Prince Daniil Gagarin had brought her earlier that day. Surely the new tsar's father, Patriarch Filaret, and his mother, the nun Marfa, had received identical gifts—given only to royalty. The gifts both pleased and befuddled her. On the one hand, how laughable it was to give a nun something that fit in more with the rich furnishings of the Terem than with the monochrome cell of a nun! "Have they forgotten who I am?" she wondered. On the other hand, she knew that these gifts meant that the tsar—this young, newly wedded tsar from a new dynasty—had not, in fact, forgotten who she was. However inappropriate these gifts might be to her circumstances, these signified that he acknowledged her as a tsaritsa—as Anna, not Daria.

A year and a half would pass, and Prince Daniil would return to the Tikhvin Convent bearing gifts for Daria again. Tsar Mikhail Romanov's first wife had died shortly after their wedding, perhaps a victim of the kind of court intrigue that had ruined Anna's marriage and consigned her to this remote monastery for a lifetime. In February 1626, the tsar had married Evdokia Streshneva, a union that would give rise to the Romanov dynasty that survived into the early twentieth century. Prince Daniil arrived shortly after the wedding, just as he had done a year or so before, with identical gifts, uttering the same speeches and returning to Moscow bearing Daria's same letter of congratulations and another copy of the Tikhvin Icon of the Mother of God. But Daria was by then in failing health and rarely left her cell. The gifts this time brought no pleasure, no solace. She lingered on a few months after Prince Daniil's visit, and passed on to her heavenly reward one cool April night, dying in her sleep, alone in her cell, the only fitting way for a nun to die.

Suggestions for Further Reading

Beketov, P., ed. *Opisanie v litsakh" torzhestva, proiskhodivshago v 1626 godu, fevralia 5, pri brakosochetanii Gosudaria Tsaria i Velikago Kniazia Mikhaila Feodorovicha s Gosudaryneiu Tsaritseiu Evdokieiu Luk'ianovnoiu, iz roda Streshnevykh*. Moscow, 1810.

Kaiser, Daniel H. "Symbol and Ritual in the Marriages of Ivan IV." *Russian History* 14, nos. 1–4 (1987): 247–62.

Martin, Russell E. "Gifts for the Bride: Dowries, Diplomacy, and Marriage Politics in Muscovy." *Journal of Medieval and Early Modern Studies* 38, no. 1 (2008): 119–45.

———. "Gifts for Kith and Kin: Gift Exchange and Social Solidarity in Muscovite Royal Weddings, 1495–1671." In *The Rude and Barbarous Kingdom Revisited: Essays in Russian History and Culture in Honor of Robert O. Crummey*. Bloomington, IN: Slavica Publishers, 2008, 89–108.

———. "Muscovite Esther: Bride Shows, Queenship, and Power in *The Comedy of Artaxerxes*." In *The New Muscovite Cultural History: A Collection in Honor of Daniel Rowland*. Bloomington, IN: Slavica Publishers, 2009, 21–42.

Mashtafarov, A.V. "Dariia." In *Pravoslavnaia entsiklopediia*. Moscow: Tserkovno-nauchnyi tsentr "Pravoslavnaia entsiklopediia," 2006. Vol. 14: 199–200.

Morozova, Liudmila Evgen'evna, and Boris Nikolaevich Morozov. *Ivan Groznyi i ego zheny*. Moscow: Drofa-Plius, 2005.

Thyrêt, Isolde. *Between God and Tsar: Religious Symbolism and the Royal Women of Muscovite Russia*. DeKalb: Northern Illinois University Press, 2001.

———. "The Royal Women of Ivan IV's Family and the Meaning of Forced Tonsure." In *Servants of the Dynasty: Palace Women in World History*. Berkeley: University of California Press, 2008, 159–71.

Zabelin, I.E. *Domashnii byt russkikh tsarits v XVI i XVII st.* Moscow, 1869.

Memoir of a Tatar Prince
Ismail ibn Ahmed

Donald Ostrowski

The fictional author of this memoir, Ismail ibn Ahmed, is a composite character created from evidence of historical Tatar princes between 1480 and 1552. Ismail's relationship with his sons is based on that of an earlier Tatar prince, Melik-Tagir, who came over to the Muscovites in 1487 but remained Muslim while his two sons, Fedor and Vasilii, converted to Christianity. The parallel of Ismail's asking asylum in the Ottoman empire is with Sheikh Ahmed, the last khan of the Jochid ulus, who had asked Sultan Bayezid (1481–1512) for asylum but was refused. Having an intermediary write a letter to the Muscovite ruler on one's behalf was done by Said Mehmed in 1502, who asked the Nogai prince Azika to do so. Azika, as does Musa in the memoir, also sent his letter with a junior kinsman, Kanbar mirza. For most of the historical parallels on which this account is grounded, I drew on the documents in volume 41 of Sbornik Imperatorskogo Russkogo istoricheskogo obshchestva *(SRIO), 148 vols. (St. Petersburg, 1867–1916). Ismail's dislike of bells has a historical parallel in Ibn Battuta's* Rihla *where he claimed he found the Christian practice of ringing bells to be aesthetically offensive. All the poetry that Ismail cites would have been available to him at the time (see "Suggestions for Further Reading"). His age (seventy years old) when writing this memoir is a little unusual at a time and place when most people did not live beyond their fifties. We do have evidence, however, of some individuals surviving longer, into their seventies and eighties in the sixteenth century. I have taken the liberty of adding explanatory footnotes as though I were editing a text from the time.*

In the name of God, the Merciful and the Compassionate, I, Ismail ibn Ahmed, write down these reminiscences of my long and varied past during the seventieth year of my life, for I do not know how many more days I will live to see. It is with mixed feelings that I watch as my two beloved sons, Kalil and Hasan, may God preserve them, ride off in the army of the Russian tsar and grand prince to attack my birthplace, Kazan. It was I who spoke the sacred words, "La ilaha illa Allah"

Drawing by M. V. Gorelik of a heavily armed Tatar cavalryman, based on archaeological finds from the field at Kulikovo where a battle took place involving Rus and Tatar forces in 1380. Tatar weaponry and armor did not change much by the sixteenth century, and so Ismail ibn Ahmed, the composite Tatar prince of this chapter, would probably have been accoutered like the individual depicted on the horse when going into battle.

three times in their little ears when they were born.¹ I could not bring myself to attend their baptism to become Christians, which they did when they entered the service of the Muscovite ruler, but I did not act to prevent it. Both they and I realized the faith of their forefathers was an obstacle to their advancement in the realm of the Christian grand prince.²

I was born in the third year of the reign of Khan Ilham.³ We had many troubles in the realm (*ulus*) of Ulug Mehmed.⁴ During most of my early years in Kazan, the khan was Mehmed Emin, who was the son of Ibrahim ibn Mahmud and the famous (some say, infamous) Nur Sultan.⁵ She had been previously married to Ibrahim's older brother Halil while he was khan.⁶ After Ibrahim died, she left Kazan to marry the dastardly Mengli Girey, khan of the Crimea.⁷ Thus, in the eyes of my family, she went from being a princess heroine to being the wife of Kazan's archenemy. The Holy Qur'an teaches us that "good women are obedient" (4:34), but Nur Sultan did not obey God's will. Or, in the words of our poet Muhammed Yar:

> The country girl had turned into a beast;
> White bones remained the remnants of her feast.

Her son Mehmed Emin was corrupt, and I blame Nur Sultan's meddling for the evils of her son.⁸ The assembly (*quriltai*) deposed him twice,⁹ but each time, after an all too brief lapse of time, the assembly, at the behest of the council of state (*qarachi beys*), restored him to the throne.

---

¹ The Muslim practice is to say the *shahada*, "There is no god but God and Muhammed is his messenger," three times in the ears of a newborn to set the infant on the proper path in life. What Ismail reports here in Arabic is the *tawheed*, the first part of the *shahada*.

² Ismail is referring here to the system of precedence (*mestnichestvo*), which ranked clans according to proximity to the ruler and individuals within each clan, all of which was dependent on their being of the Russian Orthodox faith.

³ Ilham reigned twice, 1479–85 and 1486–87. The "third year" apparently refers to the first reign and would place Ismail's birth in 1482.

⁴ Ulug (or Ulu) Mehmed founded the khanate of Kazan by 1445. He had been ousted as khan of the Jochid ulus (also sometimes called the "Qipchaq khanate" or, incorrectly, the Golden Horde by his cousin in 1435). Ulug Mehmed fled north, battled the Muscovite army at Belev in 1437, and subsequently settled in Kazan. The term *ulus* refers to his realm, also called *yurt*.

⁵ She was a Nogai princess and a great-granddaughter of Edigei, who had besieged Moscow in 1408.

⁶ Halil had been khan of Kazan from 1466 to 1467. When he died, Ibrahim, who had been chosen to succeed his brother, married Nur Sultan to secure his position.

⁷ That would have been either in later 1486 or early 1487.

⁸ Ismail seems to be overstating the case here in regard to Nur Sultan's influence, although she did in fact write a letter to Ivan III in August 1498 complaining about his support for another of her sons, Abdullatif, over Mehmed Emin and pleaded with him to do what he could to get Mehmed Emin restored to the throne. *SRIO*, 41: 272. What effect that letter had in getting him restored, we cannot say.

⁹ That would have been in 1486, when he was replaced by Ilham for a year, and in 1496, when he was replaced by his brother Abdullatif for five years. Abdullatif then fled

At one point, Mehmed Emin turned treacherously on Muscovy and, driven by greed, attacked Muscovite merchants in Kazan, who were there under a safe-conduct decree.[10] He confiscated all their wares, killed some, and sold the rest into slavery. Not only was this in violation of the *shari'a*[11] and his own promises, but also it led to immediate hardship for our people as the unsettled conditions kept merchants away from our city, which in many respects depends on the trade along the Idel.[12] Shortly after that, Vasilii ascended the throne of Muscovy and, along with Kudai Kul, sought just retribution for this cowardly attack.[13] I was a young man at the time[14] and was called out to protect Kazan for what Mehmed Emin had done. Fortunately I did not have to fight Kudai Kul, for I was assigned to the southern flank to defend against a possible attack from the Nogais in collaboration with the Muscovites.

Somewhat to my dismay, Mehmed Emin defeated the Muscovite forces and remained on the throne for many years.[15] How appropriate and how ironic to recall the words of a poem he is reputed to have written:

> The world was ruined; Islam lay broken, shattered,
> And tears like rivers flowed down every cheek.
> Now what will be his answer before God
> When he is questioned for his evil deeds?

When this corrupt son of Nur Sultan died, the assembly and council of state were fed up with the influence from Mengli Girey's successor, the Crimean khan

---

to Moscow. The *quriltai* was an assembly of notable men who advised the khan on significant matters concerning the khanate and who had the power to depose a reigning khan and select a new khan. One notes that Ismail consistently writes that the assembly of Kazan selected the khan. This is in contrast, on the one hand, to Muscovite sources, which say that the grand prince chose the khan, and, on the other, to the Crimean khans, who insisted they chose the khan of Kazan. The *qarachi beys* were the heads of the four most prominent clans in the khanate. Collectively, they acted as a council of state.

[10] That would have been June 1505.

[11] The *shari'a* is the ethical and moral code of Islam based on the Qur'an and the Sunna (the example of the Prophet, literally means "the path").

[12] Idel was the Tatar name for the Volga. In Arabic, it was Itil.

[13] Kudai Kul was the son of Khan Ibrahim and Ibrahim's first wife, Fatima, and the younger brother of Khan Ilham and Melik-Tagir. He left Kazan in 1487 and was held incommunicado by Ivan III for eighteen years. Under Vasilii III, Kudai Kul converted to Christianity, taking the baptismal name Peter, married the grand prince's sister, and became the second most powerful individual in Muscovy.

[14] Ismail would have been twenty-three or twenty-four years old.

[15] In contrast, the Muscovite sources report that the Muscovites defeated the forces of Kazan in this war, which ended in 1507. Mehmed Emin died in 1518.

Mehmed Girey. They chose as khan a candidate who was friendly to Muscovy and a close kinsman of the khan of Astrakhan.[16] But he was only a boy and no match for the political machinations of those who were won over by the Gireys with promises of wealth and influence. After three years, the assembly met again, deposed the boy khan, and placed Sahib Girey on the throne.

I go into some detail about these political developments because it is directly related to the most important decision of my life—to place myself in exile from my homeland and begin helping the Christian grand prince of Moscow. That happened thirty-one years ago. Much to my dismay I find myself still in exile and missing more than ever the sights, sounds, and aromas of Kazan, the hustle and bustle of its marketplace, the call to prayer of the muezzin, and the powerful solemnity of its Friday mosque where I had gone to worship each week.

For some time before I actually left Kazan, I had been considering the possibility of doing so. Following Kudai Kul's rise to the highest position of power within the princedom of Muscovy just behind the grand prince, I was tempted to come over to the Muscovites. Kudai Kul, who had taken the baptismal name Peter, after whom my own eldest son took his baptismal name, tried to convince me to join the Muscovites with the hope of restoring just rule to Kazan. But I could not bring myself at first to side with Christians against my homeland. My alternatives were to go over to the Ottoman sultan or the khan of Astrakhan. I never really considered the khan of Sibir, for his crowd was not highly regarded by those of us who think of ourselves as part of the civilized descendants of Chinggis Khan. Nor could I consider the Crimean court, for my family had a falling out with the Gireys, and we objected to the Gireys' influence in the realm of Ulug Mehmed.[17]

I opposed the candidacy of Sahib Girey both because my family and the Gireys had been on unfriendly terms and because I knew Mehmed [Girey], who was khan of the Crimea, would use his brother's position to expand his own influence and to oppress the Kazanian polity. Little did I realize how quickly he would do so. When the assembly and divan decided in favor of Sahib, I began to make alternate plans. One plan was to flee to the Ottomans by begging the protection of the sultan, Suleiman the Lawgiver. But the sultan declined on the basis that Mehmed Girey was his vassal and his granting asylum to me might be misunderstood. Apparently he had advisers who were aware of my family's difficulties with the Gireys. I decided against applying to the khan of Astrakhan because he was a puppet of the Gireys.

So I finally yielded to the blandishments of Kudai Kul. I asked Musa, a prince

---

[16] That was the thirteen-year-old Shah Ali (Shigalei), who at the time was ostensibly the khan of Kasimov.

[17] It is not immediately apparent which clan Ismail belonged to, but this statement that his family did not get along with the Gireys may point to his belonging to the Shirin clan, one of the largest in Kazan. They and the Gireys were antagonists for many years.

of the Nogais, to write a letter on my behalf to the Christian ruler.[18] He wrote it and sent it to the grand prince of Muscovy with a junior kinsman of his, *mirza* Ulan. Apparently, as I found out later, the grand prince of Muscovy, Vasilii Ivanovich, was concerned that his granting asylum to me would adversely affect his already worsening relations with Mehmed Girey, for he wrote a letter to Mehmed telling him what he was about to do. He did not want to provoke Mehmed into thinking he was doing something on the sly. Relations between Vasilii and Mehmed shortly thereafter disintegrated completely, so Vasilii then seems to have felt he no longer owed any obligation to try to stay on friendly terms with Mehmed. Or perhaps he just wanted to trumpet the fact that more Jochid princes were coming over to him.

The next thing I knew I received a return message from Musa that the grand prince had granted my request. I think also Kudai Kul intervened on my behalf. During the time when Kudai Kul had been held by Ivan Vasilievich, the father of Vasilii, under strict restrictions,[19] Kudai Kul and Vasilii had become "blood brothers" (*anda*). I later found out that Vasilii had convinced Kudai Kul to convert to Christianity and give up the teachings of the Prophet (may God's prayer and Peace be upon him). Vasilii was in the grips of his own struggle for the succession and prevailed upon him with the argument that the fate of the principality of Muscovy hung in the balance. He admired Kudai Kul, as did Kudai Kul him, and believed he would make a better ruler than any of his own brothers, should anything happen to him. But the old man, Ivan Vasilievich, would not allow it. He still had hopes of using Kudai Kul as a bargaining chip in the three-cornered diplomatic game among Muscovy, Kazan, and the Crimea. Vasilii's father was a shrewd player of that game and could easily, on the one hand, have sold out Kudai Kul to Mengli Girey or, on the other, supported his candidacy for khan of Kazan and, through him, have greater influence on Kazanian policy. Kudai Kul could become khan only as long as he remained faithful to the teachings of the Prophet, for the divan and assembly could be counted on to resist a Christian khan.

When Ivan Vasilievich died, Vasilii came to the throne and immediately granted Kudai Kul's petition to be baptized into Christianity. Not long after his baptism, Kudai Kul married the sister of Vasilii.[20] This marriage secured Kudai Kul's position in the hierarchy of Muscovy. But his becoming a Christian virtually eliminated his chances of ever becoming khan of Kazan. Nonetheless, I heard it said, after I came over to the Muscovites, that Vasilii had hopes that Kudai Kul would succeed him as grand prince and perhaps then unite the realm of Muscovy with that of Kazan, because, after all, Kudai Kul was a descendant of Chinggis Khan.

I did not think it possible then that a non-Muslim would ever rule in Kazan, but

---

[18] Most likely Ismail thought it would have been too risky to write such a letter himself and send it from Kazan. If it were intercepted, he would have some serious explaining to do.

[19] Ismail is referring here to the period 1487–1505.

[20] Kudai Kul/Peter married Evdokiia, the sister of Vasilii III, on January 25, 1506, just over a month after his baptism in the Moscow River (December 21, 1505).

now I find in the twilight of my life, that this very thing I said over and again could never happen is now about to happen with the Christian khan, Ivan of Moscow. It is sometimes difficult for us mere mortals to comprehend the ways of God. Yet especially when we do not comprehend His ways, His will must be done. We are required to obey and not to be led astray by unfounded doubts or idle questioning.

In any case, my worst fears concerning Sahib Girey were confirmed shortly after he came to the golden throne. His brother Mehmed began sending Crimean forces northward, took over control of the city of Kazan, and used the city as a base of operations to attack Moscow. My first role in support of the Muscovite grand prince was to lead a contingent of horsemen to harry Mehmed Girey's forces on their way from Kazan. Kudai Kul took charge of the defense of Moscow while the Christian grand prince fled for his own protection.[21] Thanks be to God, Mehmed Girey did not succeed in taking Moscow. I won't be so bold as to claim that my harrying tactics decided the outcome of the campaign. Other Jochid princes aided the Christian grand prince; and most of all, Kudai Kul's staunch defense of Moscow led Mehmed to realize he was overmatched. After demanding and receiving agreement from the Muscovites to pay him annual tribute, Mehmed took his forces back to the Crimea. Yet he continued to dominate and oppress Kazan even after his brother Sahib died three years later.

The transition to supporting the Muscovite ruler was not easy, and there were many times I was tempted to return to my home in Kazan. Most of those in the Russian court I found to be rather rude and uncultured, although I did have some interesting conversations with a certain Dmitrii Erasmus.[22] Kudai Kul was around in the beginning to remind me of why I had come over to the Muscovite grand prince. Although the Muscovite grand prince was not without his faults, he did seem interested in restoring just rule to my homeland. Kudai Kul assured me that I would not need to convert to the Russian faith, for he saw that I could not leave the faith of my fathers and my fathers' fathers. But I never thought I would be with the Muscovites so long that my own sons would grow into manhood here and want to convert. I had a number of heated arguments with them. I explained that when we returned to Kazan their Christianity would prevent their advancement. I quoted the Holy Qur'an and threatened them with eternal damnation for turning away from God. I even repeated to them the words of the poet Kol Sharif:

> My soul! Do not yield to the world.
> The world is forever constrained;
> And all those who live in this world
> To the goblet of death are chained.

---

[21] According to the Muscovite chronicles, Vasilii III repaired to Volok, just to the west of Moscow, to await the outcome of the battle for Moscow.

[22] That may well have been Dmitrii Gerasimov, who had traveled to Italy in 1525–26 and knew Latin.

Yet they countered my every argument as well as my every plea, and always brought up Kudai Kul and his conversion. They knew how much I admired that great champion. They also seemed to want to forget what they considered the "old" ways; they wanted to adopt what, from their point of view, are the "new" ways of Muscovy. During this period of dispute with my sons, I wished many times for my sons' sake that I had never left Kazan.

My dream in coming over to the Christian ruler of Muscovy was both to escape the oppression of the Gireys and to work for the establishment of justice. I had hoped that a khan of great capability and humanity could ascend to the golden throne. I did not see the possibility of that occurring under Girey rule and dominance. Instead, I saw only death and destruction for Kazan unless I and others like me took action. It was incongruous that I should look for life and constructive efforts in a Christian realm. We always had contempt for the Christians. True, they were people of the Book and we tolerated their religious practices, except for that awful ringing of bells that they are prone to—nothing like the sublime beauty of our call to prayer.[23] We Muslims should be grateful for the purity and grace of Islam. That cacophonic din in Moscow is one of the reasons I have been there only twice, both times to affirm my allegiance on the Holy Qur'an they keep in their citadel for such purposes. The first time I went to Moscow was when I first affirmed allegiance to Vasilii. The second time was to affirm allegiance to his son Ivan the current ruler when he was crowned tsar a few years ago. I have been fortunate to be able to spend most of my time in the countryside near Murom so much like the countryside of my homeland. I tend the estate and villages that the present ruler's father so generously granted me for my support. I read the literature of my homeland and take solace in the Holy Qur'an and in our great poets. The beginning of one poem, in particular, by Muhammed Yar comes to me now as describing my life here:

> One day as I was sitting in my room
> And drinking deeply from the cup of gloom,

---

[23] Ismail is referring here to the Islamic call (*adhān*) to prayer (*salat*), which the *muezzin* acclaims five times a day. The words of the *adhān* translated into English are

> God is great! God is great! God is great! God is great!
> I bear witness that there is no god but God.
> I bear witness that there is no god but God.
> I bear witness that Muhammed is the messenger of God.
> I bear witness that Muhammed is the messenger of God.
> Come to prayer! Come to prayer!
> Come to prosperity. Come to prosperity.
> God is great! God is great!
> There is no god but God.

> Burnt in the fire that blazed within my heart,
> A trembling prisoner, grieved and torn apart,
>
> I cried: "My heart, be calm. Do not torment
> My soul. Now give me peace. Relent!"
>
> My heart replied: "Remember, God commanded
> That I should rule you. Thus it was demanded."

Although I have been to the Friday mosque in Kasimov many times, for it is only 70 versts [75 kilometers] away, I don't have much to do with Khan Shah Ali and his crowd there, who are merely puppets of the grand prince.[24] They do not realize that the Christians have nothing to offer us; and, besides, we are better fighters in battle and superior in techniques of the bow, which they do not practice sufficiently. Yet I saw observance of the ways of my fathers and my fathers' fathers diminishing. I sought solace in the words of the poet Saif-i Sarai:

> The morning breeze will always chase the fleeting clouds;
> The wind of grief will ever blow throughout the land;
> But let brave men still speak their fathers' noble tongue
> And on their horses vie and triumph hand in hand.

The grand and glorious Abode of Islam (*Dar al-Islam*) with its many accomplishments and achievements in science, mathematics, medicine, and art was now receding from us under the oppressive practices of unjust rulers. The magnificent Ottoman sultan Suleiman the Lawgiver expressed concern for Kazan and even claimed it as his part of his realm (*yurt*),[25] but he was far away and had his own struggles with the Persians. The only hope I saw was that we could ally with the Muscovites, and they would help us to restore just rule to our land.

Now my own sons have adopted the infidel's cult, and they go off with the Christian tsar to conquer my (and not just my, but their) homeland for him. My only consolation is that their army is commanded by Prince Ivan Mstislavskii, the grandson of Kudai Kul. Yet only God knows when the Muslims of Kazan will be free to rule themselves again. God is great.

written 27 Jamadilakhir 959 A.H. (July 20, 1552)

---

[24] Ismail is referring to the khanate of Kasimov, which was set up under the auspices of Ivan III.

[25] That occurred in 1524 when Iskander, an envoy from Suleiman, made the claim.

Suggestions for Further Reading

Historical Anthology of Kazan Tatar Verse: Voices of Eternity. Edited and translated by David J. Matthews and Ravil Bukharaev. Richmond, UK: Curzon Press, 2000. Provides the full texts of the Kazanian Tatar poetry quoted in the text.

Keenan, Edward L. "Muscovy and Kazan: Some Introductory Remarks on the Patterns of Steppe Diplomacy." *Slavic Review* 26, no. 4 (1967): 548–58. Discusses Muscovy and Kazan within the context of steppe diplomacy.

Khodarkovsky, Michael. "Taming the 'Wild Steppe': Muscovy's Southern Frontier, 1480–1600." *Russian History* 26, no. 3 (1999): 241–97. Focuses on the relationship of Muscovy and Kazan.

Martin, Janet. "Muscovite Relations with the Khanate of Kazan' and the Crimea (1460s to 1521)." *Canadian–American Slavic Studies* 17 (1983): 435–53. Discusses the economy of the khanate of Kazan.

Ostrowski, Donald. "The Extraordinary Career of Tsarevich Kudai Kul/Peter in the Context of Relations Between Muscovy and Kazan'." In *States, Societies, and Cultures East and West: Essays in Honor of Jaroslaw Pelenski.* Edited by Janusz Duzinkewicz et al. New York: Ross, 2004, 697–718. Discusses the tsarevich Kudai Kul/Peter.

———. "Ruling Class Structures of the Kazan' Khanate." In *The Turks.* 6 vols. Edited by Hasan Celâl Güzel, C. Cem Oğuz, and Osman Karatay. Ankara: Yeni Türkiye, 2002. Volume 2: *Middle Ages*, 841–47. Recreates the social and political structure of the khanate of Kazan.

Pelenski, Jaroslaw. *Russia and Kazan: Conquest and Imperial Ideology (1438–1560s).* The Hague: Mouton, 1974. Analyzes the relationship of Muscovy and Kazan.

Gleb Vasilievich
A Prince in Fourteenth-Century Yaroslavl

Lawrence N. Langer

History is replete with people whose names momentarily surface in dusty records only to submerge again in a past largely forgotten. They are the fleeting traces of a once-lived world, tantalizing bits of information that catch the imagination, beckoning us to try to cross a great historical divide between the then and the now. Such is the enticement offered by Gleb Vasilievich, a minor appanage prince who lived in fourteenth-century Yaroslavl but whose existence was not of sufficient import to find its way into contemporaneous chronicles. Appanage princes received their principality as an inheritance from their father. Gleb lived at a time when Rus was subservient to the Mongols of the Jochid ulus (Qipchaq khanate), and when Moscow emerged as the center of political and ecclesiastical power in northeastern Rus. The Muscovite princes were successful in obtaining the title of grand prince of Vladimir, the titular head of the Rus principalities. The Mongol khans of the Jochid ulus granted such titles by conferring a patent (iarlyk) on the Muscovite princes, who often had to fight off rival claimants, such as the princes of Tver or Suzdal–Nizhnii Novgorod to the title. As the Jochid ulus declined in the late fourteenth century, Moscow increasingly asserted its political independence and secured the loyalty and subservience of many of the appanage princes.

The little information that exists for Gleb derives from later genealogical books, and all that they record is that he had three sons, named Ivan, Fedor, and Konstantin; that he was alive in 1340 (age unknown); and that perhaps he died at or witnessed the Battle of Kulikovo in 1380. There are no records of Gleb's birth, marriage, or death to be found. We do know that Gleb's father, Vasilii Davidovich, was prince of Yaroslavl and died in 1345. His mother, Evdokia, was the daughter of Ivan I "Moneybag" (Kalita)[1] *of Moscow and died three years earlier, in 1342.*

---

[1] Ivan I, prince of Moscow (1325–1341) and grand prince of Vladimir (1331–1341). The sobriquet "Kalita" means "moneybag," implying Ivan's careful policy of collecting and paying the Mongol tribute.

This miniature from a seventeenth-century manuscript in the State History Museum (GIM) depicts the *Legend about Mamai's Battle* (Skazanie o Mamaevom poboishche), from the cycle of tales about the Battle of Kulikovo in 1380. In the miniature, Rus and Tatar forces are indistinguishable from each other. Notice the severed heads, arm, leg, and headless torso along with curved swords at the bottom of the image. Prince Gleb Vasilievich, the historical person who is the subject of this chapter, may have been killed at Kulikovo.

Gleb had an older brother, Vasilii, who at some point became prince of Yaroslavl, and a younger brother, Roman, both of whom fought at Kulikovo. (See the genealogy at the end of this chapter.) Unfortunately, fourteenth-century sources provide little information about the wives and daughters of princely families or the nature and dynamics of family life; therefore, anything said about Gleb must of necessity remain speculative and can only suggest what may have occurred to an appanage prince in Yaroslavl. The life of Gleb that is presented is a composite drawn from evidence common to the lives of many other fourteenth-century princes. The events and personages described, however, are based on actual historical occurrences.

Yaroslavl was founded in 1024 on the upper Volga and its tributary, the Kotorosl River, which linked it to Rostov. Natural defensive ravines existed on both the Kotorosl and Volga embankments, and the fortress or kremlin was built on a spit between the ravines. Before the Mongol conquest, the town expanded and built a second line of fortifications, which incorporated the Savior Monastery as part of its defensive wall. The town contained a trading center and suburb with a moat, ramparts, and towers. Yaroslavl was not a large town. It may have had a population of five thousand or six thousand people, perhaps declining to four thousand during the plague years of the second half of the fourteenth century. The town was sufficiently small to traverse easily on horseback. Its inhabitants would have been familiar to Gleb.

For the purposes of this imagined biography we can posit Gleb's birth sometime in the mid-1330s. Both his brothers died in 1380 at Kulikovo, and Gleb may have perished at the battle as well, when he was in his mid-forties, an age few Russians ever lived beyond, since life expectancy for males was low, even after they reached adulthood. We know Gleb had three surviving sons, but we do not know whether he had any daughters or how many of his children may have died in infancy. Death was a constant companion of medieval life.

Gleb grew up in the shadow of Mongol rule. As was true of any of the Riurikids[2] in the northeast, the princes of Yaroslavl had to accommodate themselves to the realities of Mongol power. The princes of Yaroslavl controlled an independent appanage principality, which they bequeathed to their sons, but they were not in the line of succession to the title of grand prince of Vladimir, the titular head of the northeastern Rus principalities, who was responsible for the collection of the Mongol tribute. The Yaroslavl princes often played a political game of acknowledging whoever was grand prince of Vladimir while attempting to preserve as much of their independence as possible.

Gleb's grandfather, David, had two sons: Vasilii "the Dread" (*Groznyi*), Gleb's father; and Mikhail, prince of Mologa. Vasilii opposed Ivan I Moneybag's efforts

---

[2] The descendants of Riurik, a Scandinavian warlord who by tradition founded the line of princely rulers in Rus in 862.

to acquire the Mongol patent[3] to the grand principality of Vladimir for Moscow, even though Vasilii had married Ivan's daughter, Evdokia. In 1320, Yaroslavl and Rostov both rioted against the Mongols. Two years later, Ivan, with the backing of Mongol troops, seized and pillaged Yaroslavl, taking away many prisoners to be held for ransom or sold into slavery.

The calamity at Yaroslavl would be repeated in Rostov and Tver in 1327. When the khan summoned Prince Aleksandr Mikhailovich of Tver to Sarai in 1339 and executed him along with his son, Fedor, it becomes entirely clear why Gleb's father resisted a similar demand. Ivan I Moneybag in fact dispatched five hundred men and forcibly brought Vasilii to Sarai, but Gleb's father escaped harm.

Upon Ivan's death in 1341, Vasilii joined other princes from Tver and Suzdal at Sarai, to prevent Semen[4] of Moscow from acquiring the patent to Vladimir. The effort failed, and Vasilii found himself joining Moscow in a campaign against Torzhok, where Moscow extorted a heavy tribute of 1,000 rubles, a sum equal to the tribute owed the Mongols by the entire Muscovite principality. The possibilities of acquiring silver could always induce a degree of loyal behavior. These would have been lessons not lost on Gleb.

Following tradition, eight days after his birth Gleb was baptized and given his name day in the Church of the Savior. Did Gleb receive any education? Likely not, as most princes were illiterate or obtained at best a rudimentary ability to read from ecclesiastical tutors. He did learn the arts of combat and horse riding, probably from boyars attached to his father's household. It would have been part of his good breeding to be steeped in the horse culture of Muscovy. Hardy if rather unprepossessing, the Muscovite horses were well suited for warfare and the harsh winters of the forest and steppe. The purchasing of horses from Tatar traders and the maintenance of the herds, as well as the skills of hunting and falconry, were central to Gleb's training as a prince.

Gleb's primary education, however, meant understanding the realities of Mongol power. It was not uncommon for princes, when they reached ages as young as eleven or twelve, to be sent to the Horde (as Russians called the Qipchaq khanate). Dmitrii Donskoi[5] was eleven when he was first brought to the Horde, only to flee soon after the khan's murder. Gleb understood the necessity of preserving the flow of tribute and the importance of appearing personally with gifts to acknowledge Mongol rule. He may have been too young to accompany his father when Vasilii, together with other princes, appeared at the Horde in 1342 to recognize the succession of Khan Janibeg. Semen of Moscow became a frequent traveler to the Horde, appearing there in 1344, 1347, and 1351 and bearing, no doubt, the tribute. On one of these journeys, Gleb joined the grand prince's entourage for his first venture to

---

[3] The patent (*iarlyk*) was bestowed by the khan of the Qipchaq khanate on a Russian prince, who thereby became titular head of the princes of the northeastern Rus.

[4] Semen Ivanovich, prince of Moscow and grand prince of Vladimir (1341–53).

[5] Grand Prince of Moscow (1359–89).

Sarai, where he encountered a multitude of different peoples, reflecting the vast extent of the Mongol empire: Russians, Kumans, Greeks, Italians, Egyptians, Syrians, and others, each group with its own quarters and bazaars and religious houses of worship. He may have found the Mongol appearance strange: the men with partially shaved heads and braided plaits of hair in the rear, the women who sat astride their horses like men. He avoided the drinking of mare's milk, fearing for the loss of his soul, yet he could not but help admire the warriors bedecked with bows and arrows and curved swords.

Princes were obligated to fund urban and ecclesiastical construction, but it was expensive and Yaroslavl did not have the resources available to Moscow. Semen could afford to send money to defray the costs of repair of the Cathedral of St. Sophia in Constantinople in 1347 and to maintain the defenses and rebuild his town following such disasters as the four major fires between 1330 and 1343 or the great flood of 1347. Church construction, the painting of frescoes, or the casting of bells all drew on the resources of the secular and ecclesiastical authorities, as well as wealthy boyars and merchants. But the absence of a bishopric in Yaroslavl meant the princes bore much of the burden. They acquired most of their income through the collection of the tribute, commercial taxes, judicial fines, and transit fees along the Volga. Yaroslavl maintained an administrative and tax structure similar to that of Moscow. At the head of the princely household administration stood the chamberlain, who supervised a small group of slaves, while boyars lent their advice in council.

In 1345, Gleb's father died. He was tonsured a monk on his deathbed and buried in the Church of the Savior. Gleb was perhaps ten years old. The traditions of lateral succession[6] should have brought Gleb's uncle, Mikhail of Mologa, to the head of the principality, but the chronicle information is inconclusive as to whether Mikhail or Gleb's elder brother, Vasilii, became prince of Yaroslavl. We can only guess at the possibility of a family division between Gleb and his brothers and the family of Mikhail, a not uncommon occurrence among princely families. Nonetheless, in the following generation princely rule reverted to the children of Vasilii, while Mikhail's family carved out a separate patrimony in Mologa.

In the divisions of Yaroslavl into smaller patrimonies, Gleb received lands that lay just north of the Volga River, while his younger brother, Roman, held lands just to the west. There do not seem to be any towns in Gleb's patrimony, but he controlled several settled areas, particularly two important villages (Golovinskoe and Skomorakhov). There were also forests and easy access to the Volga and other rivers. The absence, however, of urban areas in Gleb's patrimony, and the general lack of urban centers, other than Mologa, throughout Yaroslavl probably meant that Gleb and his two brothers shared the revenues generated from Yaroslavl itself.

---

[6] Ascension to princely rule followed a pattern whereby brother succeeded brother, rather than father passing the throne to son. Following the death of the last eligible brother, succession would shift to the next generation.

The brothers were responsible for the collection of tribute within their individual patrimonies. Villages paid the tribute, either in silver or more likely in furs, and supported the upkeep of princely servitors who dispensed justice and collected taxes. In the wake of the plague, the taxes imposed on a reduced population were even more onerous.

The modest economic expansion that occurred in the 1340s in Rus was cut short by the outbreak of plague, which struck widely and deeply. The epidemic of 1352 erupted in Pskov and spread throughout Rus. The stricken populace manifested the characteristic symptoms of pneumonic plague as they spat blood and succumbed within three days. The dead were everywhere. Graves of five and ten were dug, until churchyards could no longer accommodate the dead and new graves were dug far from the churches. It is said that not a soul survived in Beloozero. A panicked populace began to distribute its wealth to the churches and monasteries in return for prayers for the dead. The plague devastated the Muscovite house of Semen, killing him and his two young sons—Ivan, aged two, and Semen, aged one—along with Metropolitan Feognost.

At the time of these epidemics Gleb was sixteen or seventeen, a marriageable age. His bride was probably no older than fifteen and the daughter of a minor princely or an important Yaroslavl boyar family. Following Semen's death in 1353, the princes gathered in Sarai for the selection of the new grand prince of Vladimir. Gleb joined them and, like the others, remained there for a year. He was now a frequent visitor to Sarai, traveling there in 1355, when the princes of Starodub and Suzdal sought to obtain the patents to their patrimonies; in 1357, following the murder of Khan Janibeg, when the princes assembled at the Horde to acknowledge the new khan, Berdibeg; and again in 1359, after the death of Ivan II of Moscow and the murder of Khan Berdibeg, when the Russian princes made their way to Sarai to confirm their positions within their individual patrimonies.

It was a time of evil portents and evil events. In 1360, Gleb watched as clouds the color of blood stretched across the sky. The next year he witnessed the moon disappearing in a sky once more turned red. The cosmology available to him drew on the tenth-century *Hexaemeron* of Ioan, exarch of Bulgaria, which by the late fourteenth century had found its way to the Kirillo-Belozersk Monastery, or evoked the complex images of the sixth-century Egyptian monk Cosmas Indicopleustes. From the *Hexaemeron*, the world would have appeared like an egg with the earth as the yellow yoke, the air as the surrounding egg white, and the sky as the shell. Cosmas's universe was based on an imagined image of the Old Testament tabernacle. The cosmos was shaped something like a quadrangle capped by a cylindrical vault with a material and corruptible world that lay just below an incorruptible sphere. Cosmas's universe was reflected in the architecture of a church, wherein the sanctuary embodied the invisible sky of the firmament. The workings of the four elements of earth, water, air, and fire brought either harmony or conflict within the material universe.

The astronomical portents that engendered fear and wonder in the monastic scribes played on Gleb's imagination as well. The light, which fled from the moon in an eclipse, was akin to the soul leaving the body. A sun's eclipse was an angel crowned with fire. In the Apocalypse of Baruch, the moon at the beginning of creation was more luminous than the sun itself, but when Adam sinned and all of creation wept at his transgression, only the moon laughed and, therefore, was condemned to see its light again and again lose itself to darkness. In 1361, Gleb saw the moon withdraw its light; and in 1371, the sky turned so red that that even the snow, water, and homes took on the terrifying hue. Such signs could only mean disaster. When the sun grew dark, Gleb knew that drought prevailed throughout the land.

Gleb and his brothers were responsible for maintaining the flow of trade along the Volga through Yaroslavl. But beginning in 1360, the Volga trade route was in upheaval as marauding raiders (*ushkuiniki*) from Novgorod appeared, challenging the Volga Bulgars and Moscow for control of the Volga fur trade. It was an era of vast changes as the Qipchaq khanate disintegrated into fratricidal wars (the era of "Great Troubles"); plague and famine ravaged much of Rus; and civil war engulfed Moscow, Suzdal, Nizhnii Novgorod, and Tver. In 1361, young Dmitrii of Moscow—together with the princes of Suzdal–Nizhnii Novgorod, Rostov, and Yaroslavl—appeared at the Horde. Gleb traveled with them.

In 1364, a terrible outbreak of plague occurred in Nizhnii Novgorod, killing fifty to a hundred per day. The plague then swept throughout all the towns in Rus. Plague again struck much of Rus in 1365, killing Prince Konstantin of Rostov, his wife and children, the bishop and other princes, boyars, and merchants (*gosti*, who may well have brought the epidemic with them). That same year plague struck Tver, and a terrible fire destroyed much of Moscow as drought also stalked the land.

This was Gleb's world. In 1366, a year when plague and drought again ravaged Moscow and raiders pillaged merchants along the Kama River and attacked Nizhnii Novgorod, Dmitrii Donskoi married Evdokia, daughter of Grand Prince Dmitrii Konstantinovich of Suzdal–Nizhnii Novgorod, but the ceremony was held outside Moscow, in Kolomna. Gleb no doubt would have attended so important an occasion.

In the wars that erupted between Moscow and Tver, Gleb threw his support to Dmitrii and tried to answer the call for help against the invading force of Lithuanians, allies of Tver, who besieged Moscow in 1368. Gleb's first concern, however, was the safety of Yaroslavl. His ability to protect his town was sorely tested in 1372, when raiders attacked and plundered Yaroslavl. It was his and the Yaroslavl princes' greatest failure.

Three years later, Moscow, together with the princes of Yaroslavl, launched a major invasion of Tver. For four weeks, the army besieged Tver, burning and plundering the suburbs and districts, taking off many into captivity, and finally storming the town itself.

After 1375, there was no longer any doubt that Dmitrii had secured Moscow's preeminent political and military position among the Russian princes. He restored order along the Volga, netting some 5,000 rubles from the Bulgars, a sum equal to the entire yearly tribute owed by the grand principality of Vladimir to the Horde. Gleb cast his lot with Moscow—he would have had no real choice, and he would have reaped the rewards, partaking in the plunder and distribution of the 5,000 rubles.

The Mongols were keenly aware of Moscow's intrusion into the middle Volga. In 1377, Arab-Shah, prince of the Horde, raided the area near Nizhnii Novgorod. Troops from Yaroslavl joined an army led by Grand Prince Dmitrii Konstantinovich of Suzdal–Nizhnii Novgorod. They arrived at the Piana River, a tributary of the Sura River. There, believing the Tatars had retreated, the Russian soldiers relaxed without their armor, drinking beer, mead, and wine. Arab-shah attacked the unsuspecting Rus and slaughtered most of the troops. Dmitrii Konstantinovich's son, Ivan, drowned in the Piana River trying to escape, but no mention is made of the loss of any Yaroslavl princes. Still, the defeat resonated among the town's populace.

Moscow's assertion of its dominant political and military place among the principalities in the late 1370s brought it into conflict with the looming presence of Mamai's Horde. The inevitable conflict between Moscow and Mamai brought their armies to the fields of Kulikovo in September 1380. As tensions rose and Dmitrii gathered a large army, he found himself without the support of Riazan (which openly backed Mamai), Novgorod, Suzdal–Nizhnii Novgorod, and Tver. These principalities had decided discretion was the better part of valor. Instead, Dmitrii looked to the retinues of those princes who were largely subject to Moscow's authority and influence: namely, Beloozero, Galich, Yaroslavl, Iuriev, Kostroma, Pereiaslavl, Rostov, Serpukhov, and Uglich.

After almost a century and half of Mongol rule and participation in Mongol campaigns, the Russian princes knew well how the Mongol army operated and were familiar with their military tactics. The Muscovite army at Kulikovo copied Mongol deployment of troops, dividing their forces into five major divisions. The largest contingent occupied the central division and was flanked by right and left wings (or hands). In front of the line stood advanced divisions, and a reserve unit remained in the rear. Another division lay in ambush in a wooded area at some distance beyond the left wing. The troops from Yaroslavl were placed under Vladimir Andreevich of Serpukhov, who commanded the reserve unit in the oak wood.

Gleb donned the traditional military gear of chain mail, which covered his torso and his thighs. A metal conical helmet protected his head with metal extensions around his eyes and over his nose. He also used light chain mail to protect the face and neck. He carried a sword and a shield that was wider across the top than at the bottom, or tapered down somewhat in the shape of a triangle. In addition, Gleb armed himself with a lance and probably bow and arrows, as well as a battle-ax, which hung at the side of his armor- and leather-plated horse. The Rus, however, faced a formidable foe. The Mongols traditionally employed cavalry charges with warriors armed with steppe recurved or composite bows that required a pull of up to 160 lbs and had a destructive range between 200 and 300 yards. Their swords were light, sharp sabers, and they carried lances with hooks to pull the enemy off a horse as well as maces.

Mongol tactics were devastating. The army was organized on a decimal system with divisions theoretically consisting of ten thousand men and subdivided into units of one thousand, one hundred, and ten. This allowed for greater coordination through the use of signal flags. In battle, rows of archers on horseback rotated firing volleys of arrows that were usually sufficient to disorganize and weaken the front lines of the enemy. This was followed by flanking movements of the right and left hands to surround the enemy in much the same manner that the Mongols had learned how to encircle animals in a hunt that stretched over a vast area. Sometimes the Mongols would feign retreats to draw the opposing cavalry into a fatal charge that caught them between the flanking divisions. The Mongols were also extremely adept at firing volleys of arrows as they retreated by turning in their saddles.

The Russians expected the initial volleys of arrows and held their ground. They had marshaled their troops on a field that was surrounded largely by a wooded area that made it very difficult for the Mongols to employ their traditional flanking tactics. This time, the Mongol left and right hands had to directly engage their Russian counterparts. After the initial engagements, much of the fighting took place on foot as many of the cavalry on both sides were forced to dismount. The Mongol right wing began to push back the Russian left wing, but in so doing they crossed in front of the Russian reserve troops, which then charged into the Mongol wing.

The attack of Vladimir Andreevich's division turned the tide of battle, but the slaughter took a terrible toll on the princes of Yaroslavl. Gleb's two brothers, Vasilii and Roman, and his cousin Ivan Mikhailovich all died at Kulikovo. It is quite possible that Gleb fought and died alongside his brothers at Kulikovo. If he survived the battle, he may have lived a few more years, perhaps succumbing to plague. In that case Gleb would have requested to be tonsured on his deathbed and to be buried in the Church of the Savior. His name would have been listed in the monastery's commemorative lists of prayers for the dead.

The deaths of Gleb and his brothers, however, are not to be found in the recorded chronicle notations. Unlike the Muscovite princes, and with the important exception of Fedor Chernyi, who died in 1299, there was no tradition of venerating Yaroslavl princes. The fourteenth-century princes of Yaroslavl slip away into an amorphous past, but this leaves a telling clue. What most concerned the chroniclers of northeastern Rus was the story of Moscow and its princes. Non-Muscovite princes appear or not only insofar as they impinge on that tale.

The world of northeastern Rus was changing. Under the guiding hand of Metropolitan Kiprian, particularly during his last sixteen years of tenure (1389–1406), the Church helped lay the foundation of a more explicit Byzantine ideology to enhance the Orthodox stature of the Muscovite princes. The tales of the Battle of Kulikovo and the cult of St. Sergius[7] from the 1430s and 1440s allowed the ecclesiastical bookmen to elaborate a central drama of Moscow's emergence as a

---

[7] St. Sergius of Radonezh (ca. 1314–92), founder and hegumen of the Holy Trinity–St. Sergius Monastery.

political/religious center of Rus. The victories of Timur[8] over the Qipchaq khanate in 1391 and in 1395/96 fundamentally altered the power relationship between the Qipchaq khanate and Rus, ultimately leading to the fragmentation and decline of the Horde. In hindsight, the bookmen could see the significance of the immense changes in Rus between 1380 and 1395.

In the late fourteenth and the fifteenth centuries, the Yaroslavl princes retained ownership over their patrimonies, but they remained subject to calls of military service by Moscow. When the principality was fully incorporated into Moscow in 1463, the princes lost their theoretical sovereignty over the principality but were permitted to reside in Yaroslavl and could continue to cede, sell, and bequeath their lands. They would be expected to render military service. By 1495, Yaroslavl princes were finding places in the court and military of Ivan III. Gleb and his brothers were among the last of the Yaroslavl princes to have ruled a provincial principality still independent, but one that stood at the cusp of a new Muscovite world. After Gleb's death, Yaroslavl was effectively a dependency of Moscow. By the end of the fifteenth century, an appanage prince would have to leave his place of birth and seek his fortune in Moscow.

Suggestions for Further Reading

There are no historical accounts of Yaroslavl in English. Suggested readings on Rus during the Mongol era:

Fennell, John. *The Crisis of Medieval Russia, 1200–1304.* London: Longman, 1983. A study of the Mongol invasions and the political turmoil in thirteenth-century Rus.

Halperin, Charles. *Russia and the Golden Horde: The Mongol Impact on Medieval Russian History.* Bloomington: Indiana University Press, 1985; repr., Bloomington, IN: Slavica Publishers, 2009. A study of Mongol influence on Russian society with particular emphasis on how Rus intellectually failed to adequately cope with the realities and consequences of the Mongol conquest.

Kollmann, Nancy Shields. *Kinship and Politics: The Making of the Muscovite Political System, 1345–1547.* Stanford, CA: Stanford University Press, 1987. An important study of the emergence of the nobility (boyars) in Muscovy and the formation of the Muscovite political system.

Martin, Janet. *Medieval Russia, 980–1584.* Cambridge: Cambridge University Press, 1995. A good basic survey of the history of medieval Russia from the era of Vladimir in Kiev Rus through the death of Ivan the Terrible.

Ostrowski, Donald. *Muscovy and the Mongols: Cross-Cultural Influences on the Steppe Frontier, 1304–1589.* Cambridge: Cambridge University Press, 1998. A controversial study of the role of the Mongols in Russia, which differs from many of Halperin's conclusions.

Presniakov, A.E. *The Formation of the Great Russian State.* Translated by A.E. Moorhouse. Chicago: Quadrangle Books, 1970. An excellent history by a preeminent Russian historian examining the rise of Moscow and the incorporation of the appanage principalities into Muscovy.

---

[8] Timur (Tamerlane; 1320s or 1330s–1405), Central Asian conqueror whose capital was at Samarkand.

34 MEMBERS OF RULING FAMILIES

Genealogy of Yaroslavl Princes

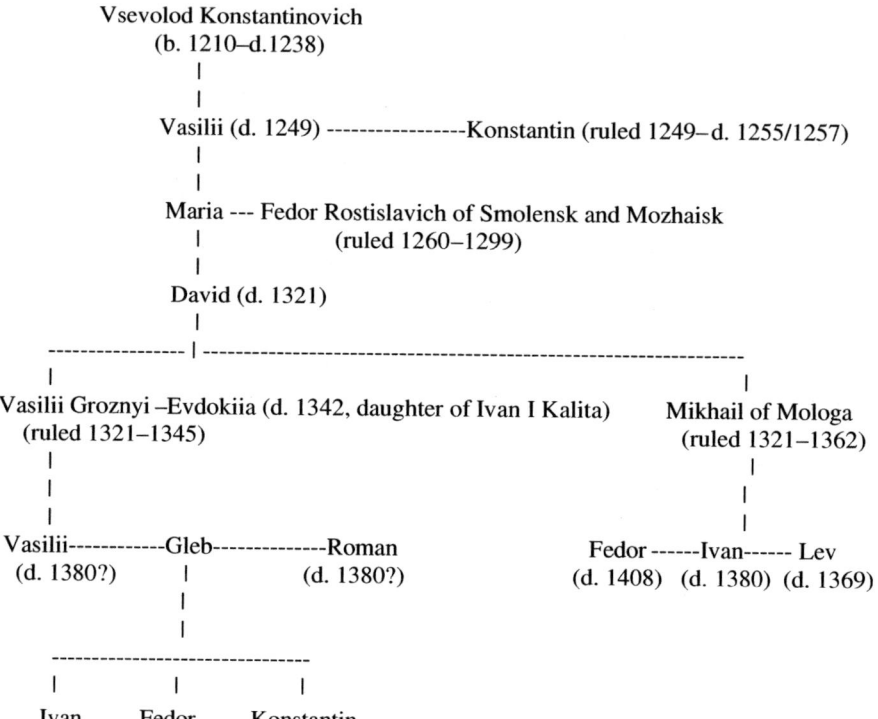

II
Government Servitors

∞ 4 ∞
A Dialogue Between Two Seventeenth-Century Boyars

Marshall T. Poe

In the words of Robert Crummey, the preeminent scholar of the early Russian nobility, the boyars (boiare i dumnye liudi) *were early modern Russia's "power elite." Together with the tsar they served, the boyars dominated the court (the center of the government), ran the army (in which they served as officers), and governed the central and local administrations (both of which they headed). Paradoxically, although they were powerful, they were not free: the boyars were "service men by patrimony"* (sluzhilye liudi po otechestvu); *as such, they were required by custom and law to serve the tsar throughout their lives. In this sense they differed from the nobilities of other (and especially European) states, states in which elites served "at the king's pleasure" and at their own. European nobles could opt out of royal service and honorably enter the clergy, the university, or the counting house. Not so the sons of boyars. To them, royal service was all: an identity, a livelihood, a way of life.*

Nonetheless, boyar status was not hereditary (unlike princely status, which was worth far less in the Muscovite scheme of things). One might well be born of a boyar and, by the nature of things, be assured a good run in the service of the tsar. But birth did not make one a boyar. Only the tsar made boyars. He did so in recognition of a number of things, including (but not exclusively or necessarily): a man's heritage, his service, his loyalty, his mind, his abilities, and his political position. Few were chosen at the beginning of the seventeenth century (typically a dozen), and most were the sons of well-known boyar families. As the century wore on, though, the number of boyars ballooned (to above forty).

By this time, the boyars were well on their way to completing the typical early modern journey from warrior class to courtier class. In earlier eras they had fought for the tsar with sword, hammer, and tong. By the later sixteenth century, however, the tsar and boyars had gained the resources to field a rather effective army of local notables (deti boiarskie), *and they had hired a class of low-status administrators* (prikaznye liudi) *to support the state apparatus (the court, or* gosudarev dvor, *and*

Drawing by Adam Olearius of a man dressed in the typical garb of a boyar, wearing a long caftan and tall fox-fur hat. Olearius was a member of an Embassy from Frederick III, Duke of Holstein, to the court of Tsar Mikhail Fedorovich in 1634. Vasilii Ivanovich and Iurii Borisovich, the two composite-character boyars whose conversation is represented in this chapter, would probably have dressed this way in public.

the army). Free of their martial and administrative duties in large part (they still served as military officers), the boyars set themselves to "executive functions," so to speak: organizing, commanding, and, the most esteemed service of all, counseling the tsar. And, of course, they spent much of their time playing the sport of all courtiers—politics.

It is for politics that they are most remembered today, for the history of Muscovy in the early modern period is largely the story of the "tsar and boyar." Indeed, it would hardly be much of an exaggeration to say that the tsar was a boyar. He was born of them, raised among them, surrounded by them, and bedeviled by them. Generally speaking, the tsar had the upper hand. After all, even the boyars were his "slaves." But the boyars were always powerful (the Muscovite enterprise could not be operated without them) and, in the minority of a sovereign (young Aleksei) or under a weak hand (Sophia), they might well run nearly riot. Having said this, it is important not to think of the tsar and the boyars as natural opponents. Rather, they were natural allies occasionally divided by policies, prejudices, or petty pretensions. The tsar and boyars ruled Russia together and profited mightily thereby. They could not rule it apart, and they knew this.

In the dialogue that follows, two old boyars (both fictional, as is everyone mentioned in the discussion), Vasilii Ivanovich and Iurii Borisovich, meet and fall to discussing their lives, careers, and the changes both have seen over the course of decades. The time is 1680, late in the reign of young Fedor Alekseevich. The Miloslavskii faction (Fedor was Aleksei's son by Maria Miloslavskaia) had attempted to solidify its hold on the court by packing the elite ranks with its allies. The result was a serious inflation of honors that threatened to destabilize the entire political system. In addition, it was well known that Fedor was sickly and might not live long. At the conclusion of his reign, the entire court expected a battle over the throne between the Miloslavskiis (under the leadership of Sophia Alekseevna, Tsar Ivan's sister, both the children of Maria Miloslavskaia, the first wife of Aleksei Mikhailovich) and the Naryshkin family (which included Natalia Naryshkina, the second wife of Aleksei Mikhailovich, and her son Peter). Everything seemed to be up in the air, and indeed it was.

Vasilii: Iurii, my old friend, how is your health?
Iurii: I am, for my sins, not at all well. The wound I got outside Smolensk in the great war with Poland is bothering me again. I feel that the Lord may call me any day, though that is His will.
Vasilii: Indeed. How is your son? Is he back from service? Belgorod is rough duty.
Iurii: He's returned and is happy to be back in Moscow serving at court, though he is still a *stol'nik*. The southern frontier is a complete mess. The stockades are in ruins, the local service men in revolt, and their serfs are pouring into the steppe. The God-forsaken Tatars are everywhere, and they are constantly dragging off peasants and selling them to the Turks. It's a disaster.

Vasilii: Yes, so I've heard. But one must take the good with the bad. And we all must serve as our master instructs. Such is God's will.

Iurii: True, we are all the slaves of God and the tsar. But this wasn't "service." It was exile. Ever since the incident in Pskov, the one with Prince Boris Alekseevich, that son of a dog, he's been out of favor at court. He's been sent hither and yon on all kinds of horrible duties, and with commoners to boot. It seems he may never make it to the council (*duma*), though I'm pulling all the strings at my disposal.

Vasilii: What incident was that? I don't recall.

Iurii: Dmitrii was appointed to serve as governor with Boris in Pskov and Prince Boris sued for precedence, claiming his family was more honorable than ours. The tsar heard the case but was deceived. Prince Boris had some clever state secretary (*d'iak*) forge service papers that "demonstrated" his kin had served under Tsar Ivan III, of blessed memory. The idiot secretaries—whom I suspect had been paid off—authenticated the documents, and the case was lost. Well, you know Dmitrii is young and foolish. So he refused to eat, grew his hair long, and let himself go to the dogs. He looked like a beggar. The tsar ordered him beaten on the square. He finally came to his senses and begged forgiveness. But the damage was done—to him and our entire family.

Vasilii: Prince Boris and his kind are the devil's servants. Take solace, at least, that Dmitrii is out of disgrace.

Iurii: Yes, thank God and the tsar. But now that the supposed service has been officially registered, we shall forever be under Prince Boris's family. This case brings shame on me and all my ancestors. We are an old family and have served for centuries, since the time we came from the Roman empire. The records show it, and I know it. Prince Boris's kind are nothing but upstarts. Everyone knows they are of the Vladimir line and did not serve in Moscow until the Troubles. Provincials!

Vasilii: Yes, it's a shame. And there are more and more of them flooding Moscow by the day. In our youth only honorable families served in Moscow, and only the most ancient of them were appointed to the council. Boyar families were truly boyar families. Now it's all confused. One doesn't know who's who anymore.

Iurii: Right you are. It's all the fault of those God-forsaken Miloslavskiis. Tsar Fedor is unable to control them, and they appointed every idiot in Moscow to the council. We can hardly fit in the hall anymore. And these new people are so rude. Who are they?

Vasilii: Riffraff, that's who. I wouldn't have anything to do with them if I didn't have to. But some of them are powerful. They are in the chancelleries, serve as governors, and some have even been appointed to the rank of *okol'nichii!*

Iurii: Yes, it's a disgrace. Once a man was happy enough to serve in the provinces, to fulfill God's will and the tsar's. It was honorable. You had respect, slaves, serfs, lands. If you saw the tsar even once in your life, you felt blessed. No more. Now the court is full of your "riffraff," with their pretensions and boorish manners.

Vasilii: Yes, and they are shamelessly ambitious. I was shocked when Prince Boris married the daughter of the boyar Ivan Ivanovich. How could he shame himself and his kin in such a way!

Iurii: The Koshelevs were behind it, don't you know? Ivan Ivanovich's uncle was married to Iurii Mikhailovich Koshelev's sister, before she died of the plague. Prince Boris's family and the Koshelevs are as thick as thieves. They served the False Tsar together during the Troubles and keep each other's secrets. A few words in Ivan Ivanovich's ear from his aunt, and that was all it took for him to dishonor his entire line before God and the tsar.

Vasilii: Disgraceful. And now Prince Boris himself is in line to enter the council under the wing of Ivan Ivanovich. That scheming rube has not served for more than a dozen years, and only rarely in the field. We gave our blood for the sovereign, while he and his kind hang around the court flattering one another, sucking up, and trucking with cursed foreigners. They act like women, with their flowery language, clothes, and pretense.

Iurii: Yes. I'm so sick of it I have a mind to retire to my estates, as much as it pains me to leave Moscow.

Vasilii: Have you petitioned to be released from service?

Iurii: No. And I'm not optimistic the tsar would release me. He loves to keep us old beggars on to parade us around like so many puppets. All these ceremonies, the daily visits to court, the endless standing around. It's too much, and expensive too. I've not been granted my salary for six months, my house is in ruin, and my slaves are up in arms. If I could just enter a monastery or get to my estate.

Vasilii: Estates! When was the last time you visited your estates, you old fart! You're no better than these young sissies at court. You've no stomach for country life, no more than I do. You've grown fat and happy at the tsar's table, and you'll not leave any time soon!

Iurii: Perhaps you are right. I've grown accustomed to Moscow, and certainly do not relish the idea of living among swine in some backwater. God, I remember what it was like in the provinces when I used to serve as governor. I'd order them whipped and beaten and even executed, and still they would not obey. It was all a huge headache. Leave the country to the country folk.

Vasilii: Now you're back on track, my friend. Perhaps you'd fancy a trip abroad. Why don't you finagle an appointment as an ambassador to the Habsburg lands or some such? It pays well, and you've done it before.

Iurii: God forbid. You yourself have served as an emissary and know how dan-

	gerous it is. The evil Papists are always trying to lure you away from the true path. I've my soul to worry about in this late day. I'll not risk it by trucking with cursed foreign devils. In fact, I think we should expel them all from our midst immediately!
Vasilii:	Well, you have a point, about the foreigners I mean. They are serpents. But they know how to do many useful things, things we know nothing about. They say that the foreigners have hundreds of printed books, and that they have ships that can sail to new worlds. Why, I heard one German say that they knew a way to make gold from iron.
Iurii:	Satan's work, all of it. Reading and writing books is for lowly scribes, and printing is manifestly evil. In our day we left reading to priests, those who could read that is. What is the point in all of it anyway? We need only know what God and the tsar would have us know, and no more. The end time will come soon, I know it, and then the wicked foreigners and their evil learning will be cast into the pit of hellfire.
Vasilii:	Verily. They are evil, but we need their skills and wares, if only so we needn't dirty our own hands with their foul magic. Imagine where we'd be if it weren't for the foreigners' guns? The Turks would have made mincemeat of us, not to mention the Poles and Swedes. You remember how we got chewed up in the great war with Poland.
Iurii:	All true, but nonetheless I find them, their sorcery, and their inventions are the devil's business. It would be better if we could close our borders completely.
Vasilii:	Ah, and what of all that Rhenish wine you have put up in your cellar? Would you give that up? And the silver utensils? What about the German bottles? All of that is very nice . . .
Iurii:	Oh, to hell with you and your clever words. We've all been corrupted by the foreigners. The end is nigh, I tell you. All the signs are there, just as foretold in scripture.
Vasilii:	Let us hope the end is at hand and our savior will appear. But I must say, the signs have been seen before, and all that has been proven is that the seers are blind. That business with the followers of the old rituals and their "End of Days" is behind us, Thank God. They've burned themselves up and departed to the wilderness. Surely you're not saying—
Iurii:	No, no, my friend. I've washed my hands of the Old Belief as well. And you should be careful about what you say. There are spies everywhere. If the priests were to get wind of us discussing Old Belief, there is no telling what could happen. You remember the fate of Prince Ivan Kirillovich.
Vasilii:	You are an old man! And, alas, your memory has failed you. Prince Dmitrii was exiled for insulting the tsar, not for any flirtation with the Old Belief. I remember it well. Prince Ivan was three sheets to the wind at a tavern and began to sing one of those old ditties about the pretender during the

	Troubles, you remember the one I'm talking about. The one that has the line about ass wiping—
Iurii:	Enough, enough! Stop it you old fool! You're going to get us arrested. I don't want to be tortured!
Vasilii:	No, neither do I. So enough about that. Anyway, it's late, and the guards will be closing the gates soon. Should be getting home, as should you. I hope to see you soon, my friend, God and the tsar grant.
Iurii:	God and the tsar grant indeed.

Suggestions for Further Reading

Bogatyrev, Sergei. *The Sovereign and His Counsellors: Ritualised Consultations in Muscovite Political Culture, 1350s–1570s.* Helsinki: Academia Scientiarum Fennica, 2000.

Crummey, Robert O. *Aristocrats and Servitors: The Boyar Elite in Russia, 1613–1689.* Princeton, NJ: Princeton University Press, 1983.

Dunning, Chester, and Norman S. Smith, "Moving Beyond Absolutism: Was Early Modern Russia a 'fiscal-Military' State?," *Russian History/Histoire Russe* 33 (2006): 19–44.

Keenan, Edward L. "Muscovite Political Folkways." *Russian Review* 45, no. 2 (1986): 115–81.

Kollmann, Nancy S. *Kinship and Politics: The Making of the Muscovite Political System, 1345–1547.* Stanford, CA: Stanford University Press, 1987.

———. *By Honor Bound: State and Society in Early Modern Russia.* Ithaca, NY: Cornell University Press, 1999.

Ostrowski, Donald. "The Façade of Legitimacy: Exchange of Power and Authority in Early Modern Russia." *Comparative Studies in Society and History* 44, no. 3 (2002): 534–63.

Poe, Marshall T. "Absolutism and the New Men of Seventeenth-Century Russia." In *Modernization in Seventeenth-Century Russia.* Edited by Jarmo Kotilaine and Marshall T. Poe. London: RoutledgeCurzon, 2004, 97–115.

———. "Tsar Aleksei Mikhailovich and the Demise of the Romanov Political Settlement." *Russian Review* 62, no. 2 (2003): 537–64.

———. *The Russian Elite in the Seventeenth Century.* 2 vols. Helsinki: Academia Scientiarum Fennica, 2003.

———. "What Did Russians Mean When They Called Themselves 'Slaves of the Tsar'?" *Slavic Review* 57, no. 3 (1998): 585–608.

———. "The Imaginary World of Semen Koltovskii: Genealogical Anxiety and Falsification in Seventeenth-Century Russia." *Cahiers du monde russe* 39, no. 3 (1998): 375–88.

Thyrêt, Isolde. *Between God and Tsar: Religious Symbolism and the Royal Women of Muscovite Russia.* DeKalb: Northern Illinois University Press, 2001.

5

The Power of Knowledge
Vita of the Secretary Andrei Putilov

Sergei Bogatyrev

In the sixteenth century, the increasing political and social complexity of the Muscovite state caused profound transformations in its administration. The grand-princely household evolved into a complicated chancellery system with formalized procedures and a considerable degree of redundancy. Through the chancellery system, the rulers of Muscovy mobilized military forces, collected taxes, handled diplomatic relations with other states, and governed their growing territory during the formative period of the Russian autocracy. The staff of chancelleries, secretaries, became the main functionaries of the monarchy. This piece involves a fictional character, the secretary Andrei Putilov. His prototypes were the influential high-ranking officials Putila Mikhailov, Afanasii Demianov, and the brothers Andrei and Vasilii Shchelkalov (the two later also appear under their own names in this essay).

The main sources of our information on sixteenth-century secretaries are diplomatic and military chancellery records, many of which were published respectively in the series Collection of the Imperial Russian Historical Society *(Sbornik Imperatorskogo Russkogo istoricheskogo obshchestva) and the series* Deployment Book *(Razriadnaia kniga). The chronicles published in the* Complete Collection of Russian Chronicles *(Polnoe sobranie russkikh letopisei) tell us about the participation of secretaries in political events and court ceremonies. Various documents from the monastery archives provide valuable information on the cultural and spiritual life of secretaries, their kin ties, and their immovable property. Similar data can be found in the documents deriving from the private archives of Muscovite cavalrymen, which were published in the series* Collection of Russian Acts *(Russkii diplomatarii) and* Acts of Serving Landowners *(Akty sluzhilykh zemlevladel'tsev).*

A monk was standing in his monastery's church (*minster*). He looked at the icons, which always reminded him of written texts. Like writing, icon painting was a ceremony that required knowledge of the rules and understanding of the meanings of symbols. Every icon painter and every scribe had to spend long hours learning the

Ivan Bilibin designed this costume of a counselor secretary (*dumnyi diak*) for Sergei Diaghilev's production of the opera *Boris Godunov* by Modest Mussorgsky at the Paris Grand Opera, May 19, 1908. The libretto for the opera was based on Alexander Pushkin's play *Boris Godunov*. The subject of the present chapter, the composite character Andrei Putilov, would have dressed in a way not dissimilar to Bilibin's concept.

secrets of their trades, but the results were always rewarding. After a long period of training, an icon painter and a scribe became initiated into a world of power: icons were windows to the world of almighty God; and written texts conveyed the power of the mighty ruler, the grand prince of Moscow whom the man used to serve as a secretary.

The man, Andrei Putilov, was born into the family of the Yaroslavl rank-and-file cavalryman Mikhail Putilov in 1526. The local cavalrymen retained their hereditary lands in Yaroslavl after its annexation by Grand Prince Ivan III of Moscow. His son Vasilii III began to summon local Yaroslavl landowners to his court by granting them service estates. However, Andrei's father, Mikhail Putilov, was not among them, for he could not afford expensive armor and a thoroughbred horse. Instead of joining the elite regiments commanded by the grand prince and his closest boyars, Mikhail served together with his neighbors under the command of a local military governor. Mikhail also retained connections with his neighbors during peacetime by concluding deals on land with them, by acting as a suretor in transactions, by occasionally borrowing and lending small amounts, and by participating in joint prosecution of vagabond bandits and runaway peasants. Each of the cavalrymen had also vouched for one of his neighbors to the grand prince of Moscow.

The Putilovs did not limit their contacts to the circle of their neighboring landowners. The family traditionally cultivated ties with local monasteries by generously donating villages, money, and church books to the monks. The Putilovs were especially close to the Savior's Transfiguration monastery in Yaroslavl, since Mikhail's uncle, Iona, was archimandrite of the monastery. Located in the town of Yaroslavl, the monastery enjoyed the patronage of the princes of Yaroslavl and was a place of burial for many members of the local dynasty. In the early sixteenth century, the monastery thrived. The monks received generous tax exemptions from the grand prince of Moscow, and a new minster was built in the monastery in 1515–16.

Mikhail Putilov thus had relatives and good friends among the local clergy and cavalrymen. In early 1535, Mikhail took part in a campaign against the Grand Duchy of Lithuania and was severely wounded near Orsha. Mikhail received several villages from the grand prince of Moscow as compensation for his sufferings. He never fully recovered from the injury, however, and could not perform military service any longer. He had to mobilize his connections in the local community to secure the future of his only son, Andrei, who was only nine years old at the time. Mikhail compiled a will in which he asked his uncle, Archimandrite Iona, to take care of the boy until he grew up. To back up his plea, Mikhail granted a village, a horse, and several icons to the monastery. Mikhail also donated twelve church books to the monks and emphatically asked the archimandrite to teach Andrei to read and to write.

Mikhail took these precautions just in time. Soon after the compilation of his will, he died, leaving Andrei to the care of the archimandrite. In the beginning, the boy helped the novices and monks in various chores in the large monastery household.

Later, the archimandrite instructed the monastery treasurer to teach Andrei the basics of grammar. Andrei thus spent the formative period of his life in the monastery, learning how to read and write using the Psalter and the Book of Hours under the guidance of the treasurer. When Andrei had acquired a good command of reading and writing, the treasurer involved the boy in keeping the monastery household books. Unlike church books, which were written in ornate Church Slavonic, the monks used the so-called "chancellery language" in their household registers, a plain and businesslike language, which was also the language of official documents of the grand-princely court. Thanks to the supervision of the treasurer, Andrei not only became functionally literate but also acquired a good command of working with texts written in various styles.

These skills proved to be essential for Andrei's future career. The Savior Monastery enjoyed the patronage of many top-level members of the grand prince's court, especially those originally from the Yaroslavl principality. Among them was Prince Ivan Ivanovich Kubenskii, a member of the Yaroslavl dynasty. Prince Kubenskii had matrimonial connections with the ruling line of the Riurikid dynasty through the marriage of his father, Prince I. S. Kubenskii, to a niece of Grand Prince Ivan III. Prince I. I. Kubenskii began serving at the court of the grand prince of Moscow in 1518 by fulfilling various appointments connected with the sovereign's household. By 1524, Prince I. I. Kubenskii became a majordomo, head of the Great Household Office (*Bol'shoi dvorets*), which exerted administrative and supreme judicial authority over various categories of lay and church population across the country, oversaw the local agents of the grand-princely power, and governed the territories belonging to the crown. Prince I. I. Kubenskii often accompanied the grand prince in his journeys in the provinces.

Though the Kubenskii princes forfeited their hereditary lands in the Yaroslavl district, Prince I. I. Kubenskii retained close connections with the local Savior Monastery by making generous donations to the monks and by paying frequent visits to the monastery on feast days. During one such visit, the archimandrite asked the prince to act as a patron for Andrei at court. In his capacity of majordomo, Prince Kubenskii had at his disposal a staff of secretaries (*d'iaki*) and clerks (*pod'iachie*). The need for such professional administrators became especially acute in the 1530s, which saw an extensive program of land surveys aimed at integrating the territories of former appanage principalities into the domain of the ruling line of the dynasty. In the 1540s, the central authorities began to use a new taxation unit, the *chetvert'* (1.35 acres), in land surveys. The introduction of the *chetvert'* signified an important development in the taxation system. It left less and less uncultivated land in the central part of country, and the ruling circles switched from taxing separate households to taxing particular amounts of arable land. The Great Household Office was the first to make use of the *chetvert'* when it began to use it in surveys of crown lands. Later, this unit found its way into surveys of lands of other status. Because of its responsible and diverse tasks, the Great Household Office was in constant need of young, literate, and energetic cadres. This is why Prince Kubenskii was interested in getting Andrei, who was literate and had experience in document making, into his office.

Thanks to the protection of Prince Kubenskii, Andrei Putilov received the position of clerk in the Great Household Office in 1541. Initially his task was to rewrite documents compiled by more senior clerks and approved by a secretary or the majordomo. Given his experience in the monastery treasury, however, Andrei Putilov climbed the chancellery hierarchy very fast for a newcomer. Soon he was entrusted with the responsible mission of preparing documents for the secretaries and received access to the chancellery archives. Here he learned that his position gave him considerable power over people who petitioned the central authorities for additional parcels of land or appealed land disputes.

Since court proceedings by the mid-sixteenth century heavily relied on oral and written evidence, judges usually requested extracts from older surveys of corresponding territories. It was up to the clerks working in the archives to decide which case to process first and how widely to search for the documents. Experienced litigants completely comprehended the situation and bribed the clerks processing their petitions to speed up the process. Money coming from petitioners was an essential source of income for officials like Andrei Putilov. Some petitioners noted that newly appointed clerks were often more greedy than their older colleagues. Other litigants pointed out that the favor of some experienced clerks was sometimes even more important than the position of a secretary. Petitioners offered officials not only money, but also salt, game, fish, eggs, utensils, and even icons. It should be noted that such gifts were not only bribes in our modern sense but also functioned as means of reciprocal exchange between the parties, since a clerk receiving a gift assumed certain responsibilities towards the petitioner.

As with every member of the court, Andrei Putilov had to muster for military actions and campaigns. Starting in 1541, he joined regiments gathering annually in the border towns of Kolomna, Riazan, and Serpukhov to repel possible attacks by Tatar troops. At the beginning of 1545, Andrei participated for the first time in a large-scale campaign against Kazan, which marked the beginning of a new series of military and political attempts to establish Muscovy's hegemony over that Tatar khanate. Though the Muscovite commanders failed to coordinate their efforts, the grand prince and his advisors were generally pleased with the results of the campaign and invited the participants to submit petitions for rewards.

Andrei Putilov used this opportunity to apply for promotion to the post of secretary in the Military Office, which later became known as the Military Chancellery (*Razriadnyi prikaz*). The Military Office, which crystallized within the court in the 1530s, was responsible for keeping records of military service. The books kept in the chancellery were essential for the prosperity of members of the court, for they could hold most of their lands only as long as they showed up for military campaigns. The documents of the Military Office also fixed the status of the elite cavalrymen in accordance with the system of precedence (*mestnichestvo*). An inappropriate appointment taken by one member of an elite family could harm the honor of the entire clan. This is why the deployment records guaranteed the position of a clan at court and served as the main evidence during precedence disputes between elite cavalrymen. The officials of the Military Office were also involved in the compilation of genealogical books, another essential source for precedence rules.

Given the important functions of the Military Office in the court administration, the central authorities sought to secure independence of the office from influential boyar clans by appointing its heads from nonelite families on the basis of professional skills rather than pedigree. Correspondingly, the secretaries running the Military Office were known among the elite as very influential officials. After joining the staff of the Military Office, Andrei Putilov became close to the important secretary Vasilii Grigorievich Zakharov.

The secretary Vasilii Zakharov formally held a rather modest place in the chancellery hierarchy, but his real influence was far greater than it may seem. He had access to the highest levels of the court elite and was deeply involved in struggles among various groups of boyars. In 1546, he accused several leaders of the household chancelleries, including Prince I. I. Kubenskii, of high treason. Prince Kubenskii was executed as a result of Zakharov's accusations. Andrei Putilov was fortunate enough to secure the favor of Vasilii Zakharov before he attacked Andrei's former patron. Thanks to his connections among the chancellery personnel and professional skills, Andrei thus managed to retain his position at court despite the fall of his former patron from Yaroslavl. Andrei Putilov even strengthened his position in the Military Office since his new patron, Vasilii Zakharov, became very close to Ivan IV after Ivan's coronation as tsar in 1547.

In the 1550s, the Military Office was busy preparing numerous campaigns launched by the tsar against Kazan and Astrakhan. Throughout the decade, Andrei accumulated substantial experience in compiling and managing deployment documentation, something that enabled him to intervene even in the *sancta sanctorum* of military service, the system of precedence. Andrei manipulated some deployment registers and records of court ceremonies to benefit his friends at court by putting their names in more prestigious places. He could even add his own name to the records of a wedding at court.

Doctoring official records was a risky but profitable business. Andrei acquired good friends and patrons among the cream of court elite. Among those who made use of Andrei's service were such top-level courtiers as the prominent boyars Sheremetev and the princes Golitsyn. When other boyars discovered his frauds, Andrei usually blamed clerks of the Military Office for inaccuracy and ill will toward him. The secretary could easily frame his clerks, since they were heavily dependent on Andrei. Some of them even called him "sovereign" (*gosudar'*) and styled themselves as Andrei's "fosterlings" (*vskormlenniki*).

Andrei's involvement in keeping deployment registers also offered him good opportunities for making connections with provincial cavalrymen. In his capacity as a secretary of the Military Office, he often participated in mustering provincial cavalrymen in different towns. During one such muster in Ruza in 1546, Andrei met the Pushechnikovs, a clan that had hereditary lands in the Ruza and Yaroslavl districts and occupied a prominent place in the Ruza cavalrymen community. Andrei entered into an agreement with the local felony elder (*gubnoi starosta*) Nikifor Vasiliev *syn* Pushechnikov. Using his connections in the central chancelleries, Andrei helped Nikifor to secure his rights to several hereditary estates (*votchiny*) belonging to Nikifor's late relatives in Ruza province. In exchange, Nikifor agreed to share the ownership of the largest estate, which included a large village with two churches, with Andrei. Andrei also acquired the large estate of Nefimonovo, which included nine villages, on the Istra river in the Ruza district.

Andrei's contacts with the Pushechnikov family soon went beyond material interests. In 1549, he married Anastasia, the daughter of Nikifor Pushechnikov, and brought her to Moscow. Andrei had a homestead in the capital, in a borough adjacent to the kremlin. After marrying Anastasia, he moved to a larger homestead on the same street. His marriage and move was noticed by the monks of Moscow monasteries, who always thought to maintain close relations with important members of the court like Andrei. The monks of the Chudov (Miracle) Monastery in the kremlin sent the secretary an icon of Archangel Michael as a gift to commemorate his move to the new house. Soon, Andrei fathered two children, Nikita and Maria.

Apart from the estate in Ruza, Andrei also had lands in the Kashira, Viazma, and Yaroslavl districts. Chancellery service did not often allow him to visit his remote estates, however, and he appeared there only occasionally, mostly after participation in a military campaign. Otherwise, Andrei spent most of the year in the capital or at Nefimonovo, though he was always in touch with the stewards of his estates to secure regular deliveries of payments in quitrent (*obrok*) from all his lands. Andrei erected a church of Simeon the Receiver of God at Nefimonovo. Though Andrei's activities were concentrated in the capital, he also cherished memories of his home, Yaroslavl. This is why he ordered the building of two chapels honoring the Yaroslavl miracle workers Fedor, David, and Konstantin in the church at Nefimonovo. The church at Nefimonovo had a large iconostasis, thirteen icons, and a large number of icons of local saints, as well as over ten church books, including canons to the Yaroslavl miracle workers.

With the outbreak of the Livonian War in 1558, Andrei became fully occupied with organizing military troops; the distribution of ammunition, supplies, and salaries; collecting and processing intelligence; and instructing commanders in Livonia. Andrei's obligations also included administration of occupied towns, organization of building and renovation of fortifications, the establishment of a postal system, and the distribution of lands and urban homesteads among Muscovite cavalrymen in annexed territories. These tasks brought Andrei in constant contact with Prince I. F. Mstislavskii and other members of the tsar's council, to whom the secretary referred many military and administrative issues.

In September 1562, the tsar summoned his councilors and secretaries of the Military Office to the palace to discuss a large-scale campaign against Sigismund II of Poland, the tsar's main rival in the Livonian War. Before the meeting of the war council, Andrei and his clerks prepared two registers of available military forces on the basis of recent town military musters. The first register included elite members of the sovereign's court, retinues of several princes, cavalrymen from various towns, people of the Tatar princes serving at the court of Ivan IV, and servitors of the metropolitan and other church hierarchs. All these forces were distributed among six elite regiments of the tsar's army and the ordinance detachment. Another list specified gathering points for various provincial detachments and military commanders responsible for mobilization in different towns. On the basis of the lists submitted by Andrei to the council, the tsar and his councilors determined that the troops should be ready on December 6 (the so-called "autumn" St. Nicholas's day). Several days later, the tsar again invited Andrei to the palace and gave him oral orders, which specified the decisions taken by the council. Andrei had to officially inform boyars about their military appointments in the future campaign and to arrange the sending out of instructions to the provincial governors. The tsar, of course, did not bother to formulate the exact text of the documents, leaving it up to Andrei. On receiving the tsar's order, the secretary quickly prepared and sent a letter to the governors telling them to select young and energetic cavalrymen who possessed horses and armor for the campaign. Every cavalryman had to have a bow and arrows, a pike or a "boar spear," a battle axe, and, given the time of the campaign (winter), a pair of skis. (It is unlikely that these instructions were always fulfilled because the weapons distribution was often sparse within the regiment.) According to the secretary's instructions, all cavalrymen had to be skillful in using the bow, the musket, and skis.

In October and November, Andrei was involved in intensive correspondence with military commanders about the situation in the border territories. Local commanders forwarded to the secretary reports of spies and plans of the territory between Velikie Luki and Polotsk, a major town blocking the road to Vilno, the capital of the Grand Duchy of Lithuania. Using these documents, Andrei and other secretaries of the Military Office prepared a detailed plan for the campaign. They submitted the plan to Prince V. S. Serebrianyi, a member of the tsar's council and a talented commander, who was known for efficient use of artillery in the battles of the Livonian War. Prince Serebrianyi and Andrei came up with the idea to attack Polotsk with overwhelming military force backed by intensive artillery fire.

The campaign against Polotsk, for which the Military Office mobilized over a hundred thousand people, began on November 30. Secretaries from all major chancelleries, including Andrei, accompanied the tsar on the campaign. Andrei was responsible for the work of a marching chancellery (the so-called "tent," *shater*), which compiled the tsar's itinerary for the official chronicle and kept records of numerous ad hoc appointments made during the campaign. He also participated in judging several precedence disputes that occurred in connection with these appointments. As a result of a two-week siege and fierce fighting, Polotsk capitulated on February 15, 1563.

After the taking of Polotsk, the tsar ordered Andrei's patron, the secretary Vasilii Zakharov, to stay in the town together with the newly appointed governor. As for

Andrei himself, he returned safe and sound with the tsar's troops to Moscow, but now he had no influential protector in the capital. Fortunately for Andrei, the tsar did not forget the secretary's active participation in the preparation of the successful Polotsk campaign. After his return to Moscow, Ivan IV allowed Andrei to go on vacation and to visit his estate in the Ruza district. The tsar also permitted the secretary to establish a marketplace at Nefimonovo, something that promised a considerable increase in Andrei's income.

Andrei now did not have to worry about how to maintain his family. He could not wait to see his wife Anastasia, who was expecting another baby and lived in the countryside. The treasurers provided the secretary with a free pass, which entitled him to use two carts at every postal station on his way from the capital to his countryside estate. Andrei was looking forward to a wonderful time at Nefimonovo, but he rejoiced too soon.

Andrei never saw his wife alive again. Anastasia died two days before his arrival while delivering a girl, who was too weak and followed her mother the next day. Andrei found only his son and daughter at home, deeply shocked by the loss. After the burials, he took his children and hastened back to Moscow, not wishing to stay at the countryside estate that reminded him of Anastasia. He hoped to find peace in routine chancellery work in the capital but faced more trouble there. In April 1563, the tsar ordered Andrei to accompany the ambassador Afanasii Nagoi on a diplomatic mission to the Crimea. Ivan IV was eager to use the victory under the walls of Polotsk to increase his political influence in the Crimean khanate, whose loyalty was essential for the tsar's struggle with the Polish king. Traveling to the Crimea, however, was always a dangerous enterprise. Though Andrei had never visited the Crimea before, he had heard a lot about the khan's court from other secretaries who traveled there. The way to the khanate was unsafe; and negotiations at the court of the khan required endurance, flexibility, and quick reactions. Every mistake could be fatal for the whole mission and sometimes even to the life of a diplomat. Aware of the risk associated with the journey, Andrei prepared a will, in which he bequeathed his estates to his children.

Thanks to the diplomatic skills of the head of the mission, Afanasii Nagoi, and generous gifts to the khan and his courtiers, the mission began well. In early 1564, the khan agreed to conclude an alliance with the tsar. The political situation was highly unstable, however, for the tsar's opponent, the Polish king, was also very active in the Crimea. Afanasii Nagoi had to stay at the court of the khan for ten years, trying to mitigate the activities of Polish diplomats and to secure the loyalty of the khan to the tsar. Andrei, who acted as Afanasii's secretary, had the chance to return to Russia earlier. In 1567, when relations between Muscovy and the Crimea were peaceful, the khan agreed to release a large group of Muscovite captives held in the Crimea. Andrei had to accompany the captives to Russia.

Andrei faced an unpleasant reception in Moscow, where he arrived with the captives in the summer of 1567. When he entered the capital, he was immediately arrested and thrown into prison. While in the Crimea, he had heard about bizarre things taking place in Russia. Muscovite merchants visiting the Crimea reported that Tsar Ivan IV had established a new court and had taken vast territories under his personal governance. The new arrangement was called the *Oprichnina,* from the old word *oprich,* meaning "except." Some landowners were deported from the Oprichnina territories; and many boyars, provincial rank-and-file cavalrymen, and Andrei's colleagues in the chancelleries were executed. There were rumors that the tsar had turned into a raving torturer, but Andrei did not believe them. He thought that the tsar was sick, as had happened before, and that some evil boyars had seized power and ruled in the tsar's name.

One night Andrei and several captives were taken into a torture chamber (*pytochnyi dvor*). Here the secretary saw the tsar for the first time after more than three years. Andrei noticed that Ivan's hair had turned thin and white. The tsar surprised Andrei by ordering him to be unchained and then instructing him to keep records of the investigation. The captives, former servitors of the boyar Prince I.F. Mstislavskii, were tortured by fire. The tsar asked them who among his boyars had plotted against him and listed the names of the most prominent boyars and princes: Prince Mstislavskii, the Shuiskiis, the Sheremetevs, the Iurievs, Vasilii Ivanovich Umnoi-Kolychev, Prince Tulupov, and Prince Serebrianyi, among others. Under torture, the prisoners accused many of the boyars of high treason—including their master, Prince Mstislavskii. Andrei was shocked by the names mentioned by the tsar, for those boyars occupied top positions at court. It was clear that nobody was safe now from the tsar's wrath.

Next day Andrei was released, but he could not forget what he had seen in the chamber. And his troubles were not over. Soon after Andrei's release, two of the captives whom he had brought to Moscow, the cavalrymen Semen Likharev and his sister Elena, accused Andrei of raping Elena in the Crimea. Some Muscovite envoys to the Crimea indeed forced captive women into sexual relations by taking advantage of their vulnerable position, but Andrei had always believed that it was a sin. It turned out that the Likharevs had an influential patron in Moscow, the secretary Vasilii Shchelkalov, who was brother-in-law to Semen Likharev. Vasilii Shchelkalov and his elder brother, Andrei, occupied the highest positions in the chancellery hierarchy by the end of the 1560s. Vasilii Shchelkalov ran the Felony Chancellery (*Razboinyi prikaz*), and his brother concentrated on the administration of military service. The Shchelkalovs openly told Putilov that he had no chance of returning to the Military Office, because Andrei Shchelkalov wanted to become the head of that chancellery. This is why the Shchelkalovs had instructed their Likharev relatives to implicate Putilov. Relying on the support of the Shchelkalovs, Elena Likhareva confirmed the accusations in court. Since women's word was usually honored in suits about rape, Putilov was sentenced to pay the Likharevs fifty rubles, half of what he earned annually, as compensation for injuring the honor of Elena.

Andrei Putilov's life was ruined. He had acquired mighty enemies at court and could not rely on the patronage of the tsar, whose behavior had become unpredictable. Andrei's son, Nikita, left the house and became a member of the Oprichnina court of the tsar. Like all members of the Oprichnina, Nikita donned black clothes and spent most of his time at Aleksandrovskaia Sloboda, the Oprichnina residence of Ivan IV. Members of the Oprichnina were ordered to limit their contacts with relatives remaining outside the Oprichnina, and Nikita was reluctant to maintain relations with his father.

Andrei's daughter, Maria, turned seventeen. It was high time to find a husband for the girl, but she developed a strange disease, which caused severe and regular attacks of fever. The only chance to secure Maria's future was to conceal her poor health. Andrei entered into negotiations with the parents of Prince Aleksandr Vasilievich Volkonskii, whom Andrei knew from his time in the Military Office. He promised the Volkonskiis a homestead worth fifty rubles, clothes worth seventeen rubles, and a horse with harness worth fifteen rubles as dowry. After long bargaining, the parents of the groom agreed to the marriage and, fortunately for Andrei, they did not demand an examination of Maria's health.

After the wedding, Andrei renewed his old contacts with the Savior Monastery in Yaroslavl. He donated sixty rubles to the monastery, one of his estates in the Yaroslavl district, and a horse. For this gift he asked the monks to permit him to take monastic vows in the monastery. Andrei joined the Savior Monastery in 1569, changing his lay name to the monastic name Aleksandr. The change of name signified a symbolical break with life beyond the walls of the monastery. Andrei left behind a royal court that was shaken by the Oprichnina upheavals, and chancelleries in which the Shchelkalov brothers mercilessly destroyed their opponents. Andrei was tonsured a monk, praying to God to pardon his numerous sins and the sins of those who had been so hostile to him. He also compiled a will, according to which after his death all his villages would go to his son, Nikita. Andrei's serfs were to be released. The Savior Monastery would receive thirty rubles, for which the monks were to commemorate Andrei several times during the year. In 1570, Andrei Putilov died.

Officials like Andrei Putilov were responsible for formulating and articulating the policy of the ruling circles. Thanks to their expertise and professional knowledge, Andrei Putilov and his colleagues greatly contributed to the development of legal procedures, to the codification of law and to the regulation of service relations at court. People like Andrei also influenced the policy of the Muscovite ruling circles by supplying information to decision-making centers and through direct participation in the decision-making process. The work of chancellery secretaries expanded the application of literacy throughout various social groups of Muscovite society and thereby made this society more coherent.

Suggestions for Further Reading

Bogatyrev, S.N. "The Clan of the Diaks Shchelkalov," *Historical Genealogy* 5 (1995): 60–70.
    A case study of the careers of two influential secretaries, their patronage, and kin ties.

Brown, Peter B. "Muscovite Government Bureaus." *Russian History* 10, no. 3 (1983): 269–330. A thorough review of the Muscovite chancelleries and their functions.

Poe, Marshall. "Muscovite Personnel Records, 1475–1550: New Light on the Early Evolution of Russian Bureaucracy." *Jahrbücher für Geschichte Osteuropas* 45, no. 3 (1997): 361–77. A study reassessing the expansion of formalized documentation and administrative literacy in the first half of the sixteenth century.

∞ 6 ∞

Larka the Clerk

Peter B. Brown

Larka Lvitskii (a.k.a. Illarion Savinov Lvitskii/Levitskii) was a real seventeenth-century person. We have documentary evidence on his place of work, career trajectory, workplace colleagues, wages, marriage, and mentalité. Thanks to an imposing amount of material on the operation of the seventeenth-century Muscovite central administration and its officialdom, we can make a large number of empirically based inferences concerning Larka's physical and mental universe. He lived and usually worked in Moscow. Larka's experiences were typical of other government clerks (sing., pod ′iachii), and his life story is a microcosm of theirs. His work contributed to the demarcation of Muscovite lands and the state's control over them.

*Larka Lvitskii was a lifelong clerk in the Service Land Chancellery (*Pomestnyi prikaz*), Muscovy's land office and largest chancellery, in existence from 1555/56 to 1720.*[1] *He labored there for at least a quarter of a century, from 1623, the earliest date we have for his employment, until September 1651, the last date we possess for his Service Land Chancellery tenure.*

Larka was the proverbial small fish in a large pond, and though a competent clerk, he was not a very distinguished one. He never earned more than eleven rubles, even though forty rubles was the maximum earnable in the Service Land Chancellery, as was true in almost every other chancellery.

Larka probably was born during the rule of the first non-Riurikid tsar, Boris Godunov (1598–1605), and endured childhood and perhaps adolescence during the Time of Troubles (1598–1613), when the central administration, like the rest of the government, eventually collapsed. Regardless of his date of birth, he either

---

[1] The Service Land Chancellery initially distributed and supervised only military land grants (sing., *pomest′e*) for the maintenance of the *dvorianstvo* and *deti boiarskie*, the famous provincial service cavalry (the middle service class), called into being during Ivan III's reign and lasting into Peter the Great's reign. Over time, the Service Land Chancellery became involved in recording land surveys, land ownership, and land alienation throughout Muscovy, not only for military land grants but for several other land categories as well.

Engraving based on a drawing by Adam Olearius of a young man dressed in the typical garb of a government clerk (*pod´iachii*). Olearius was a member of an Embassy from Frederick III, Duke of Holstein, to the court of Tsar Mikhail Federovich in 1634. Larka Lvitskii, the historical person who is the subject of this chapter, "wore a long, plain caftan, probably from ram skin or wool, that cost between 1.5 and 3 rubles (10–50 percent of his cash entitlement), reaching down to his ankles and having long sleeves extending beyond the hands."

had personal memories of this catastrophe or heard vivid accounts of it from his family. These must have fortified his commitment to the rigorous Muscovite code of state service. In the early 1620s, Larka had a three-ruble salary entitlement and, thirty years later, one for eleven rubles. We can make several inferences about Larka's Service Land Chancellery career prior to the early 1620s, knowing what we do about the initial, unpaid apprenticeship that aspiring chancellery clerks typically endured between ages ten and fifteen (the age of majority), for some or all of these years. During this period, the apprentice clerk, like Larka, learned to write the Middle Russian hand with its multitudinous variations in letter formation and letter combinations, and memorized a large number of specific administrative terms and the documentary formulary associated with them. Once satisfied with Larka's apprenticeship, his superiors promoted him to junior clerk (*mladshii pod'iachii*), the first of three formal ranks in the chancellery clerkdom, followed by those of middle (*srednii*) and senior (*starshii*) clerk, the last of which Larka never achieved.

Larka, before the onset of adolescence, may well have obtained the rudiments of literacy at home, from a father, uncle, or brother or from one of the few literate Muscovite churchmen. Larka's Muscovy was an overwhelmingly illiterate place, for only 2–3 percent of the population could meaningfully read and write. This reality highlights the exceptional skills that men like Larka were regarded as having.

Larka's "book learning" would have encompassed primers, abecedarias, brevaries, and psalters. Russian Orthodoxy greatly colored his mental universe, to the extent that his rudimentary and ritualistic comprehension of his faith would allow him.

Any incoming Service Land Chancellery official, whether junior clerk or boyar, had to take an oath of probity, with many stipulations. There were variations on the oaths, though all conveyed the same sense of unassailable conduct and devotion to work expected of everyone entering government service.

The following oath is probably similar to the one Larka took:

> And while I . . . am in the Service Land Chancellery, . . . I will spend day and night [working] with my coworkers without surcease, I will be prepared [to carry out] whatever assignment the sovereign has, I will obey [my] superiors in every way, and I will not drink or commit illegal acts; and, after having received the sovereign's pay, I shall not depart from Moscow without the sovereign's permission. And without receiving permission from my superiors to leave, I will not travel anywhere nor break open trunks nor chests nor boxes; nor will I break or alter seals; nor will I steal the sovereign's and plaintiffs' records. . . .
>
> I will not display favoritism to anyone in any way, and I will not be prejudiced against anyone on grounds of enmity in any way. And I will safeguard the sovereign's funds of any sort. And I will not take advantage of anything of the sovereign's for personal gain, and I will not use the sovereign's treasury for my own gain, and I will not loan the sovereign's funds to anyone and I will not accept anything, either bribes or presents, from anyone. And I will not hand over or reveal to anyone official privy business of any sort.

After proving his basic competence, Larka received his first promotion, probably at age fifteen, to junior clerk. Junior clerks almost always performed basic tasks such as rough copying, filing, document retrieval, and other scut work. More exalted jobs—such as composing, dictating, signing documents, and writing final copies—were the lot of the older, more experienced, and more respected middle and senior clerks. Junior clerks typically earned between one and five rubles, so Larka's first surviving salary attestation of three rubles indicates he had been a junior clerk for a while. By 1623, he was in his late teens or early twenties.

In the 1620s, Larka spent appreciable time in reconstructing records lost and destroyed during the Time of Troubles, which caused the annihilation of major portions of the chancellery archives as well as the destruction of town records. The 1611 Moscow fire and its 1626 sequel especially ravaged land records.

The three main categories of records that Larka would have reconstructed were census books (*perepisnye knigi*), cadaster books (tax rolls—*pistsovye knigi*), and recording books (*dozornye knigi*). Such labors meant spending considerable time traveling to provincial towns and rural areas on special assignments for surveying and record compilation. Larka was no stranger to such tasks, for chancellery clerks from whatever bureau routinely performed field service—for example, staffing diplomatic missions, shepherding payrolls to military units, assisting in the organization and deployment of military servitors, helping town governors in a myriad of civilian and military jobs, and engaging in prisoner-of-war repatriation. Such trips caused risky privations for Service Land Chancellery clerks, who suffered disease, starvation, generalized debilitation, long separation from family members, and even death.

That Service Land Chancellery clerks were social creatures is evident from Larka's 1626/27 marriage to the daughter of fellow Service Land Chancellery clerk, Ilarion son of Postnik Sharapov. Larka's father-in-law earned in the year of Larka's nuptials but five rubles and may well have been an "under-performer," despite his greater age and putatively greater work experience. Sharapov was probably in his thirties, if not early forties, but had yet to advance beyond junior clerk, and he disappears from the records after 1632.

We do not know the name of Larka Lvitskii's wife, her age at marriage, the number of children she might have borne, nor the age at which she died. Larka's wife certainly did not work in the chancelleries or in any of the service castes. She was humble, diligent, devout in religious belief, and obedient to her husband. She was also illiterate, as most women of her time were not provided even the informal education male children sometimes received.

In 1630/31, Larka worked in the Moscow Desk, a subdepartment, with the same entitlement as before. In that year, he accompanied the Service Land Chancellery head *okol'nichii* Semen Vasilievich Prozorovskii, to Kaluga and Mtsensk, southwest of Moscow, to assemble military servitors. One year later, Larka got a raise to seven rubles and, in 1631–32, to eleven rubles. Now in his late twenties or early thirties, Larka had become a middle clerk. Toward the end of his career, he headed the top of the bottom quarter of the clerks' pay scale. The mean cash entitlement for Service Land Chancellery clerks was 11.6 rubles, close to the amount he was receiving at quite an advanced age by Muscovite standards.[2]

It must be stressed that the designated cash salary allotment—more accurately, service compensation entitlement (*oklad*)—was what one was *entitled* to receive, not what one automatically received annually. To take possession of salary money entitlement, any member of the Moscow and provincial service classes or one of their helpers—be he boyar or junior clerk—had to petition, often several times, to jolt the executors of such requests into action. This was necessary because chancellery officials were monopoly service providers and had in their demeanor a certain arrogance and obduracy. Intensifying these attitudes were the autocratic Muscovite political system and its enormous stress on hierarchy, subordination, and deference to rank. Larka, as did other petitioners, melodramatically and beseechingly used the self-abasing, diminutive form of his personal name (Larka, Larishka), as if referring to himself as a child before sternly paternalistic authority. Also in the introductory protocol, he addressed himself as a slave (*kholop*) and inserted stock-in-trade, self-abnegatory expressions to further underscore his abjectness and helplessness.

Here is part of one such petition that Larka penned:[3]

> While I am working at your official business, I lack the means to provide for myself, (and) I am dying of starvation. All my property was destroyed in the Moscow fire of the 134th year [1626]. And in the present 135th year [1627], I have agreed to marry the sister of Service Land Chancellery clerk Larion Sharapov, but there is no way I can cover the expenses. Order, Sovereign, that my sovereign's salary be augmented from [money authorized for] compensation schedules that are now unclaimed, and that on account of my [destroyed] property I be issued [this money] in the current 135th [1627] year.

Whether Larka received the money remains unknown. But after a while, Larka would be joined by his father-in-law, petitioning about similar woes. Sharapov, who wrote up his own plea of destitution in September 1632, was lucky and received the money he desired.

Partially compensating for the unpredictability in receiving entitlement monies were the special payments, from revenues internally generated within a chancel-

---

[2] The mean salary in Larka's bureau was close to his salary. How could that be if Larka's compensation placed him at the 75th percentile? This occurred because there were in almost every chancellery several people earning 20, 25, 30, 35, even 40 rubles and above. Their compensation amounts skewed the mean upward.

[3] The editors of the volume, who included Larka's petition, shortened it by omitting the introductory protocol.

lery, that clerks obtained for events such as marriages or children's christenings, personal need, major religious holidays, or the tsar's name day. Larka acquired his share of special payments that particularly helped compensate for his junior clerk's wages.

A twenty-year hiatus separates 1631–32, on the eve of the Smolensk War (1632–34), fought between Russia and Poland, and 1651, the last citation for Larka. One of the most dramatic events affecting the Service Land Chancellery, and one that Larka may have witnessed, was the Moscow riots of June 1–3, 1648, resulting in half of Moscow being burnt down.

In September 1651, Larka made a circuit journey about Moscow, and after that we hear nothing more of him. By now he was in his late forties or early fifties, well beyond the median life span of some thirty years for Muscovite men. Given the talent scarcity and lack of age-based retirement for Muscovite servitors, Larka may have worked until he dropped dead on the job. He may have labored a few years longer, until 1655, the year of the bubonic plague outbreak that hit Moscow hard.[4] The plague felled as much as 75–80 percent of the capital's chancellery workforce. If we speculate that Larka had not stepped down earlier, then probably he would have succumbed in 1655.

As was true for 95 percent of all chancellery clerks, Larka stayed a clerk, never advancing to the rank of state secretary (*d'iak*). Larka's three-ruble entitlement in 1626–27 was but 4 percent of state secretaries' mean cash entitlement of seventy-five rubles for that year; his eleven rubles of the early 1650s was 15 percent of mid-1650s state secretaries' cash entitlement. Yet Boyar A.V. Sitskoi, the top Service Land Chancellery tribunal official in the mid-1620s, had a cash entitlement of several hundred rubles and probably had estate resources generating an even higher income stream.

Socially, financially, and professionally, Larka ranked far below the elite, who, along with the tsar, directed the Muscovite state. In the early 1650s, there were 665 clerks, 65 state secretaries, and 67 Duma members, of whom 29 were boyars. The cliché of the base of the pyramid being very wide and the tip of it being very narrow is apt here. From another perspective, however, Larka was very much a part of this "apex." In the early 1650s, the Moscow military service class and chancellery clerks numbered twenty-five to thirty thousand, or .0025 percent (25/10,000s) of Russia's population of ten to twelve million. Decrees of 1640 and 1658 limited the recruitment base of state secretaries and clerks to their offspring and banned the clergy, townsmen, provincial military service groups, and others from joining, though members of these proscribed groups continued to vie for and receive chancellery appointments. To the vast majority of the Muscovite populace

---

[4] The gathering in Moscow of large numbers of military servitors, in response to the outbreak of the Thirteen Years War (1654–67), fought in the main between Muscovy, the Polish-Lithuanian Commonwealth, and Sweden, led to this epidemic.

bound to the land as serfs and tied to masters as slaves, becoming a chancellery clerk was inconceivable.[5]

These two decrees de jure converted Larka's professional colleagues into what for some time they effectively had become—a hereditary caste. Certainly, the 1640 legislation increased Larka's sense of social privilege and entitlement and perhaps even a desire to "lord it over others." In short, Larka belonged to a privileged minority but at a definite cost in personal tranquility, for the proficiency demanded of clerks was taxing, as was the uncertainty regarding promotion and advancement, which were not at all automatic. Major budgetary recisions during the 1640s, 1670s, and after resulted in the dismissal of large numbers of chancellery clerks. The first of these Larka confronted, but luck was with him and he remained employed.

Larka's station in life was precarious because of a certain unpredictability about duration of tenure, conditions of work, and social status. Larka was very much an individual who expressed his feelings passionately, albeit stereotypically, as evidenced in his 1627 petition. But his prerogatives, skimpily deeded out by the regime, were limited and could never be taken for granted; this helps us comprehend a certain defensiveness and edginess in Larka's petition.

Throughout the seventeenth century, other clerks, in writing similar pleas, habitually projected the same mood. The intense, and at times ferocious, pace of Service Land Chancellery work is reflected in this collective 1632 Service Land Chancellery petition, written in the name of all Service Land Chancellery clerks, including Larka:

> [We,] your slaves, the Service Land chancellery clerks, [petition]. Sovereign, we, your slaves, without surcease attend to your sovereign's business. We, your slaves, in accordance with your sovereigns' edict, are compiling a land register at this moment, and we work day and night over this land register without (ever) leaving the chancellery. We have compiled already a land register of some monastery and church lands; more than 900,000 *chet*s [1,215,000 acres], and more than 60,000 *chet*s [81,000 acres] we have recorded [and are intended] for widows and minors. These land registers were sent to Service Land Chancellery Boyar Prince Dmitrei Mikhailovich Pozharskoi and to State Secretary Grigorii Volkov. Right now, we are working over these same land registers, and through attending to your sovereign's business [working] over these land registers, have incurred great debts because we, your slaves, were not issued your sovereign's pay for the present 140th year (1631/32).
>
> Sovereign, those colleagues of ours working in various other chancelleries and in the tax collection chancelleries have less of your sovereign's assignments than [we do] in the Service Land Chancellery. They do not prepare land registers and all of them, our colleagues in the chancelleries and in the tax collection chancelleries, were all issued in full your sovereign's pay for the present 140th year [1631/32].

---

[5] Throughout the seventeenth century, clerks working in provincial administrative offices derived from these same social groups; sometimes, central offices would summon provincial clerks to work in Moscow, or they might accompany a town governor (*voevoda*) back to the capital after he had completed his term.

How did Larka survive? The minimal yearly cash income to survive in Moscow was around eight rubles. Prices remained fairly constant throughout the seventeenth century; inflation, with little exception, did not exist. Yet if Larka until the early 1630s was entitled to receive from three to seven rubles, clearly he was earning less than a subsistence wage. One method to increase income was through accepting bribes, strictly forbidden but widely resorted to. Certain chancellery venues, above all judicial ones, seemed more prone to have their clerks engaging in bribery.

Depending on its location, land was a form of wealth in seventeenth-century Muscovy, and litigants sued over land. The Service Land Chancellery dealt in land. Service Land Chancellery clerks assessed and recorded large volumes of service and hereditary land, capitalized in varying degrees. Stakes could be high enough for a plaintiff or a defendant illicitly to offer money to clerks as a means of effecting a favorable outcome and to influence-peddle with the chancellery judges; these practices took place within the Service Land Chancellery but probably were not excessive. Bribery of central officials engaged in circuit tours of the countryside was no novelty either. To what degree Larka accepted bribes, if at all, is unknowable.

What we term *bribery* is actually an umbrella term for a variety of practices, accorded varying degrees of official tolerance, that Larka would have broken down into *pochest'* (good-will gesture, token of good-will expressed before a deal is made), *pominok* (gift once a deal has been made), and *posul* (an outright monetary bribe to an official). The government eyed the first two less suspiciously than the last. This cultural acceptance of bribery was a remnant from a pre-1550 era when administrators widely practiced *kormlenie* (feeding) or reserving for their own personal use money and kind siphoned off from local populations.

Larka, to minimize costs, could have lived at his parents' or relatives' home in the early stage of his career. As an apprentice, he would either have received one or two rubles (a practice that withered as the century wore on) or would not have been assigned to a service category (*verstan'e*), and therefore, would not have received a cash entitlement at all. As a very low-salaried or even nonsalaried minor, he would have lived in someone's home where he was provided room and board. Larka would have had a brush with rising social expectations, as did other central officials. Most of his career coincided with the reign of Tsar Mikhail Fedorovich (1613–45), a weak ruler dominated by banal oligarchs, especially from the early 1630s onward. Chancellery officials' financial impropriety then became blatant.

Larka certainly would have known of the famous complaint the townspeople lodged at the 1642 Assembly of the Land, and he may have been one of the complainants' targets. The Assembly delegates lamented:

> Your sovereign's state secretaries and clerks are paid your royal monetary salary and with land and hereditary estates. And they attend constantly to your sovereign's affairs without surcease and enrich themselves with much wealth through superfluous charges. They have bought many estates and have constructed many of their own homes, great homes made from stone, which, under previous sovereigns of blessed memory (whose blessed memory may not be abused) even people of exalted birth, who would have been worthy to live in such structures, never owned such homes.

The recitation above of temptations for Larka seems at odds with the impeccable standards demanded of all chancellery officials. There were a multitude of laws in the 1649 *Ulozhenie*, Muscovy's most significant seventeenth-century law code, ferociously proscribing clerk misconduct, such as misspelling the tsar's name or altering the tsar's title, writing down false testimony, altering documents, and taking bribes to influence cases. Punishments included execution, severing of the hand, knouting by a thick leather strip (one blow of which was sufficient to kill a man), beating by the bastinado, getting fired from work, and paying monetary damages. Many of the *Ulozhenie*'s statutes were culled from pre-existent laws; all of them were common knowledge, and perhaps Larka obeyed them. Small—by our standards—clerical mishaps, such as sloppy but otherwise innocent work performance, nonetheless could spark hugely unpleasant judicial inquests against a hapless clerk. Chancellery clerks accused of some impropriety were invariably tried within their own institution. Somewhat belying the above-mentioned directives' forcefulness was the government's inconsistent enforcement of them, but the threat was real nonetheless.

Clerks could stubbornly defend their sense of honor in court against family or other personal insults, whether verbal or physical. Clerks could and did sue, and were entitled to collect damages, including a dishonor (*bezchest'e*) payment. The level of self-esteem and alacrity in defending one's honor would vary from person to person; perhaps Larka was dogged in sticking up for himself. The harshness of the climate, work regime, diet, and other elements of the Muscovite physical regime combined to produce chronic irritability and explosive tempers.[6] Muscovites, as noted in travelers' accounts and in court case records, were prone to let curse words—above all the famous "mother oaths"—tumble out of their mouths, and maybe Larka absorbed his share of them on the street; for all we know he may have responded in kind.

Though he may not have lived to hear of this later 1650s case, undoubtedly there were others similar to it earlier. In this example a Little Russian [Ukrainian] Chancellery clerk was badly beaten by a drunken neighbor and called a "son of a bitch." The clerk sued for restitution, though whether he received satisfaction is unstated.

What also makes this case interesting is the description of the aggrieved clerk's house; it was a standard Muscovite *dvor* (complex household), consisting of a yard in front with house in back. Larka may have lived in and even owned a similar dwelling; however, since the median price of a Moscow complex household during his career was a few score rubles, how could he have afforded the dwelling, assuming he actually purchased it? Unless he inherited his household, he most plausibly would have had to raise cash from his wife's family or from bribes. Then, too, he might have received a special cash distribution for house construction.

What else do we know about Larka's material existence? What did he look like? As was true not only of Russia at this time, clothing was intended both for comfort and

---

[6] Larka's diet, for example, consisted of hardy, rough, nutritious, and boring food such as onions, cucumbers, beets, cabbage, barely salted fish, and some meat.

to broadcast profession and social status. What Larka did for a living was recognizable instantaneously. He wore a long, plain caftan, probably from ram skin or wool, that cost between 1.5 and 3 rubles (10–50 percent of his cash entitlement), reaching down to his ankles and having long sleeves extending beyond the hands. In his earlier days as an apprentice, he more likely could have afforded a caftan made from dyed sackcloth, costing sixty kopecks. He also wore an elongated, triangular cap; and his boots, handy for walking through snow and mud, reached as high as his lower calves. The quality and price range of these two items were appropriate for men of his caste, and he probably received a special clothing allotment to purchase his things.

What he could not wear, for example, would be the high, cylindrically shaped black fox or beaver hats boyars donned, nor would he have worn their gaudy caftans, made from silk, damask, and satin and costing from 5.5 to over 10 rubles (0.5–2 percent of a boyar's cash entitlement), nor the prominent, upright, stiff collars that boyars sported. Caste status mores and cost precluded this.

What were Larka's place of work and workday routine like? The Service Land Chancellery for much of the seventeenth century was located in a number of complexes, housing other chancelleries, within the Moscow kremlin. During his tenure, Larka would have worked in a two-story building located between the Archangel Cathedral and the Spassky Gates. The Service Land Chancellery would have been allocated a few large rooms for tribunal sessions, clerks' workspace, and document storage. By the 1650s, the Service Land Chancellery was in a block "C"-shaped building on Ivan's Square behind the Archangel and Dormition Cathedrals. Finally, in 1670, the government ordered Larka's former employer, along with other chancelleries, to relocate to Kitai-Gorod, the commercial district next to the kremlin.

The office Larka worked in was stuffy, poorly lit with tallow and wax candles, at times drafty, and probably quite smoky, thanks to wood fires in the colder months.[7] The rough diet contributed to the Muscovite affliction, noted in travelers' accounts, of phlegmy breath and passed gasses, which must have exacerbated the duress of working in a crowded Service Land Chancellery office.

In such work conditions Larka very well might have developed chronic pulmonary maladies. His eyesight along with his finger and wrist joints may not have remained intact as he aged; there are a plenitude of chancellery documents with belabored, even tiny penmanship, indicating that the writer had to hold the paper on which he was writing within a few inches of his face and suggesting age-related maladies for which there were no real cures. If Larka's eyes did go bad, he might not have been able to acquire spectacles, as few appear to have been available. Folk remedies were virtually the only medicine. Since administrative literacy was so scarce, there was no age-related retirement, and Larka would have had to remain on the job until he died, became incapacitated, or otherwise convinced superiors that he was finally useless to them. When writing, Larka, with his inkpot tied to a cord around his neck, usually

---

[7] Splinters (long, thin pieces of wood) were used sometimes for illumination.

kneeled or sat cross-legged. Sometimes, he sat on a stool and huddled over a crude wooden table. Since he wrote his drafts rapidly, every few seconds he jabbed his quill pen in the inkpot for a refill. In essence, Larka was a work machine.

The chancellery workday adjusted itself seasonally, but it was a long one, about twelve hours. Mechanical clocks were few and expensive, and thus people relied greatly on sundials, provided that the sun was visible. A series of edicts during the seventeenth century instructed chancellery workers as to when they had to show up for work and when they could leave. Larka and his colleagues had to show up one to two hours after first morning light, worked into the early afternoon, took a long lunch and afternoon rest, and then returned to work and remained at their stations through the evening and for several more hours into the night. Consequently, during the winter, Larka would spend considerable time working inside while it was black outside, given the paucity of wintertime sunlight and the amount of time he spent indoors.

Larka eventually graduated from junior clerk and had the opportunity to write up more than rough copies. As a middle clerk, he could pen final copies (*belovki*). Since he never attained the rank of senior clerk, he never experienced the executive pleasure of supervising subordinates like himself, could never become a designated signatory clerk (*pod'iachii s pripis'iu*) who signed documents, and never had any possibility of promotion to tribunal-level duties as a state secretary.

In addition to writing up documents in scroll form—such as edicts, memoranda, and rescripts—and filling in the pages of a large variety of individually tailored record books, Larka devoted an immense time to locating documents, most of which were in scrolls. This ponderous undertaking, consuming inordinate amounts of Larka's time, meant unrolling scrolls, many of which were scores of yards long, on the floor of a cramped and crowded office. Scroll pages were attached to one another by gluing together overlapping edges and became detached easily. Larka had to have the patience of Job in matching up corresponding sheet ends, each pair of which bore the upper and bottom halves of the state secretary's or senior clerks' signature, and reattaching them.

Such is our description of Larka. What Larka knew could easily fill the proverbial volume, although what we do not know about him is likewise germane. We know virtually nothing of his personal life. His dates of birth and death, data on his children, and his personal reflections—boilerplate petitions excepted—remain unknown. Since Muscovy was not a Protestant country, there were no family Bibles into which family patriarchs inscribed family trees and other seminal events. Nor were there parish records that might have noted such personal matters. Literacy was low, and the Orthodox Church never promoted Bible reading. There was no tradition of Renaissance letter writing; not unsurprisingly, we find no diaries and very little personal correspondence in the Russia of Larka's day. Native religious disposition—Russian Orthodoxy frowned on learning in general—no formal educational system, and an appallingly low rate of literacy conspired to make silence and resistance to more forward ways of thinking an unignorable characteristic of seventeenth-century Muscovy. From another perspective,

Larka's cognitive ability, gained through his professional expertise, was a forward-looking and progressive development.

What did Larka know, and what effect might his knowledge have had for seventeenth-century Russia and after? Larka's expertise in land matters, gained from surveys, recording in the field, and writing up large numbers of highly individualized instruments, meant that he had accumulated a vast amount of knowledge about Russian terrain, various forms of land tenure, social conditions, and the laws and norms associated with them. In short, he came to acquire a considerable amount of statistical, administrative, and physical environmental information. This constituted a formidable body of synthesizable knowledge that was generative and had the capacity to stimulate an even greater appetite for broader knowledge. These experiences and connections are not explicitly stated in Larka Lvitskii's documentation, but they are readily inferable from the data we have on him and his milieu.

Sixteenth- and seventeenth-century Muscovites' acculturation into governmental paperwork underlay Imperial Russian educational accomplishments, for through incremental steps Russians became caught up in a self-reinforcing and increasingly complicated interactive process of documentary detailing and reflective thought that slowly enlarged Russian appetites for information. Unbeknownst to him, Larka, in his own way, was a hero of Russian culture.

Suggestions for Further Reading

Brown, Peter B. "Peering into a Muscovite Turf-War (How Do We Even Know It's There?): Boyar Miloslavskii and the Auditing Chancellery." *Russian History* 25, nos. 1–2 (1998): 141–53.
———. "Salaries and Economic Survival: The Service Land Chancellery Clerks of Seventeenth-Century Russia." *Jarhbücher fur Geschichte Osteuropas* 51, no. 1 (2003): 32–67.
———. "How Muscovy Governed: Seventeenth Century Russian Central Administration." *Russian History* 36, no. 4 (2009): 459–529.
Crummey, Robert O. *Aristocrats and Servitors: The Boyar Elite in Russia, 1613–1689.* Princeton, NJ: Princeton University Press, 1983.
Demidova, N.F. *Sluzhilaia biurokratiia v Rossii XVII v. i ee rol' v formirovanii absoliutizma.* Moscow: Nauka, 1988.
Hellie, Richard. *Enserfment and Military Change in Muscovy.* Chicago: University of Chicago Press, 1971.
———. *The Economy and Material Culture of Russia, 1600–1725.* Chicago: University of Chicago Press, 1999.
———. *Slavery in Russia, 1450–1725.* Chicago: University of Chicago Press, 1982.
Olearius, Adam. *The Travels of Olearius in Seventeenth-Century Russia.* Translated and edited by Samuel H. Baron. Stanford, CA: Stanford University Press, 1967.
Plavsic, Borivoj. "Seventeenth-Century Chanceries and Their Staffs." In *Russian Officialdom: The Bureaucratization of Russian Society from the Seventeenth to the Twentieth Century.* Edited by Walter McKenzie Pintner and Don Karl Rowney. Chapel Hill: University of North Carolina Press, 1980, 19–45.

III
Military Personnel

"My Brilliant Career"
Autobiography of a Career Army Officer

Carol B. Stevens

"My Brilliant Career"[1] *is a fictional autobiography from late-seventeenth to early-eighteenth century Russia. Its author, Andrei Beklenshev, is an unusually successful career army officer. Below, he recounts his rise from a marginal social and economic position, as a southerner with pretensions to "nobility," to the relative heights of a senior Russian field officer whose noble status is secure and hereditary. His story opens with his father's concerns about family, status, and village, typical of the late seventeenth century. Andrei's perspective changes. He becomes absorbed by military life with its frequent marches, rapid relocation, and even its tedium. In the process, his family and land become less important to him. Andrei's use of non-Russian "professional" words, which he learns in the army (*amunitsiia, ofitser, *and* frunt*), is indicative of his new self-image.*

We have examples of secular writing from this period, and Andrei writes in a typically flat and uninflected tone. Officers like Andrei were often the first members of their families able to read and write. When asked toward the ends of their careers to write accounts of themselves, they had little experience with autobiographies, and they typically wrote bald recitals of events and places, with few emotional and self-reflective interpolations. Thus Andrei refers to his own Orthodox faith but never discusses it or explains its importance. Similarly, Andrei has considerable contact with West Europeans and their ideas, but their impact is clearer in his vocabulary and behavior than it is from his own account of his time in northern Germany and the Baltic.

Both the style and content of Andrei's narrative are inspired by first-person military accounts stored in the Russian State Military-Historical Archive in Moscow (f. 489 op. 1 and f. 490 op. 2) and by the literature of the period. Variations in spelling, capitalization, and punctuation reflect the style of this period, before

---

[1] My apologies to Miles Franklin, whose 1901 novel entitled *My Brilliant Career* shares nothing with the following, except his title that is appropriate to both.

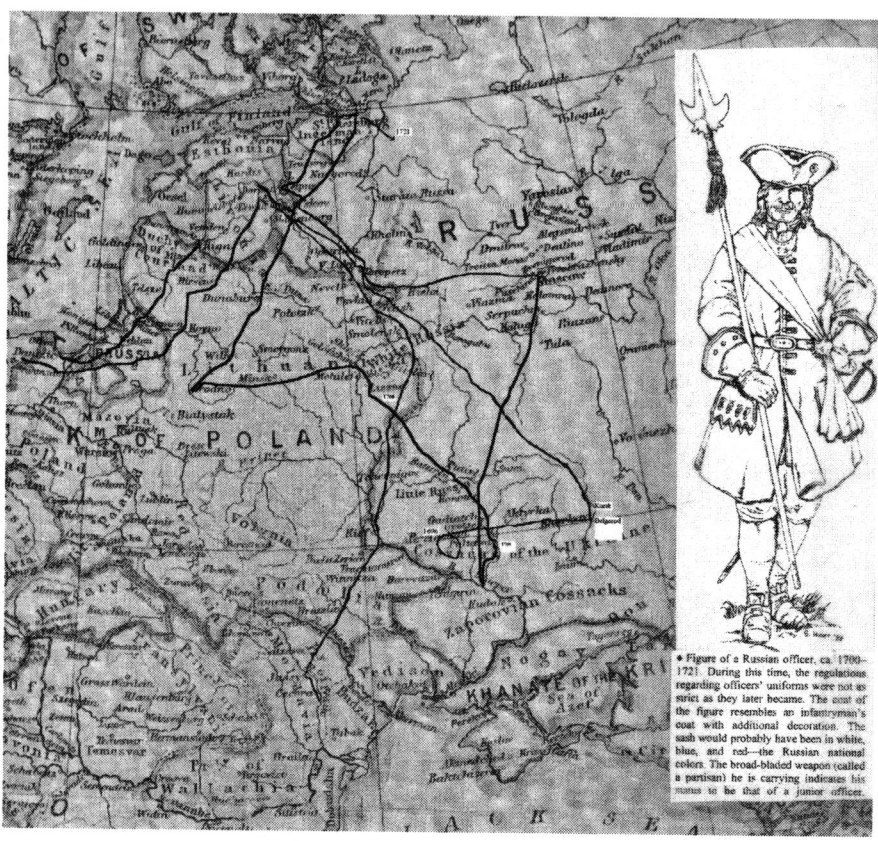

◆ Figure of a Russian officer, ca. 1700-1721. During this time, the regulations regarding officers' uniforms were not as strict as they later became. The coat of the figure resembles an infantryman's coat with additional decoration. The sash would probably have been in white, blue, and red—the Russian national colors. The broad-bladed weapon (called a partisan) he is carrying indicates his status to be that of a junior officer.

Military itinerary of Andrei Beklenshev, a composite of an army officer, who traveled from the Baltic and western Russia to the steppe and present-day Romania and Ukraine between 1695 and 1720. He participated in the battle of Poltava (1709) against the Swedes, at the Pruth River (1711) against the Ottoman Turks, and in the siege of Stettin (1713), again against the Swedes. The drawing depicts a uniform similar to the one Andrei would have worn. The drawing of the Russian officer is by S. Hart in *Eighteenth Century Notes and Queries*; the map is from Eugene Schuyler's *Peter the Great Emperor of Russia: A Study of Historical Biography* (1884).

orthography and grammar became standardized. Troop movements, supply shortages, taxes, the hunt for recruits, and even the rumors mentioned in Beklenshev's account are documented in the sources.

Andrei's wife, Nadia Beklensheva, was illiterate, as one would expect. Letter writing did not come naturally to her. On the rare occasions when she sent a letter to her husband, she paid a scribe on the town square to write it. Her husband kept the letters (which are modeled on the very limited extant correspondence of women connected with the Bezobrazov, Golitsyn, and the royal families) but voiced little emotion about them besides his own increasing distance from his Kursk home.

In the year 7187 (1680), I, Andrei Nikita's son Beklenshev, was born the second son of a provincial service family in Kursk province. Until then, my father left in different years to serve in the sovereign's cavalry regiments, and we plowed our own fields without peasants to help. Soon after, my father was assigned to a garrison nearby, defending our villages against Tatar raids. Such duties were less honorable than a battle regiment, but he plowed the land with my brother every spring.

When His Highness Prince Vasilii Vasilievich Golitsyn, at Tsarevna Sophia Alekseevna's command, led the first attack on the Crimea,[2] my father was restored to the active cavalry and served against the fearsome Tatar. Alas, he returned without honors, although he suffered much from starvation and disease after Tatars burnt the steppe grass. At home, my mother hoped that I would take to wife her friend Anton's daughter, Anya, but Anya's father cared only for family position and more peasants.

In 7188 (1695), at fifteen, I went with my father to be reviewed for service against the infidel Turk.[3] Anya's father was the reviewer, and he had many acres in Kursk province and elsewhere. He inspected our few trusty weapons and horses, and he recorded our small estate without peasants. Against these, my father's faithful service in garrison and campaign counted for little. I was assigned to an infantry regiment, although we gave gifts to avoid such disgrace, and my father returned to the garrison.

With my father's blessing, I served first under the command of the boyar Boris Petrovich Sheremetev. He had led southern troops before, and my father admired and revered him. Now Russian regiments moved west toward Little Russia,[4] and mine with them. My regiment, Colonel Gavril Burfa's, stood apart and guarded against Tatar counterattack against Little Russia. Few eyes followed us; most watched the tsar at Azov. Still our tasks were of no little danger and difficulty.

---

[2] An alliance among the Papacy, the Polish-Lithuanian Commonwealth, Venice, and the Holy Roman Empire was at war with the Ottoman empire. To divert the empire's Tatar allies and fulfill its obligations to the alliance, Russian armies attacked the Crimean khanate in 1687 and 1689.

[3] Peter I's first campaign to take the Turkish fortresses near the Black Sea.

[4] The seventeenth-century Russian name for Ukraine.

The Tatars attacked far in the west. They kept close together, moved very rapidly without straying, and so they were hard to catch. My regiment saw some action. I did not know my musket well, and there was little gunpowder. Some men learned as we fought. My father and brother at home said that groats, hard biscuit, and oats were demanded for the army, if one man in the family was not at work building river barges. Despite my service, they had much hardship to avoid those contributions, and the food collected did not come to Ukraine. Our kasha was thin, and later there was hunger.

With Hetman Mazepa, General Sheremetev went down the River Dnieper toward the Turkish fortress of Ochakov on its lower reaches, but above that came more forts: Kazi-kerman and Arslan-Ordek on each side of the river with Shagin-kerman, Mubaret-kerman, Mustreb-kerman, and Shakh-kerman nearby. They gloriously took Kazi-kerman, and two of the smaller fortifications were destroyed by the enemy.

Before the mud came in 1696, I was wounded in the arm and struggled home to my father's farm. As I recovered, my marriage to our dear neighbor, Nadia daughter of Aleksei, was arranged and took place; her family's small lands and ours now ran together. For my wounds, I avoided service at Taganrog and barge building. I still had little time on our land.

In spring 7190 (1698), after review, I joined the infantry regiment of *stol'nik* Colonel Afanasii Nikitin Nelidov. Under his command, we garrisoned the important palisade fortress at Belgorod. The colonel was a good Orthodox man; he did not deny me the company of men of my own rank. My dark green uniform reminded me of treacherous musketeers, but with a strange and foreign three-cornered hat. An officer kept our muskets except on the battlefield. We paid for these things from salaries we were promised. My company was drilled by a foreign captain, and he was rude and unsuitable for servicemen of our rank. *Stol'nik* Colonel Savva Vasilievich Aigustov's regiment was also in Belgorod, and he noticed me. I took the place of a second lieutenant in his troop lost on the city palisades. When the inglorious events of Narva took place and Russian troops were basely deserted by their foreign commanders,[5] we were still in the south. Colonel Aigustov marched us north to garrison Pskov, where the fortress is all of stone and very fine and large with cannon for the towers. A letter from Nadia came then with news, as my service took me far from home:

> My dear husband, I long for news of you; may God keep you well and safe while you fight. For us things go poorly. There is a new review of military men here, mixing those of all ranks together and recording their lands and men. Our neighbors who stayed behind and did not go to serve are now ordered to serve with men with no lands nor claims to them; they build the fortress at Taganrog, taking horses, a cart and supplies for two months, and there is much complaint, hardship, and unhappiness about the

---

[5] In 1700, the Russian siege of Swedish Narva was relieved by Swedish troops commanded by Charles XII in person. The treachery of Russia's foreign officers was a common, if erroneous, explanation for the defeat.

kind of service. In many families near ours all but one of the men are gone to serve in the army. Some sell and scrape to buy substitutes, but it is very expensive. Some have been restored to the cavalry forces, but they serve in fortresses nearby. This is good, but without pay or help that is a great hardship. We need you here but can find little news of you or your return among soldiers who pass by. Pray send us news of yourself, that you are well and uninjured.

I was commanded by order of the illustrious General Sheremetev to transfer immediately to Matvei Treiden's regiment. Nearly half the men died at Narva when the enemy attacked. After, the regiment marched to Novgorod and then Pskov, where I came up with it. In 1701, we marched under Prince Repnin's command to Derpt. After the events at Derpt, we turned back to Pskov and thence returned to Novgorod, and our command shadowed the Swedish corps under General Krongort.

I was at the attack and storming of Schlusselburg, which the Swedes call Noteburg. Our infantry service was hard and dangerous. Men standing in the lines had little training or protection, and we issued small amounts of powder to the men with their muskets. We left camp with others to forage for food, as there was little there. I remembered my family's accustomed place: the freedom of the cavalry, capturing tongues (*iazyki*),[6] skirmishing with enemy patrols and dashing across the field of fire. In Kursk, we knew that excitement well. Cossack forays were no little help here, although not against a fortress. We lost many men at Schlusselburg, but few Swedes defended the fortress, while we were twelve thousand strong. The illustrious General Sheremetev gave me a lieutenant's commission for my actions, and perhaps my attentions to my former colonel helped. My pay grew, and the battlefield bonus paid debts, purchased supplies, and some was left to send to Nadia in Kursk. I was assigned an orderly. My family held land without peasants, but as an *ofitser* I got a servant who was a soldier in the regiment. My new commission brought hope for distinction and better fortune. At home, Nadia wrote, things changed little, but I was far away from their struggles:

> Dearest husband, I have hoped these years to hear that you are well and calm, honored and prospering, and there has been no one to give us news as you serve in such distant places, and now I hear that you were in many battles and came safely away with your life and your health. I rejoice that you were safely delivered. Our daughter, Natalia, who was born healthy and strong, is now two; all here are safe, praise be to God. Life for many is hard. There are demands for recruits and supplies and money to support them every day, but the land is no richer. We have paid and paid, and no longer have anything to offer. Your father is old and surely no longer suited to service, and I am like a widow though my brother and yours are doing the plowing and your mother is here. Nearby there is little help. More and more families lose the few men remaining to do the plowing, and, since men of our kind too are mostly gone, we are fearful of Tatar attack. Please send us news of your health and may you prosper.

---

[6] Informers.

After Schlusselburg, we went to Nyenskans and in the summer stayed at Piterburkh (St. Petersburg), where we guarded and built the new capital. Although the place commanded the river, it was desolate and muddy with marshy land. The work was hard and long, and unsuitable for officers. However, His Highness Tsar Peter himself built boats and served in all ways manual and military, surprising many, and service in these days took many different forms, so that such work was seen well by our commanders. The soldiers built wooden buildings; we escorted carts of food and workers who wished only to escape this desolation. Stonemasons arrived daily from Novgorod to lay foundations for long-lasting buildings, but how stone will stand in the swamp I did not know. Mud was everywhere, and the wind off the marshes was sharp. We trained the men in military science. I hoped to be noticed for my willing actions as for bravery, for not to every man does God give the chance to fight in many battles.

The regiment did not stay in Piterburkh, where the work continued for many years, but moved toward Derpt. As we marched, we saw a Swedish ship stranded in the lake. We attacked and took it; with others, I was wounded. The medical orderly tended us, and we were moved toward Pskov. My regiment went to Narva, because of siege experience and the need for more men. Our new artillery, made of bell-metal taken straight from churches and monasteries, opened the attack. The storming of the fortress took nine hours, and only good came from such Blessed metal, and the battle was won. After that, Field Marshal Sheremetev brought the troops to Pskov, but I did not rejoin my regiment. Instead, for my wounds and service, I was transferred as a captain to Lieutenant General Adam von Shonbek's Regiment, but why this regiment I did not know. Nadia again wrote the country news, but my honorable service and suffering brought little reward there:

> Dearest husband, May the Lord's grace be with you and may He bless you always, Amen. There are many letters that I send you, and for my sins you do not answer them, when I tell you of our life and our situation. I have heard nothing of yourself and your health—perhaps there is no time or I do not know. I no longer know what to do. Your parents have abandoned us; they leave behind responsibilities and want and live within the city walls of Kursk. We send them food and help when we can. Your brother too is on his way to join a regiment, since God willed that he should at last be called into the wars after the new military lists were written. There is no one left to help us and we can farm but poorly even with my family's help. Saving seed from the year's crop will be difficult, and we gather as much as we are able, since we are lucky to have such land and the building of the millpond may help. Men from Kursk demand more contributions from our holding and no longer can Anton Alekseevich intercede for us, for he too is gone to do other service and no longer returns in the fall. We fear a Tatar attack further south. It is said that the garrisons are rebellious, so it may be that even the defenses are useless. For a long time, no Tatars have been so far north, but if they come here we can only abandon everything and join your parents within Kursk. We know not what to do. For the love of God, do not now forget us, but remember our problems and my letters and please send us word and advice and help us.

Our regiment with others, and with the Poles who supported his Highness King Augustus and His Majesty Peter Alekseevich, together guarded Lifland and the east at Grodno, while the Swedish army of King Charles moved against Saxony and King Augustus. My father feared Polish fighters sorely, but now they quibbled among themselves and did not fight; perhaps it was difficult against King Charles.

Then we marched east and to the south. Under command, we burned villages and destroyed crops, leaving nothing for the winter, although some food was buried. The enemy searched for food and water far from their line of march, and our Cossacks attacked them. We moved south to the edge of the steppe, far from damp, dismal Lifland. The cold froze men and horses to death, and our own troops had little food. Supplies and men and more moved westward to quell the troubles[7] in the east. The time was hard and anxious. The steppe fortresses were not so large as in my youth, but small and crowded with many men as we waited for attack along the southern front (*frunt*). Many soldiers ran off, but many stayed. As for us, officers (*ofitsery*) did not desert. The treachery of (the Cossack leader) Mazepa did not change our path.[8] We were not the regiments to destroy Baturin.

In 1709, we followed the Swedes under General Kreits by winter path. Battalions were commanded to fall on Golk, and I led one company. We went overland by summer routes to Poltava, and I with my regiment. Near Poltava, the men built earthen walls around the camp, and at the battle, we stood inside waiting. The Swedish infantry drew up in front of us. They had already lost many men, and our own dragoons came up behind. The Swedes ran at us at full force, as we emerged before the walls, but neither their dragoons nor their artillery helped them as before. So we in the front line commanded the men to fire with good courage and great effect. With God's help, the men stood stolidly and shot well and fewer were lost than expected, though many died. After the battle, His Excellency Field Marshal Sheremetev rewarded me with a commission as major. The treacherous Cossacks were trapped on the riverbank in the pursuit, and we had our revenge on them and great feasting after all was done; there were many Swedish prisoners.

There was no second battalion command open in my regiment, and I was on furlough (*vakantsiia*) and then with a training regiment for fresh recruits. I continued in this work for two years. Soldiers guarded the recruits as they came from the countryside, but they ran away back to their villages. There was talk of shackling or branding them, but sometimes not so many were lost. Most were peasant boys with no knowledge of arms and fighting, not such as I when I enrolled. There was more money for food than before, but most men ate groats boiled with salt.

---

[7] For example, a rebellion led by the Cossack Kondratii Bulavin against the violation of traditional Cossack freedoms in 1707–8 split the Don Cossack camp, and its suppression was savagely carried out by two contingents of Russian troops led respectively by V.V. Dolgorukii and P.I. Khovanskii.

[8] Ukrainian Hetman Mazepa joined Charles XII of Sweden in March 1709, but Russian troops destroyed Mazepa's capital, Baturin, and the supplies the Swedish army needed so badly.

78 MILITARY PERSONNEL

In 1710, a fearsome plague struck and killed soldiers in the training regiments, although I was, thanks be to God, myself spared. Soon after I marched to Lithuania with recruits for garrisons in Reval, Riga, and Vyborg, and the plague was there. There were cities with Orthodox households, and a blessed Orthodox church, but Catholic churches too and Uniate, and Jewish temples. And new troops were also raised for the South, where the Turkish armies and the Tatars threatened.[9] These concerns do not trouble women much; Nadia wrote only their worries and sufferings at home.

> Dear husband, I give thanks to God that He has allowed me at last that which I so desired, that is some greater news of you. The soldier who came from your regiment says that the great battle with Sweden is over at last and, led by Tsar Petr Alekseevich himself, you are honored and your life is preserved. More and more army men return to the South, because of rebellion and new worries about Tatars, and it is said that more regiments from the front will soon arrive; may your regiment be one of these and you yourself return to your homelands with them after so many years. I have more news. Your sister Iulia is of an age to marry and it is proposed by your parents that I arrange it, because we also have no word or news from your brother since he left. I have no dowry to offer for her but that small sum you sent from the army (with that soldier who came) and perhaps also if we sell something. It has not been easy to live peacefully. New collections for the army are most demanding and insistent that we pay instead of your service and your brother's. It would be well if you showed more concern to write to us and tell us the tale of your life away for so many years—soldiers from the army pass near Kursk often—and suggest to me or send me more help in caring for these family matters when no one else can do so.

At last I took command in the Kiev Infantry Regiment. We marched south; these days were accursed. Locusts came on the troops in clouds and they would not leave though we fired arms and burned lines of powder and shot cannon. I did not know why this portent, but not a few disasters followed. Our Christian allies in Wallachia failed, and the Moldavians who came had nothing. We did not know how many Turkish arms we faced, but we met them across the river. So we remained under arms till nightfall, pulling back to the river in haste. Many horses were lost. We burnt carts and supplies with no horses to pull them, under command, and left nothing for the enemy. We were in the Turkish action.[10] Our infantry squares were fiercely attacked but held. Without the carts, the ammunition lasted four days, and likewise with the food and fodder. Still we drew back with drums and colors. We took food even from the Turks and could not defend the weak and stragglers behind the army. There was little praise for any action. Many foreigners departed after the Turkish battle from their little faith in the Russian army, but new commands and promotions did not open. Life in distant Kursk was also accursed; my father died in these times, may God preserve his soul.

---

[9] The Russian empire expected the Ottoman empire and its vassal, the Tatar khanate of Crimea, to declare war.

[10] A typically oblique reference to the only major encounter of this Russo-Turkish War—Russia was badly defeated on the River Pruth in 1711.

My husband, May God help us that things have come to such a place. Last month your blessed father breathed his last, and your mother returned with me to our land. All around, soldiers hunt for those who have land and yet who do not serve nor send their sons. They say that lands will be taken and three times on the road home we were stopped. Your brother and his son we do not know their fates, nor yours for some long time though we hear that you are far away in unchristian lands. . . . May He preserve you and bring you home to help us here.

In 1712, I was seconded to another regiment under Prince Menshikov in Pomerania. At the fortress of Demin, I commanded the garrison. At that time, a Swedish force passed near the fortifications, going toward the Stettin. I left some men in the fortress and gave chase. The Swedes divided into small units, and we formed pursuit parties. Although there was skirmishing and we had no little difficulty and risk, there were too few men to block the Swedish passage everywhere. Evil reports reached Fieldmarshal Sheremetev that through inaction I permitted reinforcement of Stettin. A well-born Colonel Denisov relieved my command, and with him many more men. Military valor, loyalty, and obedience are not valued as before; now title (adres) and courtliness are needed, but I still serve with pride and patience.[11]

I was at Stettin in 1713 from the beginning of the attack, but after it was taken, it was given to the Danes. I went to Viazma in 1714, and wintered in Lifland and then to Riga. Next, I was sent from Riga into Poland, where we passed a very severe winter when Tsarevich Petr Petrovich was born, and then to Mecklenburg. I went with the transport ships to Copenhagen and returned. In 1717, we wintered in Lithuania, and in 1718 in Gdansk.

I was many years in glorious action away from home. For my infirmity, wounds, and years of loyal service, the War College granted my petition to retire in 1720. I am commanded to the steppe once more, to train frontier militia—small landholders without peasants like my father. They will need much to be battle ready. My own lands supplement my pay, for the census states that I hold fields still in Kursk province. But I have no news these many years of my family (*familia*), their fortunes, or the land. And the land that was left after my father, that land should be my elder brother's, but I know nothing of his fate. I have served without ceasing with first one regiment and then another, as commanded, never leaving to return to my home nor to tend my lands and see my family. My wife's dowry fields and our lands are in I know not what condition. I leave for Belgorod tomorrow.

Suggestions for Further Reading

Bushkovitch, Paul. *Peter the Great: The Struggle for Power, 1671–1725*. Cambridge: Cambridge University Press, 2000. Emphasizes the political context for Petrine change and, in particular, the continuity between Peter and his predecessors.

---

[11] Social standing probably was more important in promotion toward the end of Peter's reign. Promotions in any case slowed after 1711.

Engel, Barbara Alpern. *Women in Russia, 1700–2000*. Cambridge: Cambridge University Press, 2004.

Frost, Robert I. *The Northern Wars: War, State, and Society in Northwestern Europe, 1558–1721*. New York: Longman/Pearson, 2000. Places the Petrine war against Sweden in the context of general European military change and conditions in the Polish-Lithuanian Commonwealth.

Hughes, Lindsey. *Russia in the Age of Peter the Great*. New Haven: Yale University Press, 1998. Contains discrete sections on the military events and reforms of Peter's reign.

Keep, John L.H. *The Soldiers of the Tsar: Army and Society in Russia, 1462–1874*. Oxford University Press, 1985. Contains a social history of the Petrine military.

"Letter from Tsaritsa Proskovia, May 1722," and "Letter to Peter I from Anna Menshikova, ca. 1705." In *Russian Women, 1698–1917: Experience and Expression*. Edited by Robin Bisha et al. Bloomington: Indiana University Press, 2002. Letters of women connected to the Russian royal family.

Ostrowski, Donald. "Peter's Dragoons: How the Russians Won at Poltava." In *Poltava 1709: Revisiting a Turning Point in European History*. Edited by Michael Flier and Serhii Plokhy. Cambridge, MA: Harvard Ukrainian Research Institute (forthcoming).

Pushkareva, Natalia Lvovna. *Women in Russian History: From the Tenth to the Twentieth Century*. Translated by Eve Levin. Armonk, NY: M.E. Sharpe, 1997.

Stevens, Carol Belkin. *Russia's Wars of Emergence 1460–1730*. London: Pearson Longman, 2007.

"The Tale of the Russian Sailor, Vasilii." In *The Literature of Eighteenth-Century Russia: An Anthology of Russian Literary Materials of the Age*. Edited by Harold B. Segel. New York: Dutton, 1967. This tale is one of few relevant fictional accounts that probably dates from the time of Peter.

The Travel Diaries of Peter Tolstoi: A Muscovite in Early Modern Europe. DeKalb: Northern Illinois University Press, 1987. The diary of a fifty-year-old (noble)man sent by Peter I to study in Europe in the late 1690s. Both his writing style and the content of his diary are useful in understanding Beklenshev's very different life.

The Life of a Foreign Mercenary Officer

W.M. Reger IV

Written in the dialogic tradition of the Renaissance, this portrait presents two types of foreign mercenary officers active in seventeenth-century Russia. Colonel William Allen is a composite character representing a distinct type of mercenary officer: those recruited from abroad, who served in the tsar's army either for the duration or for a portion of the Thirteen Years War (1654–67), or for their entire lives. The events and experiences described by Colonel Allen and Captain Edvart are historical, not fabricated, but did not necessarily happen to the historical Allen and Edvart. Some of the opinions attributed to Allen's character are distilled from my reading of the sources and do not necessarily derive from any explicit statement in the historical record. His friend, Boldvin Edvart (Baldwin Edwards), and their mutual acquaintance, Mikhail Kro (Michael Crowe) represent a second type of officer, the nemchins, *who were typically either born of Russian mothers, raised in Russia, or officers of very low status from the West. The term* nemchin *was often used in a derogatory sense. I have retained the Russian versions of the names Edvart and Kro to emphasize the distinction between them and the officers from the West. The merchant Andrew Smith is intended as a naïve interlocutor and comedic foil. I made an effort in this portrait to use authentic names and phraseology typical of the period of the mid- to late seventeenth century. Capitalization and punctuation follow the somewhat eclectic style of the period.*

The fictional conversation depicted in this portrait is set toward the end of the Thirteen Years War, when Russia employed thousands of foreign military officers. The government of Tsar Aleksei Mikhailovich Romanov had already begun to dismiss or turn away unnecessary officers, anticipating peace, though certain key individuals and their sons would remain in Russian service until the time of Peter the Great. These officers played a principal role in the formation of Peter's military ideas, and helped Peter transform the Russian army from a force dependent on hired foreign professional soldiers to a state with the apparatus in place to create its own modern army without relying on foreign expertise. This portrait is drawn primarily

Генералъ Патрикъ Гордонъ.
Первый устроитель арміи Петра.

The caption under the portrait reads: "General Patrick Gordon. First Organizer of Peter's Army." Gordon (1635-1699) was a Scot born in Aberdeenshire who entered Russian service in 1661 during the Thirteen Years War (1654–67). He later went on to teach Peter I about military and technical matters. Gordon left a 6-volume diary, parts of which serve to create the composite portrait of the subject of this chapter, Colonel William Allen, a mercenary officer who, like Gordon, was recruited from abroad. The portrait is from an 1859 edition of excerpts from Gordon's diary.

from documents found in fond 210 of the Russian State Archive of Ancient Acts, the published collection of documents entitled Akty Moskovskogo gosudarstva, *vols. 2 and 3, and* Passages from the Diary of General Patrick Gordon of Auchleuchries in the Years 1635–1699 *(1968). It also relies heavily on secondary material discussed in the* Suggested Reading *section.*

Shortly before dusk one evening in Moscow in late September 1666, three men sat down to an intimate dinner of roasted pullets in the rented rooms of the eldest of the three, Colonel William Allen, recently returned from a bloody campaign in the Dnieper river valley. His visitors included Andrew Smith, a merchant who was new to Russia, and Captain Boldvin Edvart, a fellow officer known to Colonel Allen since boyhood, also recently returned to the capital from the siege at Bobrovsk. The three were waiting for Susanna, the Colonel's German maid, to bring the platters of food. Mr. Smith felt unsettled over difficulties he had encountered entering the country, and began the conversation by inquiring of the Colonel whether he also had trouble upon his arrival in Russia.

"As I recall," replied the Colonel, "we arrived on the 25th of September 1654, about four months later than hoped. At the border we could not find sufficient cartage to carry our people and gear."

"How many were in your party?" asked Mr. Smith, who was in Moscow with a large shipment of wine, which he hoped to sell at a profit.

"We were eight officers altogether; including wives, children, and servants, a total of thirty-two souls. We were held up in Pleskau because that charlatan monk-turned-soldier Jean De Gron managed to commandeer our carts, which obliged us to sit on our hands until a petition could be sent to Moscow asking for more carts. Finally, the order came to the local chancellery office to provide us with the eighteen carts it required to carry our food, clothing, books, weaponry, tools, and equipment, as well as those not mounted on horseback. Once here, we encountered difficulty in hiring lodgings in the Stranger suburb.[1] Still, we were admitted to kiss his Tsarish Majesty's hand at his country house in K——,[2] and were back in the city before the first real snows fell."

"Was this your first journey to Muscovy, then?" asked the merchant Smith, who felt extraordinarily peckish and wondered when Susanna would serve, and whether a military man living so far from civilization could keep a decent table.

"Actually, no. I came here years ago as a young lad with my father, who later died in battle against the Cherkassy.[3] After his death, my mother and I returned home to England, where she remarried. When my stepfather refused to grant

---

[1] The term used by Patrick Gordon and others to describe the neighborhood outside Moscow where foreigners lived during the seventeenth century.

[2] In keeping with literary style of the period, I have opted to record Russian personal and place names with an initial only.

[3] Circassians.

me a portion of his estate, I left home and became a soldier like my father. I attached myself to a certain Irish gentleman who did service under the French king, and in time I rose to the rank of lieutenant in the French army. The fortunes of war carried me to Germany and a number of petty princelings, before coming to Vienna, where I encountered the Russe[4] ambassador, L—, who promised a steady salary in the Tsar's service. I thought at the time that my experience would qualify me for command with the Russe army, and I presented seven letters testifying to my abilities and experience. The boyar Prince M—, however, insisted that nothing be left to chance with any of the incoming officers. I, and the officers who entered Russia with me, were ordered to undergo an inspection of our martial abilities. I marched with the long pike and the musket, and executed all the parade turns for the examiners—who, by the way, were countrymen of mine. I also fired muskets and pistols to demonstrate my marksmanship. Sadly, not all our officers were so adept. After I was examined, a Scotsman named Stuart, while attempting to reload his musket, shot and killed two clerks who were attending the prince. The Russes were furious, as you might imagine, and refused to give him an officer's rank and pay. I satisfied the prince, apparently, because I was enrolled for colonel on the following Monday, with a full salary of 45 rubles a month.[5] I was promised a gratuity of some cash and goods for a welcome, but it was held up because the clerk expected a bribe, which is the usual, even *expected* practice in these parts. Still, I refused to pay it, and made considerable trouble for him with the boyar of his Office until he delivered my payment. When they finally delivered the gratuity it was in their cursed copper coin, and so hardly worth my trouble."

"How long after your successful examination did you receive a command?" asked Smith, tearing both legs from the nearest pullet before the flustered maid could set the platter on the table.

"Almost immediately. The Russes gather the soldiers and then assign them to a colonel for training and arming. My regiment was formed from a number of elements. I had fifteen hundred men with banners, drums, and muskets who were thrown together from various infantry regiments. Some of them were little more than bandits or deserters brought to Moscow to be reintegrated into service. Others were members of the musketeer militia, who were to be rearmed and retrained. Quite often we retrain their native musketeers who typically have neither the weaponry nor the discipline to make effective soldiers. Some had even been horsemen from the Tatar tribes, who came to us mere beggars, without mounts,

---

[4] The contemporary term used by Gordon and others meaning Russian.

[5] Monthly pay of foreign officers varied according to the rank and experience of the individual. A sergeant might receive two to four rubles, a captain nine to eleven rubles, and a colonel anything from ten to fifty rubles. Forty-five rubles was an impressive sum for a colonel only recently employed.

sick, and little knowledge of the language. Quite a soup for a first command, but it was their practice to do so—even De Gron commanded Cossacks among his Russe soldiers."

"How do you like commanding your own regiment in his Tsarish Majesty's army?" asked Captain Edvart.

"To be honest, it is nothing like what I imagined; much more challenging than I had supposed. The Russian army has no proprietary colonelcies, no absentee colonels, so with the rank comes considerably more responsibility than many colonels in Europe bear. I am responsible for teaching them everything from field maneuvers and how to stand and march in formation to making bullets. I must also make certain the Russes give us the powder and shot we need to keep the men in training—not to mention defend themselves in battle. You cannot conceive the equipment a regiment requires: muskets, carbines, pistols, pikes, gunpowder, holsters, bandoleers, cartridges, match,[6] not to mention the axes, shovels, mattocks, hammers, and carts. Then there are the great guns, the food, cloth, tents, medicines, and so on. We depend entirely on the Russe scribes and clerks for every necessity, and the government seeks always to restrict any effort at ingenuity. I find it difficult to practice the art of war in such circumstances, where bribery accomplishes more than merit and where we are restrained, even on the field of battle. Even when we have the expertise and opportunity to push our advantage, if we act without direction from above—by which I mean the Tsar or his representatives—then we risk censure or worse. I know of one officer, Snevins, who was chastised for manufacturing grenades during a bombardment, when his men ran out of bombs to heave at the enemy."

"I heard you've been having some trouble yourself of late," said Captain Edvart.

"Yes, but certainly nothing I can't handle. If you're referring to the insurrection last month in my regiment, for which I was fined a year's salary—I still maintain my innocence in that affair. I had no idea executing a deserter would so entirely destroy the discipline of my men. If the Tsar had opened his state warehouses when we petitioned for sustenance, I could have fed my men and they would not have been tempted to run away to their homes or set fire to their billets."

"Actually, William, I was speaking of your contention with Prince K—."

"Oh, that? As I said, I have fought and bled for many of Europe's princes since leaving England, but never in all my years of service have I seen such abject ignorance of the arts and disciplines of war as exhibited by Prince K—. His cavalrymen were shooting at my sentries, if you can believe it, and in the presence of a hostile enemy force, no less. I always endeavor to keep my men well trained, though they are deserters and infidels: I think every respectable officer should do so. The average Russe, with discipline and a stern hand, will march and die like any

---

[6] Match is a slow-burning wick used to ignite the gunpowder in a musket or cannon.

Englishman or German, and I will be damned if Prince K— will waste them like straw after all my preparations. I told him that if he did not punish the cavalrymen who killed my sentries, and put a stop to the practice, I would arm my troops and give the command to shoot their tormentors on sight. Of course, he scoffed at my threat, but I rejoined that if he was to allow such a great misconduct, then I could not possibly remain under his command."

"Is it true, then, what I have heard, that you deserted your post?"

"Oh, yes. I ordered my drummers to sound 'to arms,' and my regiment assembled immediately in the square, in good order, and then I marched them straight out of the town."

"Certainly you have doomed yourself with the Tsar then!" exclaimed Mr. Smith, as he helped himself to more of the Colonel's excellent wine.

"Not at all. I have my orders and instructions directly from His Majesty and Prince K— knows it well. That cross-grained fellow cannot touch me. These people place great store in the scribbling of the scribes and clerks; petitions, writs, orders, and decrees are what they respect and give attention to. I know my duty to His Majesty's cause, and to my men, and I am all too willing to wave my papers in Prince K—'s face. His cries of treason mean nothing to me. In fact, I have just heard from Colonel Crawford that the Tsar has commended my service in a letter to Charles II. I doubt Prince K— will be able to persuade the Tsar against me, but, as you may have heard, my quarters were destroyed in a fire last month, and frankly, I suspect it happened with the connivance of the Prince."

"Do you feel estranged from your native land, serving the Tsar, all these frozen miles away?" asked Mr. Smith.

"It is difficult, to be sure, but thankfully Europeans come and go regularly, and bring word when they do. I receive a number of gazettes and scholarly works from abroad, and thus remain aware of the affairs of the world. My family and I correspond regularly with our friends and family, and we hear constantly of the wars and calamities that befall Europe. I am convinced our letters are translated and scrutinized before they leave the country, however, because the Russes mistrust us, though I have been in service more than a decade here. I also correspond with a number of Europe's leading minds on a variety of subjects, most especially world and military affairs. I received a letter from a nephew recently, for example, in which he discussed a strange new engine of war[7] whereby horsemen may break through lines of infantry, even though they may defend with pikes."

"Tell me, William," said Captain Edvart, "How is it that you have been able to train your men so well and keep them loyal to you?"

"Yes," chimed in the merchant Smith, as he forked up a second slice of the Colonel's favorite pudding. "I have heard it said that many in this country despise

---

[7] The term "engine of war" might refer to any number of mechanisms designed to enhance fire power, assault walls, or give advantages on the battlefield.

the European officers, for their customs and religion, and for the upset they cause in the army among the gentry servitors, and will not follow them."

"True enough. One essential thing for organizing our regiments is finding officers who speak the native tongue. When I arrived I had the good fortune to encounter young William Brackett, my sister's son, who began as a bugler, and who has been engaged for a number of years with Mungo Carmichael's infantry regiment as first captain.[8] Mungo had no qualms about letting young William go; it is our practice to bring our relations under wing when we attain command. I convinced Prince M—, with whom I had become intimate, to transfer him to me, and I made him a lieutenant colonel. Of course, I had to bribe several clerks in the Stranger Office, and we are still contesting his corresponding raise in pay, but he has been a great help to me. He knows the Russe language, and has brought along other officers, who speak it, too. Now, when I give an order, my officers repeat it in the soldiers' own tongue, and they perform according to my desires."

"Would I know any of these officers?" asked Captain Edvart.

"Mayhap you know one who was, like yourself, born here in Moscow—Kro by name."

"Do you mean Mikhail Kro? We studied together in the Apothecary Chancellery to become physics."

"Yes, he mentioned as much; a fine lad. I knew his father years ago in Vienna, but we lost touch right before Rakoczy made his move against the city in *anno* '45. He was a good officer. Apparently, he was recruited into the Tsar's employ secretly, because it went against their treaty with the Commonwealth, came here, and married a native girl, for which he was required to accept the Russe faith. I would never have done so, as I have no wish to indigenate.[9] My wife dearly hopes to return to England after the war. The more enlightened Russes, as you well know, Boldvin, look upon us Europeans as scarcely Christian, while the common folk consider us pagan through and through. My advice to anyone, Mr. Smith, is to look for marriage among their own kind, and leave the natives to themselves."

"I quite agree, Colonel," nodded the merchant, sipping his wine with a companionable smile on his flushed face.

The colonel continued, "Young Mikhail was raised in the Russe faith and speaks like a native, his mother having been the daughter of a Muscovite merchant. He'll serve me well as a major, and take good care of our weaponry. He can cipher, read, and write in Russe, German, and English, and those rapacious thieves in the chancelleries who would look for every chance to cheat us out of arms, munitions, and supplies do not intimidate him. Because I knew his father, we have become especially fond of one another, and he keeps me aware of what our quartermaster, the

---

[8] The first captain is the officer who commands the Colonel's company in the regiment.

[9] *To indigenate* was a contemporary term meaning to "go native" or to convert to Orthodoxy.

black rogue, is up to. I'm going to put Kro over the disbursement of pay. The men like him well, and trust him, so they won't riot because they suspect he's robbing them. He'll also keep the damned brutes from breaking or selling their muskets to buy brandy and vodka, and get beastly drunk while on duty."

"He sounds like an excellent clerk, Colonel, but can he lead men in battle?" asked the merchant, slicing cheese to eat with the cracked nuts passed around the table in a Dutch porcelain bowl.

"Many say that we *nemchins* are not capable of command," added Captain Edvart with some heat, "but it is not necessarily the case."

"Kro commands his company as well as any man, Mr. Smith. He has taken his company to reconnoiter the Poles on several occasions without incident. He did have some difficulty maintaining control over his men during that fiasco at Kopys when the men, in their zeal for blood, did not obey clear orders to refrain from attacking without a specific command from the Tsar himself. Major Kro was unable to restrain his company and keep them in position inside our fortified trenches around the town. But then many of the European officers disregarded the commands of the boyars and let their men engage. The real problem with a man like Kro is simply his unfortunate Russe parentage, which the Europeans look down upon as less worthy."

"Why then does Kro not turn his back on the Greek Church and reunite with the Protestants?" asked the merchant, as he poured a third glass of wine. "I understand General Baumann and others are establishing churches here in the Suburb. Perhaps he could find a pastor willing to help him along and renew his exercise of the Protestant faith."

"I'm afraid that would be impossible, Mr. Smith. The Russes, for one thing, would look very unfavorably on such a course of action, and consider it an act of extreme disloyalty to the Tsar, punishable perhaps by exile to Siberia. The Tsar never looks favorably on an officer who wishes to leave his service, least of all one who has accepted the Russe faith."

"Yes, it does seem the Tsar wants to keep as many of his hired officers in his service that he can. Overall, as far as I can see, he makes good use of their abilities," admitted Captain Edvart.

"I must agree, Boldvin. Many of the older officers, who have been in the country for decades, write much to the Tsar and his advisors, to instruct them in the ways of war, as it is waged in Europe. The Russe must be instructed specifically, even in the most mundane matters, such as the shot and powder requirements of a full regiment for practice shooting, guard duty, and for battle. We must instill a sense of the organizational principles governing the movements and fighting techniques of a modern army. His Tsarish Majesty finds our disciplined regiments useful for hunting bandits, thieves, and even traitors, and we have put down riots, as well, if you recall some years ago that fracas over the copper coinage. During times of war, we inspect their fortified towns and even design and build modern fortifications. Our designs, of course, have the advantage of being informed by the latest military architectural principles currently held in Europe, the idea of which is to maximize firepower, while diminishing the enemy's capacity to destroy our defenses. The greatest trouble is that the Russe do not take well to any sort of criticism or advice from us. I was sent once to Nevel to evaluate its defenses, and the Russe governor took such offense at my report that he refused to arrange for laborers to construct the improvements I recommended."

"How do you find the Russe officer as a warrior?" asked the merchant, shifting uncomfortably in his chair, crossing and recrossing his legs, and looking frantically about the room.

"For the most part he is difficult to manage, ignorant of his duty, hostile to ourselves, and corrupt through and through, bent on sucking the very blood from his troops, if he has half a chance, but again, I must insist that there are exceptions. Some of them know their duty and have risen to prominent command positions in our regiments by their merits and lights. Most of the Russes in the regiments hold the rank of captain or below, and thus must take their orders from us, which they contend is too difficult to bear. Many of them are landless members of the gentry, so they are proud and do not take orders from foreigners gladly. Still, I can name several occasions when European and Russe have worked well together on the battlefield."

"It sounds as though the Russes have little love for or trust in their hired officers from Europe, but occasionally we hear of officers who attain administrative positions. Is it possible for foreign officers to rise in government?" asked Mr. Smith, over his shoulder from the corner of the room where he stood using a chamber pot.

"The usual practice is to appoint officers who have converted to Orthodoxy, men of distinction like your countryman, Alexander Leslie, now known by his baptismal name, Avram. Primarily, however, men whose families have been Orthodox and in Russe service for generations—like the Livonian families of the Fahrensbachs and Traurnikhts—gain the choicer preferments. The war, however, has placed several Protestant officers in the position of governor over towns held by the Tsar. I myself was governor for a time at S— B— when the governor suffered a stroke and could neither speak nor move his extremities. When I reported this to Prince D—, who was my superior at that place, he appointed me governor of the town. I was given the keys to the treasury, armory, and all the storehouses, and made responsible for making certain the local gentry appeared for service, and for maintaining the artillery, munitions, and food supplies. All was well until the new Russe governor arrived, and began to make changes in my own officers; that I could not abide and we quarreled. He sent me to the town of S— in chains to answer charges of treason, but in the end Prince D— favored my cause and all was well. I take some satisfaction in knowing that, should the Tsar not permit me to depart after this war, I will surely advance to high charge in his army."

"Has it truly been difficult for Europeans to leave the country?" asked Mr. Smith, as he pulled his pipe from his coat pocket. He was about to light it when the Captain reminded him the Muscovites frowned on the use of tobacco, so he merely sucked on it sullenly, wishing he were back in London, where everyone, he was certain, sat smoking by a fire.

"If one is of the Russe faith, or especially valuable to His Majesty's service, it is next to impossible to escape. Many officers leave on errands of state—to recruit more officers, purchase weapons, or perform some diplomatic mission—but they are impelled to return because their families remain behind. Now that this damnable war is about to end, however, His Tsarish Majesty has begun to dismiss officers, and to refuse the engagement of newly arrived cavaliers. Colonel Gordon tells of seeing hundreds of discharged officers along the road to Europe."

"I am under the impression that the Russes depend heavily on their hired officers for conducting not only this war, but also for maintaining their relations with the West. What are your thoughts, Colonel?" asked the merchant, sucking his pipe violently and finding no comfort in the taste of old smoke. He sorely missed his after-dinner pipe.

"We are in the service of the Tsar. Though I am a soldier trained and experienced in arms, and willing to serve on the field of battle any prince who will guarantee my rank and pay, the Tsar sees me as his servant, even as his slave, to do with according to his pleasure. My brother officers and I are servitors more than we are independent soldiers of fortune. Our special abilities on the battlefield are only complemented in his eyes by our ability to speak and write European languages, and thus serve him as translators, interpreters, or diplomats, or by our talents in trade and industry. An acquaintance of mine, for example, Colonel Justus van Kerkhoven, a Dutchman, complained to me that the Tsar saw him as more of a merchant than a soldier because he was sent so often abroad to purchase arms. I have myself some knowledge of the manufacture of munitions, and was required some years ago to oversee an iron mill where the Russes produced grenades and other explosive devices. The Tsar retains us as long as possible out of his belief that we are in many ways useful to him, and thus free him to a degree from reliance on his boyars, but I believe his confidence in our abilities blinds him to our weaknesses."

At that point the Colonel grew pensive and the conversation lagged. The merchant fell helplessly into a deep slumber, and the Captain signaled the Colonel's servant that he and Mr. Smith would be taking their leave, and would she have their horses brought around. Helping the merchant to his feet, the Captain and the Colonel managed to perch him on his willing horse, and then bade each other adieu as old friends who knew they would certainly meet again somewhere on the battlefields of eastern Europe.

Suggestions for Further Reading

Informative discussions of the foreign mercenary officers serving in seventeenth-century Russia published in English include the works of Richard Hellie, Carol Belkin Stevens, and Chester Dunning. Several useful articles have been penned from time to time by Paul Dukes as well. In addition, three as yet unpublished dissertations offer solid scholarly data on the foreign mercenaries and their lives and impact on Russian military affairs.

Hellie, Richard. *Enserfment and Military Change in Muscovy.* Chicago: University of Chicago Press, 1971. A classic work. Places the foreign mercenary officers in the context of Muscovy's fitful efforts at military reform throughout the century.

Lahana, Martha Luby. *"Novaia nemetskaia sloboda:* Seventeenth-Century Moscow's Foreign Suburb." Ph.D. diss., University of North Carolina, 1983. Discusses the German Suburb, the foreign community where many mercenary officers and their families made their homes.

Margeret, Jacques. *The Russian Empire and the Grand Duchy of Muscovy: A Seventeenth-Century French Account.* Translated by Chester Dunning. Pittsburgh: University of Pittsburgh Press, 1983. Dunning's translation of Margeret's memoir from the beginning of the century offers an eminently readable insight into the life of a foreign mercenary officer. Autobiographical material in English exists also for individuals such as Patrick Gordon and Paul Menezius.

Ostrowski, Donald. "Melchier Sternfels von Fuchshaim in Muscory." *Russian History* 35, nos. 3–4 (2008): 395–408. Analyzes a chapter in Grimmelshausen's seventeenth-century novel *Simplicissimus*, in which the protagonist, a German, enters the Tsar's service as a mercenary.

Phipps, Geraldine. "Britons in Seventeenth-Century Russia: A Study in the Origins of Modernization." Ph.D. diss. University of Pennsylvania, 1971. Places British mercenaries in the broader context of the experience of Britons in Russia.

Reger, W.M., IV. "Baptizing Mars: The Conversion to Russian Orthodoxy of European Mercenaries during the Mid-Seventeenth Century." In *The Military and Society in Russia, 1450–1917*. Edited by Eric Lohr and Marshall Poe. Leiden: Brill, 2002, 389–412. Discusses the conversion of European mercenaries to Russian Orthodoxy.

———. "In the Service of the Tsar: European Mercenary Officers and the Reception of Military Reform in Russia, 1654–1667." Ph.D. diss. University of Illinois, 1997. Examines the military expertise and impact of the mercenary officers on Russia's fighting capacity during the Thirteen Years War.

Stevens, Carol Belkin. *Soldiers on the Steppe: Army Reform and Social Change in Early Modern Russia.* DeKalb: University of Northern Illinois Press, 1995. A well-researched discussion of the Russian army's logistical concerns along the southern borders during the final decades of the century.

9

Vasilii Zotov
A Military Colonist on the Southern Frontier

Brian Davies

In the summer of 1635, the Military Chancellery decided a new garrison town should be built at the confluence of the Lesnoi Voronezh and Polnoi Voronezh rivers about 250 kilometers southeast of Moscow to block the Nogai Road and protect Riazhsk, Shatsk, Lebedian, Riazan and other districts against Tatar raids. The project of building and settling this new town, Kozlov, was entrusted to the military governor (voevoda) Ivan Vasilievich Birkin and the Moscow courtier (dvorianin) Mikhailo Ivanovich Speshnev. Birkin and Speshnev were authorized to settle a garrison of three hundred Cossacks, two hundred musketeers, and as many middle service class cavalrymen (deti boiarskie) *as the district plowland fund could accommodate. For this purpose they were to invite volunteers from all across the southern frontier. Ordinarily eligibility for enlistment was restricted to "free men who have never been in service or in draft as taxpayers, and who never tilled the land for someone or served someone under a deed," but for this occasion Birkin and Speshnev were permitted to enroll volunteers who could show under vetting that they or their fathers had been in service before 1613—the end of the Troubles—and had subsequently suffered ruin and lost their legal freedom. A flood of volunteers from across southern and central Muscovy soon headed for the new town of Kozlov, drawn by this unusual dispensation and the abundance of fertile land. By January 1639, over two thousand men had been settled in permanent service at Kozlov.*

More than half of the Kozlov colonists were deti boiarskie. *But they differed from the traditional middle service class of central Muscovy in that they were yeomen* (odnodvortsy) *with smaller* pomest'ia *and no peasant tenants. Typical of those accepted into the Kozlov yeomen was Vasilii Grigoriev syn Zotov. He presented himself for vetting by Governor Birkin and the clerk Osip Prutskii on 15 April 1636, the day after his arrival at Kozlov, and gave the following account of himself.*[1]

I am Vasilii Grigoriev *syn* Zotov, a free man never before enrolled in the sovereign's service. My father, Grigorii Filatov *syn* Zotov, was a patrol Cossack in the sovereign's town of Dedilov. He worked zealously for the sovereign's interest and tried to do his best for me and for my older brothers, but he was killed when Sagaidachnyi's Cherkassy raided Dedilov.[2] I was then seven years old. My oldest brother, Fedor, was of age for contract into the patrol Cossacks and took over my father's croft at the patrol Cossacks' settlement; I remained in his household and tried to earn my bread. When I entered my fifteenth year, I began to see I would not receive contract into the Cossacks or musketeers at Dedilov, for I had two older brothers, the Cossack contingent was fixed in size, and there were too many other hungry young men—sons, brothers, dependents of free men—seeking service. I did not want to work all my days supporting my brother on his small croft, so with his blessing I went out on my own. The places to the southeast drew me—Epifan, Riazhsk, and Dankov—for I knew something about them from my father and grandfather, who had patrolled them for the Sovereign, and everything told me they were places with good land, if wild, and opportunities for service on the Sovereign's bounty.

At Epifan I found no Cossack service, only work for board in the household of a *syn boiarskii*, Klimentii Fedotov *syn* Avderikhin. After two winters I went to Riazhsk, where many Cossacks serve, but I found no service there. I began to think of going downriver to Borshchev Monastery or even further to the forts and camps of the Don Cossack Host, but I never found the means and company to do this and finally decided it was too dangerous. So I went to Dankov—this was about eight years ago—and settled on the *pomest'e* of Your Lordship's deputy governor Mikhailo Ivanovich Speshnev. I lived under him of my own free will, as a free man, without indenture, on agreement that in return for my labor I would hold my own little croft—two quarters per field, in three fields—at his village of Pokrovskoe.

---

[1] Vasilii Zotov is a composite of Lipovka village's original fifteen settlers. His story is reconstructed from the following sources: Russian State Archive of Ancient Acts (RGADA), f. 210, Razriadnyi prikaz, Knigi prikaznogo stola, no. 2 (7145 g.), l. 87 ob.; f. 1209, Pomestnyi prikaz, Kniga pistsovaia pis'ma i mery Ivana Birkina da Mikhaila Speshneva (7145–7147 gg.), ll. 40–40 ob.; f. 1209, Pomestnyi prikaz, perepisnaia kniga goroda Kozlova i Kozlovskago uezda, pis'ma stol'nika Il'ii Danilovicha Miloslavskago da pod'iachego Artemiia Afanas'eva (7154 g.), ll. 349–50, 356 ob. See also: "1636 goda [sic] sentiabr' 5. Nakaz iasel'nichemu i voevodam Ivanu Birkinu i Mikhailu Speshnevu," *Izvestiia Tambovskoi uchenoi arkhivnoi komissii* 41 (1897): 151–58; and Brian Davies, "Service, Landholding, and Dependent Labour in Kozlov District, 1675," in *New Perspectives on Muscovite History: Selected Papers from the Fourth World Congress for Soviet and East European Studies*, ed. Lindsey Hughes (London: St. Martin's Press, 1993), 129–55.

[2] Cherkassy: Ukrainian Cossacks; Hetman Petro Sahaidachnyj's Cossacks invaded Muscovy in 1618–19 on behalf of Crown Prince Władysław.

94

Painting of the steppe border, titled *On the Patrol Border of the Muscovite State* (1907), by Sergei Vasil'evich Ivanov (1864–1910). Ivanov's painting provides the sense of what Russians call *prostor* or *razdol'e*, for spacious vistas, open views, and expanse that the steppe offers, not dissimilar topographically to the American Midwest. It was on this border that the town of Kozlov was founded and that the subject of this chapter, Vasilii Zotov, helped develop and protect against Tatar raids.

It was from His Lordship's, Mikhailo Ivanovich's, other Pokrovskoe tenants that I heard of the Sovereign's gracious bounty waiting at the new borderland town of Kozlov. This was in the summer of last year, year 7143 (1635). We learned of it even before the criers came to the villages and marketplace, when we heard that His Lordship Mikhailo Ivanovich had received the Sovereign's order to go with Your Lordship to the Voronezh River to found a new town to defend the Sovereign's borderland towns from the Busurman.[3] I reached agreement with His Lordship Mikhailo Ivanovich to find someone to take over my plowland at Pokrovskoe and follow His Lordship to the new town on the Voronezh, to enroll in the Sovereign's service there.

I left Pokrovskoe in late winter just before Shrovetide to avoid the mud and mire. I was able to leave so soon because Denisko Rukin had already agreed to take on my allotment and do the spring plowing, and I had no family and few chattels to slow me. But the journey was still hard, and we had to keep watch against Tatars and ruffians. I traveled with some of these fellows, as they will tell you. Ovdokim Vasiliev *syn* Skvortsov, here, is likewise from Dankov, the son of a Dankov Cossack. We started out together. These other men and their families joined us on the road. Some of them are from even further off, from Riazan and Tula. They will give you their testimonies. We have arrived only yesterday, and have come before you to relate our stories and ask permission to enroll in service at the Sovereign's new borderland town of Kozlov.

My father and his father before him were in the Sovereign's service. I swear that I am a free man, never before in service, never a deeded peasant or bondsman. These men will give surety on me. His Lordship Deputy Governor Mikhailo Ivanovich Speshnev will also vouch for me when he returns. May our Sovereign Tsar and Grand Prince of All Rus Mikhail Fedorovich favor me, his slave, and bestow his bounty and have me taken into his service, into whatever formation is suitable. And I am ready to take the oath of fidelity and service to our Sovereign Tsar and Grand Prince of All Rus Mikhail Fedorovich.

Governor Birkin and clerk Prutskoi were satisfied with this account and administered Zotov the oath of allegiance. They placed Zotov on surety bond to settle at the village of Lipovka, about ten kilometers east of Kozlov town.

Zotov was now recognized as a novitiate (novik) *eligible for eventual initiation* (verstanie) *into the Kozlov* deti boiarskie. *The other members of Zotov's party were all found eligible to enroll, although a landlord in Riazan district would later claim two of these men as deeded fugitive peasants and they would have to defend their status in remand hearings in the governor's court.*

Zotov could not claim his pomest'e *allotment at Lipovka until he had demonstrated his fitness for and commitment to military service and had undergone*

---

[3] Busurman: the Muslims—i.e., Crimean Tatars or Nogais.

initiation to confirm his land and cash entitlements. Only a fortunate few settlers had undergone initiation at Moscow before coming to Kozlov; the majority had to wait until June 1637 when Governors Birkin and Speshnev conducted a mass review. It was at this review that the additional five-ruble settlement subsidy promised all enlistees was finally paid out. The long wait for entitlement rates and settlement subsidies imposed considerable hardship on most enlistees. They got by in various ways. Those relocating from service households in the nearer frontier districts could bring down stores and return to their former homes to claim part of the family harvest. Others had to sell off gear or mounts to buy grain (for which they had to travel to the granaries in Voronezh, some 180 kilometers to the southeast).

Zotov was unusually lucky. Although the vast majority of Kozlov settlers were young men, his nearest neighbor at Lipovka, Tomilo Ivanov syn *Ukolov, was an older man, an* Elets syn boiarskii *allowed to resettle at Kozlov in reward for his services as a guide and escort to diplomats going down the Don to the Crimean khanate. Ukolov needed help putting his land under first cultivation and had an unmarried daughter, Domna. Zotov provided such help, shared Ukolov's harvest, and by spring had received Domna's hand in marriage.*

At the June 1637 review, Zotov stood for initiation along with 337 other novitiates and gave the following testimony:

You have on table my account of myself, as I dictated to the notary, and the account written by our Lipovka elected assessor [*okladchik*] Tomilo Ivanov *syn* Ukolov.

I cannot claim past rank [*chin*], for I am a novitiate never before in service in any of the Sovereign's towns.

As for family precedence [*otechestvo*], I have had none, being the son of a patrol Cossack and scion of Cossack and musketeer forebears. But the Sovereign has graciously given me enrollment in the ranks of his *deti boiarskie*, which will set a mark of precedence honor for me and for my descendants and for which I am most thankful. And I wish to say that my father had his own small honor in serving the Sovereign zealously and faithfully, fighting the Busurman and Litvak[4] and not sparing his own head.

Tomilo Ivanov *syn* Ukolov has given testimony as to my service capacity [*sluzhba*] that I am of good health, unweakened by any wounds. I have built on my lot at Lipovka and have sown my winter rye and spring oats. Although still solitary on my plowlands, I am able to appear for service whenever the Sovereign commands, with a good mare, with saber and bow, and in a helm and *kuiak*;[5] and when the Sovereign gives out the arquebuses coming from Moscow I will be diligent

---

[4] Litvak: Lithuanian.
[5] *Kuiak*: a leather jerkin sewn with thin iron strips.

in learning to shoot and will take good care of the Sovereign's arquebus and not waste His powder and shot.

I have already given much service to my Sovereign, from the time of my arrival, in rank with my comrades, not sparing my own head. I helped His Lordship Mikhailo Ivanovich Speshnev search out the Tatar trails and the tracks and places for our patrols and ranger beats. I helped put up palisade and dig wolf traps at Urliapovo Ford, and I and my comrades take shifts guarding that ford and guarding part of the German's great earth wall that was built by the men on loan from Riazhsk, Shatsk, Voronezh, and other of the Sovereign's towns.[6] I helped burn the high grass beyond the wall to deny cover to enemy scouts, and I helped guard the mowing parties sent across the river. I also helped to finish building the town cathedral consecrated to the Protection of the Most Holy Mother of God (Pokrov presviatoi Bogoroditsy). Upon alerts I have ridden with Captains Krasnikov and Bykov to give pursuit to Tatar warbands and to beat them and free captives and take tongues for questioning.[7] And I have many times served as an orderly to His Lordship Mikhailo Ivanovich Speshnev.

And in April of last year I fought when that large raiding party—some five hundred Tatars, they say—came to Kasimov Crossing and tried to pull down the fences there and pass on into Rus. I was with his Honor Ivan Vasilievich Birkin and the Cossacks and *deti boiarskie* when we fought those Tatars. We battled them from noon to early evening, and two of our men were killed and one wounded. But we pushed the enemy back across the river and put them to flight, wounding many of them and killing others, so that by the grace of God and the Sovereign's good fortune those Tatars did not pass on into Rus. And in that battle I took a horse for myself, and helped my neighbor[8] Rodion Afanasiev *syn* Vorypaev capture a Tatar. That Tatar must be a princeling, for he was richly caparisoned, although nearly black of skin; and he was sent on to Moscow, to the Sovereign's Military Chancellery, for questioning.

And in November, when patrol riders brought news of a raiding party sighted on the steppe east of the Pol'noi Voronezh, I was the orderly to Captain Krasnikov and rode with him and two hundred other men in pursuit of the enemy. Those Tatars were returning from a raid on villages outside Riazhsk and were heading back to the Matyra steppe. We followed their tracks to the east and south, and toward midday we found their camp on the Chelnovaia River below Lysye Gory. Only a few Tatars were in camp, but we knew there must have been many off

---

[6] Kozlov's twenty-five-kilometer earthen steppe wall was built according to a plan by Jan Cornelius van Rodenburg, a Dutch engineer who had entered Muscovite service during the Smolensk War.

[7] *Iazyki*: "tongues," prisoners who turned informant.

[8] *Siabr*: "neighbor," household head and fellow member of an *odnodvorets* village commune, holding his *pomest'e* as shares within a communal block allotment.

gathering firewood, for we saw many horses picketed—almost as many as our own. When those Tatars returned and broke camp, we followed them, but at a safe distance and keeping within the wood along the river. But after dusk bad weather set in—cold rain, turning to sleet, and then snow, which covered over the enemy's tracks, and the captain decided not to try to give further pursuit lest some larger raiding party be waiting for us out there in the darkness. He sent me back to Your Lordship to report he would be turning back; and he and his command came back to Kozlov on the following day. Those Tatars did not pass back into Rus but went south, and there were no more sightings of the enemy that month. . . .

At this review Zotov was finally issued his five-ruble settlement subsidy. More important, he finally received his initiation—he was henceforth listed among the Kozlov deti boiarskie *of middling novitiate grade. This was the grade awarded to the majority of Kozlov's first wave of middle service class colonists. It carried an entitlement to the Sovereign's bounty (*zhalovanie*) of four rubles' cash per year and* pomest'e *of 100 quarters per field. These were only entitlements, however: Zotov's actual land grant at Lipovka was just 50 quarters (*chetverti*) per field, as was the case for the majority of Kozlov yeomen, and he often went years without receiving his cash bounty in full.*

Unlike the classic pomest'e *of a* syn boiarskii *in central Muscovy, the* pomest'e *of a southern yeoman like Zotov was not a discrete consolidated holding; rather, it consisted of shares in a communal block allotment—that is, several narrow strips of plowland and haymeadow interspersed with those of Zotov's fellow household heads* (siabry) *in Lipovka village. These strips were assigned by lot and were subject to periodic redistribution. They could not be alienated without the consent of the Lipovka commune.*

Zotov's pomest'e *was surveyed and confirmed for him sometime before 1639. The testimony Zotov gave confirming his acceptance of the surveyor's work shows the size and composition of his holdings were typical for a Kozlov yeoman.*

"At the hamlet of Lipovka, in Oleshenskii bailliage, under Lipovka Hill at Oleshenka Creek, fifteen households. And in these households . . ."

I, Vasilii Grigoriev Zotov, hold a house-lot measuring twenty by seventy *sazheni*,[9] on a grant of twenty-three quarters per field of wild steppeland, in three fields, and another twenty-seven quarters per field of waste outland on Trostenka Creek in Ilovaiskii bailliage. I have 120 ricks of haymeadow between and beyond my fields, and a stand of wood for 100 *sazheni* out from my house-lot. I plow my land and mow my hay at Lipovka across the boundary and rick, with my fellow neighbors (*siabry*) of Lipovka. And I hold various appurtenances in accordance

---

[9] *Sazhen'*: seven feet or 2.133 meters.

with my grant, and for lumber and for fishing, hunting, and beekeeping I go into the great Voronezh and Khobotets forests in common with the men of the town and of the district.

Your Lordship, I and my comrades wish to say again that we hope for the Sovereign's gracious verdict upon our petition to him, which we turned over to you in the assembly house last spring. In the year 7145 Sovereign Tsar and Grand Prince of All Rus Mikhail Fedorovich favored us, his slaves, and ordered us given rights to the forest appurtenances—beehive, tree, and beast's den—in the wood along Oleshenka Creek and the Voronezh River, which appurtenances used to be held by the peasants of Prince Dmitrii Pozharskii's Goretovo *votchina* across the Voronezh River, under lease from the Great Household Office. And as those leases brought no large return to the Sovereign's treasury and were needed by us, thy slaves, for our sustenance, the Sovereign ordered them taken off lease and given over to us. But those Goretovo peasants still hold on lease the fishing rights along the Voronezh, and they refuse us access to water there for our cattle and horses, and refuse us the right to fish there, and they assault us and chase us out. Last year they assaulted our comrade Frol Shavtsov, and beat him and tried to drown him in the Voronezh. Your Honor, please speak for us to Moscow, and we will send in another petition begging our Sovereign's mercy and grace and asking that those fishing leases be ordered taken away.

*The year 1646 saw a general census enumerating urban settlement (*posad*) taxpayers,* pomeshchik's *peasant and cottar tenants (*bobyli*), the peasants on parish church allotments, and the boarders and undeeded dependent laborers residing in* pomeshchik *households. In Kozlov district this census was conducted by* stol'nik *Ilia Danilovich Miloslavskii and the clerk Artemii Afanasiev. When they came to Lipovka they questioned Tomilo Ukolov, who was again serving as Lipovka's elected assessor. Ukolov testified that Lipovka still held fifteen households, none of which had peasant or cottar labor. Vasilii Zotov confirmed this in turn:*

I have no peasants or cottars, not one soul, and never did have. We are all yeomen here at Lipovka, like most men in Kozlov district. If you want to find peasants, go to Staeva Poliana—that's really the only place they are, under the Kartavtsovs and Krasnikovs.

My grant is fifty quarters per field, in three fields, but I work no more than ten quarters in all because that suffices to feed me and because I have but my sons Fedka, nine years of age, and Grisha, seven years, to help me. Some five years ago, I did have a boarder, an itinerant from Elets, but he was next to worthless and stayed but one year and then went south to the Don, probably to try to join the Host. We do not keep many itinerants here in Kozlov district, for they can find households of their own in the Sovereign's service in the other borderland and steppe towns or they can go to the Cossack forts on the lower Don.

In fact, Miloslavskii found only 204 peasants and cottars living on pomeshchik *land in all of Kozlov district.*

Zotov was typical of Kozlov yeomen in cultivating no more than ten quarters on average (five quarters per field, in two fields, with the rest lying fallow). It took some 200 to 382 man-days and horse-days to plow, harrow, and sow a field of fifty quarters, and another 245 man-days to reap it; a yeoman without tenant labor simply could not manage this, especially given his heavy burden of military service. And few Kozlov yeomen (odnodvortsy) *in 1646 had sons old enough to be fit for such labor, for most of the volunteers settling at Kozlov ten years before had been young novitiates just starting families.*

Fortunately, the southern frontier's rich black soil was more fertile than the leached grey podzol of central Muscovy, and Kozlov yeomen were not yet subject to heavy grain taxes; so ten quarters was enough to feed a family, especially when supplemented by gardening, fishing, hunting, and gathering. By Kozlov standards Zotov was a man of middling means. His cabin, barn, sheds, threshing-floor, and tools would fetch some six rubles total at auction; his standing and threshed grain and his livestock—two horses, one cow, two pigs, some chickens—might bring in another fifteen rubles.

Moscow saw no need to long maintain entitlement norms and grant norms at their 1630s levels, given that a grant of fifty quarters per field was more than a yeoman could work and that population growth required that a reserve fund of land be maintained for future pomest'e *grants to the next generations of yeomen. By the 1670s, the typical Kozlov* pomest'e *entitlement was but half of that awarded in 1636, and grant sizes had also halved—most grants were now under twenty-five quarters per field. By itself, this would not have endangered yeoman economy. But starting at mid-century, yeoman households came under increasing pressure from new service obligations. An increasing number of sons were taken off their fathers' plowlands to perform campaign duty* (polkovaia sluzhba) *in the new formation infantry and cavalry regiments operating far off in Ukraine. Many of these recruits were fated never to return to Kozlov. On top of this, new dues increasingly akin to the taxes borne by the unfree men of draft* (tiaglye liudi) *were imposed on Kozlov servicemen, and the weight of these dues grew heavier over the course of the protracted war in Ukraine.*

Zotov had some inkling of the seriousness of this problem as early as 1653, when he had the following conversation with his Lipovka neighbor Ivan Tashlykov. Tashlykov subsequently reported the gist of this conversation to Governor Pushkin.

We'll turn off here to Khomutets—Agafia Parfenovna will put us up for the night; she's a good soul and may even share a drop with us.

I need to talk to you, Ivashka, and I beg you not to pass my words on to anyone else—it could get us both in great trouble.

Our Lipovka chose me as assessor—we old buzzards did, along with the younger lads, all together as one, and I'm proud of that. I'm trying to do my best for us all.

But we're under a great new burden now, and there's nothing I can do to protect us. It's the Sovereign's decree. It's not like the days of that old son of a bitch Roman Fedorovich, who set us to digging away like navvies, carrying earth in our shirts while he stood above barking mother-oaths at us.[10] We were finally able to take care of him, and we got away with it. Even the Military Chancellery recognized he'd gone too far, and he ended up in the Sovereign's disgrace again.

This new campaign duty is different. It goes back on their word that we'd always serve here at home, that we could hold our lands for protecting Kozlov and stopping the Tatars from passing northward into Rus. It's a burden, maybe a killing one, but it's the Sovereign's decree and they're intent on seeing it through. Governor Pushkin has taken my son Fedka into this new German-style infantry regiment. He's taking your son Demka, too. This is very bad. Fedka is my falcon; Domna—the Lord rest her soul—put all her strength into him, and I was counting on him. He may never come back. That leaves me with just Grisha, who's but fourteen and has weak eyes. How we'll manage I don't know.

And who's to say they won't come back sometime for Grisha too? This war is going to be against the Poles (*Liakhi*), and that's bad. It could last a long time and grind up many men. I know the Sovereign sees the chance to take the Cherkassy under his lofty hand, but what's that to us? Who are they? They speak strangely, they dress like Turks; I don't think they can really be of our faith. Fighting for them pits us against the Pole today, and maybe against the Tatars and Turks someday. I fear things won't go well and we'll face ruin.

The new recruits are supposed to assemble next week for the march to Iablonov. This may be the last time we see our sons. Ivashka, I have to tell you, I hear rumors. I hear they may not march; they may refuse. I'm not involved in this, but some of our comrades in the Boborykin matter are. I won't name names—I think you know who that means. This is very bad. I fear the worst. We must be ready for this.

Governor Pushkin managed to suppress mutiny in the regiment with some preemptive arrests. After a month's delay the regiment marched at Iablonov.

Fedor Vasiliev syn Zotov died at the battle of Ozernoe in November 1655. Grigorii Vasiliev Zotov was eventually taken into the infantry as well, but not until the levy of 1662. His father died two years later.

Suggestions for Further Reading

Davies, Brian. *State, Power, and Community in Early Modern Russia*. New York: Palgrave Macmillan, 2004.
———. *Warfare, State, and Society on the Black Sea Steppe, 1500–1700*. London: Routledge, 2007.

---

[10] Zotov refers here to the 1647–48 petitions drive and mutiny, which succeeded in driving Governor Roman Fedorovich Boborykin from Kozlov.

Hellie, Richard. *Enserfment and Military Change in Muscovy*. Chicago: University of Chicago Press, 1971.

Keep, J.L.H. *Soldiers of the Tsar: Army and Society in Russia, 1462–1874*. Oxford: Clarendon Press, 1985.

Stevens, Carol Belkin. *Russia's Wars of Emergence, 1460–1730*. London: Pearson Longman, 2007.

———. *Soldiers on the Steppe: Army Reform and Social Change in Early Modern Russia*. DeKalb: Northern Illinois University Press, 1995.

IV
Church Prelates

10

A Seventeenth-Century Prelate
Metropolitan Pavel of Sarai and the Don

Cathy J. Potter

In the nineteenth century, Pavel M. Stroev combed the archives of the Russian empire to compile a list of all the prelates and heads of monasteries of the Russian Orthodox Church from its origins in Rus through the eighteenth century. The task took almost forty years, and Stroev did not live to see the resulting publication, an important reference work that continues to be used and amended by scholars today. For most of these individuals we know little more than the dates, often uncertain, of their elevation and transfer. Some prelates do emerge out of the shadows in a clearer outline. The more active, powerful, and influential are drawn more vividly in the chronicles and their accomplishments can be traced in official records, documents, and decrees. The notorious continue to live in reports of investigations and court cases. The particularly holy and charismatic were honored with Lives (vitae) and often records of the miracles attributed to them in life and posthumously. Early Lives were highly stylized, intended to portray a saint rather than a unique individual.

By the seventeenth century, the line between hagiography and biography began to blur. The "emergence of the individual" that scholars have detected in this period revealed itself not only in the well-known "autobiography" of Archpriest Avvakum but also in the more personal information included in the Lives *of saintly men and women, wills and testaments, graveside speeches and panegyrics. The abundant polemical works of the time were also more personal, although not necessarily more accurate or objective. As a result of these changes, we have more biographical information about more prelates in the seventeenth century than previously. Nonetheless, in no case do we have information for any one prelate sufficient for a complete biography.*

The portraits of the prelates that appear below are based on real individuals, active in the second half of the seventeenth century in a process of church reform initiated during the tenure of Patriarch Nikon (1652–58/1667). Nikon's approach to church reform stimulated violent opposition within the clergy itself, an opposition culminating in a schism that spread to the laity. In 1658, Nikon abandoned

This seventeenth-century Kolomenskii sakkos ("sackcloth") of Patriarch Nikon, with gilded satin, taffeta, velvet weaving, and embroidery, is in the Moscow Kremlin Museum; it likely came from the Ottoman empire. Sakkoses were worn by prelates to represent the "tunic of disgrace" that Christ wore during his trial; this sakkos is quite elaborate. Patriarch Nikon is associated with the Church reforms of the mid-seventeenth century, but his high-handedness and lavish ways offended many both within and outside the church. The subject of this chapter, Metropolitan Pavel of Sarai and the Don, along with his able assistant Epifanii Slavinetskii, were among those tasked with continuing the reforms after Nikon walked away from his patriarchal position in 1658.

the patriarchal throne, but it was only in 1666/67 that a church council formally removed him as patriarch. The central figure, Metropolitan Pavel of Sarai and the Don, was a historical figure and did serve in that post from 22 August 1664 until his death on 9 September 1675. The other prelates and clerics who appear in the narrative were also real individuals and the situations described are based on real historical events reported in the sources. Where needed, plausible invention has fleshed out the story and provided details that are missing. The scene itself is imagined. The result is a fictionalized historical reality that I hope is true to the spirit if not precisely to the letter of the sources.

The old man leaned over the table to look more closely at the translation a young monk was preparing. "Well, Epifanii," he said, straightening and turning to an elderly monk standing amid stacks of books and manuscripts at the front of the room, "the New Testament is complete and ready for the Printing Office. Will we live to see a solid translation of the Old?" "God willing, your Grace," Epifanii replied, looking up from his work to smile at his old friend and colleague, Metropolitan Pavel of Sarai and the Don, now more commonly known as the Krutitskii metropolitan.[1] "Yes, God willing," the metropolitan repeated softly.

It was late August in Moscow in the year 1675. The late afternoon sun lingered, gathering in pools on tables and gilding the dusty manuscripts and the men poring over them, but the light would soon be gone and the scholar-monks began to stretch and straighten their work areas. A murmur of voices rose and fell as men clustered in small groups discussing problems encountered with the work of translation as they prepared to depart. Metropolitan Pavel moved from group to group, now and then contributing to a discussion, occasionally bending over with a dry cough, as he waited for Epifanii to finish. Together the two men walked out into the courtyard of the metropolitan's complex, located on a steep embankment overlooking the Moscow River. To the northwest the Moscow kremlin nestled along a bend in the river. Nearby the bell tower and the golden cupolas of the Church of the Transfiguration hovered over the walls of the New Monastery of the Savior where Pavel had taken his monastic vows more than two decades earlier.

Pausing, Pavel turned to survey the grounds and the building he had just left. Pavel had restored the Krutitskii metropolitan's complex and bought a plot of adjacent land. When he made the purchase, the site was a garden laid out in the Dutch fashion, replete with fountains. He supervised the removal of the gardens and the construction of a building. Pride was a sin, Pavel thought, but he could not repress the feelings of delight and satisfaction that the sight of the building evoked. It was designed as a cultural center, a meeting place with rooms for learned discussion and debate. Now it housed the men working on a new scholarly translation of the

---

[1] *Krutoi* in Russian means steep or sharp. The name Krutitskii metropolitan was taken from the location of the metropolitan's palace, located on a steep bank overlooking the Moscow River.

Bible from the Greek language into the Slavonic language, a task that the church council had entrusted to him and his friend, the highly respected and erudite monk at his side, Epifanii Slavinetskii.

The two men strolled along a path in companionable silence. The setting sun was still warm, but a sharp breeze warned of the winter to come. Feeling weary, Metropolitan Pavel sat down on a nearby wooden bench. Epifanii remained standing a few steps away, deep in thought, his hands clasped behind his back. Seated, Pavel allowed himself to lean against the back of the bench. Eyes closed, his mind wandered over the years past and he marveled at the workings of Providence.

Pavel had been born in the early decades of the seventeenth century to humble but hardworking and pious parents. Materially, these had been difficult years as Russia struggled to recover from the devastations of the Time of Troubles. Pavel's mother had died giving birth to a sister, when Pavel was still a small child, barely able to walk. He had been raised in the home of relatives. When he was old enough to begin learning his letters, his father placed him in the charge of an elderly and learned local priest. Pavel's father could neither read nor write, but he was determined that his son would learn. How surprised and pleased he would be, Pavel thought, to know how greatly his respect for learning had shaped his son's life. Certainly when he had sent Pavel to the local priest to learn his letters, he could not have imagined that someday his son would master the Greek and Latin languages as well as Polish and be respected as a scholar, having risen to the very top of the Muscovite clerical hierarchy. Thinking of the past, Pavel was touched by a sadness, tempered by time. His father had been killed by a band of marauders shortly after Pavel's marriage and his installation as a deacon in a nearby local church.

Pavel's early years had been materially difficult, but spiritually these were times of great ferment. Russians at all levels of society understood the Time of Troubles as God's righteous punishment for their sins. In these desolate years, the chronicles said, God had turned his face away from Russia, appalled by the godlessness, the immorality, of his people. At last, God relented. A new tsar was elected and Russians of all ranks united to drive the invading enemies from the Russian land. This was only the beginning. To keep the Russian land safe forever, Russians must truly repent, abandon their sinful ways, and embrace a true Christian life.

Truly this was a cause to inspire the young and energetic. The people must be taught the error of their ways, enlightened as to the true path. What better way to do this than by preaching and teaching the faith? What more worthy career than the priesthood? Many of Pavel's colleagues and contemporaries had followed a similar path: from humble origins they entered the ranks of the parish clergy. Some went on to monastic careers and later achieved positions within the church hierarchy.

The most famous of these was the deposed patriarch, Nikon. Shusherin, the author of Nikon's *Life,* described his parents as "simple people." Nikon had begun his career as a member of the parish clergy. Later, persuading his wife to enter a convent, he embarked on a monastic career. He rose to the important post of metropolitan of Novgorod and ultimately was consecrated patriarch of Moscow.

Pavel's colleagues, Metropolitan Ilarion of Riazan, Metropolitan Ilarion of Suzdal, Metropolitan Iona Sisoevich of Rostov, and Bishop Aleksandr of Viatka, followed similar career paths. Pavel, sighing, thought too of former associates and friends, Avvakum and Ivan Neronov, activist members of the secular clergy, who in their zeal had split the Church.

A slight smile brightened Pavel's face as he remembered the ardor and ideals of his youth, remembered the shining eyes of the young woman who eagerly and sympathetically listened to his plans and dreams. He had married that young woman shortly before being appointed deacon at a local church. The secular clergy in Russia were required to be married, but Pavel did not recall even thinking of this requirement. In Evdokia he had found a partner, modest and chaste, to assist him and support him in his chosen career. Young, talented, and energetic, Pavel quickly moved up the ranks from deacon to priest. In 1651, he was appointed archpriest at the Church of the Reception of the Blessed Virgin's Icon from Vladimir in Moscow. According to one legend this church had been built on the spot where the grand prince and the people of Moscow met and received the icon of the Mother of God. This miracle-working icon was brought from Vladimir in 1397 to ward off a threatened attack by Tamerlane, the fearsome and feared Mongol leader. Pavel remembered Evdokia's joy and excitement when he had told her the news of his appointment. Moscow! The center of Russia! A place of limitless possibilities, where great changes were afoot and plans were being formed at the very highest levels to reform the Church and spread learning and enlightenment in the service of the faith.

In 1654, tragedy struck. An epidemic swept Moscow; Evdokia and Pavel's two sons died. How different his life might have been, Pavel thought, had Evdokia lived. In Russia at that time, only married men could serve in the secular clergy. The prelates, however, were chosen from the black or monastic clergy, a vocation requiring celibacy. With one hand, God had taken away; with the other He revealed new spheres of action to Pavel. Grieving over his loss, Pavel entered the New Monastery of the Savior (Novospasskii) as a monk. In 1659, he was named archimandrite of the important Miracle (Chudov) Monastery in Moscow, the center of the patriarchal administration. Pavel rose rapidly, from monk to archimandrite of an important monastery and then to Metropolitan of Sarai and the Don in 1664.

This was an important position. The Krutitskii metropolitan lived on the doorstep of the patriarch and assisted him. In 1664, with the Nikon affair still unresolved and the patriarchal throne essentially empty, this metropolitanate was particularly important. Even before his elevation to metropolitan, Pavel served as *locum tenens* of the patriarchal throne, and he would be called to fill the role again before a new patriarch was selected following the deposition of Patriarch Nikon in 1666.

Reflecting on the past, on personal loss as well as professional fulfillment, Pavel's thoughts turned once again to his father, and he silently thanked him for the love of learning he had instilled in his son. It was study and the diligent effort required to learn both Greek and Latin that had filled his early days in the monastery and, along with prayer, preserved him from indulging in unmeasured sorrow. It was Pavel's passionate pursuit of knowledge and his developing erudition that contributed to his rapid promotion in the Church and that gained him the respect and esteem of other likeminded clerics.

Pavel raised his eyes to look at his friend and colleague. Epifanii Slavinetskii had come to Moscow in the middle of the seventeenth century from Ukraine in response to Tsar Aleksei Mikhailovich's search for scholars knowledgeable in both the Greek and Latin languages. The tsar was seeking educated men, able to assist in the translation of the Bible from Greek into Slavonic. Until the closure of the Nikon affair, Epifanii's time was absorbed with the issue of church reform. Now, Pavel thought with satisfaction, he could concentrate on the important translation work.

Pavel thought with affection of the lively and talented Simeon Polotskii (from Polotsk). Simeon was another learned monk who had fled to Moscow from the turmoil of military campaigns in the contested territory of White Russia. He was a gifted author of verse and plays but also of powerful and effective sermons. Simeon's facility with words was greatly appreciated, and he enjoyed considerable influence at the tsar's court. Pavel felt humble as he thought of how much he had learned from these two men. How fortunate he had been in his friendships.

"So Archbishop Iosif will be removed from the see of Kolomna?" Epifanii asked, as he seated himself on the bench beside the metropolitan.

"Yes," the metropolitan replied, recalled from his musings. "Iosif must go." Metropolitan Pavel frowned, recalling the unpleasant scenes at court and around Moscow. Iosif had participated in church councils held in 1674 and early 1675. The new patriarch, Ioakim, had led debates aimed at clarifying jurisdictions within the episcopal sees and the patriarchal domains. The council also discussed future plans to increase the number of sees and reduce the size of the existing ones to improve pastoral care and supervision. Only in this way could opposition to the Church be pacified and the schism mended. Archbishop Iosif signed the acts of the councils, indicating his agreement with the decisions taken. Immediately thereafter the Kolomna prelate could be heard around Moscow, loudly criticizing these very decisions and maligning Patriarch Ioakim. "The new patriarch is rude and ignorant," the archbishop shouted scornfully at one evening gathering. "At the church council he just sat there, stroking his beard, with nothing to say . . . all he can do is read sermons . . . and no one listens."

At the very least, such indiscretions would have merited a stern reprimand, but they occurred against the background of numerous complaints about Iosif's harshness to the clergy in his see. Those guilty of minor infringements were beaten unmercifully with whips, imprisoned in chains for days, and tortured with freezing water. In the cathedral church itself during the liturgy, Archbishop Iosif had beaten an archpriest until the blood flowed, simply because he had omitted a word from a prayer. Called to account before a church council and confronted with his victims, Iosif blustered arrogantly about his Episcopal rights but could offer no defense.

As Pavel recalled the shameful scene, words recently spoken in the course of a service installing a new prelate flickered across his mind: "Teach your spiritual children and correct them according to the rules of the holy fathers and according to the measure of their sins. Persuade them with discussion and do not give penance beyond their strength." The metropolitan sighed. How could bishops so brutal, so remote from the example of Christ, expect to enlighten the clergy under them, much less simple Christians?

"Iosif will be reassigned to the Cathedral of the Archangel in the Kremlin," Metropolitan Pavel continued. "No one will be subordinate to him, and he will be supervised."

"Mild," Epifanii commented, "and probably prudent."

"Yes, but it doesn't solve the problem of the see of Kolomna," said Pavel. "Religious dissidence is spreading in the area. People are sneaking into the forests to build their own chapels and worship with the old printed liturgical books. Some of the parish clergy are abetting them. The former Patriarch Nikon made a martyr of Bishop Pavel of Kolomna when Pavel questioned the liturgical reforms. Then he appointed Aleksandr in Pavel's place, only to have him oppose the newly printed liturgical books as well. Temporarily abolishing the see of Kolomna and sending Aleksandr to Viatka, a primitive backwater by anyone's standards, nourished his resentment and did nothing to persuade him of his error. It probably didn't contribute to the spiritual well-being of Christians in Viatka either. Bishop Aleksandr only recanted his support for the old texts under severe pressure once Patriarch Nikon was deposed. God forgive me, but one can't help but wonder about the sincerity of his repentance. I think it no accident that he left Viatka and retired to a monastery as soon as Patriarch Ioakim was elected."

"No," Epifanii agreed, "Aleksandr knew that Ioakim was committed to further reform, that he shared our vision. Ioakim was discreet, but everyone knows he supports the liturgical reforms. More important, he advocates a strong church, united behind the patriarch and capable of acting in genuine symphony with the government—the question is, can he achieve it? Archbishop Iosif's outburst doesn't bode well for the future. Iosif underestimates the patriarch. He sneers at the sermons, but no one who has heard Ioakim preach could doubt his sincere commitment to the teaching role of the episcopacy. And how else is it possible to teach the faith?"

"Brother Simeon from Polotsk, the tutor to the tsar's children, has written several sermons for me and for Ioakim," Metropolitan Pavel said. "They explain to people how to be good Christians, with vivid examples from their own lives. They're good and effective; the patriarch intends to have them printed and distributed to the clergy."

"Simeon is intelligent and talented," Epifanii acknowledged. "But Aleksandr can't recognize it. In his view—and he is not alone—Simeon is from the West and contaminated by the teachings of the Jesuits, although he doesn't think much of the Greeks in Moscow either. He is convinced that only in Russia has the faith remained pure. He's of the old school; literate, perhaps, but not educated. He wants to be lord in his domain, answerable only to God and the tsar, and he's inclined to think that Christianity can be inculcated by the knout. Moreover, he's not the first man, nor will he be the last, to confuse his own convictions with God's will."

"True!" The metropolitan laughed. "Members of the Russian clergy do not lack conviction! If only we could direct those convictions along more beneficial paths." Pavel thought of his own efforts, more than a decade ago now, to persuade Archpriest Avvakum and some of his followers to submit to, and to recognize and accept the authority of, the patriarch and the church council. Avvakum and Ivan Neronov had led the opposition to the church reforms implemented by Patriarch Nikon and attracted many of the clergy to their side. Metropolitan Pavel winced as he recalled his failure. Worse, he thought to himself—faced with the audacity and intransigence of the zealots he had lost his temper. He lowered his head in shame at the memory. Would patience and teaching have prevailed? Could the schism have been avoided? No, Avvakum closed his ears to reason and would never have admitted error. Nonetheless, the memory of his own unseemly lapse saddened him.

Pavel's mind wandered further, to an instance of his own intransigence, his own disobedience. It was not only the schismatics who held fast to their convictions and beliefs, convinced of their righteousness. At the conclusion of the important church councils of 1666 and 1667, confronted with a version of the council decisions asserting that the tsar was above the patriarch, he and Metropolitan Ilarion of Riazan had resisted, demanding this phrase be removed. It undermined the pivotal notion of a symphony, a balance between church and state. It was the cornerstone of the church reforms.

When their demands were ignored, they signed the acts of the council, noting beside their signatures that they approved *only* the deposition of Patriarch Nikon. Both had been removed from their posts for that action and excommunicated, forbidden to participate in the liturgy. They repented and were restored to their posts but, Pavel interrogated his conscience, had his repentance been sincere?

Unable to resolve the question satisfactorily, he thought of Ilarion, who had died a little more than a year ago. He grieved for him as a friend and missed him as a colleague in the struggle to reform the Church and spread enlightenment (*prosveshchenie*). Ilarion had come from the same region and the same background as Patriarch Nikon and his staunchest opponents, Avvakum and Ivan Neronov. Like Nikon he had taken monastic vows in the Monastery of St. Makarii of the Yellow Waters, later becoming archimandrite of that same monastery. Ilarion had understood Avvakum and Ivan Neronov, had even felt an abiding affection for them, although he rejected the path they had taken. Metropolitan Ilarion had opened his mind to enlightenment. Although in his forties, he embarked on a study of the Greek language, determined to master it and gain access to the Holy Writings in the original.

Turning back to Epifanii, Pavel picked up the threads of the conversation, shading it with his own unspoken thoughts. "Perhaps what we need is more humility," he said, then continued pensively, "Aleksandr was wise to retire from the see of Viatka.

From the patriarch's standpoint it means one less obstacle to a united Church. Iona, his replacement, shows great promise. He is a good and pious man, sufficiently educated and energetic as well. Would that we had ten more like him. I don't know who will be sent to Kolomna."

"The decision should be made quickly," Epifanii observed, "or someone will be running to the tsar seeking the post and creating more problems for the future. In theory our tsar wants a strong and glorious Church as a fitting partner for a strong and glorious kingdom; in practice he tends to act as head of both. Two years ago Archbishop Stefan of Suzdal asked for the privilege of wearing a *sakkos*[2] while serving the liturgy. The tsar granted his request without even consulting Patriarch Pitirim. It caused much grumbling among some of the other bishops who were not so privileged."

"Yes." Pavel sighed. "Too many years without a patriarch, or without a patriarch the tsar respected. Patriarch Nikon had so much promise—and charisma. The tsar truly loved him. But what great damage he caused. When Patriarch Pitirim died, the tsar refused even to attend his funeral. Pitirim too blatantly displayed his desire to be patriarch in those difficult years after Nikon abandoned his post. He compromised himself and even he recognized it, repenting most sorrowfully at the end. God no doubt will forgive him, but I am afraid the tsar and many others found forgiveness difficult." The two men fell silent, lost in their own thoughts. Then they rose, exchanged a few affectionate words and parted.

Metropolitan Pavel went directly to his private apartment to pray in accordance with the rule he had adopted over twenty years ago when he took monastic vows. Following prayers, he dined alone this evening as he had much work to do. He limited his meal to bread, fruit, and a small portion of vegetables. Then he removed to his library and sat for a moment, looking out the window.

Tomorrow he would go to the Kremlin. He would stay at the Monastery of the Miracles for several days. He remembered his tenure as archimandrite there. He looked forward to seeing old friends, to sharing the latest ecclesiastical gossip and participating in scholarly debates. He had important business at the Printing Office and would consult with the patriarch. There was much to discuss. Moreover, the feast honoring the holy Archangel Michael was approaching. It would be appropriately and ceremoniously marked with a full service in the Cathedral of Michael the Archangel in the Kremlin. The tsar was expected to attend with other members of the royal family and leading boyars. Metropolitan Pavel along with several other prelates and a full complement of lower clergy would assist the patriarch at the service. Simeon Polotskii was composing a sermon for the occasion. Shaking his

---

[2] The *sakkos* is a liturgical vestment, the bishop's chasuble, resembling the Western Church's dalmatic. It was worn by Eastern Orthodox prelates during the service and adopted by Patriarch Nikon. Initially in Russia, the privilege of wearing it was reserved to the patriarch.

head, he turned to the book on the table before him. Soon he was absorbed in a tract by St. John of Damascus.

Metropolitan Pavel did not travel to the Kremlin the next day, nor did he assist in celebrating the mass for Michael the Archangel. That night he fell ill and was unable to rise from his bed in the morning. His condition deteriorated over the next few days and his friends and colleagues attended at his bedside. Earlier Simeon Polotskii had assisted him in recording his spiritual testament. As he lay dying, Metropolitan Pavel himself wrote the directions for the disposition of his property and signed it in front of witnesses. Pavel's property was modest, with the exception of a rich library containing books and manuscripts written in Greek, Latin, and Polish. He had little property to dispose of, but he could bestow blessings on those, both lay and clergy, who had served God and the Church well; this he did generously. Blessings he had in abundance and he distributed these generously. On Sunday, following the liturgy, Patriarch Ioakim hurried to Pavel's bedside to grieve for his dying friend and mentor. He wept at the bedside. On September 9, 1675, Pavel repented of his sins, confessed and took the Eucharist. He then was anointed and according to reports died "lifting up his heart and saying, into your hands, Lord, I commend my spirit."

Epifanii Slavinetskii died two months after his friend Metropolitan Pavel. With him died the last of the generation of churchmen most intimately involved in shaping and promoting the so-called Nikonian reforms in the face of strenuous opposition. Ironically, the former patriarch Nikon, as well as leading members of the opposition that Nikon's methods of reform evoked, still lived albeit in exile and deprivation. The strong autonomous Church that the reformers had envisioned proved illusory. By the eighteenth century, the patriarchate was abolished, the church administration incorporated into the state. The image of the prelate as an imitator of Christ, teaching the faith and enlightening all Christians, proved stronger as an ideal, even if the reality proved difficult to achieve.

Suggestions for Further Reading

There is little available in English on the prelates of the early Russian Church. Most historians exploring the seventeenth century have been attracted to the opponents of the Nikonian reforms, the so-called Old Believers, looking askance at the bishops who are perceived through the writings of the schismatics. The books listed below offer various viewpoints on the schism and its spiritual context. The few translations of sources available do not truly depict the situation in the seventeenth century.

Bushkovitch, Paul. *Religion and Society in Russia: The Sixteenth and Seventeenth Centuries.* Oxford: Oxford University Press, 1992. Analyzes the changes unfolding in Russian spirituality in the defined period. Many of the prelates and clerics who appear in the present narrative played an important role in these changes and much useful information can be found here on their lives and activities.

Lupinin, Nickolas. *Religious Revolt in the XVIIth Century: The Schism of the Russian Church.* Princeton, NJ: Kingston Press, 1984. Offers useful information about the context of the schism. Sympathetic to the dissidents.

Michels, Georg B. *At War with the Church: Religious Dissent in Seventeenth-Century Russia.* Stanford, CA: Stanford University Press, 1999. Offers useful information about the context of the schism. Sympathetic to the dissidents.

Shusherin, Ivan Kornilevich, *From Peasant to Patriarch: Account of the Birth, Uprising, and Life of His Holiness Nikon, Patriarch of Moscow and All Russia.* Trans. and annotated by Kevin Kain and Katia Levintova. Lanham, MD: Lexington Books, 2007. Annotated translation of the Life of Patriarch Nikon.

Solov'ev, Sergei M. *Istoriia Rossii s drevneishikh vremen* [History of Russia from the earliest times], 15 vols. Moscow: Izdatel'stvo sotsial'noiekonomicheskoi literatury, 1959–66. Incorporates massive amounts of archival material and weaves the lives and activities of Russian bishops into his larger narrative. The majority of Solov'ev's work is now available in English translation published by Academic International Press, with the remaining volumes scheduled to appear soon. [Sergei M. Soloviev, *History of Russia,* in fifty volumes. G. Edward Orchard, general editor. Gulf Breeze, FL: Academic International Press, 1976–).]

Vernadsky, George. ed. *A Source Book for Russian History.* New Haven: Yale University Press, 1972, 361–63. Includes an extract from the spiritual testament of Patriarch Ioakim.

Zenkovsky, Serge A. ed. *Medieval Russia's Epics, Chronicles, and Tales.* 2d ed. New York: E.P. Dutton, 1974, 399–448, 517–19. Includes translations of the "autobiography" of Avvakum and several samples of the work of Simeon Polotskii.

∞ 11 ∞

Vasilii Kalika, Archbishop of Novgorod
(r. 1330–52)

Michael C. Paul

This sketch is taken from primary sources, particularly the Novgorodian First Chronicle, a portion of which was composed under Vasilii Kalika's auspices. While we know from that chronicle that Vasilii Kalika did have a nephew named Matvei (he is specifically said to be the son of Vasilii's sister) and that he was among the Novgorodian emissaries to the 1339 treaty with King Magnus Erickson of Sweden, nothing else is known of him. I have taken the liberty of making him a member of his uncle's entourage throughout Vasilii's archiepiscopate (certainly a credible situation in the medieval Church) and have made up his patronymic, which is also unknown. There was also a Greek iconographer named Isaia, who painted the frescoes of the Church of the Entrance into Jerusalem under Vasilii's patronage in 1338. Whether he had any ties to the Hilandar Monastery is not known, so the correspondence between the fictional Serbian monk Georgi of that monastery and Matvei is imagined, though certainly not implausible given the South Slavic Influence and the importance of Mount Athos in medieval Orthodox culture. The other people, places, and events in this sketch can be found in the various Novgorodian chronicles, as well as in a few other sources. For example, the letter of Vasilii Kalika to the Bishop of Tver has been inserted into the Sofia First Chronicle and was reprinted in the first volume of Pamiatniki literatury drevnei Rusi. *Some of the artwork mentioned is still extant, such as the Vasilii Gates, which Ivan the Terrible removed from Novgorod and had hung at Aleksandrovskaia Sloboda. We know Vasilii died at the Monastery of St. Michael the Archangel at the confluence of the Uza and Shelon Rivers while returning from Pskov. Given the circumstances, it is likely he died of plague, but the exact events that transpired at the monastery on the day of his death are not recorded, and I have taken some license in describing these events.*

Archbishop of Novgorod Vasilii Kalika wearing a white cowl. Detail of a fresco dating to the fourteenth century from the Uspenie (Resurrection) Church on Volotovo Field near Novgorod. Archbishop Vasilii is donating a church, which he is symbolically holding in his hands, to the town of Novgorod. The church was destroyed in World War II but now is being restored. One explanation for Vasilii's wearing a white cowl as opposed to the black cowl that other bishops and archbishops wore is that he was a parish priest (white clergy) rather than a monk (black clergy) as most other prelates of the time were.

The Vladyka[1] had come a long way from Novgorod the Great to end up here, at this the little Monastery of St. Michael the Archangel, where the Uza flows into the Shelon southwest of Novgorod the Great on the road east from Pskov. From his position as a simple priest of the Sts. Cosmas and Damian Church, he had for twenty-two years helped lead one of the greatest Russian cities and had overseen one of the wealthiest eparchies in Eastern Christendom; he had supported great building projects and sponsored great works of art; he had negotiated peace with princes and kings; and he had worked with great prelates to protect the Orthodox faith. In the process he had attained honor for himself and his city. Physically the distance from St. Michael's to Novgorod was not very far, maybe sixty versts as the crow flies—two days journey down the Shelon River and along the western shore of Lake Ilmen to Novgorod—but the Vladyka's heart and mind had traveled far afield since he had been chosen archbishop, and so it seemed as if it had been an age—as though the priest of Sts. Cosmas and Damian had been an entirely different man from what Vasilii Kalika had become.

All had seemed well when they left Pskov that Sunday morning. In fact, the Vladyka's relationship with the city had never seemed better. After initially being rejected by that city at the time of his consecration, he had traveled there in the third year of his archiepiscopate and baptized Prince Aleksandr's son, Mikhail. A few years later, however, the city would not receive him or allow him to sit in judgment over cases in the church courts in Pskov, and he returned home cursing the entire city. But while the city broke political ties with Novgorod the following year, he remained their bishop—the archbishop of Novgorod the Great and Pskov. Later, after Aleksandr's execution at the Horde, he brought Prince Mikhail to Novgorod and taught him to read and write, so his relations with the Tver princes and with Pskov had improved so much that he left Pskov with a sense of triumph. But after he and his entourage had traveled the thirty versts to Proshchenik, he took ill; they pushed on a little further and stayed the night just east of Proshchenik, but in the morning he was worse, and Monday was a hard journey that brought them to this place.

Now the courtyard of the monastery was full of men who seemed ill at ease and out of place—the *Sofiane*—the "men of Holy Wisdom": priests, deacons and monks, copyists, clerks, stewards, and others, some of them chroniclers and iconographers, who made up the archiepiscopal administration in Novgorod the Great and accompanied the archbishop on his journeys—journeys that had taken him from his election by the *veche,* the boisterous and sometimes violent city assembly in Novgorod,[2] to his consecration in Volynia, and from there to

---
[1] *Vladyka* (lit. "master") is a term of respect for a Russian bishop; it is equivalent to the Greek *despotes,* used for Greek prelates, and does not denote any political power.

[2] The *veche* or city assembly in Novgorod, Pskov, and a few other cities has a rather confused and controversial composition and history. Some imperial Russian scholars saw it as a democratic institution, whereas Soviet-era scholars such as Valentin Ianin regarded it as controlled by the boyars, at least by the fourteenth century. More recently, Jonas Granberg has argued that it was not as institutionalized as most modern historians have believed.

Moscow, whence they brought the grand prince to be enthroned as prince of Novgorod. They had been with him to Pskov before, and most recently they had traveled with him up north to the frontier with Swedish-Finland, to the island of Orekhov, where Lake Ladoga empties into the Neva. There he had built a great stone fortress on the site of a wooden one that Grand Prince Iurii had established a generation before to guard against the Catholic Swedes, who had just recently burned the first one.

Counted among the *Sofiane* was Matvei, Vasilii's sister's son, who had accompanied the Vladyka on many of his journeys and had been changed by them just as his uncle had. He had first traveled with him down to Vladimir-in-Volynia for his archiepiscopal consecration and had witnessed much of what the great man had been through; much had been exciting and he was proud to be part of it, but there was also much sadness. Orthodoxy was seemingly beset from every side during Vasilii's archiepiscopate, and Vasilii suffered much. Matvei had, of course, experienced much of this and reflected on it, so that when he received a letter a few months back from a Serbian monk at the Hilandar Monastery on Mount Athos near Thessalonika, he had a ready reply. The monks there had heard of Vasilii from Isaia the Greek, a monk and iconographer whom Vasilii had commissioned to paint frescos for the Church of the Entrance into Jerusalem in the archiepiscopal compound twelve years earlier. Isaia had told them of Vasilii, of Novgorod, of the Russian far North. Isaia's experience had so amazed him that he spoke of it to the other monks, but they did not believe him and had been admonished by the hegumen for gossiping. Then one monk, Georgi, had written to ask Matvei, who he had heard was a close aide of the archbishop, to see if it was all true—if Vasilii was so learned and holy, if Novgorod's storied wealth was real, if fur-bearing animals indeed rained from the sky as Arab writers had said, and if Orthodoxy was under siege in the northern land just as it was under attack from the Ottomans. Matvei had begun to gradually write down a reply over the past few weeks and hoped to have a scribe write out a fine copy of it on parchment to send to Mount Athos:

> Greetings from Matvei Vladimirovich to the monk Georgi of the Holy Monastery of Hilandar on the Holy Mountain:
>
> I marvel that word of my uncle and spiritual father has traveled so far from Novgorod the Great to you and your brethren in Greece, and I will tell you as best I am able of the Vladyka. Here they call him Vasilii Kalika—Vasilii the Pilgrim—and have done so ever since he made a pilgrimage to Jerusalem, saw the tomb of Christ, the bones of Adam, and the place where Jesus fasted in the desert near the Jordan and planted a hundred fig trees that still grow there to this day. The Vladyka told of this to Bishop Feodor of Tver when he tried to convince him that paradise was very real—a physical place that God had set in the East, as it says in Genesis, and which Chrysostom spoke of in his homilies—and that it still exists since nothing God has made ever really perishes. He also wrote to Vladyka Feodor that other Novgorodians have seen paradise too—Moislav the Novgorodian and his son Iakov saw it during one of their trading journeys and returned to tell us that they had seen the luminosity and heard the joyful singing of paradise after having been blown off course in the Northern Sea. My uncle has studied the lives of the saints, and wrote that several great

saints had seen paradise too: Macarius the Great lived twenty *poprishches*³ from it, and St. Ephrosinius had received three apples from paradise.

My uncle was baptized with the name Grigorii and was married and ordained a priest as a young man; he served at the Church of St. Cosmas and Damian on Slave Street north of the Detinets, as we call the great fortress in the middle of Novgorod the Great where the Cathedral of Holy Wisdom and the archiepiscopal palace stand.

Matvei paused to think—they called his uncle "the Pilgrim." Now his earthly pilgrimage was coming to an end in a cell in the small monastery a third of the way home, where he had been brought stricken with the great plague that had engulfed Pskov, the second city in his eparchy, to which he had traveled in hopes of saving it. Vasilii had set out without hesitation after the Pskovians had sent emissaries to him begging him to come, and upon arriving there he had blessed the Pskovians—his children; he had led them in procession with crosses and icons around the city, accompanied by Archimandrite Mikifor and all the hegumens of the monasteries and the priests of the city; he had celebrated the Divine Liturgy and led them in many prayer services in the Trinity Cathedral in the Krom or fortress in Pskov. He had also prayed at St. Michael's, at the church of the Mother of God at the Snetogorsk Monastery north of the city, at the Church of St. John the Evangelist, and again at the Trinity Cathedral, but it had done no good at all it seemed.

> I did not know my uncle well at that time. His wife had recently died, and he had entered the Monastery of the Holy Angels outside Novgorod. He was elected archbishop of Novgorod by the veche eight months after his immediate predecessor, Archbishop Moisei, who still lives, took the *schema*⁴ in the Kholmov Monastery in the environs of Novgorod. My uncle was tonsured a monk in January, taking the name Vasilii, and while he waited for emissaries from the metropolitan to arrive, he sent word to me, asking that I join him to aid him during his archiepiscopate.
>
> The metropolitan's emissaries arrived in Novgorod during Holy Week to call my uncle to Vladimir-in-Volynia in the southwest of Rus, where the metropolitan then resided. But we set out with several of the city's boyars only toward the end of June and arrived in Vladimir on the Day of the Assumption of the Mother of God (August 15). Vasilii was consecrated archbishop of Novgorod on August 25 by Feognost, a Greek appointed by the patriarch, in the company of other bishops.
>
> You have asked if Orthodoxy is under threat here, and in answer I would point to the difficulties the Vladyka faced even before his consecration; the godless Lithuanian Grand Prince Gedeminas along with Prince Aleksandr Mikhailovich of Pskov had sent their own candidate, who arrived in Vladimir just as we entered the city. This

---

³ A *poprishche* (also *pop"rishche*) is a unit of distance calculated by the church for the purposes of travel per diem. It is equivalent to twenty *versty* or thirteen miles.

⁴ Russian: *skhima*. A degree of monkhood. After tonsuring, if the hegumen feels a monk has reached a certain degree of spirituality, then that monk may be allowed to take the Little *Schema*. After further spiritual development and again with the approval of the hegumen, a monk may take the Great *Schema*. Corresponding garb accompanies each degree of monkhood.

candidate, the hieromonk Arsenii, bore all their hopes that the metropolitan would name him bishop of Pskov and separate that city from the Novgorodian eparchy of which it was and remains a part. But Feognost, shrewd as a serpent, took Archimandrite Lavrenii and, of these three candidates—my uncle, Arsenii, and Lavrentii—the council chose Vasilii to be archbishop of Novgorod the Great and Pskov.

Matvei paused again as his quill was dull. He took a penknife to cut a clean point. He went on to write that it could be said, then, that Vasilii's election was a canonical one, even if the role of the veche in his election in Novgorod called that into question. Even his uncle had admitted that the civil authorities should have no say in episcopal elections, but that hardly mattered now, and it was not as if other cities and princes did not have a hand in episcopal elections across Christendom. He picked up the pen again and continued, proudly telling the monks on Mount Athos:

> A bright star appeared over the church where Vasilii's consecration took place, a great sign of divine blessing, it was said, even though it did not end the dispute with Pskov and Lithuania. Arsenii and the Pskovians, angered at being rebuffed by the metropolitan, went off to Kiev and induced the Lithuanian Prince Fedor with fifty men accompanied by a *basqaq,* as the Mongols' tax officials are known, to attack our party as it passed by Chernigov on the way back to Novgorod. We fought off the prince and his men, and God punished Fedor by killing off all his horses.
>
> The Lithuanians, this time Grand Prince Olgerd [Algerdas], attacked Novgorod itself just six years ago after one of our mayors, Ostafei Dvorianets, had called the Lithuanian a dog. The grand prince with his brothers seized several of our towns, including Luga, Opoka, and the fortress of Porkhov to the west.

Matvei paused again; he remembered how he had watched in horror as a Novgorodian mob killed the mayor. They explained their actions by saying that "because of you they took our districts."

"Three years later, Casimir of Poland seized Volynia. He 'did much injury to Christians, and he converted the sacred churches to the Latin service hated of God,'" Matvei concluded, using the words that the chronicler had used in the entry for that year.

> But the greatest threat to us has been the Swedish king, Magnus Eriksson, a great crusader, who has threatened our northern borders and trade routes with the Germans for more than a decade. Four years ago he marched his army up the Neva River and forcibly converted the Vod and Izhora peoples, shaving the men's beards so they looked like boys, as is the custom among the Latins. He then sent his emissaries to the Vladyka in Novgorod and challenged him to debate his "philosophers" at a "conference" on the true faith.
>
> "If your faith is better, I will adopt your faith," he told us. "If mine is better you will adopt mine and we will be as one person. If not, I will come against you with all my force!"
>
> The Vladyka consulted with Mayor Fedor Daniilovich, with Avraam the *tysiatskii,* and with the whole town; their reply was a defiant and good one in defense of the True Faith: "If you wish to debate which faith is better, ours or yours, go to Caesargrad

(that is, Constantinople, as we know it here) to the patriarch, for we have received our Orthodox faith from the Greeks. With you we will not budge on our faith, and whatever offense there is between us, bring a helmet to the conference."

Matvei himself had traveled on his uncle's behalf to deal with the Swede even before this latest, most serious, incursion. In 1337, one of the king's men had raided the Vodskaia Fifth (*piatina*)[5] and had killed many of the Karelians who paid tribute to Novgorod in furs; the raiding continued for two years before a peace conference was called.

Before this latest attack, which still threatens us to this day, I was sent with the city's mayor and other boyars to make peace with the Swedes on the old terms that Grand Prince Iurii had drawn up in 1323 on the island of Orekhov. My uncle gave me strict instructions to save the Orthodox Karelians in his care. While many had already died in the war, the Vladyka told me to see to it that in addition to the old terms, I was to insert a clause stipulating that we would not hand over any Orthodox Karelians who crossed over from the Swedish side; the devil-worshipping Karelians who came over from the Swedish side would be hanged as troublemakers, just as the Swedes would do to the pagans crossing over from the Novgorodian land who were caught on their side of the frontier—but the Vladyka was very clear: the Orthodox among the Karelians were to be protected.

After this treaty, we had nine years of peace before the Swedes came up the Neva into our land, and in that time the Vladyka did what he could to defend the city. Even prior to his consecration, while still archbishop-elect, he strengthened Novgorod's defenses—building the Detinets wall along the river. After his consecration, he reinforced the embankments around both sides of the city, and after the Swedes had burned the fortress of Orekhov, he went up and built a stone fortress there.

Matvei remembered how unwilling Vasilii had had been to go—how he had hoped the Lithuanian princes would defend Novgorod after they had been granted Orekhov and other towns for their maintenance—Ladoga, Korela, and half of Koporie—but they had not done so. The Novgorodians had then called on the grand prince in Moscow for help, and Matvei recalled their desperate plea: "Defend your patrimony according to your kissing of the cross;[6] the king of the Swedes is coming against us!" Grand Prince Semen had apparently come as far as Torzhok before turning back. His brother, Ivan, arrived in Novgorod a little later, but he lingered in the city and never went north to the fortress itself; receiving word that it had fallen to the Swedes, he returned home. So Vasilii had finally gone.

Matvei continued his letter:

After the Swedes had captured and burned Grand Prince Iurii's wooden fortress, the Novgorodians asked our Vladyka to go rebuild the fortress there, and my uncle set out

---

[5] An administrative division of Lord Novgorod the Great.
[6] Promises and agreements were sealed by the kissing of the cross or icons of the saints.

with his master builders—who had honed their skills building the Detinets, the bridge over the Volkhov River, the Church of the Mother of God in the Zverin Monastery north of the city, and the Church of the Entrance into Jerusalem in the archiepiscopal compound, which the Vladyka commissioned Isaia to paint. This is the Isaia who has told you so much of us. The Vladyka also had the Church of the Annunciation in the Gorodishche, the prince's compound south of the Market Side of the city, rebuilt after Grand Prince Simeon had ordered it demolished, and rebuilt the Church of St. Paraskeva in the marketplace after a fire. These masters built a fine fortress to protect the Orthodox Novgorodian land. They had only just completed their work when Pskov was struck by pestilence. Then the Pskovians sent men who called the Vladyka to them, so we do not know what the Swedes will do next, though we have faith that this new fortress can withstand another assault by these accursed men.

Matvei thought of the difficulties arising elsewhere in Rus; Grand Prince Ivan Daniilovich, had turned on Novgorod within a year of Vasilii's consecration. Having come from the Horde, he demanded silver from the Kama district to pay the tribute to the khan. When he did not receive that, he marched to Torzhok and from Epiphany to the second week of Lent looted the southern part of the Novgorodian land. The Vladyka had sent Archimandrite Lavrentii of the Iuriev Monastery, and Novgorod for its part had sent two boyars to negotiate with the grand prince, but he would not listen to them. The next year, Novgorod sent Vasilii himself to make peace with Ivan. He and two Novgorodian boyars found the grand prince at Pereiaslavl, and the boyars offered the grand prince five hundred rubles to renounce his privileges in Novgorod, but Ivan would not take the money and did not listen to the Vladyka's appeal for peace. Another year passed before the grand prince made peace with Novgorod and visited the city.

But within four years, Ivan demanded more—a second tribute in a single year—leading the Novgorodians to complain, "this has never happened among us since the beginning of the world—you have kissed the cross to Novgorod and agreed to the old fees according to Iaroslav's Charter." Ivan's son, Semen, was not much better than his father. He too attacked Torzhok within a year of coming to the throne, and the Novgorodians sent Vasilii with Tysiatskii Avraam and other officials to make peace with him. They gave the grand prince a thousand rubles, and he agreed to Iaroslav's Charter.

There were troubles in Novgorod too. Matvei had seen his uncle face down the various boyar clans and the popular elements that they incited from time to time. He had seen how the common people themselves rose up in riot and how at times there was open war in the streets of the city, and how hard the Vladyka had suffered trying to bring peace to the city. In 1337, a mob had attacked Archimandrite Efim, and he had to take refuge in the Church of St. Nicholas on the Market all night until the crowd dispersed. Matvei thought it better not to write of all this—to tell others of arguments at home—but he did jot down how, in 1342, looting was so bad after a huge fire in the city, that the Vladyka and the hegumens of the monasteries called a fast and held processions and prayer services at various monasteries around the city.

He left out how, later that same year, Mayor Ontsifor Lukinich had stirred up the commoners (*chernye liudi*), against another mayor, Fedor Danilov, and his associate Ondreshko. Ontsifor accused them of having killed his father, Luka, as Luka was campaigning in the northeast, "Beyond the Portages" as they called the unorganized territories from where Novgorod's great fur wealth came. When Fedor and Ondreshko fled to Koporie, the fortress on the Gulf of Finland near the border with Estonia, Ontsifor had appealed to the Vladyka, who in consultation with the boyars sent Archimandrite Esif to bring the two men back to answer the charges. When Fedor and Ondreshko arrived in Novgorod, Vasilii called the town together before the Cathedral of Holy Wisdom—a "Vladyka's veche" as they called it— where the two men denied having killed Ontsifor's father. They then fled across the great bridge and called their own supporters to a veche at Iaroslav's Court south of the marketplace. The situation remained tense throughout the day and into the night as the two crowds faced each other across the great bridge. The next morning, Ontsifor asked the Vladyka to speak to the veche on the Market Side. But, without waiting for Vasilii's diplomatic efforts to bear fruit, Ontsifor then crossed over with armed men and attacked the veche on the Market Side, seizing Fedor and Ondreshko and locking them in one of the churches in the marketplace. It was pandemonium on the Market Side by that point, and the ensuing melee drove Ontsifor from the city. It took most of the day for the Vladyka, with his vicar, to calm the crowds on both sides of the city and bring peace. To write of that might offend the boyar clans in Novgorod, were they to ever hear of it, or might make his readers think less of Novgorod. In recent years, there were even murmurings that heresy was loose in the land—of men in Pskov and Novgorod who denied the authority of the Church, the power of the sacraments, the Trinity itself, but Matvei did not know what to think of those rumors and thought it best not to write of them. His uncle had not said much of them and so there was not much to tell his readers.

> Not all has been storm and strife. Tell the brethren, as Isaia has told you, how the Vladyka has beautified his city; how he refurbished the Cathedral of Holy Wisdom several times—putting up a new cross and covering the roof with lead soon after coming to the archiepiscopal throne. He raised an iron fence. He hung a beautiful set of gilt bronze doors, which people called the "Vasilii Gates" in his honor, and brought in a master from Moscow to cast a new bell. After a fire, he repaired the iconostasis, including new Holy Doors, and had a set of festal icons painted. Indeed, he himself is an iconographer as well as a great patron of the arts, a diplomat, a theologian, a pilgrim and traveler, and a great churchman, and has left us some beautiful works by his own hand.

In fact, Matvei felt that Vasilii had resurrected the archiepiscopal office in Novgorod. "One has to go back to Archbishop Martirii 250 years ago," he wrote, "to find an archbishop who built or rebuilt as many churches in Novgorod the Great as has Vasilii Kalika. Vladyka Antonii built two churches just before the Mongols came and devastated our land; Vladyka Kliment built a chapel over the Detinets gates in 1296; Vladyka David built the Church of St. Nicholas in the Nerev End forty years ago, and Archbishop Moisei built the main church of the Derevianitskii Monastery just three years before Vasilii's own election. Although these archbishops did these things, Vasilii did more."

Matvei thought of what else Vasilii had done. No other Novgorodian archbishops, in fact, had built fortifications either in the city or elsewhere in the Novgorodian land, and he had used his own men and personally overseen the rebuilding of the great bridge over the Volkhov after it had been swept away by floodwaters in 1338. Beyond his architectural endeavors, he had also taken on more power than had been held by any of his predecessors, certainly not any in the last century. In addition, his courts heard cases that no other episcopal court in Russia or perhaps all of Orthodoxy ever judged.[7]

Matvei paused. There was commotion in the courtyard as priests went in to give the Vladyka last rites. Matvei had been with the Vladyka through so much and had written down all he had seen and done, how he had grown up with the Vladyka, traveled far and wide on his behalf, and negotiated with the Swedish king in Vasilii's name. Matvei felt, as many of the other Men of Holy Wisdom must have felt, that they did not belong in this small monastery so far from the city—a place of solitude, at the core so far away from the grand monasteries, churches, icon workshops, and scriptoria of the great city. They wanted to push on—to Great Novgorod; more so, they wanted to see their archbishop in all his glory, wearing the white cowl he donned as a former parish priest turned bishop—a member of the "white clergy" as they called them—and in the polystaurion, the chasuble covered with crosses, that had been a special gift from the metropolitan, a sign of special status among the Byzantine clergy. Arrayed thus, he was every bit the great prelate who had revived the House of Holy Wisdom, the archiepiscopal office and administration, after it had fallen into more than a century of decline. He was fully a city father, helping to lead the great northern metropolis—he was their Vladyka—the great builder and defender of Orthodoxy against pagan and Catholic foes, and a true leader of Novgorod as it stood against the avaricious grand princes.

They would eventually push on, of course, but no longer with the Vladyka. He died at the ninth hour on July 3 in the 6,860th year from the creation of the world according to the Constantinopolitan reckoning. In mourning—indeed, there was a great sense of loss, because some of the younger monks knew no other Vladyka— they would carry Vasilii Kalika's earthly remains back to the great cathedral he had adorned in the heart of the city he had helped lead through so much. There, clad in his white cowl and polystaurion, they would bury his body in the southern gallery with the other bishops and archbishops of Novgorod, the funeral presided over by Moisei, his predecessor and successor. Then Novgorod would have to find a new archbishop. Once things had calmed down, Matvei could then return to his letter,

---

[7] A number of documents dealing with land transactions are in the archiepiscopal archives and they seem to have judged some purely secular cases, sitting on a court of appeals or referral court with secular officials (according to the Novgorodian Judicial Charter).

finish it, and send it off to Athos in hopes that they would believe all the marvelous things they had heard of Vasilii Kalika and his city.

Suggestions for Further Reading

The Chronicle of Novgorod. Edited and translated by Robert Michell and Neville Forbes. New York: AMS Press, 1970, 126–45. An imperfect but still useful translation of the Novgorodian First Chronicle.

Ostrowski, Donald. "Images of the White Cowl." In *The New Muscovite Cultural History: A Collection in Honor of Daniel B. Rowland*. Edited by Valerie Kivelson, Karen Petrone, Michael Flier, and Nancy Shields Kollmann. Bloomington: Slavica, 2009, 271–84.

Paul, Michael C. "Archbishop Vasilii Kalika, the Fortress of Orekhov, and the Defense of Orthodoxy." In Alan V. Murray, ed. *Clash of Cultures on the Medieval Baltic Frontier*. Farnham, UK, and Burlington, VT: Ashgate, 2009.

"The Tale of the White Cowl." In *Medieval Russia's Epic's Chronicles and Tales*. Edited by Serge A. Zenkovsky. 2d ed. New York: E.P. Dutton, 1974, 323–32.

Weickhardt, George. "The Canon Law of Rus', 1100–1551." *Russian History* 28, nos. 1–4 (2001): 411–46.

V
Monks

∞ 12 ∞

Holy Images for the Grand Prince

Michael S. Flier

Of all of the artisans working in Muscovite Rus, icon painters were perhaps the most respected but the least described. By the very nature of their profession, they were understood to do God's work with dignity and modesty, for the faith and not for fame and fortune. Most holy images, whether painted on walls in fresco, affixed to wall surfaces in mosaics, or painted on wooden panels in tempera, come down to us without the name of an artist. We do not have detailed descriptions of the artists' techniques or their training, and so we must work backward from the experiences of contemporary icon painters to understand the nature of the art they had to master. Modern technical analyses have revealed some of the methods employed to obtain specific visual effects of light, shade, and color that dazzled the eye of the medieval beholder. As with all artisan trades, we know that the intricate knowledge of materials, tools, composition, and the theology behind the holy image was passed down orally, from master to disciple over the centuries.

The icon (from the Greek, eikon, *meaning "image"), was an art form developed by the Byzantine Greeks on the basis of the early Christian painting of the late Roman empire. By the time icon painting was brought to Rus in the late-tenth century, however, the Byzantines had developed a complex theology of the holy image that retreated from naturalistic depiction of the material world toward greater abstraction. An icon came to be understood not only as a symbolic representation of the holy but as a dynamic window to the celestial world beyond the reach of sinful man. Using a flattened composition and inverted perspective to underscore the transcendental nature of the heavenly kingdom, the artist represented its inhabitants obliquely, inaccessible to the direct comprehension of the senses.*

When an Orthodox believer prays to a saint depicted on an icon, he or she participates in a mystical connection established by the image with the holy person addressed. The link to the holy confirms the icons themselves as holy. Each saint or canonical scene is painted with individualizing attributes of clothing, facial features, gestures, and background, which, together with golden halos behind the

This icon from the workshop of Feofan Grek (Theophanes the Greek; Moscow, early fifteenth century), held in the Tretyakov Gallery, Moscow, was the namesake icon of the Cathedral of the Savior-Transfiguration in Pereiaslavl-Zalesskii. It depicts the Transfiguration of Christ before Peter, James (son of Zebedee), and John (the Apostle), who have followed him up a mountain, traditionally held to be Mount Tabor. Christ is flanked by Elijah on his right, and Moses, holding the tablets, on his left. The disciples are shown reeling below from the brightness of the light. The Transfiguration, celebrated on August 6, is described in the Gospels of Matthew 17:1–9, Mark 9:2–8, and Luke 9:28–36.

heads of the holy and an obligatory inscription, fulfills the Orthodox requirement of iconographic recognizability. An icon can be considered holy only if it represents faithfully the holy personage or scene intended. Model books with details of such iconographic attributes were a relatively late phenomenon.[1]

Only a few icon painters in Muscovite Rus were possessed of such singular talent that their names have come down to us in written documents, such as chronicles and correspondence. We are fortunate to have a rare letter from around 1415, written by the hagiographer Epifanii the Most Wise to Kirill, the archimandrite of the Savior–Afanasii Monastery in the city of Tver. The letter, which survives in a single seventeenth-century copy, is filled with admiration and respect for Feofan Grek (that is, Theophanes the Greek), one of the master icon painters of Orthodox Christian art. In addition to Feofan's intellectual brilliance and knowledge of theology and philosophy, Epifanii underscores the artist's great skill in painting from memory in quick strokes, without the aid of sketches like his less talented peers, constantly moving about while painting and conversing with visitors about spiritual and philosophical matters.

Probably born in or near Constantinople around 1340, Feofan emigrated to Rus by the 1370s and is credited in the Novgorod III Chronicle with painting the remarkable frescoes in Novgorod's Church of the Savior on Elijah Street in 1378. The reconstructed Trinity Chronicle has him heading a team that decorated several major churches in Moscow itself in the late-fourteenth and early-fifteenth centuries, including the Kremlin's Cathedral of the Archangel Michael in 1399 and the palace church, the Cathedral of the Annunciation, in 1405.

In the fictionalized account below, a team of assistants—Feofan's workshop— prepares for the arrival of the master, now around sixty-five years old, along with two other icon painters who have agreed to help him with the Annunciation decoration: the elderly Prokhor of Gorodets, and the monk Andrei Rublev, some twenty-five-years-old at the time. Gleb Ivanov syn, the thirty-eight-year-old head of the workshop, is explaining its operation to a twelve-year-old apprentice, Nikita, who has just been recruited to shore up the team following a terrible accident that had occurred the week before.

"Nikita," Gleb said, "what good fortune that I saw your father at the matins service this morning. After I explained our situation, he readily agreed to let you join our workshop. We truly need you to help us, for we have a serious problem. I must tell you that Grand Prince Vasilii Dmitrievich—may God grant him a long life—has commanded that his palace church here in the Kremlin be decorated. We have been busy preparing for Masters Feofan, Prokhor, and Andrei to begin their work. We have brought all our materials and tools to the site. We have set up our workbenches and gathered the loads of plaster, wood, and the various pigments we need for all

---

[1] A sixteenth-century model book by Dionysios of Fourna is traditionally viewed as the earliest one extant.

phases of the project. Alas, our poor Grisha just last week was assembling the scaffolding to be used for painting frescoes on the walls of the nave of the cathedral and the platform he was standing on gave way. He fell some fifteen arshins[2] to the stone floor, broke his neck, and died instantly. May God have mercy on his soul! Without any money coming in now, his poor wife and five children have had to abandon Moscow and go live with relatives in Kolomna. The Lord knows how they will survive. But you, Nikita, you must listen carefully to what you are told and learn quickly. We simply don't have time to waste. We must begin our work on time!"

"I will do my best, my lord. Of course, I am eager to join your team, but I must tell you, I'm worried about working for a master so great as Feofan. I am at a loss about what to do! Where do I begin? I have never done anything like this before!"

"The first thing you must realize is that you are now engaged in God's work, helping us to create holy images. They are the result of our devotion to Christ our Lord. You must remain pure of heart and dedicate yourself to the glory of our life-giving Trinity and Mary, our Most Pure Mother of God. You must leave your childish games and notions behind, and do all that you can to be a truly good person worthy to help make the images of God's holy saints. Do you swear before all that is holy to do this without reservation?"

"Yes, my lord, I do," Nikita replied.

"Good, very good," said the relieved Gleb. "Now let us pray that God might grant us the strength and the wisdom to accomplish all the tasks before us in decorating this beautiful cathedral. It is a great responsibility, and we must do it especially well—for Master Feofan, for the grand prince, and for Christ our Lord and all his saints." They knelt before an icon of Christ the Savior and prayed together for a very long time.

Rising to his feet, Gleb turned to Nikita and said, "Now we must get started by showing you the various tasks our team must carry out. You first must see how the boards are prepared to make panels for the painting of icons. It is more complex than you might think. As a beginning apprentice, you will have to master this task—actually a whole series of tasks—before taking on more difficult ones. Now, about the wood. You use wood from trees like linden, birch, beech, ash, and oak because they have less resin than other trees and don't warp as much. You cut the boards out of the center of the thickest part of the trunk, since that is the strongest. They must be dried for many months and finally saturated with a special solution[3] to kill any parasites remaining in the wood. When a board is ready, you hollow out two or more strips on the back and insert wedges of even harder wood to act as braces that also resist warping. Then you take a chisel and knife to the front to hollow out a central, rectangular depression, called the ark, which is the

---

[2] One arshin = 0.71 meters or 2.3 feet. Fifteen arshins is nearly thirty-five feet.
[3] The solution was mercury chloride.

base for the layers beneath the actual painting. The area around the ark serves as a frame for the icon itself. Next scratch the surface of the ark with diagonal lines for good contact. After that apply layers of sturgeon glue to the surface. You let the adhesive dry each time. Then, finally, glue a sheet of very fine linen to the ark. Smooth out all the air bubbles and let it dry for at least a day. Then you are ready to add the white gesso ground to the surface of the ark. The gesso is made of fine alabaster powder mixed with glue and is applied in several layers. After each one dries hard, you must polish down any uneven or rough spots until the final surface is perfectly smooth. This is the surface that will take the paint. But you must be careful, Nikita! Any mistake along the way will lead to cracks and the paint will flake off. That must not happen!

"Once the surface is properly prepared, the master will draw or trace the overall composition onto the gesso ground with a lead stylus or charcoal. Then, under his supervision, different members of our icon painting team will use their talents to paint various parts of the icon. Some are trained to do garments; others, background buildings and vegetation; yet others, hands and feet. The most difficult part of the image is, of course, the face. All the facial features—expression, shading, skin tones—require such great skill, they may be done only by the master himself."

Nikita recoiled in fear. "How will I ever learn all this? My head is spinning!"

"You will, my son, you will," said Gleb. You will repeat each step again and again and again for months on end until they are all as familiar to you as your own five fingers. You will work together with Luka and Matvei, who will make sure you do everything the right way, the Orthodox way.

"Now in addition to preparing the boards, the workshop must make sure that the very materials used for painting are ready. The pigments are taken from various minerals or organic matter found in plants, animals, and even insects. The mineral substances themselves have to be ground to a powdery form so that they can combine well with egg yolk and a bit of water or vinegar to create egg tempera. The colors produced with the tempera are very rich and filled with brilliant light, and they bond well with the gesso ground. Always keep in mind that the pigments are very expensive and must be handled with great care. Now, once the painting is finished and the surface is covered over with several protective coats of linseed oil, the rich colors will shimmer in the light and make an image worthy of veneration. Of course, it will be many years before you are ready to handle the pigments for the actual painting, but once you do, you will understand how miraculous they can be.

"As you might imagine, we will have to prepare many more boards than usual for this project. We have been told that the iconostasis[4] will be very high, that it will have more tiers than usual. Nikita, you are used to your parish church that

---

[4] The iconostasis is a large screen of icons, typically multitiered, that separates the church sanctuary that contains the altar from the nave, where the congregation stands during services.

probably has a single Deësis tier of three icons and some festival icons.⁵ But in this royal cathedral we will have to make large panels for each of the icons by gluing together a number of boards. Master Feofan will paint the Deësis tier, which will also include on either side of the Deësis, icons of the archangels Michael and Gabriel, the apostles Peter and Paul, and the church fathers Basil of Caesarea and John Chrysostom, all facing in toward the Savior to plead for mercy for mankind.

"Masters Prokhor and Andrei will paint the icons for the Festival tier above, that is, the icons of the major feast days of the church, including the Annunciation, Christ's Nativity, and the Entry into Jerusalem on Palm Sunday. These icons have many scenes from the lives of our Lord and the Mother of God, scenes that tell wonderful stories from the very Gospels themselves.

"Above the Festival tier will be a Prophet tier, with images of the prophets from the Old Testament, who predicted the coming of the Messiah: prophets like David, Solomon, Daniel, Ezekiel, and Isaiah. And above that there will be a Forefather tier with images of such ancient holy men as Abraham, Isaac, and Jacob.

"I don't yet know who will paint the cathedral's namesake icon of the Annunciation, which, by tradition must be placed on the lowest, Local tier, to the right of the icon of Christ that always stands to the right of the Royal Gates before the altar. But there is no doubt that when all these icons are in place, the high iconostasis will be an astonishing sight to behold! It will present the entire story of our faith in beautiful holy images.

"But, Nikita, look around you; we don't paint images only on boards! The walls and vaults and cupolas offer us space to paint holy images of great size. And you use a different system of painting from what you do on wooden panels. You first burn limestone in an oven and then plunge it into water. There it dissolves into a thick paste called lime putty. When lime putty is mixed with sand it forms lime plaster, which can easily be spread on walls, smoothed out, and then left to dry, forming a hard surface. While the plaster is drying, an artist can apply pigments dissolved in water directly to the wet surface and they adhere, binding the color to the plaster itself. Entire color images can be painted on the wet plaster in this way until it dries and will no longer take the color.⁶ Usually our team will put several layers of plaster on the walls to be decorated. You mix the first layer with coarse sand to make a rough surface that will dry and become a solid base for the next layer, made with slightly finer sand. You can put each of these base layers on with

---

⁵The central composition of an Orthodox iconostasis is always the Deësis (from the Greek for *supplication*), consisting of a central icon of Christ in Judgment, flanked by an icon of the Mother of God on the left (stage right), and an icon of Saint John the Forerunner (John the Baptist) on the right (stage left).

⁶Muscovite documents describe mural painting with such collocations as *podpisyvati* or *raspisyvati tserkov'* ("fully decorate a church"). The word *fresco* is an Italian term that entered Russian only at the beginning of the nineteenth century.

a mason's trowel over an entire wall and let it dry. When the painting layer of plaster is ready to be applied, you use very fine sand. And you plaster only a small portion of the wall, just the amount of wall that can be painted before the drying is complete, in about ten hours. While the plaster begins to dry, the artist must take a brush with a reddish pigment and paint freehand the basic outlines of the entire image to be done. Once the base drawing is finished, he and his assistants must quickly set to work and paint the entire image in quick strokes before the plaster sets. As you can imagine, this takes unimaginable skill and a sure, steady hand. Not a moment can be wasted!

"I was just about your age, when fate brought me from my little village to Novgorod. There I was taken in by the foreman of Master Feofan's workshop as an apprentice and learned everything I could about the painting of images over many years. I saw with my own eyes, how the Master decorated the walls in the Savior on Elijah Street. He used mostly a reddish-brown pigment together with black and white, but what he produced was vivid and awe-inspiring—as if God himself were painting through him! The Pantocrator[7] in the main cupola cast a stern face over the entire nave below—terrifying! And the huge archangels and the forefathers glaring down made me feel the Lord's power in the universe. Painting such figures on a curved surface like a cupola or a vault is especially difficult, because the artist has to adjust the composition so that the image won't be distorted from below. And he seemed to do it with such ease, perched high over the nave of the church on the scaffolding. It is a miracle! And now, all these years later, I have become the foreman of our workshop. My destiny is tied to Master Feofan forever! And just last week I learned that he will paint new images here on the cathedral's south wall, images of the Apocalypse. That is why we were setting up the scaffolding, when poor Grisha . . ."

"I don't understand," Nikita responds. "What is apoca . . ."

"A-po-ca-lypse," Gleb replied, drawing out each syllable. "It means the End of the World! Saint John writes in Revelation that there will be a tremendous struggle in the universe between the forces of good and evil, and that the Savior, on a white horse, will lead Archangel Michael and the heavenly host to a great victory over the evildoers. But all kinds of terrible things will appear before that victory, such as earthquakes and fire and plagues and fearsome beasts from Satan himself, like a dragon with seven heads and ten horns! And the destruction and the blood! Horses with the heads of lions! It is horrifying! When Christ returns for a second time, he is finally victorious, evil is cast out, and the New Jerusalem descends to earth and the Last Judgment begins, the General Resurrection of the dead. What we all have to face at the end! And Master Feofan will paint all those images in our cathedral, on this very wall!"

---

[7] The Pantocrator image of the Almighty is usually a head and upper torso of Christ holding the Gospel in his left hand and raising his right hand in blessing.

"But why?" stammered Nikita, wide-eyed, "after all, we see the Last Judgment every time we leave the church![8] Why do we need to look at more images of such terrible things at the end of the world?"

"Well, do you know what year this is?" asked Gleb.

"No, I don't," replied Nikita, slightly flustered. "I know it is March, and that Maslenitsa and the Great Fast will be here soon."[9]

"Then let me tell you—it is the year 6913 from the time the world was created by God.[10] The Psalms teach us that a day in the sight of God is like unto a thousand, and thus a year is like a millennium. And so a great week in the sight of God is seven millennia. The Apocalypse, the End of the World, will happen when we reach the fateful year 7000. That is why the Church doesn't even bother to calculate the tables for Easter[11] past that date—human history will end! We must all think about what is coming and be ready to see the Lord return for the second time. No wonder the grand prince wants Master Feofan to paint the Apocalypse in his own palace church!"

Suddenly there was a commotion at the entrance to the cathedral. Nikita spun around and spotted many of the workshop artisans surrounding a tall man, gray and wizened, with a flowing beard and bright blue eyes, who was making his way into the nave.

Gleb turned to Nikita, patted him on the back, and said, "Now, Nikita, you are one of us. Let's go to greet Master Feofan!"

Suggestions for Further Reading

There are a great number of books in English devoted to Orthodox icons and church architecture. The following provide general introductions to the two topics.

Alpatov, M.V. *Early Russian Icon Painting*. Moscow: Iskusstvo, 1974.
Beckwith, John. *Early Christian and Byzantine Art*. Harmondsworth, UK: Penguin, 1970.
Belting, Hans. *Likeness and Presence*. Chicago: University of Chicago Press, 1994.

---

[8] The western wall of every Orthodox church is devoted to the Last Judgment, the final image a believer will have to contemplate before leaving the nave.

[9] In Rus, the passing of specific years was the business of chroniclers and chancery clerks, not the majority of the populace, who kept track of the passage of time with references to major natural events (fire, earthquakes, eclipses, droughts, floods) and to church holidays. Maslenitsa refers to the week before the Great Fast of Forty Days ("Great Lent"), followed by Holy Week and Easter. During Maslenitsa only dairy products are allowed, no meat or fish, but there are great celebrations in anticipation of the severe restrictions to come.

[10] The Byzantine Greeks and therefore the inheritors of their culture in Old Rus and Muscovy believed that the world was created 5,508 years before the birth of Christ. The year 6913 corresponds to 1405 in the Western, Julian, calendar, which was not adopted in Russia until 1700.

[11] The annual date of Easter is not fixed, but movable, calculated on the basis of the interaction of solar and lunar cycles. For this reason, the Christian churches East and West produced Easter tables to allow the calculation of the exact date each year.

Cormack, Robin. *Byzantine Art*. Oxford: Oxford University Press, 2000.
——. *Writing in Gold: Byzantine Society and Its Icons*. New York: Oxford University Press, 1985.
Cormack, Robin, and Delia Gaze, eds. *The Art of Holy Russia: Icons from Moscow, 1400–1660*. London: Royal Academy of Arts; Frankfurt: Schirn Kunsthalle, 1998.
Evseyeva, Liliya, et al. *A History of Icon Painting: Sources, Traditions, Present Day*. Translated by Kate Cook. Moscow: Grand Holding Publishers, 2005.
Faensen, Hubert and Vladimir Ivanov. *Early Russian Architecture*. New York: G.P. Putnam's Sons, 1975.
Grierson, Roderick. *Gates of Mystery: The Art of Holy Russia*. Baltimore: Intercultura, [1995].
Hamilton, George Heard. *The Art and Architecture of Russia*. 3d ed. New York: Penguin, 1983.
Ivanov, Vladimir. *Russian Icons*. New York: Rizzoli, 1988.
Kondakov, Nikodim Pavlovich. *Icons*. New York: Parkstone International, 2008.
Krautheimer, Richard. *Early Christian and Byzantine Architecture*. Baltimore: Penguin Books, 1965.
Kyzlasova, Irina, ed. *Russian Icons 14th–16th Centuries*. Leningrad: Aurora Art Publishers, 1988.
Lazarev, Viktor. *Old Russian Murals and Mosaics from the XI to the XVI Century*. London: Phaidon, 1966.
Lowden, John. *Early Christian and Byzantine Art*. London: Phaidon Press, 1997.
Maguire, Henry. *The Icons of Their Bodies: Saints and Their Images in Byzantium*. Princeton, NJ: Princeton University Press, 1996.
Milner-Gulland, Robin. "Art and Architecture of Old Russia, 988–1700." In *An Introduction to Russian Art and Architecture*. Edited by Robert and Dimitri Obolensky. Cambridge: Cambridge University Press, 1980. Vol. 3: 1–70.
Opolovnikov, Alexander, and Yelena Opolovnikova. *The Wooden Architecture of Russia: Houses, Fortifications, Churches*. New York: Harry N. Abrams, 1989.
Ouspensky, Leonid. *Theology of the Icon*. 2 vols. Crestwood, NY: St. Vladimir's Seminary Press, 1992.
Ouspensky, Leonid, and Vladimir Lossky. *The Meaning of Icons*. Crestwood, NY: St. Vladimir's Seminary Press, 1983.
Ousterhout, Robert G. *The Master Builders of Byzantium*. Princeton, NJ: Princeton University Press, 1999.
Rice, David, and Tamara Talbot Rice. 1974. *Icons and Their History*. Woodstock, NY: Overlook Press.
Rodley, Lyn. *Byzantine Art and Architecture: An Introduction*. Cambridge: Cambridge University Press, 1994.
Safran, Linda, ed. *Heaven on Earth: Art and the Church in Byzantium*. University Park: Pennsylvania State University Press, 1998.
Tradigo, Alfredo. *Icons and Saints of the Eastern Orthodox Church*. Translated by Stephen Sartarelli. Los Angeles: Getty Publications, 2006.
Uspensky, Boris. *The Semiotics of the Russian Icon*. Edited by Stephen Rudy. Lisse: Peter de Ridder Press, 1976.

For the theology of the icon, see especially the following.

Baggley, John. *Doors of Perception: Icons and Their Spiritual Significance*. Crestwood, NY: St. Vladimir's Seminary Press, 1988.
——. *Festival Icons for the Christian Year*. Crestwood, NY: St. Vladimir's Seminary Press, 2000.

Limouris, Gennadios. *Icons, Windows on Eternity: Theology and Spirituality in Colour.* Geneva: WCC Publications, 1990.
Quenot, Michel. *The Icon: Window on the Kingdom.* Crestwood, NY: St. Vladimir's Seminary Press, 1991.
———. *The Resurrection and the Icon.* Crestwood, NY: St. Vladimir's Seminary Press, 1998.
Tarasov, Oleg. *Icon and Devotion: Sacred Spaces in Imperial Russia.* Translated and edited by Robin Milner-Gulland. London: Reaktion Books, 2002.
Temple, Richard. *Icons and the Mystical Origins of Christianity.* Shaftesbury, UK: Element, 1990.

For albums of various schools, see the following.

Laurina, Vera, and Vasily Pushkariov. *Novgorod Icons 12th–17th Century.* Leningrad: Aurora Art Publishers, 1980.
Lazarev, *Old Russian Murals*, cited above.
Lazarev, L.N. *Moscow School of Icon-Painting.* Moscow: Iskusstvo, 1971.
———. *Novgorodian Icon-Painting.* Moscow: Iskusstvo. 1976.
Maslenitsyn, S.I. *Yaroslavian Icon Painting.* Moscow: Iskusstvo, 1983.
Milyaeva, Liudmilla. *The Ukrainian Icon.* Bournemouth, UK: Parkstone Press; St. Petersburg: Aurora Art Publishers, 1996.
Yamshchikov, Savely. *Pskov: Art Treasures and Architectural Monuments 12th–17th Centuries.* Leningrad: Aurora Art Publishers, 1978.
Yevseyeva, L.M., I.A. Kochetkov, and V.N. Sergeyev. *Early Tver Painting.* Moscow: Iskusstvo, 1983.

∞ 13 ∞

Three Scholars at the Kirillo-Belozersk Monastery
A Teacher, a Student, and a Librarian

Robert Romanchuk

The great Kirillo-Belozersk (Kirillov–White Lake) Monastery was founded in 1397 in the far Russian North as a "desert" hermitage dedicated to the Dormition of the Virgin by Kirill of White Lake, a conversant of Sergii of Radonezh, hesychast, and former hegumen of Simonov Monastery. At the time of Kirill's death in 1427, its patron was the prince of Belozersk-Mozhaisk, and its titular head the archbishop of Rostov (to whom Kirillov was administratively subordinated by 1478). Social and administrative reforms took place under Hegumen Trifon (r. 1434/35–47/48), a monk of the Mt. Athos-linked Spaso-Kamennyi (St. Savior on the Rock) Monastery and later archbishop of Rostov (r. 1462–67). At this time, apparently, the monastery adopted an Athonite cenobitic (communal) rule.

During Trifon's hegumenate (and for several decades afterward), a Byzantine-style secondary school functioned at Kirillov, where translated textbooks of grammar, semantics, geography, and history circulated. Novices like Aleksei, the future saint Aleksandr Oshevenskii, studied with well-read masters such as Oleshka Palkin, who was remembered well into the sixteenth century. But the school's lasting legacy was a bibliographical trend in the 1480s whose representatives, such as the elder Efrosin, preserved and catalogued significant parts of the literary inheritance of Bulgaria, Kievan Rus, and Serbia, and edited important new works of Muscovite literature (e.g., the epic Zadonshchina*) and history (the* First Sophia Chronicle*). Kirillov's great library—one of the largest in Muscovy, with 1,304 books by 1621—has come down to us almost intact.*

A SECONDARY-SCHOOL TEACHER: LORD ALEKSANDR-OLESHKA PALKIN, 1440

Introduction

Primary schooling—"letters" (*gramota*) or "writing" (*pisanie*), training in instrumental literacy commencing with the letters, progressing to their combination in

This fifteenth-century miniature depicts a centaur holding a sword and standing over the monogram of the monk Efrosin, one of the subjects of this chapter. Painted by Efrem Trebes at Efrosin's request, the image has been preserved in the archive of the Russian National Library in St. Petersburg. The centaur's significance (as something that can only be captured by skill) is discussed in this chapter.

syllables, and culminating in the reading aloud of the Psalter—was reasonably common in Muscovy, as elsewhere in medieval Europe. Great towns such as Novgorod had primary schools (*uchilishcha*), while in smaller towns a scribe (*d'iak*) might offer such schooling; some larger monasteries had a *d'iak* on hand to teach letters to beginning monks. In the West and Byzantium, a few students went on to secondary school, to study the language arts of grammar, rhetoric, and sometimes philosophy. Grammar (*gramatikiia*) was always the commonest of the language arts, and the only one taught in Muscovy. It focused on the technical grammar (declension and conjugation) and vocabulary of high-style writings, as well as "historical" (informational) knowledge, with the goal of training students to read a text "with understanding." Secondary schools were extremely rare and ephemeral among the Orthodox Slavs—even in comparison with Byzantium, where, in the words of Thomas Conley, "such educational institutions as did exist . . . came and went."[1]

The erudite Kirillov scribe Oleshka Palkin, who flourished at Kirillov under Hegumen Trifon (r. 1434/35–1447/48), was named Aleksandr in the world. He had started a family before he took monastic vows, and his son Stepan (Stepych) Aleksandrov *syn* Palkin was a secular scribe. While the sixteenth-century *Life of Martinian of White Lake* describes him (using the name "Olesh Pavlov") as a primary-school teacher at Kirillov, the materials found in Oleshka's own books indicate that he headed a secondary school there in the 1440s. He copied and taught from various academic books in translation: the Serbian Church Slavic grammar called the *Eight Parts of Speech*, the *Dialectica* (or *Philosophical Chapters*) of John Damascene on semantics, the *Homilies* of Gregory Nazianzenus—models of good style—with classroom *scholia* explaining the classical references, a Serbian *Lexicon* of Slavic archaisms and Greek technical terms, and a *Geographica* and *Short Chronograph* used in Byzantine secondary schools—taken together, a grammar curriculum in Slavic.

The following fictional text represents Oleshka's colophon (that is, a scribal afterword) to a nonextant codex of the *Grammatica* and *Dialectica*, explaining how it reached Kirillov and what it contains. It is based largely on Oleshka's colophon as preserved in the St. Petersburg manuscript RNB Pog. 989, with material added from other colophons that he wrote and the learned writings enumerated above.

Text

Christ is the beginning and end of every blessed deed, begun and completed in Him.
Amen.

This divinely inspired book was brought from the Serbian land by the venerable monk Kassian, who was called Rumiantsev, after his lineage. It was brought to the

---

[1] Thomas Conley, "Byzantine Teaching on Figures and Tropes: An Introcution," *Rhetorica*, 4 (1986): 356.

monastery of the Divine Transfiguration of the Holy Savior [i.e., Spaso-Kamennyi] at the behest of the venerable hegumen Dionysios, who had puissant preeminence and a deep intellect, and was made bishop of the city of Rostov for his good deeds. After forty years passed [i.e., around 1430], the hieromonk Trifon was at great Spaso-Kamennyi, where he was taught by Hegumen Kassian (whom Lord Hegumen Gennadii, student of the venerable Dionysios, taught). It happened that while he was at Kirillov, the monastery of the Honorable Assumption of the Ever-Virgin Theotokos [in 1434], the venerable hegumen Khristofor departed to the Lord. At this time the hieromonk [i.e., priest-monk] Trifon took the post of superior at Kirillov, while this book remained at great Spaso-Kamennyi.

The Spaso-Kamennyi Monastery was located seventy versts from Kirillov and had links with both Kirillov's princely patrons and Mt. Athos. Its Greek hegumen Dionysios was a cenobitic reformer who cultivated learning at his monastery, seeking out erudite Church Slavic books. Trifon, whose "alma mater" was Spaso-Kamennyi, appears to have been forced on the unwilling Kirillov brethren by the prince of Belozersk-Mozhaisk. Of the itinerant Russian monk Kassian Rumiantsev we know almost nothing.

This book contains the writing of the blessed John Damascene concerning the *Eight Parts of Speech* which we speak and write: the name [i.e., noun], verb, participle, article [i.e., anaphoric/relative pronoun], pronoun, preposition, adverb, and conjunction, in the letters of the Serbian language. It was translated by Bulgarian, Greek, and Serbian translators, who did not condescend to put it into the Rus language; indeed, a word is fine in one language, but in another it is not fine. In this book are also other, *Philosophical Chapters* [i.e., the *Dialectica* of John Damascene], which he sent to Kosmas, bishop of Masuma [*sic*: Maïuma]. They have much knowledge and great meaning but are not all, nor to all, understandable; but in much, and to many, they are difficult to understand and require experience. But, as the holy and great Lord John Damascene writes: let us search, let us examine, let us inquire. "For every one that asketh, receiveth: and he that seeketh, findeth; and to him that knocketh, it shall be opened" [Matt. 7:8]; and "Ask thy father, and he will declare to thee: thy elders in knowledge and they will tell thee" [Deut. 32:7]. If, then, we are lovers of learning, we shall learn much, for it is of the nature of all things that they may be apprehended through industry and toil, and before all and after all by the grace of God, the Giver of grace.

All the early extant copies of the Eight Parts of Speech *treat only the first four parts; the last four were added or restored in the seventeenth century. Attributed to John Damascene, it was in fact the work of Serbian monks. The* Dialectica *taught how to define a term or concept. John links heuristic study (what we would call scholarship) to interpretation with his gloss on Matthew and, citing Isocrates, sets this study alongside Christian grace.*

Philosophy is knowledge of things which are in so far as they are, that is, a knowledge of the nature of things which have being. Again, philosophy is a knowledge of both divine and human things, that is to say, of things both visible and invisible. It is concerned with that term which has meaning, is articulate, and is universal, or, in other words, common and predicated of several things. And as man is created in God's image and worthy of the dignity of the word, it is necessary not to leave him without a teaching about its parts, of which it is composed. For even if the word is composed in the soul without these parts, the God-bearing fathers teach that for the second birth of the body—manifested with the lips and the voice and the other organs of the body—it needs these parts too, for its composition. For without the latter, it is impossible to clarify one's word concerning the former. And this is part of the art and science called grammar.

The first two definitions of philosophy given here (from the Dialectica*) are Aristotelian and Stoic. The convoluted apology for the study of grammar, found in the preamble to the* Eight Parts of Speech, *may ultimately derive from Stoic doctrines that treated grammar as a model of the cosmos (here, the body or microcosm) as well as from patristic theories of matter.*

Philosophy, again, is a study of death, whether this be voluntary or natural. Death is of two kinds: the one being natural, which is the separation of soul from body, whereas the other is the voluntary one by which we disdain this present life and aspire to that which is to come. Still again, philosophy is the making of one's self like God. Now, we become like God in wisdom, which is to say, in the true knowledge of good; and in justice, which is a fairness in judgment without respect to persons; and in holiness, which is to say, in goodness, being that by which we do good to them that wrong us. Philosophy is the art of arts and the science of sciences. Philosophy, again, is a love of wisdom. But, true wisdom is God. Therefore, the love of God, this is the true philosophy. Monks who understood this book were true lovers of wisdom, such as Lord Trifon, who became hegumen after the venerable Khristofor. And so Trifon wished to copy and to read in common this book of Serbian writing with the *Eight Parts of Speech* and *Philosophical Chapters*, and he took it from great Spaso-Kamennyi Monastery.

Here are Platonic (two of them), Aristotelian, and etymological definitions of philosophy from the Dialectica. *In the monastic culture of the desert—as in Russian traditional culture to this day—"artifice"* (khitrost') *had mostly negative connotations; but in John's works, and for the scholarly Kirillov monks, its meaning was favorable, that of an acquired skill. To "read in common"* (chesti vo zbore) *apparently meant to read in class, as distinct from common reading* (chesti na sobore) *in the liturgy or at the table.*

At Kirillov, the monastery of the Honorable Assumption of the Ever-Virgin Theotokos, the lover of this book strove with great labors, at times thanks to his learning, at times reading it repeatedly and only then understanding its meaning, leaning over it and putting his faith in God and in His Ever-Virgin Mother, and in prayers to the holy and great Lord John Damascene. And that lord hegumen named me, the wretched reader of books and poor copyist, the rude *ipaktit* [*sic*: *epaktit*] Oleshka, called Palkin, overfull of all rudeness and physical weakness, who have purified neither my intellect nor my mind, a lord [i.e., a schoolmaster]; and he ordered me to copy this book and to read it in common. Even before this I often happened to look into this book and desired to collect a good word, if only a little, like a drop from the ocean; but I feared my ignorance and lack of intellect and did not dare to copy it all, nor to read it to many.

*"The lover of this book" is Oleshka's circumlocution for Trifon. "Lord" (*gospodin*) was more usually an honorific for the hegumen, but in a teaching context could mean "[school]master." The rare Slavic word* epaktit *(which Oleshka spells* ipaktit*), deriving from the Greek* epaktos, *"foreign," means "stranger" (i.e., in the world: cf. Ps. 118 [119]:19). Note also Oleshka's learned "humility topos"—borrowed from John Damascene himself!*

But when I saw the zeal of that Godly man—for Scripture writes that the one without a suitable leader strays from the path [cf. Isaiah 3:12, Matt. 15:14, Luke 6:39]—so I too, truly rude, renounced my rudeness: by the exhortation of the hegumen it was as if I was placed on the path. Having applied my sin-serving right hand to the corruptible ink, I placed my hope in God and in His Ever-Virgin Mother and in the holy and great Lord John Damascene. In the year 6949 [i.e., 1440], the love of this service reached its end of paper and ink, on the 4th day of the month of December, the Feast of the holy and great Lord John Damascene, the day having ended, at the third hour. May those who happen upon it have it as their purpose to bring their intellect safely through to the final blessed end, which means to be guided by their sense perceptions up to that which is beyond all sense perception. The ignorant writer implores those who read this after me: do not begrudge my rudeness, but remember me in your holy prayers, for God's sake. Amen.

*Byzantine time marks twelve o'clock at sunrise and sunset and counts the years from the creation of the world, while the year begins in September. Note, finally, how learning is seen as a kind of purification of the intellect (*um, *Greek* nous*) that helps the scholarly monk approach God. Such ideas would have justified secondary schooling at Orthodox monasteries.*

A SECONDARY-SCHOOL STUDENT: ALEKSEI FROM VAZHEOZERSKAIA (SAINT ALEKSANDR OSHEVENSKII), 1445

Introduction

Male children, perhaps around the age of ten, might be sent to learn letters from a scribe At some monasteries (such as Kirillov under its founder), they might even be offered up by their parents for the monastic life in order to learn letters. The practice of accepting beardless boys into the monastery was curtailed at Kirillov under Trifon. It appears that Trifon raised the minimum age of novices to sixteen or seventeen, following Byzantine practice, and no longer encouraged elders to train them in "desert" fashion, one-on-one in their cells. By the same token, some novices would have had the opportunity to study grammar with a master such as Oleshka Palkin. The *Life of Aleksandr Oshevenskii* paints a vivid portrait of the novitiate at Kirillov during these years. The future monk (and saint) Aleksandr was born Aleksei in 1427, in the village of Vazheozerskaia in the White Lake region. At age eighteen he set off for Kirillov to stay. His father Nikifor was a petty landowner (although not an aristocrat), a fact that may have eased Aleksei's entry into an institution that was ever more attuned to worldly symbols of status.

The *Life of Aleksandr Oshevenskii* relates two levels of education that its hero received: the study of letters, referred to as "learning in part," and a more thorough study of books (cf. the Greek term for the "language arts," *enkyklios paideia* or "rounded learning") under a Kirillov scribe, almost certainly Oleshka Palkin. However, the version of Aleksei-Aleksandr's *Life* that has come down to us, compiled in 1567 by Hegumen Feodosii of the Oshevenskii Monastery, tells us little about the higher level of study. This may be due in part to the *Life's* textual history, which itself reads like a novel. After Aleksandr's death, his brother Leonid-Leontii dictated a version of his *Life* to clerics at Oshevenskii, which Aleksandr had founded. It remained there until around 1530, when it was stolen, in turn, by a fugitive hegumen and the highwaymen who killed him on the road. In the meantime, Aleksandr's nephew Isaak used to reminisce about his uncle to Feodosii's father, the local priest in Vazheozerskaia; and when the family moved to the Onega region, one of Leonid's clerics, the monk Kornilii-Kirill, would recall for them stories from the lost *Life*. Feodosii eventually took the tonsure at Oshevenskii, became hegumen, and reconstructed the *Life* on the basis of the tales remembered from his youth, those he heard at the monastery, and the *Life of Aleksandr Svirskii*—a northern saint with no connection to Kirillov and no great learning besides, but whose story Feodosii used to structure his narrative.

The following excerpts from a fictional redaction of the *Life of Aleksandr Oshevenskii* are based largely on Feodosii's version in the St. Petersburg manuscript RNB Sof. 463, with interpolations from the translated *Life of Theodore the Stoudite* (for the passages on "philosophy"), the *Life of Martinian of White Lake* (for Oleshka's name and his work), the epistles of Nil Sorskii, and the *Apophthegmata patrum*.

Text

[. . .] The blessed child Aleksei's parents gave him over to learn letters and the holy books from one of the teachers there [i.e., in the village of Vazheozerskaia], a certain scribe. As the child learned Holy Scripture as quickly as one already taught, his teacher began to marvel at his quick learning and success and said to himself, "Indeed, he has been given knowledge of books from God, and not from my teaching." All this was according to the divine dispensation, for "every best gift and every perfect gift is from above, coming down" from thee, "the Father of lights" [James 1:17]. Indeed, the blessed one would pray before icons of the Savior and his most pure Mother: "Lord Jesus Christ, give knowledge to my intellect and open the eyes of my heart, and tell me hidden and secret things [cf. Ps. 50 (51):6], so that I understand things out of thy law, for I am a stranger in the earth; hide not thy commandments from me [Ps. 118 (119):18–19], but give me knowledge of everything sought in thee, as thou art blessed for the ages. Amen."

Aleksei's prayer derives from a very ancient and popular prayer, dating back to at least the fifth century, said by Byzantine monks before reading and schoolboys before studying the Greek letters. From the tenth century on, Georgian and Slavic monks used it as well, as texts recommending it before reading began to be translated and recompiled in those languages. The "eyes of the heart," the seat of the intellect, are opened in order to see spiritual realities and to correctly interpret the book at hand.

[When he turned eighteen,] the blessed one's parents wished to arrange a lawful marriage for him. But the blessed Aleksei only desired and thought of how and by what artifice he might escape from all evil lusts, and approach God. And when he heard from his mother and from others about the monastery of Kirill the wonderworker, and its fasting brethren, and the other desert monasteries where monks worked for God and saved themselves, the thought came to him to go to Kirillov Monastery to pray to the Savior and his most pure Mother, and to bow before the coffin of the wonderworker. And that which he thought he wished to turn into deeds, and went to his parents to ask their leave, by custom, and their blessing with a prayer. Having received their blessing, the godly youth left home, taking nothing with himself except for clothes and a little bread for the sake of his bodily needs. And he wept for a long time, but when he and his friends set off to Kirillov, he was filled with great rejoicing. Hurrying on his way, in a few days he and his companions reached the monastery; as they approached, they saw the church of the most pure Mother of God.

Trifon's monastic reforms followed a pattern established by Dionysios at Spaso-Kamennyi Monastery: architectural renewal, increase in brethren, and the imposition of a cenobitic rule. One of his first acts upon becoming hegumen of Kirillov was to build a great new central church or catholicon *out of stone: it is still an impressive sight today, although the monastery takes its present imposing profile from its seventeenth-century fortress walls.*

[. . .] The blessed youth hid from his friends, informing one of them that he wished to stay at Kirillov Monastery for a time and giving him a sealed letter for his parents. Waiting until the proper moment, he came to the hegumen [Trifon], and, falling before him, bowed down to the ground. The hegumen asked him, "Who are you, child, and what need do you have of us?" The youth said to the hegumen with great humility, "I have come, lord father, to your holiness, asking for your blessing and your prayer. I am called Aleksei, from the village of Vazheozerskaia, and my need is this: I beg of your holiness, father, that you receive me into this holy monastery. Yet I fear the common enemy, who entrapped our ancestor [Adam] and has caused many saints to waver. For should ever the enemy, having tempted me, abscond with me and carry me off from the truth of God, then I will resemble someone who has descended into a ditch: the ditch is called the depth of Hell and the darkness of sin. May I not be a shame to angels and men, and a laughingstock to cunning demons! And if, lord father, your holiness orders me to stay and serve the holy brethren, I will test my youth here for three years, and become a monk."

Aleksei refers to a three-year probationary period for novices, adopted by Trifon from Emperor Justinian's legislation. When Trifon was expelled in 1447/48, Aleksei apparently had to repeat his probationary "service" under Hegumen Kassian (r. 1448–70), becoming a monk after seven years.

The hegumen, looking at Aleksei with his inner eyes, saw his humility and the purity of his soul; having heard his words, which were spoken not simply but from Holy Scripture, he asked, "Child, have you studied the holy books?" The youth answered, "I have learned a little, father, as a youth, in part and carelessly." The hegumen then said, "Even this, child, will be of great help to your salvation." The hegumen accepted him, blessed him, and sent him to the treasurer for clothing, shoes, and everything else necessary. The treasurer gave the youth variegated garments, adorned with red and purple and various other colors; and the cellarer gave him a cell, which he was to share with another novice. The blessed Aleksei and his cellmate paid great heed to their service, as it is fitting to do, laboring every day with their hands. Indeed, the novices and brethren alike gave themselves over to philosophy through works. But some also cleaved to philosophy through words, cultivating study insofar as was necessary; being makers of words, they compiled various works, and left a great memory in this life. One was a certain man named Oleshka Pavlov [*sic*: Palkin], the monastery scribe. His task was to write books and to teach students letters and the art of grammar, and he was very skilled in these sciences.

Aleksei's dress vividly distinguishes him from the tonsured brethren—in later periods, novices would wear a part of the monastic habit. Apparently following an Athonite tradition, novices under Trifon performed the same "service," or manual labor, as the monastery servants; indeed, they may have been called beltsy *("laymen"), like the servants. "Philosophy through words" is a circumlocution for the language arts. As was probably the case at Byzantine monasteries that hosted schools, at Kirillov one and the same teacher would have taught both primary and secondary students.*

The hegumen [Trifon] called the blessed youth and said to him, "Child, for the love of God do me this kindness: learn the art of grammar." And he sent him to that scribe [Oleshka], who was very knowledgeable and experienced and familiar with Holy Scripture. Aleksei came to the scribe and bowed to him with great humility, saying: "I have come to you, lord, at the order of the hegumen, so that you teach me like a peasant and an ignoramus." The scribe, seeing the youth's humility and submission, accepted him with love and began to teach him, not as a student but as a blood brother, because of his great humility and obedience. The godly youth began to practice ascesis severely, laboring with his cellmate in fasts and wakefulness and prayers, and with the scribe they would often read books in common. The youth obeyed and honored his teacher in everything, never disobeying him in anything, but heeded the sweetness of his word and would not let a single word of his fall to the ground. He studied all that is excellent and learned all that is sound and was adorned with truth and innocence. Most of all, he loved the purity of the soul, in which each will see the Lord, recalling the words of the Lord: "Blessed are the pure in heart, for they shall see God" [Matt. 5:8].

In this passage, filtered through the commonplaces of hagiography, some elements of the bookishness and memorial work of secondary schooling (as well as the transcendent goal of this learning) have been preserved, but most of its content (texts read, exercises performed, etc.) has been lost.

One brother, tempted by a demon, went to the hegumen and said: "Those two novices over there who live together live wickedly, heeding the life of this world. They do God's work by means of corrupted knowledge, according to human ways of thinking. They do not truly wish to humble themselves in fear of the Lord and withdraw from the reasoning of the flesh but rather live by their own passionate wills and not by Holy Scripture. They strive for beauty and physical comfort, finding the knowledge useful for the profits of this world, and attending to the teachings that crown the body. For writings are many, but not all are divine; one cannot look with one eye at heaven, and with the other at the earth. Woe to the heart thinking dually, and to sinners walking on two paths!" But the hegumen knew that a demon was playing with him, and he called the blessed youth [Aleksei] and his cellmate to him, and conversed with them. And at evening he sent them back to their cell and said, "They are sons of God and holy persons." But he said to the steward: "Shut this slandering brother up in a cell by himself: he is suffering from the passions of which he accuses them." And the godly youth and his cellmate stayed awake all night, singing hymns of praise to the most pure Mother of God.

This screed against education, framed by a story from the Apophthegmata patrum *(Sayings of the Desert Fathers), is compiled from the letters of the Russian hesychast Nil Sorskii, who was educated at Kirillov but rejected the learning of its masters at the end of the fifteenth century. Some of the passages may, in fact, be directed against the elder Efrosin.*

AN ACADEMIC LIBRARIAN: HIEROMONK (PRIEST-MONK) AND ELDER EFROSIN, 1505

Introduction

Librarianship at Kirillov, much like in the medieval West and Byzantium, began as an effort to organize liturgical works—that is, those read in the liturgy or at the common table. In the 1480s, the learned monks of Kirillov compiled a catalogue of its liturgical books, which consisted of an inventory list followed by two different analytical registers of the miscellaneous books (*soborniki*, "collections"). The first, liturgical register systematized the liturgical texts in 43 books according to the church calendar, using indexing symbols. The second, academic register meticulously described all the individual texts—957 in total—in 24 of these miscellanies, providing titles, *incipits* (beginnings), foliation, and chapter numeration in a well-ordered format. As Nikolai Nikolskii (who published the catalogue) remarked, the Kirillov librarians' efforts "hold their ground to this day in the scholarly description of early manuscripts. . . . We are dealing not with an ordinary monastery library's cataloguer but a bibliographer exceptional for his time."[2]

Several of the books in the academic register belonged to figures linked to education: one to Oleshka Palkin and three to the Kirillov hieromonk (priest-monk) and elder Efrosin, who flourished in the last decades of the fifteenth century. Efrosin was Kirillov's most outstanding master. He had probably been a landed aristocrat before his tonsure—in one theory, Prince Ivan Dmitrievich Shemiachin (ca. 1437–?), son of Dmitrii Shemiaka, foe of Vasilii II in the Muscovite civil wars. He copied out rare and recent texts, such as Feodor Kuritsyn's *Tale of Dracula* and Sofonii of Riazan's epic *Zadonshchina*. His approach to the material of natural and human history was that of a secondary-school teacher. Editing traditional writings, he would strip them of their "spiritual sense"—that is, their allegories (doctrinal meanings), tropologies (moral meanings), and anagogies (mystical meanings)—while preserving their "literal" or informational content. He copied out other treatises devoted entirely to classroom topics such as geography and cosmology, made definitional and historical glosses to terms and texts, and compiled chronographic registers. He would comment on the state of texts and correct them, cite specific folia in a given codex or other codices containing sought-after writings, and compile their tables of contents. He was probably Kirillov's chief bibliographer, responsible for the academic register.

The following fictional text represents an analytical catalogue of Efrosin's miscellanies, which so far as we know he never compiled. It is modeled on or compiled from materials in the St. Petersburg codex RNB Kir.-Bel. 101/1178 that

---

[2] N.K. Nikol´skii, *Opisanie rukopisei Kirillo-Belozerskogo monastyria, sostavlennoe v kontse XV v.* (St. Petersburg: Sinodal´naia tipografiia, 1897), xx.

150 MONKS

contains the Kirillov catalogue, Efrosin's colophon to the Moscow manuscript GIM Uvar. 338 (894) (365), and other writings—scholarly, apocryphal, medical, and enigmatic—that he read and copied.

Text

Lord Jesus Christ, Son of God, have mercy on me, a sinner. Help me finish this book; for nothing can be without your help. Here are [among] the miscellanies of the hieromonk Efrosin at Kirillov Monastery.

I wished to capture by some artifice the rational objects [i.e., made of words] that I wrote in my books. As John Chrysostom said: O man, you have received all things from God: knowledge and mind, art and intellect, and all things on the earth have been subordinated to you. Man, may you have intellect in your head and thought of the heavenly kingdom; in your eyes, a gaze toward God, and if turned down, then to the earth, in which we will walk for a little while. If, man, you hold to these things, you will be a child of the light of day, a son of the heavenly kingdom, an inheritor of eternal joy, and a citizen of Jerusalem on high. [*Marginal note:* Concise statements such as apophthegms, since they do not set forth the nature of a thing, are not definitions. A definition is a concise statement setting forth the nature of the thing in question.] What is man? Man is, he says, a rational mortal animal, receptive of intellect and science.

*Efrosin assimilated the favorable sense of "artifice" (*khitrost'*), using it in his version of the apocryphal tale of how Solomon captured the Centaur; here I imagine him "capturing" a text in a book by means of bibliography. Furthermore, and following John Damascene's practice in the* Dialectica, *Efrosin often tried to "capture" terms with definitions, as may be seen in dozens of marginal notes and glosses in his books. The lines attributed to John Chrysostom, from an anthropological work that served as a kind of "creed" for the Kirillov scholars, do not offer a definition of man but an apophthegm (or saying). The definition of definition is John Damascene's, while that of man is Aristotle's (via Ps.-Chrysostom or the* Dialectica*).*

Here is the first artifice of German [Podolnyi], for the capture of objects [in books]. [*Marginal note:* In 7009 (i.e., 1501), German departed and lived beyond the monastery for two years, four months, and three weeks.] A given feast day is indicated by the sign: as many times each sign appears, this will be the number of objects for each feast. Here is German's second artifice. A given object is indicated by the [numeration of the] quires: read the number given in the circle, and it [i.e., the object] will be in the middle of that quire; you simply count the points [around the circle], which are the number of leaves [from the start of the quire to the object]. And here is my artifice. A given object is indicated by its name, beginning, [chapter] number, and leaves: read the beginning and number, and the number of leaves: simply find the number, or count up the leaves, and the object will be at that leaf. [*Marginal note:* A lying *fert* Θ holds nine leaves, both recto and verso, while a standing *fert* Φ holds five hundred.]

Efrosin's acquaintance German Podolnyi, who owned the codex with the library catalogue, lived at, or nearby, Kirillov from perhaps 1468 to 1509. He was doubtless a librarian, as one of the hands in the catalogue is his. Here I attribute to German the liturgical register (his "first artifice") and an unusual bibliographical epitome (his "second artifice"), which may be considered examples of stillborn library technologies; the instructions for interpreting the epitome are found in the codex with the library catalogue. Efrosin apparently devised the academic register, on the basis of his study of Byzantine bibliographical writings. His joke on the numerical values of the letters Θ *and* Φ *was current in East Slavic seminary culture for a long time (Gogol refers to it obliquely in a note to chapter 4 of* Dead Souls*).*

[*Excerpt from the analytical register of the volume called the* Pilgrim Book:]

A Discourse on Women, Good and Evil	67.	
A good woman is like eyes in a body . . .		7 leaves
The Writing of Sofonii, elder of Riazan	68.	
The *Zadonshchina* of Grand Prince . . .		7 leaves
From the *Pilgrim Book* of Hegumen Daniil	69.	
And lo, God showed me to see . . .		5 leaves
The Book Called *Pilgrim*, of Hegumen Daniil	70.	
Lo I, the unworthy hegumen Daniil . . .		57 leaves
These Are the Words of the Holy Fathers	71.	
A lazy man is worse than a sick man . . .		2 leaves
And These Are the Signs of Thunder	72.	
Thunder coming from the east means . . .		1 leaf
From the *Palaia*, the *Judgments of Solomon*	73.	
1. There was a foreign queen named . . .		1 leaf

This is a description of ff. 116–96 of Efrosin's manuscript RNB Kir.-Bel. 9/1086 (which he elsewhere calls his Pilgrim Book), *in the format of the academic register. Two texts near the beginning of the book are numbered and both sections of Daniil's* Pilgrimage *have been foliated, so the thought of Efrosin cataloguing it is not far-fetched. Efrosin probably used parts of this book, in particular Daniil's* Pilgrimage, *in his grammar teaching.*

[*Colophon:*]
I am well pleased, having finished the last line—one word in 23 lines. I wrote this in deep old age, so that those who come after may find the objects in my books. [*Marginal note:* On gray hair. If you have white or gray hair, burn up the horn of a black bull and mix it with lamp oil, and rub it in and your hair will turn black.]

Take up these books and read often that which you know. And go to those wiser than yourself to ask about the unknown. If you do not receive knowledge from the human intellect, then may God see your effort, and grant you knowledge and fulfill your desire. [*Encrypted passage:* A king said to a virgin: Give me *yours*, and I will place *mine* inside you; and in turn I will take *mine* back to myself, and give you *yours* back again. Do not think that what is said here is shameful, if you have knowledge; or learn from them who know.] I, the sinful Efrosin, finished this in 7013 [i.e., 1505], on the Feast of the Annunciation of the Holy Mother of God, March 25, a Tuesday, at the fourth hour. O Heavenly Mistress, you are the helper of all; help me, a sinner. Glory to God, and health to the master.

Efrosin's joke plays on the double meaning of "word" (slovo)—both unit of speech and discourse (on a page with 23 lines)—while his recipe for hair dye apparently derives from the Serbian medical tradition. His riddle is found, encrypted with a simple substitution cipher, in the codex with the library catalogue. Shame on you for thinking it has an indecent meaning, for its allegorical (doctrinal) meaning is the Annunciation, its tropological (moral) meaning refers to the monk at study, and its anagogical (mystical) meaning concerns the soul and the Last Judgment. His closing formula resembles that of the Igor Tale, *which some scholars consider was written in the later fifteenth century at Kirillov—perhaps even by Efrosin. If he is using the word "master" (ospodar') as monks under Trifon used gospodin, then he may be wishing health to himself, the monastery teacher. Cheers!*

Suggestions for Further Reading

Chase, Frederic H., Jr., ed. and trans. *Saint John of Damascus: Writings*. The Fathers of the Church: A New Translation, vol. 37. Washington, DC: Catholic University of America Press, 1958. The *Dialectica* of John Damascene.

Cribiore, Raffaella. *Gymnastics of the Mind: Greek Education in Hellenistic and Roman Egypt*. Princeton, NJ: Princeton University Press, 2001. On similar themes in a very different context (Greco-Roman Egypt).

Ivanova-Sullivan, Tania D. "Interpreting Medieval Literacy: Learning and Education in Slavia Orthodoxa (Bulgaria) and Byzantium in the Ninth to the Twelfth Centuries." *Medieval Education*. Edited by Ronald B. Begley and Joseph W. Koterski. New York: Fordham University Press, 2005. Discusses primary schooling and monastic reading in the Orthodox world.

Lur'e, Ia.S. *Russkie sovremenniki Vozrozhdeniia: Knigopisets Efrosin, D'iak Fedor Kuritsyn*. Leningrad: Nauka, 1988. An alternative reconstruction for those who read Russian.

The Monastic Rule of Iosif Volotsky. Translated, edited, and with a commentary by David M. Goldfrank. Revised and expanded edition. Kalamazoo, MI: Cistercian Publications, 2000. Provides a broader context for study of late fifteenth- and early sixteenth-century monasticism.

Nil Sorsky: The Authentic Writings. Translated, edited, and with a commentary by David M. Goldfrank. Kalamazoo, MI: Cistercian Publications, 2008. Provides a broader context for study of late fifteenth- and early sixteenth-century monasticism.

Romanchuk, Robert. *Byzantine Hermeneutics and Pedagogy in the Russian North: Monks and Masters at the Kirillo-Belozerskii Monastery, 1397–1501*. Toronto: University of Toronto Press, 2007. Further discussion of the themes and figures developed in this chapter.

———. "The Idea of the Heart in Byzantium and the History of the Book." *Textual Cultures: Cultural Texts*. Edited by Orietta Da Rold and Elaine Treharne. Rochester: Boydell and Brewer, 2010. On primary schooling and monastic reading in the Orthodox world.

Ševčenko, Ihor. "Gleaning 6: Oleško Palkin's Colophon in RNB, Pog. 989. Textological Concerns and Erudition of a Late Fifteenth-Century Muscovite Bookman." *Paleoslavica* 11 (2003): 255–61. A Byzantinist's perspective on Oleshka Palkin.

Worth, Dean S. *The Origins of Russian Grammar: Notes on the State of Russian Philology Before the Advent of Printed Grammars*. Columbus, OH: Slavica Publishers, 1983. On the *Eight Parts of Speech*.

∞ 14 ∞

Greeks in Seventeenth-Century Russia

Nikolaos A. Chrissidis

This contribution is based on two historical individuals, the merchant Chatzekyriakes Vourliotes (1640s[?]–after 1709) and the hierodeacon Meletios (?–1686). The composite portrait (including the dialogue scenes) is fictional, but virtually all the details are based on documentary evidence. I have used the letters of Vourliotes to various individuals, charters permitting Eastern Orthodox clerics to come for alms to Russia, gifts donated to the Monastery of St. Catherine by the tsars, the actions and testament of Meletios, and information on the educational, commercial, and political activities of Greeks who traveled to, or resided in, Russia during the second half of the seventeenth century.

Greek–Russian contacts increased exponentially after the Time of Troubles. In addition to trading, Greek merchants acted as messengers and informants. Eastern Orthodox clerics of all ranks visited Moscow in search of alms and/or of employment as teachers or editors of liturgical books. Patriarchs, in particular, repeatedly visited the tsar's court by invitation and played an important role in the internal ecclesiastical affairs and in the foreign policy initiatives of Muscovy. The events recounted in this portrait take place in the period between the 1650s and the 1680s, after the onset of the reformist policies of Patriarch Nikon of Moscow (patriarch, 1652–67).

It was a quiet night in Moscow, and the Greek hierodeacon[1] Meletios had just finished reading the Psalms and saying his evening prayers. The cell was cold and damp. Outside, the only light came from the moon's reflection on the snow. Even after so many years—over twenty-five now!—in Moscow, Meletios was still not used to the freezing Muscovite winters. Even though the Monastery of St. Nicholas (the traditional place of residence for visiting Greek and other Orthodox clerics in the Russian capital) had been repeatedly renovated and expanded, his accommodations still left a lot to be desired. Certainly, this monastery could not

---

[1] A monk ordained as deacon.

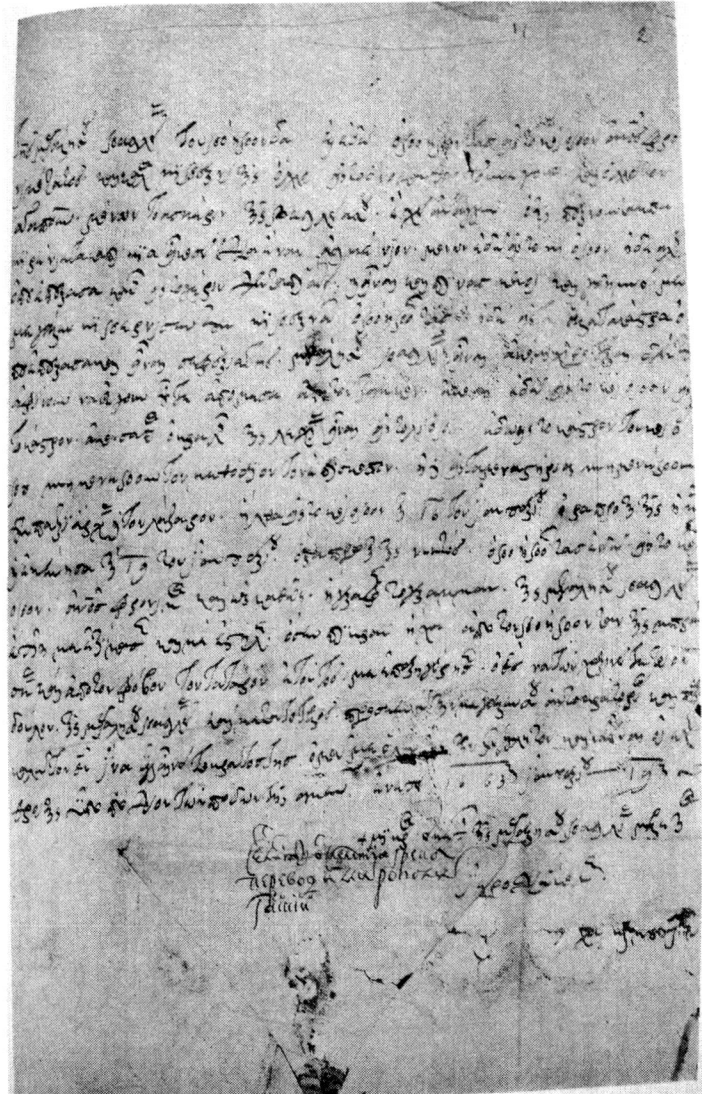

Photograph of original autograph letter by hierodeacon Meletios (?–1686) to Tsar Aleksei Mikhailovich (r. 1645–1676), dated 1663 and sent from Kiev. This is an example of the epistolary reports Meletios sent to the tsar during his travels to the Orthodox East while on assignment by the Russian government in order to shore up support for the tsar's policies towards Patriarch Nikon (patriarch 1652–67). Meletios, one of the subjects of this chapter, was a historical figure who went to Moscow in 1655 "with two main objectives: to seek alms for his monastic community . . . St. Catherine's Monastery on Mount Sinai; and to petition the tsar to take the monastery under his protection." The letter is in the holdings of the Russian State Archive of Early Acts (RGADA).

be compared with the more prestigious Moscow kremlin monastic establishments. They were far richer, owning extensive amounts of lands throughout Muscovy. And of course, the tsars had been especially munificent to them, since they were one step from his palace. Many of Meletios's colleagues in the Muscovite Printing Office lived in those monasteries and had far better accommodations. "But why complain," Meletios chastised himself. "You are a monk, and in any case, you have not fared badly!"

***

A native of the island of Chios in the Aegean Sea, Meletios indeed had not fared badly since coming to Moscow in 7163 (1655). He had first traveled there with two main objectives: to seek alms for his monastic community, the esteemed and revered St. Catherine's Monastery on Mount Sinai; and to petition the tsar to take the monastery under his protection. Ever since the Ottoman conquest, the Turks had exacted heavy taxes from all their Orthodox subjects. Churches and monasteries in the Ottoman dominions faced enormous debts due to the exactions of the local Turkish officials and of the patriarchates under whose jurisdiction they fell.[2] The situation had worsened, especially ever since the Turks had been engaged in a fierce war against the Venetians over the island of Crete.[3] The Muscovite tsars and the Moldavian and Wallachian princes were the main potential outside sources of financial support for their cash-strapped coreligionists in the Ottoman empire. Meletios knew that many Orthodox clerics (Greeks, Serbs, Bulgarians) had made the trip north to seek alms and the tsar's generosity since the time of blessed Tsar Ivan Vasilievich[4] roughly a hundred years earlier. Such visitors became so frequent by the time of Tsar Aleksei Mikhailovich[5] that the Russians had decided to institute stricter rules and regulations about the frequency of these visits. As for the tsar's protection, that would probably be more difficult to achieve: for one, the patriarch of Jerusalem would be loath to see the monastery slip from his control, and, of course, the Muscovites knew or would guess that quickly. Meletios was aware of all these problems, and he realized that he would have to play his hand deftly in arguing his case.

Meletios remembered that the first time he arrived at the Muscovite border, the governor (*voevoda*) of Putivl, the entry point into the Muscovite realm, was quite thorough in checking his credentials. He had asked to see letters of introduction from his abbot, as well as the tsar's charter granting his monastery rights to send monks

---

[2] The Ottoman Turks conquered Constantinople in 1453. Parts of the Balkans and the Eastern Mediterranean fell to the control of the Turks at different times, both before and after this date.

[3] The Turkish–Venetian war, 1645–69, ended with the Turkish conquest of the island.

[4] Reigned 1533–84 (as tsar from 1547).

[5] Reigned 1645–76.

periodically to Russia. Both the charter and Meletios's letters were authentic and had checked against the records kept in Moscow. But as both he and the governor knew, many such letters were forged by clerics in Wallachia and Moldavia, where, for a fee, a scribe could create almost any letter of introduction. While Meletios was waiting for confirmation from Moscow of his right of passage, he had seen as many as ten clerics being turned back at the border, because the clerks of the Muscovite Chancellery of Foreign Affairs did not verify their right to seek alms from the tsar. This, despite the respectful but firm protestations of the clerics who bewailed the expenses of travel and the dire economic conditions of their monasteries. Their pleas for mercy and for help in the name of Orthodoxy and of common hostility to the Turks went nowhere. Even offers to bribe the governor would not work, since he knew that he might get into trouble were he to admit foreigners (even Orthodox ones!) into the tsar's realm without proper credentials and without the right of passage. The tsar's government ran a tight ship in this regard, especially in times of war. Many a time in the past, Greek clerics had claimed that they were bringing important news of "state importance"—for example, information on Ottoman war plans, or messages from the princes of Moldavia and of Wallachia concerning foreign policy issues. The governor had then allowed them speedy passage without delay, but once the clerics had arrived in Moscow, these claims were often proven false or highly exaggerated. In addition, rumors of the plague were periodically reaching Muscovy, and the governor was particularly careful not to allow in persons from plague-stricken areas. Spies were another constant concern. Even the pleas of merchants, in whose company the clerics usually came, did not work with the governor. He knew many of these merchants personally since they often came to Muscovy to trade in precious stones, Ottoman fabrics, and wine, and he always had a cut of the products for himself. Some of the merchants even brought ransomed Muscovite prisoners of war! But orders were orders, and the governor was not willing to risk his head with something as serious as the tsar's edicts. His predecessor in the post had, after all, been executed for bribery and corruption!

Meletios had started off from Constantinople in the company of merchants himself. The trip took him through Bulgaria, Wallachia, and Moldavia, all regions of the sultan's realm. It was in Wallachia that he had to wait for at least three months. The Tatars were raiding the Polish lands, and travel was extremely dangerous. It was, of course, much better to wait in the relative comfort of a Wallachian monastery before venturing through Moldavia and into the Cossack lands. Many of Meletios's compatriots were doing the same, among them well-educated monks and bishops from throughout the Eastern Orthodox world. Even though they recognized Ottoman suzerainty, Moldavian and Wallachian princes styled themselves after the Byzantine emperors of old times and were eager to support and patronize clerics in the fashion of the emperors of years bygone.

Once the news came that the situation had stabilized, Meletios started off on the journey to the Muscovite border through the Cossack lands in the company of one of his compatriot merchants from the island of Chios, Kyriakes Vourliotes.

A skillful trader and a true benefactor of the church, especially of St. Catherine's Monastery on Mount Sinai, Kyriakes had made the pilgrimage to the Holy Land, and for this had acquired the privilege of adding the prefix "Chatzes" to his baptismal name; hence the name Chatzekyriakes by which everybody knew him. He was stationed in Lwów and had become good friends with the Polish king, and with the princes of Wallachia, whose courts he supplied with all kinds of goodies from the East. Chatzekyriakes was also heavily involved in the ecclesiastical and commercial activities of the Greek brotherhoods of Lwów and of Nizhyn, both of them important centers of the Greek merchant diaspora of the time.

Chatzekyriakes was eager to help his compatriot. Meletios brought with him several holy relics, highly prized gifts for the Muscovite tsar and patriarch. Also, he carried several pieces of cypress wood and a good number of miracle-working icons: rumor had it that the Muscovite patriarch was quite taken by icons from the East; and the Muscovites particularly appreciated cypress wood for icon making of their own. It was only fitting that the visiting Meletios bring gifts to the only independent Orthodox monarch and the head of the Russian Church, as a sign of gratitude for the expected munificence to his monastery.

Chatzekyriakes made sure to secure these items (you never knew when thieves might strike) and briefed Meletios on the habits of the Muscovites in dealing with foreigners, even coreligionists. "The Muscovites are suspicious of foreigners, and the government keeps an eye on them at all times," Chatzekyriakes told Meletios. "Be sure to do what they tell you to, once you cross the border, and do not attempt to make contact with the locals unsupervised. This will undermine your credibility in the eyes of the guards who will accompany us to Moscow. You will be given a daily money ration at the expense of the government, according to your clerical rank. Do not try to have it raised, even if you feel that it is beneath your dignity or rank. Only by order of the tsar can it be increased, and you would have to petition the tsar directly, which always takes a long time. Muscovites think that Greeks are greedy and crafty, and it won't help you to start complaining the moment you set foot in Russia." Chatzekyriakes also told Meletios that once in Moscow, he would be first taken to the Chancellery of Foreign Affairs to be registered and debriefed. "They will ask for your documents and for any news from Turkey. Be truthful and careful in your answers. The scribes there keep good records." Meletios would probably be given some more attention, Chatzekyriakes predicted. He came from such an old and prestigious monastery as St. Catherine's and he was well educated. "Once they learn that you can read and write the ancient languages Greek and Latin, they may even ask you to stay there and work translating books. The current patriarch is eager to have as many Greek books as he can." That is why, Chatzekyriakes continued, he himself was bringing so many Greek and Greco-Latin books (many of them printed in Venice, but also several in manuscript) with him this time around. A short while ago, the Russian patriarch had even sent a Russian monk all the way to Mount Athos to collect books. "Well, maybe you will be able to find a job there," Chatzekyriakes told Meletios. "How would you like to stay in Moscow for a time?"

Meletios was not surprised at this last remark. He himself had heard the rumors about the Russians asking for translators and even teachers of Greek and Latin for some time now. Apparently, the Russian patriarch had embarked on a major project of correcting the Russian liturgical books against Greek originals. Very few people knew Greek well in Russia, and even fewer were able to translate from Greek to Slavic directly. Through the grapevine, Meletios had previously heard that quite a number of Greek graduates of the colleges in Venice (in one of which Meletios himself had studied) and Rome had found their way into Moscow in search of such a job. But he had also learned that a number of them had gotten into trouble for one reason or another, had been accused of heresy, and had been sentenced to exile to the monasteries of the "sea of darkness"[6] or Siberia. Not a very enticing prospect! In any case, he would need to consult with his abbot and secure permission to leave the monastic community for a long time. "Oh well," Meletios thought, "it was far too early to know!" For the time being, he had two things in his mind: to secure alms and, if at all possible, a declaration of formal protection for his monastery from the Russian tsar. If anything else came up, he would deal with it in due course.

"Oh, and don't get offended if some Muscovite priests do not allow you to enter their churches. This happens to us, merchants and other laymen, all the time in the provinces, but even in some Moscow churches," Chatzekyriakes said suddenly, taking a sip from his water pipe. That *was* surprising for Meletios, who eagerly asked for more details. Chatzekyriakes explained that a number of Muscovite parish priests were convinced that the Greeks had lost their Orthodoxy because of the Ottoman conquest. "Russians are fiercely proud of being the only truly Orthodox people in the world. They think that they have preserved Orthodoxy pure and that is why God has granted them an independent state under the control of the tsar." The Greeks, in contrast, for their sins and their treacherous dalliances with the heretical Roman Catholics, had lost their empire. And living under the godless Turks, they naturally corrupted their Orthodoxy, according to the Muscovites. "Thus, some priests forbid not only Roman Catholics, Lutherans, and Calvinists from entering into their churches but also Greeks and other Orthodox peoples who live under Ottoman control."

Another reason for such attitudes, Chatzekyriakes continued, was probably the fact that the current efforts by Nikon, the Russian patriarch, to revise the liturgical books did not necessarily have broad support among the clergy, both high and low, either in Moscow, or in the provinces. And since the patriarch insisted that the revision was done to bring the Muscovites to conformity with the old Greek originals, there was rising resentment against the Greeks. "Be careful how you tread on this issue," Chatzekyriakes warned Meletios. "What do I know, I can just read and write a little myself, and I half understand what the old Greek texts say.

---

[6] The White Sea.

I am just a merchant, not a learned hierodeacon like you. But I hear that there is a lot of turmoil in Moscow over this issue."

Meletios asked Chatzekyriakes about another matter that was becoming increasingly important: the potential for Russian help in the liberation of the Orthodox from the Ottoman yoke. Several Greek clerics were discussing the possibility of an alliance among the Russians, the Cossacks, and the Moldavian and Wallachian princes against the Turks. Some of them, Meletios was told, had even sent letters urging the Russian tsar to claim the throne of the illustrious Byzantine emperors and free the Orthodox from Turkish tyranny. Rumors were going around that such plans had been vetted for some time now. "Do you know, Chatzekyriakes, the prophecy that the Greeks will be liberated by the 'blond peoples' from the North. Do you think the Russians will be them?" Surely, now that the Cossacks had pledged allegiance to the tsar, this prospect looked even more enticing. Chatzekyriakes looked up at his compatriot in a doubtful manner. "The Russians are hard pressed in the south. The alliance with the Cossacks is still young. And don't forget the Tatars. They still control access to the Black Sea areas. The Russians have their hands full for the time being. Maybe some time in the future, but not before they are securely in control of the Cossack and Tatar lands. And not before they have dealt with their Polish and Swedish flanks." Chatzekyriakes took another sip from the water pipe and added: "Oh, and no smoking in Moscow, especially for clerics, father. The Muscovite government prohibits the trade and use of tobacco."

It took them about two weeks to reach Moscow after crossing the border. Near Kaluga, they had an unfortunate incident when thieves stole seven of their horses, which delayed their trip. They filed a report with the governor of Kaluga, who captured three of the thieves, jailed one of them, and ordered the other two to retrieve the horses. But after waiting five days, nothing came of it, and they had to continue their trip and hope that the governor would send the horses later.

From afar, Moscow looked like a big city, with the high domes of the kremlin churches glistening in the sky. As Chatzekyriakes had said, once they arrived they were taken to register with the scribes of the Chancellery of Foreign Affairs. Meletios's documents were once more checked against the records of previous visitors from his monastery. The scribes asked him about any important news from the Ottoman empire. What was the sultan up to at the time? Had there been any large movements of troops in the direction of Russia? Who was currently the patriarch on the ecumenical throne? Was it true that the Turks were bringing patriarchs up and down almost every year? What was the mood in the Cossack lands? What about the war with the Venetians? Meletios could hardly answer all these questions, but he did his best. Yes, the Turks were bringing patriarchs up and down almost every year. The Jesuits were conspiring to infiltrate the Orthodox lands and place people favorable to them on the patriarchal throne. The Turks were hard pressed by the Venetian resistance on Crete. There had been no signs of a plague in the last two years.

Once debriefed, Meletios was assigned a cell in the St. Nicholas Monastery.

That was over thirty years ago, and he still occupied the same cell! Meletios smiled, thinking to himself how many things had come to pass since then. His first six months in Moscow were spent in long monastic rituals and masses, from morning to night. Even though Meletios was used to monastic life, nothing had prepared him for his encounter with Muscovite devotional practices. These people had legs of iron! They could stand for six hours in a row in freezing cold churches, praying and chanting and skipping not one page from their books. And they expected their visitors, Meletios among them, to do the same. Meletios could not remember ever standing for such a long time in his life. Although the St. Nicholas Monastery followed the Greek typikon,[7] and celebration of the mass was not as long, woe to him if he ever visited another of the monasteries of the capital. By the end of the first week, he knew he was in for a lot of standing. Chatzekyriakes was right, these people are indeed fiercely pious, Meletios soon concluded.

In the meantime, he was waiting for an audience with the tsar. This was no ordinary occasion and everything was choreographed and directed in minute detail. He was brought before the tsar, held on both sides by boyars. He was not allowed to approach very close before the tsar nodded to him. Meletios was told to kneel and have his head touch the ground. He duly did this, then presented a series of documents: a letter of introduction, with the full title of the tsar written in golden letters; a petition for financial help; a petition from the Sinai monastic brotherhood to the tsar to take the monastery under his protection; a list of the gifts Meletios brought with him; and finally, a number of letters of absolution of sins (indulgences) for the tsar and his family signed by the patriarch of Jerusalem. Meletios handed them to a boyar, who then passed them over to a scribe. The scribe had already prepared a Russian translation of the documents and read out loud the letter of introduction and the list of gifts. The tsar then thanked Meletios for the gifts and the letters of absolution and asked for the father's blessing. All in all, the audience lasted not more than ten minutes.

His audience with Patriarch Nikon lasted far longer. The patriarch was especially pleased with the gifts Meletios brought him, chief among them relics and two woodcuts: one depicting the Monastery of St. Catherine, and another with images of the Holy Sepulcher in Jerusalem. Nikon was especially taken by that last one!

Over food cooked "in the Greek manner," Nikon inquired about the affairs of all Greek Orthodox Churches and about the Holy Land, in particular. Were the French trying hard to wrest control of the Holy Sepulcher from the Greeks? What were the Turks doing about it? Who had the keys to the churches in the Holy Places? When Meletios brought up the matter of placing the monastery under the tsar's protection, Nikon was evasive. This was a matter of particular importance, a very serious one, and he could not do anything about it without the tsar's approval.

---

[7] Here, *typikon* refers to rules on the order and content of services in the liturgical year.

Nikon became increasingly interested in Meletios's educational background and his knowledge of the theology of the Eucharist. When he found out that Meletios could read Greek and Latin, he was especially pleased. "You know, blessed father," Nikon said, "I may be a Russian, but my faith is Greek." Nikon stressed that the Russians had first learnt their faith from the Greeks, and that the Greeks could still teach the Russians a lot. Would Meletios consider staying for a time in Moscow to help with the revision and translation of the liturgical books?

By the time this invitation was thrown on the table, Meletios had been in Moscow over six months. He had been treated well. Although many ordinary Russian priests in Moscow, and even a number of high-ranking clerics in the kremlin, had treated him suspiciously (Chatzekyriakes was right about that!), many others welcomed him. He had secured at least one of his objectives: the tsar had offered the monastery five hundred rubles for the eternal commemoration of the Romanov family by the monks, and renewed the charter of passage for alms for the future. His efforts on the second objective, the tsar's protection, were less successful. The tsar had little time for such a matter in the middle of a war against Poland. The patriarch, on the other hand, would not move without the tsar's approval in a matter that touched on not only ecclesiastical relations but foreign policy as well. After all, Meletios realized after a certain point, the last thing Nikon wanted to do was alienate the patriarch of Jerusalem: the Russian patriarch would still need the support of the other Orthodox patriarchates in his revision program. Conferring formal tsarist protection on St. Catherine's could certainly wait.

***

Meletios made sure to light another candle. It was dark in the cell, and he needed much more light to be able to write. He was about to start writing his will. He had accepted Nikon's invitation to stay in Moscow. He had written to his abbot on Mount Sinai and secured his permission to do so. At first, Moscow seemed far too much of a provincial backwater to a graduate of a Venetian college. Most Muscovite clergymen, even those in high-ranking places, were unschooled in philosophy or theology and certainly had no knowledge of Greek and Latin. Oftentimes, Meletios longed for the intellectual stimulation of a theological debate or a philosophical discussion. But once he started as a low-ranking scribe in the Printing Office, things started looking up. With time he rose through the ranks to become an editor and corrector. He learnt Russian himself, and he also taught Greek and Latin to some of his colleagues, and even to some of the young scions of important boyar families. He instructed members of the patriarchal clergy in the art of Greek chanting. He wrote reports on the rituals of Greek monastic communities and of the other Orthodox patriarchates at the request of Nikon. He composed theological tracts on the issue of transubstantiation; he even had heated discussions on this topic with some Ukrainian and Belarusian colleagues of his in the Printing Office. He acted as a carrier of important correspondence between Tsar Aleksei and the

Eastern patriarchs, once the tsar decided to have Nikon removed from office. He was present in the great church councils, which ratified Nikon's revisions but also deposed him. Meletios managed to survive Nikon's fall, because, as a conduit of contact with the Eastern patriarchs, he had served the tsar well.

Since he had no family, and he was getting paid quite well, Meletios had saved a lot of money five years into his stay in Moscow. All these years, he made sure to keep in contact with Chatzekyriakes. He even invested money in Chatzekyriakes's trade activities, and now, over thirty years after he first set foot in Moscow, Meletios had almost two thousand rubles in his possession. Admittedly, he had gotten into trouble occasionally because of some of those deals. For example, when Chatzekyriakes procured for him five hundred letters of absolution signed by the abbot of St. Catherine's, Meletios was severely reprimanded by the patriarch of Jerusalem for helping the Sinai abbot infringe on the prerogatives of the Jerusalem see. But Meletios managed to weather all difficulties. He was, after all, needed for his services; and he had friends in high places.

Here he was now. He felt old and infirm, and he had started thinking about what to do with the money he had accumulated. Some years ago, Chatzekyriakes had suggested donating a large part to St. Catherine's monastery. That was a good idea, and Meletios could thus secure eternal prayers for his soul. After all, it was St. Catherine's that embraced him after his return from his studies in Italy. He might as well do something for them. But Meletios also had something else in mind, a pet project of his own, if you will. Why not use the remaining amount to fund the establishment of a school, a college like the one in which he had studied in Venice? The Russians certainly needed it, and Meletios himself had witnessed that need firsthand. He sounded out Patriarch Ioakim[8] on this issue and the patriarch had clearly expressed interest in it. Meletios could thus be remembered in Moscow as a patron of the arts as well.

Meletios started writing the will: "I, humble Meletios, servant of God, hierodeacon of the Monastery of St. Catherine's, in the year 7194 (1686) . . ."

Suggestions for Further Reading

Alexandropoulou, Olga. *Ho Dionysios Iverites kai to ergo tou "Istoria tēs Rōsias."* Herakleion: Vikelaia Dēmotikē Vivliothēkē, 1994 (in Greek). A study of the life and writings of Dionysios Iverites, one of the major Greek players in the affair of Patriarch Nikon. Good for understanding the life, career opportunities, and activities of Greek clerics in Russian service in the seventeenth century.

Fonkich, Boris L'vovich. "Meletii Grek." *Rossiia i khristianskii Vostok* 1 (Moscow, 1997): 159–78, for the fullest reconstruction of Meletios's life. Includes publication of his testament in both Greek and Russian versions.

———. "Russia and the Christian East from the Sixteenth to the First Quarter of the Eighteenth Century." *Modern Greek Studies Yearbook* 7 (1991): 439–61. An overview of cultural contacts.

---

[8] Patriarch between 1676 and 1690.

Iorga, Nicolae. *Byzantium after Byzantium.* Translated by Laura Treptow. Portland: Center for Romanian Studies, 2000. A classic survey of the ecclesiastical, cultural, and political history of Orthodox Southeastern Europe, with emphasis on the Moldavian and Wallachian lands.

Isaievych, Iaroslav D. "Greek Culture in the Ukraine: 1550–1650." *Modern Greek Studies Yearbook* 6 (1990): 97–122. A consideration of Greek cultural activities in the Polish-Lithuanian lands with particular emphasis on the Greek brotherhoods.

Kapterev, Nikolai F. *Kharakter otnoshenii Rossii k pravoslavnomu vostoku v XVI–XVII stoletiiakh.* 2d ed. Sergiev Posad, 1914. The standard (if biased against the Greeks) monograph on Russia's relations with the Orthodox East in the sixteenth and seventeenth centuries.

Kraft, Ekkehard. *Moskaus griechisches Jahrhundert: Russisch-Griechische Beziehungen und metabyzantinischer Einfluss 1619–1694.* Stuttgart: Franz Steiner Verlag, 1995. An overview of Russo-Greek contacts in the seventeenth century based primarily on secondary literature.

Longworth, Philip. *Alexis: Tsar of All the Russias.* New York: Franklin Watts, 1984. A study of the reign of Tsar Aleksei.

Papastratou, Ntorē. *Ho Sinaitēs Chatzēkyriakēs ek Chōras Vourla. Grammata, xylographies 1688–1709.* Athens, 1981 (in Greek). A study of the merchant Chatzekyriakes Vourliotes, whose extensive commercial and personal relations extended over much of Poland-Lithuania, the Ottoman empire, and Russia in the second half of the seventeenth century. Includes publication of his personal letters and images of woodcuts whose production he facilitated at the request of St. Catherine's Monastery.

Scheliha, Wolfram von. *Russland und die orthodoxe Universalkirche in der Patriarchatsperiode 1589–1721.* Wiesbaden: Harrassowitz, 2004. An overview of Russian contacts with the Orthodox Churches after the creation of the Russian patriarchate.

Stoianovich, Traian. "The Conquering Balkan Orthodox Merchant." *Journal of Economic History* 20, no. 2 (June 1960): 234–313. Also published in Traian Stoianovich, *Between East and West: The Balkan and Mediterranean Worlds.* New Rochelle: Aristide D. Caratzas, 1992. Vol. 2: *Economies and Societies. Traders, Towns and Households,* 1–77. An overview of commercial activities of Orthodox merchants in the Balkans and Eastern Europe (including Russia).

15

Akakii Balandin of Novgorod-Volotovo and Solovki Monasteries (1526–95)

David M. Goldfrank

This sketch is taken from primary sources. The places, historical events, leading ecclesiastics, church fathers, Russian cleric-writers, and their works mentioned herein are all genuine. The names, except where indicated, are fictional but taken from records of monasteries. For example, in 1553, a certain "elder Akakii" had, as issue from the Solovki (Solovetskii) storerooms, "two cassocks, two tunics, boots, covers, trousers, leggings, a pair of mittens, socks," while one "Kassian" was a council elder in 1593, and another monastery priest in 1597. Vassian Gusilov was the scribe of a Psalter held by the Iosifov-Volokolamskii Monastery library in 1545; the late sixteenth-century Iev Balandin owned a hymnal (stikhiry) *later belonging to that monastery. My especial thanks to Jennifer Spock for sources and ideas concerning the Solovki Monastery and to Hugh M. Olmsted for his perceptive comments. What is specific to the Solovki comes from its Rule and records. Other aspects of the monastic experience described here are grounded in the collectivity of surviving rules and other documents from a variety of Russian cloisters. Novgorod, Pskov, Kazan, Narva, Solovki Monastery, and the Otnia Hermitage all had the significance that their roles here indicate. The modest suburban Novgorod Volotovo Monastery, with inspiring frescos painted in the 1370s by Feofan the Greek, was as likely a place as any for our imagined Akakii to commence his life as a monk. Tsar Ivan IV (r. 1533–84) and his government did act as depicted here, for he inflicted a series of butcheries against the population, from the highest ranking to the lowliest, especially during the Oprichnina years, from 1565 to 1572.*

It is the summer of 1573 in the gatehouse of Solovki Monastery. The council elder (*sobornyi starets*) Kassian Gusilov is about to start questioning Akakii Balandin. Clothed in monastic garb, Akakii has journeyed all the way from Novgorod—six hundred miles—on horse, foot, and boat and has inquired about joining the brother-

A sixteenth-century icon of the founders of the Solovki Monastery, the saints Zosima and Savvatii. The twenty-two miniatures around the border tell the story of the founding of the monastery—first how two monks, Savvatii and German, traveled to the island of Solovkii to follow an ascetic life, then how after Savvatii's death in 1435, German traveled to find another man to carry on the tradition, that man being Zosima, who laid the foundation of the monastery. Although Savvatii and Zosima never met, they are inextricably entwined in Russian Orthodox tradition. Akakii Balandin, the subject of this chapter, is a composite character who undertakes a spiritual, intellectual, and physical journey from the Novgorod-Volotovo Monastery to the Solovki Monastery in the second half of the sixteenth century.

hood. In the ad hoc capacity of what might be termed today the admissions officer for applicants without patronage, Kassian has cleared several dozen new brothers over the past ten years. He has seen a variety of combinations of age, health, class background, geographic origin, skills, prior experiences, psychological makeup, and expectations from monasticism and from Solovki. At first glance, the newcomer, robust and about forty-five or fifty years in age, will be a boon for the abbey; that is, so long as his character matches his appearance.

From the initial gate inspection, regularly conducted to prevent strong drinks and other forbidden items from entering the cloister precincts, Kassian already knows a thing or two about Akakii. In his traveling sack are some biscuit and dried fruits, spare clothing, boots, and carpenter's tools. In addition, most carefully wrapped in leather for protection from the elements, are three manuscript books: a *Chasoslov* (book of prayers for various times of the day), a *Lestvitsa* (John Climacus's *Ladder of Divine Ascent* with some standard glosses), and a personal *sbornik* or miscellany. Kassian is ready to assume that the first two signify the candidate's spiritual development from a devout layman accustomed to regular prayer to a serious monk, concerned with combating temptations as they arise and ready to advise others when appropriate. The absence of a Psalter may mean that he has already memorized it. Taking stock of Akakii's muscular hands, visible health, and self-control, as well as his reading material, Kassian surmises correctly that this hearty fellow is a literate, disciplined artisan, trained from youth, who had close ties with model clergy while he was still a layman.

Kassian will want to examine the miscellany as well, for it will reveal the candidate's tastes and inclinations, and it may contain some new works. Solovki bookmen are eager to have an up-to-date library and stay abreast of literary life in the leading Russian cities and cloisters further south. Kassian and his comrades will not be disappointed, as the miscellany includes some recent sermons, admonitions, epistles, and a saint's life written by Novgorod's and Pskov's best writers and spiritual guides, but he will have to await the proper moment to inquire into this manuscript.

The books also represent part of Akakii's personal capital, which he will formally donate to the monastery, if the elders and hegumen accept him. He could enter without a cash or material donation, since his skills and vitality assure that he can build his own cell and contribute far more to the central treasury than the cost of his food, clothing, expected old-age care, and modest yet guaranteed commemorative prayers after he dies. But books were among the most valuable items commoners could give to a monastery, and hegumens normally allowed brethren lifetime possession of this technically "common" property, which they donated. Solovki, in fact, did not even adhere to the fiction of common property over such items, which entitled the former owner to a year of special memorial litanies per ruble of value. Akakii in turn will be able easily to borrow books from other monks, since he has several of his own to lend and a skill to share.

As for icons—no cell could be without at least one modeled on the celebrated

Vladimir Bogomater (Virgin) for private devotions—some had their own icon rows. Daring dissidents in Novgorod, as well as the occasional visiting Protestant from abroad, might assert that Russians worshiped idols, but Akakii believed what he had been taught, when he once asked for an explanation. Icons are reminders, through which supplications go straight to the addressee, and this is what makes them holy objects, effecting numerous healings and cures. The Icon of the Sign or Praying Virgin had rescued Novgorod from attack in the deep past, and the tender Vladimir Bogomater, holding the infant Christ, had likewise protected Moscow. Prayers at icons were sometimes answered, and when they were not, who was he to question God, the unknowable?

Akakii had taken several favorite icons when he had set out from Novgorod but sold them along the way to cover his traveling expenses and keep his cash reserve. Procuring new ones, however, would hardly be a problem, since, as Kassian surmised, Akakii was an excellent tradesman—to wit, a carpenter skilled in making boards from logs, in roofing, and even in joining. If admitted, he would have no trouble convincing one of Solovki's professional artists to paint several icons in return for expert carpentry work. That was the least of his worries. His first need was to convince Kassian to make a favorable recommendation to the hegumen and the co-governing council elders for admission into the brotherhood.

Kassian also assumed correctly that Akakii had some money concealed in his clothes. He would be foolish not to have done so, since even at Solovki, someone might steal all his belongings, and he might require cash if he could not join the brotherhood. Everybody knew that the rules of obedience and common property had limits, and if strictly enforced everywhere on every monk would ruin most cloisters. "A monk with possessions is no monk," went the saying, but almost everyone took that to mean a huge stash of coin. Monastic Rules were guides toward salvation, not rigid manuals to be followed to the letter. Even saints were not perfect.

Entering the room where Kassian was waiting, Akakii had been praying and thinking at the same time. A man of deep faith who always kept his promises to God, he remained confident of divine succor, despite several great disappointments and tragedies earlier in his life. With seven years' experience in Novgorod's suburban Volotovo Dormition cloister behind him, he figured that his mastery of monastic etiquette and his proper balance of practical skills and nonattachment would work in his favor. But he might have to make a persuasive explanation of his breaking his initial vow of obedience and leaving Volotovo.

"Lord Jesus Christ, Son of God, have mercy upon me, a sinner," he muttered to himself, as Kassian commenced their conversation: "Lord, save Thy people," followed by "Wherein lies thy matter, Brother?"

"By the grace of God, and with the prayers of His Most Pure Mother, I wish to enter the dwelling of the wonderworkers Zosima and Savvatii and submit to the authority of the superior and the elders—as the Lord so wills through them, so shall I be."

Kassian soon dispensed with all but the most basic formalities and began to question the supplicant: "How camest thou to be a monk?" and Akakii calmly recounted his story.

"Pray for me, my reverend lord, a sinner. My father, may the Lord have mercy on his soul, was a competent and sober but barely literate carpenter. He heeded my mother, may the Lord have mercy on her soul, and sent us to deacon Foma, may the Lord have mercy on his soul, to teach us to read. The literate tradesmen always fared better—in work and at court—and she craved to hear the psalms, gospels, and prayers at home. I loved reading these divine words and wanted to become a deacon or priest myself, but the Lord commands obedience, and my father trained me as a carpenter. When I was seventeen, he arranged my marriage with the virtuous Marfa, a girl my age from a silversmith's family. The Lord blessed us with two healthy sons right away, though later only one more child, a daughter, survived. Working with my father until he died, may the Lord save him, I supplied several monasteries with planks and roofing boards. That is how I met the saintly elder Gelasii of Volotovo, who now rests with the Lord.

"For my sins, blessed father, the Lord afflicted me in my fortieth summer, and I almost destroyed my own soul. My wife, may she be saved, died in childbirth along with the baby, and, like Job, I questioned God's judgment before, by His infinite grace, I came to my senses. In my despair and negligence, I did not cry out to the Lord. But I eventually took counsel with the blessed Gelasii. 'Grieve not,' he said. 'but thank the Savior for taking Marfa in a state of virtue, with no unconfessed sin. If thou followest the commandments, thou willst see her again with the Lord. Ill luck and good fortune are twins that occur together. Remember that the same year our Orthodox tsar's armies captured Kazan, the plague captured Pskov.' With Gelasii's prayers and the intercession of God's Most Pure Mother, reason returned to me, but I was at sea like the children whom St. Nicholas rescued and knew not what to do.

"The saintly Gelasii, honorable father, reminded me of the Lord's two paths for salvation of us sinners. I could remarry to avoid carnal transgression or renounce the earthly for the heavenly—but only if I could detach myself from the happy but transient life I had known. I wavered, but I wished not to know a strange woman nor in any way succumb to lust. During meals at the Volotovo refectory, where the reverend brethren bade me dine, whenever I worked for them, I listened attentively to the lives of the God-bearing saints, both the ancient and our new Russian wonderworkers. I believed that monastic discipline was best for my soul and the Orthodox Christian community but did not wish to abandon my young daughter, whom the Lord had entrusted to me. My own sons could not care for her. I had trained them as carpenters, but work had become scarcer in Novgorod. One was in Narva, building houses for our merchants and soldiers. The other was with our Orthodox tsar's army in Livland and Lithuania making siege engines. Then, by the grace of God, my sister and her husband, a silversmith trained by my mother's father, agreed to take the girl as their own, for the Lord had taken away their children in the plague—may He save all of them.

"Still, oh, reverend elder, I feared for my attachment to my family, my friends, my trade, and the nature of my flesh. Would I not some day want to marry again? Would I miss the festive banquets with my brother tradesmen? Could I really renounce all and follow Him? I saw many who were monks in garb only and not at all in deed. I wondered if they would ever repent and if the Lord would shower his mercy on their former weakness. I knew that the angelic life was both lighter and heavier—lighter because of constant enclosure, instruction, and supervision; heavier because one big slip after tonsure and vows might doom my soul.

"The saintly Gelasii, may the Lord save us all through his prayers, gave me the *Divine Ladder* to read. 'Let the Holy Spirit instruct you with the great John's wisdom. When you finish, you will know if the Lord wants you to wear the black garb.'

"And so, most reverend lord, I opened my heart to the wondrous words of the *Ladder*. And there I saw my own struggle for renunciation, confidence, obedience to the commandments, and pure prayer. The second baptism into the angelic brotherhood warmed my soul, and I told the saintly Gelasii that I would submit myself to him and the hegumen so long as we lived. He warned me that this would not be easy. I would have to relinquish carpentry and any visits to the city until I had mastered desires and self-will, and he could not tell me how long that would take. I agreed, took leave of my family and friends, and the hegumen gave me the 'second baptism' and changed my name from Anton to the ancient soldier-martyr Akakii—may I be worthy of his name."

At this point the bell sounded for Vespers, and Kassian bade Akakii join them in the Solovki Church of the Transfiguration. There Kassian and some of the other council elders observed how Akakii stood reverently, chanted by memory in a fine low tone, and afterwards, at the substantial supper in the refectory, blessed the food, ate decorously, and listened attentively to the sacred lection. By now Kassian was ready to recommend Akakii's admission but wished to hear more of his story so as to advise the hegumen and council brothers how to receive Akakii and what work to counsel the rouser to assign the newcomer. So after the Compline service, when the monks dispersed to their cells for prayer, study, or handicrafts, Akakii went with Kassian to his stone cell, where he lived by himself and read or copied books when he was not at services or attending to monastery business.

They both bowed to the big Bogomater icon in the cell. Kassian fired his stove, and Akakii resumed his story. "The blessed Gelasii told the hegumen to give me a rundown wooden cell but would not let me refurbish it. Rather, he took away my tools and assigned me work in the bakery, kitchen, garden, and caring for the aged. He had me live with him for six months to observe his daily routine and train me. Sometimes he had me chant psalms while he prayed. As a frequent partaker of meals at monasteries, I was ready for the change in diet, with more stringent fasts and abstinence from meat, but as a tradesman, I was accustomed to heavy sleep after a long day's work. It took me a few months to get accustomed to rising in midnight for Vigils, but I soon learned to rouse myself when the clapper sounded.

I adhered to the cell rule he gave me after I moved into my own cell, but when I was not making prostrations or chanting prayers, I practiced writing by copying the psalms on birchbark. I thus learned them by heart. Sometimes I stood all night reciting them.

"When I asked Gelasii if I should try to follow the most humble and self-denying of the monks in the *Ladder*, he said that John taught differently for different monks, that I was already too old to try to follow Isaac [the Syrian], Symeon [the New Theologian], Gregory [the Sinaite], and the other great masters of stillness, who had spent their younger years training their bodies in abstinence. I, rather, should follow my proper royal road to salvation and do everything in measure, in keeping with my abilities and strength. He later gave me some paper to start a miscellany with my favorite passages from the Psalter and the *Ladder*. As I mastered the cell rule and acquired detachment, Gelasii told me to concentrate on combating pride. When I saw another monk falling short of his vows, to say to myself that I may be as sinful as he. He also procured for me other books of the holy fathers."

"Which ones didst thou choose to copy for thyself?" asked Kassian.

"Ephraim on the terrible judgment, Chrysostom on repentance, Nil Sinai on the eight evil thoughts, and several sermons of the Great Basil. They contain in brief what I thought I most needed to know, honorable father. I also had to copy my own *Chasoslov*, because when our Orthodox tsar and sanctified metropolitan set up the archbishopric of Kazan, they requisitioned service books from all the Novgorod monasteries."

Akakii saw that Kassian was listening intently and started to speak more freely. "After twelve months, the saintly Gelasii allowed me to resume carpentry, though for another year he questioned me daily about my thoughts. I set myself a personal rule that for every hour I spent working, I would spend another reading and praying. I worked both inside Volotovo and at other monasteries or churches. That is how I got to know the most wise Zinovii of Otnia Hermitage, may God preserve him to teach faith, justice, and salvation to Novgorod. The sexton had just saved from fire the relics of Archbishop Iona, may he pray for us, and they were building a new shrine for them. I was asked to do some of the woodwork and stayed at Otnia for several weeks. People often came to Zinovii for explanations of Holy Scripture.

"Zinovii was generous with words and used the alms they gave him to buy paper, pay his copyists, and donate to the poor. When his orations were read, I thought that God was speaking through him. He favored me and allowed me into his cell to read some of the sermons, letters, and lives, which others sent to him. I copied a few into my own miscellany."

"Whose writings?" asked Kassian.

"The priest Silvestr on home piety, Filofei [of Pskov-Eliazarov Monastery] on Divine Providence, Erazm [of Pskov] on love and charity, Markell's *Life* (Zhitie) of our Bishop Nikita, Zinovii himself on speedy justice, and a few others."

Akakii was careful not to mention Kornilii of the Pskov Monastery of the Caves, a strict, justice-seeking hegumen, since he and fifteen of his monks had been disgraced and executed by Tsar Ivan IV. In fact, after the execution, Akakii had removed the title pages of Kornilii's account of his monastery, and rewritten it as anonymous. Kassian had earlier heard about these brutal deaths and remained silent. He also already knew about Zinovii from his comforting missives to several disgraced clerics, who had been exiled to Solovki twenty years earlier, and about some of the other works Akakii mentioned, but not the latest from Novgorod.

"The saintly Gelasii also allowed me to take part in Novgorod's festive processions. We had a most glorious renovation of the shrine of St. Mikhail Klopskii at our Trinity Monastery, and I helped the carpenters finish the new tsar's throne for our cathedral, the House of Holy Wisdom." Akakii did not tell Kassian about his possibly heretical doubt at that time that God might grant such sobriety and such skill to the German master carpenters who directed the project and still condemn them to hellfire for incorrect beliefs. Akakii had not even told this to Gelasii but just said over and over again to himself, "We believe; we do not question what is above us."

Akakii continued: "At that time, for our sins, God's wrath visited Novgorod again—too horrible to recount. Slander abounded, and they tortured and killed, crying treason but really looking for hidden silver. My brother-in-law the silversmith and my sister and daughter fled, and I know not if they survive. So many people died that they burned rotting corpses in the big kilns. With bastinados they took all the monastery treasures. They hauled away Archbishop Pitirim in misery and sent us a new bishop who disgraced the hegumens and priests. Then they took most monastery horses and able-bodied servants into the Orthodox tsar's army and sent them to Moscow. The plague came back, and they burned and buried more dead and dying without prayers.

"I was in great despair again, honorable father. Both the blessed Gelasii and our hegumen died from strain and grief. Volotovo was in disorder. They sent us a new hegumen, a virtuous man but an unskilled shepherd. I remained despondent, thought of the great Anthony in the desert, turned to work, but it did not help. In my cell I imagined those human demons in black beating the blessed Gelasii, may God forgive his few sins. Whenever I went to the city, I cried. I finally visited Zinovii. They said that the Orthodox tsar honored him for preaching against the godless heretics and so spared Otnia. Himself shaken by these events, Zinovii reminded me that many holy monks in despair sought solitude. I built a cell away from Volotovo and lived there half a year but had little training in solitary stillness and remained despondent. I visited Zinovii again, and he suggested that I make a pilgrimage to the tombs of the wonderworkers Zosima and Savvatii at Solovki. Thinking I might never return, I took my books, small icons, best tools, gave the rest of my goods to the monastery, arranged for commemoration prayers for my parents, family, and my elder, the saintly Gelasii—may the Lord deliver them from eternal torments—and set off.

"On my way, honorable father, I encountered Solovki elders and brothers sent on assignments or returning, and they told me of your life here. One elder, Ignatii, who supervised the salt works, said that the wonderworkers Zosima and Savvatii still watch over the cloister, the islands, and the shore, and that they perform many healings. The sea is full of fish, and many here are monks in deed as well as garb. 'Can one live in a cell alone at the cloister?' I asked him? 'Some do,' he replied. This was what I desired: to partake in community services, to work, and to have privacy for reading, handicrafts, and my personal devotions. So now I trust in God, his Most Pure Mother, the wonderworkers Zosima and Savvatii, and beg the reverend hegumen, elders, and brothers to take me in and let me purchase or build a cell."

And so it came to pass that Akakii joined the Solovki brotherhood in 1573. With five rubles of his money, which covered five years of special memorial prayers for the former owner, he bought a rundown wooden cell right outside the walls of the cloister. He also gave three rubles for further commemorative prayers for his parents, family, and Gelasii, as he had done at Volotovo. The hegumen Varlaam assigned one of the older stone-working elders, the devout Dosifei, who worked in the kitchens, to be Akakii's personal elder and showed confidence in the newcomer by giving him the aged hieromonk (monk-priest) Irinarkh as confessor. The more energetic confessors were reserved for younger, newer, or more troubled monks.

Akakii immediately fit in at Solovki, as he quickly repaired his cell and enthusiastically attended the church services. The treasury supplied him with an all-important icon of the Virgin, basic household goods, candles, and firewood. With his unique experience working with German master-carpenters in Novgorod, he was given a variety of tasks in the monastery, such as repairing the hegumen's chair in the main church and the best refectory benches and making furniture for the leading elders' cells. He was also assigned to inspect the fortifications and wharves of the islands and on shore, where the monastery had salt works and other properties.

In one dramatic incident, he and several coworkers rowed furiously back to Solovki from a nearby island, where a fisherman had taken ill, and they feared he might die without confession. Solovki monks, following the written *Life* of the founder Savvatii, placed great emphasis on that final confession.

Akakii's work often kept him away from the cloister during the main liturgy, so his cell devotions were of special importance. He sometimes followed the standard "scete rule," with its individualized substitute for divine services, as well as hundreds of required prostrations and personal chanting of psalms and liturgical prayers or frequent repeating: "Lord Jesus Christ, Son of God, have mercy upon me." Other artisan monks, not to say most lay brothers, were also excellent workers but less vigilant in their devotions.

Akakii had observed life in Iuriev, the biggest cloister in or near Novgorod, and knew something of the large monastery and its services, regular festivities, and infrequent general assemblies. Still, nothing prepared him for Solovki with its three hundred monks and two hundred attached laymen, who also attended the liturgies when they could, dined in the refectory, and after they died were commemorated along with the departed monks. Observing the rouser assign work in the morning after "It is worthy" closed the Matins service, Akakii thought of Novgorod's foremen when the city walls were under repair. The upgraded Solovki bells also reminded him of Novgorod, as did the busy market that functioned on the island. But what struck him most were the work habits. Unlike Novgorod, in the city or outside the great suburban monasteries, there were no beggars. Everyone worked. And monks could do special tasks for "alms," hoping to acquire the required fifty rubles for special eternal remembrances. He sometimes thought how different life was in Solovki from that of the ancient desert fathers in the *Patericon*, but then remembered the words, "Not the place but good will toward God brings salvation."

Neither Akakii nor anyone else at the time realized that the Solovki monks had to have, as a rule, an adaptive immunity to infection, because, not understanding the nature of disease, the authorities assigned kitchen work to the sick as well as the older monks.

Akakii also enjoyed Solovki's special ceremonies. The kvas-toast to the Orthodox tsar and his family was a joyous occasion, even if an undertone, never spoken but written on faces, was anger over the murder of Metropolitan Filipp during the Oprichnina. Akakii had seen Filipp in Novgorod, when, as hegumen of Solovki, he had taken part in the celebrations for the victory over Kazan and in the public prayers for deliverance from the plague, but Akakii knew better than to mention his name, lest a slanderer denounce him. Some festive days were like a holy carnival, with the hegumen, priests, deacons, and council elders themselves preparing both dry and fried pirogi for the monastic and lay brethren. In 1581, when a new hegumen was installed, Akakii took part in the glorious welcoming of his boat as it arrived, the procession to the main church, and the cellarer and treasurer taking the new hegumen by the arms, leading him to his place of honor, placing the pastoral robes upon him, and handing him his staff.

Solovki was not free from disturbances, but Akakii did not expect perfection and kept to his own affairs. If some monks drank too much wine, that was for the council elders to reproach. If a fight broke out, he simply walked away, as he sometimes did as a layman. If lay workers under his supervision became angry, he turned the other cheek and prayed, remembering the commandment to love one's enemies and that "nothing benefits laymen as does the good order and reverence of monks." He did not even intervene when several elders became angry with the hegumen Varlaam over a penance he imposed and started to beat him in front of other monks. Unable to find the right words, Akakii said nothing and simply prayed for reconciliation.

Akakii had time at Solovki, especially in the winter, to read more of the church fathers. But he would never leave a valuable book in his wooden cell, which might catch fire, and always returned it to the stone repository. After several years there he was able to borrow a copy of Isaac the Syrian's discourses. These most sublime of the entire spiritual corpus frightened Akakii a bit, as he now feared that he had been following the wrong path, despite Gelasii's counsel back at Volotovo. Hearing of this, Akakii's confessor, Irinarkh, sent his charge to the librarian, Nikita, who said not to worry: "Isaac was the greatest teacher of prayer and visions of

God, but did not expect most monks to attain them, only to strive for total abstinence, nonattachment, charity to all, nonrendering of evil, and great faith. Most Solovki monks work, attend liturgy, keep their vows and their cell rules, and are saved. Those who wish to practice stillness as solitaries do so with the hegumen's permission, and their prayers sustain us all, but this is not incumbent on all who wear the black robe." Akakii was relieved and regained his confidence in the Solovki lifestyle.

The early 1580s, during the Swedish war, and another war in the 1590s provided some danger and excitement, with the fear of a maritime attack on Solovki itself. During the first of these conflicts, Akakii was busy inspecting defenses. But by 1590, he was sixty-four, no longer so active; engaged, rather, in lighter woodwork and praying more; never totally satisfied that he had acquired detachment but confident that he had sufficiently vanquished pride. His eyes were failing him, so he no longer read, but he did do his share of kitchen tasks. In 1587, as a safety measure against fire, the council brothers had given Akakii a younger monk as a cellmate, and the latter took over most of their daily chores. He also sometimes chanted psalms as Akakii prayed, just as Akakii had for Gelasii at Volotovo.

Akakii declined slowly. At times he imagined he had died and was passing through the aerial tollbooths with demons questioning him about various sins and trying to pull him into the hellfire, and with angels defending him as he sought to join the ranks of the saved. This was exactly as the Last Judgment frescos depicted the immediate fate of souls after death on the west walls of churches, and he had seen this countless times as he exited services. He also imagined meeting his parents, his wife, and his children who had died as infants, all of them now "where the saints dwell." And he wondered from time to time what had happened to his children. (In fact, the son attached to the army had been killed in action by a misfire of a Russian cannon. The other remained in Narva when the Swedes took it over in 1581 and became a Lutheran, the original religion of his local wife. Akakii's daughter somehow survived the turmoil of the 1570s and the early 1580s; by the early 1590s, she was married to a Pskovian merchant and the mother of three children—but Akakii knew none of this, and his daughter knew nothing of him.)

The end came happily, as if scripted. Having made ample confession and offers of reconciliation to any he might have offended in his lifetime, Akakii passed away peacefully in 1595 with a priest at his side. Our carpenter-monk left forty-five rubles worth of money and goods to the monastery. This was a little less than the required fifty, but the council elders, appreciative of his services and model life, added his name to the ledger of individual eternal commemorations "so long as the monastery stands."

Suggestions for Further Reading

The Domostroi: Rules for Russian Households in the Time of Troubles. Edited and translated by Carolyn Johnston Pouncy. Ithaca, NY: Cornell University Press, 1994. See especially chapter 12 for the ideal home piety at the time.

Goldfrank, David M. "Recentering Nil Sorskii: The Evidence from the Sources." *Russian Review* 66 (2007): 359–76.

The Monastic Rule of Iosif Volotsky. Translated, edited, and with a commentary by David M. Goldfrank. Revised and expanded edition. Kalamazoo, MI: Cistercian Publications, 2000. My chief source for attitudes among the leadership of economically active cloisters such as Solovki, which were interested in attracting laymen as well as monks to the community.

Nil Sorsky: The Authentic Writings. Translated, edited, and with a commentary by David M. Goldfrank. Kalamazoo, MI: Cistercian Publications, 2008. The best of the native spiritual guide literature read by Russian monks. See especially the translation of the Scete Rule (listed as *Nil Sorsky/Nil Polev Codex*), representing a typical individual cell rule for a monk, and the subchapter "Centrality of Sources," for the translated classical monastic literature available to Russians of this time.

Robson, Roy R. *Solovki: The Story of Russia Told through Its Most Remarkable Islands.* New Haven: Yale University Press, 2004, chaps. 1–6.

Spock, Jennifer Baylee. "The Solovki Monastery, 1460–1645: Piety and Patronage in the Early Modern Russian North." Ph.D. diss., Yale University, 1999. Indispensable source of information for the traditions of the Solovki Monastery.

The most important of the translated literature available to Russian monks of the time is *St. John Climacus: The Ladder of Divine Ascent*, translated by Archimandrite Lazarus Moore, introduction by Muriel Heppel (London: Faber and Faber; New York: Harper, 1959) or *The Ladder of Divine Ascent*, translated and edited by C. Luibheid and N. Russell, introduction by Kallistos Ware (New York: Paulist, 1982).

Similarly useful is Saint Basil, *Ascetical Works*, translated by Sr. Mary Monica Wagner (Washington, DC: Catholic University Press, 1950) and/or *The Ascetic Works of Saint Basil*, translation and introduction by W.K.L. Clarke (London: Macmillan, 1925). Within them, see Basil's (or Pseudo-Basil's) "Ascetical Discourse" and his "Longer Rules" and "Shorter Rules."

VI

Provincial Landowners, Artisans, and Townspeople

～16～

Provincial Landowners as Litigants

Nancy S. Kollmann

This fictional account draws on the transcripts of many criminal trials from seventeenth-century Russia, presenting typical litigant behavior, judicial procedure, and norms. Many such cases are located in Moscow in the Russian State Archive of Ancient Acts in the collections of provincial governors' offices (prikaznye izby); few if any criminal trial transcripts are published. Such cases demonstrate that the local judicial system followed the procedural and sanctioning norms of the Law Code (Ulozhenie) of 1649. They also showcase the role of bureaucrats (d'iaki, pod'iachie) in providing judicial expertise, the court system's reliance on locals to staff its ranks, and the wide judicial autonomy that governors enjoyed.

Aleksei Petrovich Shubalov peered across the field where his peasants and men were sowing grain. It was springtime, and planting season was in full swing. In the near distance he saw what he knew was trouble—his neighbor Vasilii Vasilievich Glebov was riding into the field on his nag, accompanied by his two sons Fedor and Ivan, nicknamed Tretiak, followed by a motley crowd of his peasants and servants. Not again, he thought to himself. For years the two neighbors had disputed over this field. It was land that had been in the Shubalov family for decades, since Aleksei's grandfather had moved into this frontier territory in the decades after the Polish invasion. Living on this land grant from the tsar (pomest'e), his grandfather, his father, and now he and his sons had loyally served from the town of Arzamas, proud to be provincial gentry in the tsar's service. Why his neighbor claimed it, he couldn't see. Glebov said he had deeds for it, but Aleksei knew for sure they were forgeries. The two neighbors had stewed over this field for years, and Glebov seemed to have settled on harassing tactics—arguing, shouting, and occasionally raiding and trampling the crops, trying to drive him off the land. Now he was at it again.

Shubalov called his sons Petr and Andrei to join him, and his wife ran out of their farmhouse as well. Snatching up sticks and anything to brandish, calling the

Engraving of a scene of oath taking by kissing a cross based on a drawing by Adam Olearius, who was a member of an Embassy from Frederick III, Duke of Holstein, to the court of Tsar Mikhail Fedorovich in 1634. Standard practice before giving testimony in a judicial proceeding was to kiss a cross or icon to affirm that the testimony was true. In the present chapter, both of the land owners (Aleksei Petrovich Shubalov and Vasilii Vasilievich Glebov) involved in the dispute over the death of one of Glebov's peasants in a melee, are asked by the judge to kiss the cross and confirm that their version of events is the true one.

household servants, they all ran into the field to meet the menacing crowd head on. "Get off my land," Shubalov shouted, to be met by curses from Glebov and sneers from his sons. Tretiak Glebov shouted at Shubalov's wife, calling her a whore and a prostitute. Aleksei Shubalov returned with similar juicy invective, each heaping dishonor upon dishonor. All that was the way these quarrels had gone before. But this time, the confrontation got out of hand. Glebov's men beat Shubalov's serfs with cudgels and sticks; Shubalov's men defended themselves, and wholesale pandemonium set in. Everyone was fighting, punching, yelling in pain. Then a bloodcurdling cry stopped everyone cold.

"He's dead," someone shouted—the crowd gathered round a body prostrate in the trampled grain. One of Glebov's peasants was lying inert, blood running from his skull. Next to him peasants held Shubalov's elder son, Petr, by the arms. "He did it," Glebov's people shouted, "he beat him with that heavy stick. He cracked his skull." Aleksei Shubalov stared dumbly at the dead man and his son, then lifted his eyes to the elder Glebov. "See what your marauding has done! Your man is dead, just because of your stubbornness, your greed!" "Hah," Glebov yelled. "Your son has killed my man—we'll see him hang!"

"Run." He turned to one of his sons. "Go tell the governor in Arzamas. There's a dead body here and a man to arrest." And off rode Tretiak Glebov to town, while the Shubalov family closed ranks and trudged back home to contemplate what to do next.

***

Petr Alekseevich Shubalov had never been in trouble with the law before. He sat numbly in the simple main room of their house while his father stormed about, cursing Glebov. Meanwhile, in Arzamas, Tretiak Glebov walked into the governor's office and handed him a petition. Since Tretiak himself wasn't literate, on his way through town he had sought out the parish priest from St. Nicholas Church to write up the petition for him. It was addressed all in the proper style, humbly approaching the tsar in personal terms—"To Tsar and Grand Sovereign Aleksei Mikhailovich of All Rus . . . Your slave Ivashko Vasiliev *syn* Glebov beseeches you." In formulaic prose, it established the date of the offense—June 15, 1676—and described the fight and death of his father's peasant. It then asked the tsar to investigate the dead body and to arrest the perpetrator, Petr Alekseevich Shubalov. The petition ended with a typical flourish: "Tsar! Have mercy on us! Grant us your favor and your justice." Glebov asked the priest to sign and date it in his stead and paid him for his efforts.

The governor, Prince Ivan Petrovich Zaslavskii, snatched the petition from Glebov's hand with disdain and impatience. A man with the high rank of *stol'nik*, he had previously served around the country in the army and regional administration. He'd been serving as governor in Arzamas for only a few months of his year-long term. But he had already heard about the enmity between the families, and he considered the Glebovs a bad bunch. He felt sorry for the Shubalov boy; clearly the fisticuffs had got out of hand. But a dead body was a dead body. He called over his secretary. Although he, Zaslavskii, was literate, all the record keeping for his office was done by this secretary, Vasilii Volotskii, who knew the law and the bureaucratic formulae for documents.

Volotskii quickly wrote up two orders in the governor's name, while Zaslavskii called over the bailiff Artemii Lukin and the captain of the musketeers Erofei Meshcherinov. To Lukin he handed the orders to investigate the dead body. His instructions were detailed: on the way to Shubalov's estate, Lukin was to stop at the nearest village and recruit several men as witnesses to the viewing. They were to be of all social classes, and they were to accompany him to where the corpse lay in the field. There the bailiff was to describe the wounds on the body. Volotskii handed to the captain of the musketeers another document that instructed him to take a few men to Shubalov's house and arrest the accused man. Meshcherinov groaned; he knew this would be a hard detail. Sometimes these standoffs were tense, when suspects holed up in their homes and threatened a shootout with the governor's men. Or the accused men, sometimes even the whole household and serfs, ran away in advance, leaving no one on the estate to arrest. He remembered once having to arrest the mother of an accused man and bringing her to the court for interrogation, since her son had fled. Her testimony, however, turned out to be very helpful in that case, he remembered. On another occasion, the wife of the house came running out and hit him with a cooking pot when he came to arrest her husband. It took three separate visits and the sending of a special investigator from Moscow before they hauled that one into custody. Well, he doubted the Shubalovs would do any of this. It was usually the local rogues with a reputation for troublemaking that resisted arrest.

So the next day, June 16, the bailiff and the musketeer set out on their tasks. When Lukin got close to the field, he stopped at the village of Troitskoe and rounded up some locals as witnesses. The area was settled by Tatars and more recent Russian peasant immigrants; the two groups seemed to live amicably side by side, and Lukin found both Tatars and Russians agreeing to come as witnesses. He made sure he had several of the village elders in the group. With about fifteen men, he set off to view the body and write up his report. In the document he repeated the governor's order to him, named the witnesses, and then described the condition of the body: "here we found a dead body, a man, lying in the field. He had no wounds on him except on his head, where there was a gash and much blood running out. The witnesses testified that this was V.V. Glebov's peasant, Dmitrii Aidarov." Lukin had the witnesses sign the document if they were literate or delegate another man to sign in their place. The Tatars in the group signed with their marks. All was in order. Lukin dismissed them and turned for home, leaving Aidarov's family to take the body away.

Meanwhile, Meshcherinov the musketeer was feeling relieved. He'd approached Aleksei Shubalov's homestead and hailed the family. Aleksei emerged. "You want my son, do you? . . . Look, we will come with you together; I have a suit for the governor myself." And so, without a fuss, they set off to Arzamas, the son terrified at what awaited him and the father fuming.

When they reached the governor's office, Aleksei Shubalov stormed in and stuck a petition in Zaslavskii's face. He was an old hand at litigation, literate enough to know how to write a petition on his own. His petition was a countersuit to Glebov, complaining that Glebov and his men had assaulted his land, trampled his crops, insulted his wife, and injured his peasants. He demanded a trial but specified only the dishonor, since he knew that assault and injury were on both sides. The governor handed the petition to Volotskii to be recorded and immediately took some decisions about how to pursue these two cases.

Since it was a homicide case, it merited the more complex "inquisitory" procedure in which the judge, who was the governor, took the lead in collecting evidence and even used torture to ferret out information. In simpler cases the "accusatory" form could be used, wherein the plaintiff and defendant presented their witnesses and gave testimony. But Zaslavskii liked aspects of the accusatory form; and when he ran a trial, he used some of both forms. He didn't care much for judicial niceties, and the Felony Chancellery in Moscow to which he reported on this sort of case usually didn't either. So he set a date three days hence—Friday, June 19—for the dishonor dispute between the Glebovs and the Shubalovs.

Then he ordered some of the litigants—the two fathers, Aleksei Shubalov and V.V. Glebov and the son Tretiak Glebov—to be put on surety bond, a classic part of the accusatory format. A group of neighbors and kin would be asked to guarantee that each litigant would show up for the trial date set by the governor. According to the bond, if the man failed to show, he would forfeit the trial and his sureties would face a large fine, specified in the document. This sort of collective responsibility generally worked well. So that same day the governor dispatched an undersecretary from his office, accompanied by a gunner, to Glebov's village Troitskoe and Shubalov's village Azeev to assemble clients, friends, and neighbors as guarantors. They returned two days later with documents signed by dozens of sureties, and Zaslavskii ordered these copied into the official trial transcript. Since the younger Shubalov was charged with homicide, he shouldn't be out on bond. The governor had to throw him in the ramshackle jail that was attached to the governor's office to await the judicial process.

At the same time, the governor set in motion a classic part of the inquisitory procedure, the community interrogation. Whereas in an accusatory case, he would rely on the litigants to present witnesses, here he sought them out himself. He sent his bailiff Artemii Lukin with an undersecretary to the countryside to interview as many inhabitants of the villages around the site of the crime as possible; sometimes such inquiries included hundreds of people. Sometimes the community swore they heard nothing, saw nothing, knew nothing. They closed ranks to protect their own or from fear of retaliation from their landlord. Sometimes they bubbled over with details; he expected the latter would be the case in this sort of scandalous episode.

As Lukin set off, the governor called him back to remind him of the law—the 1669 Criminal Articles reaffirmed that evidence from community interrogations was supposed to focus only on eyewitness evidence, not on hearsay and character reference. Zaslavskii agreed with what the law implied, that people could use these interrogations to blacken the character of neighbors. But taking local reputation into account was an old tradition in Muscovite legal practice, and he thought it served a good purpose. He would not exclude a little bit of character reference if it came back in the reports, he ruminated. You want to hear who the village troublemakers are and how people feel about their neighbors; you want your judgment to accord with community sentiment, or you'd end up with a village angry and divided and hostile to you and the tsar you represented. No, he thought, as a judge he wanted to know about reputation, and he'd take it into account in his judgment, that's for sure.

It took Lukin the bailiff and the undersecretary several days to complete the community interrogation. They came back on June 24 with testimony from fifty-five villagers. Thirty said they had only heard secondhand reports from people who had actually been at the incident, but many of them effused about what good people the Shubalovs were, and how the Glebovs were always making trouble. Twenty-five witnesses to the event were willing to talk about what they had actually seen themselves. Fifteen men and women testified that they had heard Tretiak Glebov shouting insults at Shubalov's wife; five people said they had heard the Shubalovs shouting insults as well; two said they heard no insults. Only three admitted that they saw the blow that killed Aidarov, and they all said that it was in a completely chaotic fight. Shubalov's people expressed regret that young Petr Shubalov was caught up in so serious an affair, since the landlord was a good one. The Glebov peasants were noticeably reticent in praise for their master. All this was more or less what Zaslavskii had expected.

Meanwhile, while his men were out interviewing and collecting sureties, Zaslavskii decided that he owed it to this family to move ahead with the case promptly. Sometimes he dragged his feet with trials. He had no particular incentive to do the judicial part of his job. His primary responsibility was to collect taxes, customs, and other fees and get them safely to Moscow. He also was kept busy with maintaining the defenses and troops of this town not so far from the southern frontier. But the Shubalovs were upstanding local gentry, and they often visited him on holy days and festivals, bringing gifts to him, his wife, and family. So, on June 17, two days after the killing, he set to the investigation.

It was with some reluctance that Zaslavskii ordered up torture for Petr Shubalov. Torture was required procedure to establish premeditation and conspiracy, but he hated to put the young man through it. First, he simply interrogated him, as an undersecretary recorded the testimony verbatim. He asked Shubalov whether he had planned this killing in advance, whether he had co-conspirators. Petr Shubalov denied any of that and explained about the brawl that Glebov's men had started. Then Zaslavskii interrogated Shubalov a second time, this time in the presence of the executioner with his knout. Faced with this threat of torture, Shubalov testified in the same way. Finally the governor ordered torture, but only a very modest five blows of the knout. Again Shubalov gave the same story. Zaslavskii let it rest at that, hoping that the testimony of the community would accord with this.

Two days later, the trial date of Friday, June 19, arrived. Since he had not yet received the report of the community inquest, he could not move forward on that suit, so for the dishonor trial, he followed the familiar accusatory trial procedure. He asked each side for witnesses, and each produced a long list of their peasants and men. Then he asked whether either side would accept the opponent's list of witnesses, since they had the right to reject. Predictably, each side rejected all the proposed witnesses of the other on the grounds that the witnesses were partisan to their landlord's side. He then asked the litigants themselves. Predictably, Shubalov asserted that Glebov had insulted his wife, and Tretiak denied it. So Zaslavskii was down to the word of the two men. The only source of evidence that would resolve this was an ordeal of God—that is, taking an oath on penalty of eternal damnation. So he ordered the men to undergo the ritual of oath taking, or kissing of the cross. This involved summoning them three times over the next few weeks to the cross, giving them ample chance to deliberate over their truthfulness in this affair.

A week later, on Friday, June 26, the litigants, Zaslavskii, and his undersecretary and the priest of the St. Nicholas Church assembled to the first summons. The two litigants were presented the cross by the priest. Neither one agreed to kiss the cross then, nor to desist or change their testimony, so they were dismissed. Zaslavskii was a patient man. He knew this process usually worked if you give it time. A week after that, July 3, the second summons was announced. Again, they were presented the cross, and again each side stood firm. A week later, July 10, they assembled again. This time, they came bearing a document.

Zaslavskii knew just what to expect. In the intervening week, Glebov and Shubalov had reached an agreement. Both reluctant to risk eternal damnation, they had settled out of court rather than face actually taking the oath on the third summons. It always worked that way. In all his years in provincial administration, Zaslavskii had never seen a case where the litigants actually kissed the cross. In their settlement Tretiak did not admit saying the insults, but his agreement to pay all the court fees *and* the dishonor fee for Shubalov's wife amounted to tacit admission. It turned out to be a boon for Shubalov, because his annual cash allotment of twenty-five rubles was at the high end of provincial gentry entitlements. Since his wife's dishonor fee was calculated at twice his annual cash allotment, Glebov was out the princely sum of fifty rubles, plus another ruble in court fees. It was risky business to insult women, since everyone protected the honor of their families assiduously and women's honor was the most important part.

It remained for the judge to wrap up the case. As soon as the dishonor case was settled, he ordered Volotskii to make excerpts of the relevant laws. Volotskii had mastered the laws—the 1649 Law Code, the 1669 Newly Issued Criminal Articles and the individual decrees that were always coming from Moscow—so well that he acted as a de facto lawyer for many litigants, advising them on procedure and on strategies of presentation to best meet the standards of the law. Volotskii went right to chapter 22 of the 1649 Law Code, on the death penalty, and selected out article 71, regarding the death of a peasant by a person of gentry rank, done with no prior intent. For good measure he tossed in article 78 of the 1669 Articles that essentially repeated the same norm. He copied out a clean trial transcript. The following week, on Thursday July 16, a month after the death of the peasant Dmitrii Aidarov, when Zaslavskii could find some time in the midst of other affairs, he summoned the interested parties to his office. With the elder Shubalov and the Glebov men attending, Zaslavskii convened a hearing for Petr Shubalov, who was looking thin and gaunt from his long stay in the jail. Volotskii read aloud the full trial report, painstakingly reading all the surety bonds and the summary of the community interrogation (he attached to the report the actual transcripts of all fifty-five respondents), and the excerpts from the Law Codes and Criminal Articles. Then he awaited the judge's decision.

In announcing his decision, Zaslavskii noted that the defendant had testified with and without torture that he had killed Aidarov in a huge spontaneous brawl, and that he had had no intent to do so. The community inquiry confirmed this, the judge noted. So, since there had been no prior intent, the 1649 Law Code and 1669 Articles were clear. They mandated that unintentional homicide of a peasant by a gentryman did not merit either the death penalty or corporal punishment, but only that the perpetrator should compensate the landlord of the dead peasant with a wealthy peasant family from his own holdings. So this is what Zaslavskii ordered the younger Shubalov to do. He instructed Volotskii to add this resolution to his clean copy and to collect court fees from the Shubalovs. But he suspected that this case was not over yet.

As Zaslavskii had guessed they would, the litigants that very afternoon approached him with a document—another out-of-court settlement. Shubalov would forgive the fifty rubles dishonor payment Glebov owed him, and Glebov would make no demands for a peasant in compensation. "And from this point on we are not litigants in this case with each other, ever again," their petition concluded. Zaslavskii accepted their settlement and instructed Volotskii to add this to the official record. Zaslavskii set to the task of signing the final copy of the trial transcript. He put his name at the bottom, and then on the reverse at all the joints between pieces of paper in the scroll he signed his name with a flourish, so that the Moscow office would know that the document was authentic. He then addressed the document to the Felony Chancellery, to its Conciliar Secretary Vasilii Kiprianov, summoned one of the gentrymen assigned to his office, and sent him off to Moscow with it. He kept a copy locally and declared the case closed.

Suggestions for Further Reading

Brown, Peter B. "Neither Fish nor Fowl: Administrative Legality in Mid- and Late-Seventeenth-Century Russia," *Jahrbücher für Geschichte Osteuropas* 50 (2002): 1–21.
Davies, Brian L. "The Politics of Give and Take: *Kormlenie* as Service Remuneration and Generalized Exchange, 1488–1726." In *Culture and Identity in Muscovy, 1359–1584.* Edited by Ann M. Kleimola and Gail Lenhoff. Moscow: ITZ-Garant, 1997, 39–67.
———. *State Power and Community in Early Modern Russia: The Case of Kozlov, 1635–1649.* Basingstoke: Palgrave Macmillan, 2004, chaps. 4–5.
Dewey, H.W. "Old Muscovite Concepts of Injured Honor (*Beschestie*)." *Slavic Review* 27, no. 4 (1968): 594–603. Dewey, often in collaboration with Ann M. Kleimola, wrote eloquently on Muscovite law. See the bibliography of his works in *Russian History* 7, pts. 1–2 (1980).
Kivelson, Valerie. *Autocracy in the Provinces: The Muscovite Gentry and Political Culture in the Seventeenth Century.* Stanford, CA: Stanford University Press, 1996.
Kollmann, Nancy S. *By Honor Bound: State and Society in Early Modern Russia.* Ithaca, NY: Cornell University Press, 1999.
———. "The Extremes of Patriarchy: Spousal Abuse and Murder in Early Modern Russia." *Russian History* 25, nos. 1–2 (1998): 133–40.
———. "Judicial Autonomy in the Criminal Law: Beloozero and Arzamas." In *Die Geschichte Russlands im 16. und 17. Jahrhundert aus der Perspektive seiner Regionen.* Edited by Andreas Kappeler. Wiesbaden: Harrassowitz Verlag, 2004, 252–68.
———. "Murder in the Hoover Archives." *Harvard Ukrainian Studies* 19 (1995): 324–34.
The Muscovite Law Code [Ulozhenie] of 1649. Part 1: Text and Translation. Edited and Translated by Richard Hellie. Irvine, CA: Charles Shlacks, Jr., 1988. An excellent starting point for legal procedure.

∞ 17 ∞

Artisans
The Prokofiev Family

J.T. Kotilaine

The dramatis personae of this story are fictional, albeit representative, examples of successful artisans in a larger Russian town. They belong to a legally defined social stratum of townsmen (posadskie liudi) who lived in a special settlement (posad), often referred to as the commercial district, typically right next to the frequently fortified town center. They enjoyed a de jure (albeit not universally enforced) monopoly of most kinds of commercial activities, whether handicrafts or trade. There was a considerable amount of social mobility among townsmen, especially ones that were able to trade with foreign merchants and thus enjoyed improved access to capital. Russia did not have a domestic capital market to speak of in the seventeenth century. Often considerable fortunes were made (and not infrequently lost) within short periods of time.

The available sources on the activities of townsmen consist of cadaster books—censuses—which typically provide the exact place of residence and profession of all urban taxpayers and in some cases offer details on the scale of their operations. Customs books shed light on the nature and extent of their commercial activities. All Russian towns had customs offices that recorded the trade flows passing through. A wide range of sources—contracts, IOUs, petitions, business correspondence, and so forth—exist on the activities of foreign merchants. Comparable Dutch, English, and German sources offer additional information.

Vasia first saw the light of day on March 15, 1656, in the modest wooden dwelling of Afanasii and Tamara on Ilia Street in the Yaroslavl townsmen's settlement. The boy was promptly baptized; and a combination of gratitude, hope, and not a little apprehension filled the hearts of his young parents as they received the infant from the hands of the local parish priest. A devastating plague epidemic had swept through the city only four years earlier and the Grim Reaper had not spared Afanasii Prokofiev's home. The family's two young children, along with the grandfather Prokofii, had died. Afanasii was left tending a struggling leather-dressing workshop as outsiders shunned the infested city.

As challenging as life on the upper Volga may have seemed to Afanasii, Russia as a country had entered a new era of political stability. The all-powerful Tsar Aleksei was now in his eleventh year on the throne, and the new Romanov dynasty appeared secure. Yet not all was well with Muscovy. The government had two years earlier plunged itself into a costly and ambitious war against its historical archenemy in the West, the Catholic Polish-Lithuanian Commonwealth. Aleksei, who was eager to live up to his putative role as the sovereign of the three Russias,[1] had not succeeded in fully subduing his adversary in spite of conquering all of the Grand Duchy of Lithuania. A new drain on the country's strained resources was about to be created with an attack on Sweden's Baltic provinces, where success would be no less qualified.

The effects of the tsar's costly ambitions were also felt in Yaroslavl. A *den'ga* or an *altyn*[2] was no longer what they had been. To finance his seemingly endless campaigns, Aleksei had revamped the country's currency. New mints were set up to produce copper coin, which ordinary Russians were now expected to accept as equal in value to the old silver coins. Afanasii was not to be fooled, however. Silver was still needed, not least because the government's tax collectors came with growing frequency demanding their share of the local artisans' dwindling revenues—in silver!

Vasia had a reasonably happy childhood, even as dark clouds covered his father's horizon. His playmates grew in number, as two girls and three boys were added to an elder sister, Vera. The little yard between the family home and Afanasii's workshop became a scene for all manner of imaginary adventures. Disaster still returned with haunting regularity. Although epidemics took away two of the family's children, Vasia himself, two of his brothers, and two sisters weathered these and other calamities, grew, and even thrived. Their parents did not presume to know God's mysterious ways and were people of positive disposition, hardworking, and optimistic, even if their mother's stern brow and earnest manner often concealed this.

As soon as he learned to walk, Vasia became a frequent visitor at his father's shop. Childish curiosity slowly turned into learning as Afanasii started to tutor the boy in the craft he himself had learned from his own father. What Vasia saw was a man who haggled the best prices in his dealings with the nearby peasants and local middlemen. Not only this, he had a discerning eye and exacting criteria for quality. Even when Afanasii could afford to buy only goat hides, he carefully inspected every skin in a bundle. A bottle of vodka or mead, or some other gifts, frequently changed hands as an advantageous deal was struck and promises made to return for a similar transaction the following year.

---

[1] The Muscovite tsar styled himself as the sovereign of "three Russias": Great (Russia proper), Little (Ukraine), and White (Belarus).

[2] These were the types of coins circulating in Russia. A *den'ga* was equal to half a kopeck and an *altyn* to three kopecks.

Scene of early eighteenth-century Yaroslavl by the Dutch artist and traveler Cornelis de Bruyn, published in Amsterdam in 1711. Yaroslavl, located on the Volga River some 250 km (155 miles) to the northeast of Moscow, was an important commercial and trade center in the seventeenth and eighteenth centuries. The events of this chapter take place in Yaroslavl, where the fictional Prokofiev family manufactured leather.

Afanasii showed his son how goat and ox hides were dried and tanned, how they should be cut and presented for prospective buyers. He was a man of honesty and inculcated the same quality in his son, although the temptation to cut corners was often overwhelming. The Russian economy was sliding toward chaos, and many customers had to be turned away because they had nothing more than nearly worthless copper to offer for their purchases. For the same reason, Afanasii counted himself lucky when he managed to miss a government buyer to whom one could not say no, even though the payment was guaranteed to be in copper. At the same time, the local business elite had few qualms about capitalizing on their fellows' misery. Afanasii was a man of modest means in a city that offered a great deal of competition. Yaroslavl was a bustling commercial center, one of the largest in the country. Some eight thousand people lived here and Afanasii was one of more than twelve hundred townsmen in the settlement that had grown along the Volga. Afanasii's trade was practiced by nearly three hundred others in this town, which was the center of the country's agricultural heartland. Some of them had grown to become prosperous tradesman who were among the regular suppliers of fine *iufti* (processed ox hides)[3] to the many foreign merchants—most of them from the Netherlands and Hamburg—who passed through the city on their way to or from the northern port of Arkhangelsk, the country's leading center of foreign trade at the time.

As Vasia turned five in the spring of 1661, Afanasii suddenly struck gold. A young Dutchman calling himself Iurii Ivanov[4] called in at his shop. Vasia marveled at this strange man's unusual dress and peculiar way with the Russian language. He had seen such people only from a distance before, even though some of them owned houses in Yaroslavl and could be seen hurrying through the city's streets and markets. The father's eyes lit up, and the foreign guest was treated with the best the house had to offer.

The company Iurii claimed to represent was among the largest Dutch partnerships active in Russia, but it was experiencing some difficulty. The Dutch had had a good run in Russia during much of the Polish war. To finance the country's apparently inexhaustible appetite for Western weapons and munitions, the tsar had sold enormous quantities of grain, as well as potash, tar, and other goods to foreign merchants. Now, however, the government's reserves were exhausted, money was short, and the Russian market was disintegrating under the heavy weight of copper inflation.

Iurii proposed to pay in advance for his annual orders of quality *iufti*. The price he offered generated far less enthusiasm than the fact that Afanasii would be paid in foreign silver coin, *efimki*. Dutch money had always been a hard currency in Rus-

---

[3] *Iufti* were the most valuable type of leather available in Russia.

[4] Foreign merchants were known to Russians by their Russified names, often just a first name and a patronymic, e.g., Georg Janszoon → Iurii Ivanov. Many of them had spent extended periods in Russia. Some settled there permanently and spoke fluent Russian.

sia but never more so than now, when it promised to make the difference between destitution and financial security. Sensing an extraordinary opportunity, Afanasii hurried to accept the deal before Iurii had managed to finish his account. A small but heavy purse was emptied before the father's and the astounded son's eyes. The road to the future lay wide open.

Iurii promised to send a man within weeks to collect any surplus *iufti* Afanasii might have. There was still time to haul the last consignments of wares to Vologda and further down the Sukhona and the Dvina to the White Sea port of Arkhangelsk. The money, however, was to be spent on raw ox hides, which would be processed during the year and collected by a Dutch agent the following January. Afanasii could not believe his luck, and celebration filled the air on Ilia Street as spring was hesitantly making its way to the Muscovite heartlands.

Having recovered from the festivities, Afanasii returned to work with renewed vigor. He went around the city buying every ox hide he could lay his hands on, and he found an unexpected number of willing sellers when it became clear that payment would be made in silver. The shop was reorganized and nearly doubled in size; and Afanasii managed to get his fifteen-year-old nephew, Misha, to help. The remaining goat and other hides were taken to the basement, as the elaborate facilities for *iuft'*-making were expanded. Vasia shared his father's infectious enthusiasm and observed with great curiosity how raw ox hides were slowly turned into beautiful, fragrant red leather. The raw hides were first treated with ash in a wooden tub, something that took nearly two weeks. They then soaked for five to six days and softened for another three days. Before a month was up, the hides were tanned, planed, and fermented for another four days. To Vasia's amazement, the process was far from complete. The hides were then taken to the back of the shop to be tanned again, and not once but five times, something that took another two-and-a-half months. But even this was not the end of the story. The hides were then washed, dyed, treated with tar, and pressed and trimmed. A total of three months were required until the family could gather to admire the results of its work. Afanasii's pride was only tempered by his frustration over the fact that the pile of finished *iufti* was so far short of what had been promised, with only six months left before delivery.

Afanasii again visited his extended family and friends and found two more willing apprentices. One of Afanasii's less fortunate colleagues agreed to enter into a partnership, and a second shop thus became available for the rest of the year. More people would now be claiming their share of the profits, but costs were minimal as desperate people were struggling to find opportunities. By September, the stack of finished *iufti* had more than doubled in size. Afanasii was growing confident that the Dutch would have their order on time and, in fact, there might even be quite a lot left over.

As leaves were falling off the trees, young Vasia could note with pride that more people were paying attention to his father than before. The reaction was not invariably favorable. Evil tongues spoke of him as a lackey of the *nemtsy*,[5]

---

[5] Literally "Germans." This was a word used to refer to most West European foreigners

someone who had sold his honor for *efimki* and betrayed his own kind. In general, however, Yaroslavl was a city where foreigners were a common sight, and most people recognized them as a source of the city's prosperity. In the eyes of most Yaroslavlians, Afanasii was now a success story in the making.

After Afanasii's family, along with the rest of Orthodox Christianity, had celebrated Epiphany and life once again began to return to its routine, an agent of the Dutch company showed up with half a dozen helpers in tow. Afanasii was paid the balance for his year's work and given a slightly larger advance for the coming year. The Dutch were hoping to see Afanasii's output grow by 10 percent or even 20 percent. The bleak midwinter again gave way to joyous celebration on Ilia Street as Afanasii and his partners shared their profits and made plans.

The thriving workshop saw energetic activity as another winter gave way to spring and eventually to summer. In spite of this, Afanasii's joy was increasingly tempered with a nagging worry. The copper currency was sowing destitution all around. Many products were increasingly hard to come by. The glorious campaign in the west had turned into a rout, and the Russian forces were driven out of Lithuania. Reports of an uprising came from the capital.[6] Some leading merchants had seen their warehouses looted as people's anger and frustration burst into the open. Many feared for the worst in Yaroslavl as well.

Soon enough, disaster did indeed strike, albeit not in the way Afanasii had feared. A proclamation was read in the square stating that the government would levy yet another extraordinary tax and would purchase the year's entire output of six important commodities, among them *iufti*. The government promised to pay the going rate for the goods collected, but no one, including Afanasii, was able to believe that. The Yaroslavl *posad* saw feverish activity as people sought to dispose of their goods in time, to hide them, or to process them in a way that would allow them to escape the monopoly. Even Afanasii wavered in his commitment to honesty. He and his helpers took a couple of days to dig a large hole in the basement floor. One-third of the year's *iuft'* output found room there. Everything was wrapped in several layers of coarse linen, enveloped in timber, and covered with earth. Piles of old goat hides, barrels of various descriptions, and sundry other things were used to conceal the *iuft'* depository.

Government agents, aided with an army of inspectors, spent several weeks going through the *posad* and buying up all the *iufti*, hemp, tallow, sable furs, potash, and white ash they could find. One day, four of them showed up at Afanasii's door. Vasia hid fearfully behind his father's back watching as the government's men took out every last *iuft'* hide stored in the workshop. They even inspected the barrels in

---

at the time. For instance, the foreigners' settlement in Moscow was called the *Nemetskaia sloboda*, the "German" quarter.]

[6] This was the famous Copper Riot (*Mednyi bunt*) of July 25, 1662, which began with popular complaints about the economic crisis and ended in a bloodbath as the government suppressed it.

the basement but remained unaware of the hidden treasure underneath them. The men's leader finally pulled out a large bag of coins and paid Afanasii with a generous handful of copper. In lieu of one-half of the money that had been promised to him, however, Afanasii received a mysterious piece of paper promising that he would receive the remainder a year later.

The Christmas fast was observed with uncharacteristic rigor that winter as the family was again reminded of what life had once been like. Neither Iurii nor his men returned that winter. There were no *efimki* to be found, although the government resumed minting real silver coins. Dejected, Afanasii told his relatives to return home, as he was forced to turn his attention to his old goat hides.

Even as it remained a struggle, life slowly began to return to normal. Many of the goods that had been hoarded during the years of high inflation now returned to the market. Money was again a proper measure of value, and Afanasii could begin to rebuild his business with the expectation of reasonable stability in his life. When the Russian year ended (on August 31), the government monopoly of the six key exports was finally lifted, and Afanasii could even tentatively entertain the thought of returning to *iuft'* production.

As the family began to ready itself for another Advent season, a familiar face appeared at Afanasii's door—Iurii Ivanov! The Dutchman was apologetic for the unpredictable events of the past two years and hoped that Afanasii would understand that the special laws had made it impossible to complete previously agreed-upon deals. Now, however, the Dutch company was both able and eager to resume its operations on their former scale. Iurii again placed a purse of *efimki* on the table, proposed to revive the old arrangement, and wondered if Afanasii had anything to sell right away. The visitor was taken to the cellar, the barrels removed, and the now vintage *iufti* revealed. Iurii was overjoyed and produced another purse to make the difficulties of the previous two years vanish from memory.

Finding partners and helpers in Yaroslavl in 1662 was easy enough. The ups and downs of the past decade had produced far more losers than winners, and Afanasii's access to cash once again elevated him to borderline prosperity. Cautious after the sharp reversals of fortune he had experienced, Afanasii preferred to rely primarily on his extended family to staff his workshop.

Even as the Dutch returned year after year, the specter of uncertainty returned periodically to test the confidence of Yaroslavlians. The Russian economy had been severely weakened by the Polish war. The government's coffers were empty and even the elite merchants[7] were left looking for new opportunities beyond government contracts. By contrast, many of the Dutch and Hamburg merchants active in Russia were associated with large partnerships at home. Their broad range of business interests effectively isolated them from the vagaries of individual markets,

---

[7] Muscovy had three special corporations of privileged merchants who enjoyed exceptional rights in return for the obligation to perform government service, usually once every six years.

making many of them virtually unassailable. Not surprisingly, the Russian merchant class was growing increasingly dismayed at the situation, and rumors were soon circulating of an appeal to the tsar.

Vasia was now eleven years old and already actively helping his father in the busy workshop. He had an excellent understanding of how *iufti* were made and could easily imagine that one day he could take over the family business and join the local business elite. Little did he know that his family's life was about to be turned upside down yet again.

Great celebration broke out at the end of 1667 when it was announced that the long war in the west was finally over. Perhaps in anticipation of this return to normalcy, the Muscovite authorities had lent an unusually sympathetic ear to the merchants' petitions and passed a New Commercial Code, a major piece of legislation that significantly strengthened the rights of Russian merchants vis-à-vis their Western counterparts. The Dutch were now expected to pay higher customs duties, which had to be settled in *efimki*. Perhaps even more alarmingly from Afanasii's perspective, they were supposed to conduct their operations in officially designated border towns: Arkhangelsk, Novgorod, Pskov, or towns of the southern and western periphery. Travel to the interior was to be permitted only with special passes. Afanasii began to worry whether he would even see Iurii and his *efimki* again. By now, he was an established operator with a strong reputation, and he could probably weather any adversity more easily than five years earlier. But he was not rich, and annual operating expenses still required virtually all of his available capital.

Great was Afanasii's relief when Iurii appeared in January 1668 to pick up the year's output and make agreements for the following year. The usually jovial Dutchman was in an uncharacteristically somber mood, however. He tried to assure Afanasii that all was as it should be. Iurii's company was a large venture with friends in Moscow, and he had all the right papers to make sure that it could continue its operations without any interruption. But his answers seemed unusually evasive when Afanasii tried to question him about the hatred that Russian merchants and the government seemed to harbor for the Dutch. Afanasii's fears were confirmed when neither Iurii nor any one of his agents came at the agreed-upon time in January 1669 to pick up the results of Afanasii's efforts. The entrepreneur, who was now thirty-six years of age, began to worry that he might have to start all over again.

In April, a man calling himself Tikhon Afanasiev appeared on Ilia Street. He was a quiet, unassuming type, not much different from Afanasii in appearance or dress. Tikhon was from Vologda and brought greetings from Iurii. He apologized for the problems with fully honoring the contract but assured Afanasii that there was a reason for everything. The Dutch merchants in Russia were now regrouping with their Hamburg counterparts under the auspices of a large company. The plan, Afanasii was told, was to make sure that they could continue to operate as freely as possible. To attain this goal, they had to find new ways of conducting their business, as a whole range of barriers had been erected between Arkhangelsk and its hinterland.

Tikhon indicated that Afanasii would in the future have to deal primarily with Russian merchants, quite possibly Tikhon himself, but he would still be paid in *efimki* at the regular rate. Many Dutch merchants now preferred to rely on their Russian associates for conducting their business in the Muscovite interior, since the latter were naturally exempt from the higher duties the Muscovite authorities had started to levy.

The uncertainty that had marked the late 1660s and the first half of the 1670s was, if anything, exacerbated when Tsar Aleksei returned to his maker in 1676. He was succeeded by a son, Fedor, who was widely rumored to be feebleminded. The men who assumed the reins of power in the Moscow Kremlin were even more suspicious of foreigners than their predecessors, and the Dutchmen who had once been such a common sight on the streets of Yaroslavl were nowhere to be found. Their now invariably Russian agents returned at regular intervals, but Afanasii feared the worst. A couple of years later, the government formally ordered all foreigners out of the Russian interior, and the stakes in the confrontation between the two sides were raised a notch higher, even though the measure was soon reversed.

Afanasii, fearful of repeating past mistakes, decided to begin to diversify his clientele to make himself less dependent on Iurii's company. Vasilii entered the state of matrimony at the age of nineteen, having, to everyone's delight, developed an interest in the daughter of Afanasii's fellow leather-dresser Arkadii. The marriage gave the two men a reason to formalize a tentative plan to pool their available resources so as to turn Afanasii's workshop into a real manufactory. The building was more than doubled in size. The two partners started working there full-time, along with Vasilii and three of Afanasii's relatives.

Given the financial commitment that the new venture represented, it was crucial to make sure that the growing output could be easily sold at reasonable prices. Arkadii knew a couple of important local merchants through family connections, and two of them were willing to commit to a formal arrangement envisaging annual deliveries and mutual credit as needed. Moreover, Arkadii's son-in-law had made a couple of trips to Riga and looked likely to regularize his business dealings in Sweden. At the same time, the workshops of the capital, Moscow, seemed to have an inexhaustible demand for Yaroslavl leather.

An era of political uncertainty in Moscow ended when—after an interregnum—Aleksei Mikhailovich's son Peter became the ruler of Russia. Peter finally turned his back on the intense xenophobia of the preceding two decades. He had a great deal of interest in Western ways and he developed close relations with several members of the Dutch merchant community. Some of the more draconian measures of the New Commercial Code were quietly lifted, and Westerners were once again welcomed in the Russian interior. *Iufti* had decisively established themselves as Russia's leading export product, and a number of Western merchants now flocked to Afanasii's factory. He was an obvious supplier and operated on a larger scale than most of his competitors.

New life was blown into the old arrangement with Iurii's company, although

Iurii himself had departed to spend the twilight of his life in Amsterdam. Another partnership of Dutch and Hamburg merchants became regular customers under a similar arrangement, and Afanasii could now delight in the sight of foreigners trying to outbid one another in an effort to secure a new source of *iufti*. The 1690s became an era of prosperity for Yaroslavl and Afanasii's *iuft'* factory alike. Afanasii himself was now an old man who had outlived most of his childhood playmates, his partner, and even his wife. He withdrew from active involvement in the factory as years of hard work began to take a toll on his once-robust constitution. His thoughts turned increasingly to the afterlife and other mainly theological matters. He devoted his time to church services and pilgrimages in the region. But still, almost every morning, with a cane in his hand, he would tour the premises of the firm he had built. He watched with unconcealed delight and pride when Vasilii replaced the old family dwelling with a handsome stone building, having added the lot next door to his possessions. As he looked back on his eventful life, Afanasii Prokofiev could note with satisfaction and gratitude that he had laid the foundation for a major company. An artisan dynasty had established itself as the last Muscovite century neared its close and the confident new tsar led his troops to another momentous battle.

Suggestions for Further Reading

The existing English-language literature dealing with townsmen and trade—whether domestic or international—is quite small. The following works shed some light on aspects of the issues treated in this essay.

Bushkovitch, Paul. *Merchants of Moscow, 1580–1650*. Cambridge: Cambridge University Press, 1980.
Hellie, Richard. "The Stratification of Muscovite Society: The Townsmen." *Russian History* 5, no. 2 (1978): 119–75.
———. *The Economy and Material Culture of Russia, 1600–1725*. Chicago: University of Chicago Press, 1999.
Hittle, J. Michael. *The Service City: State and Townsmen in Russia, 1600–1800*. Cambridge, MA: Harvard University Press, 1979.
Kotilaine, J.T. "Competing Claims: The Changing Orientation of Russian Foreign Trade in the Seventeenth Century." *Kritika: Explorations in Russian and Eurasian History* 4, no. 2 (2003): 279–311.

∞ 18 ∞

A Poor Townswoman Accused of Witchcraft

Valerie Kivelson

This story is a composite tale, based closely on the records from two trials of alleged witches in the late seventeenth century. Muscovite records, predominantly generated by state administrators or churchmen and reflecting their particular interests, do not usually devote much space to describing people's domestic or emotional lives. Trial records offer a rare point of access to the lives of ordinary people and take us into the usually opaque realm of the serf- and slave-owning household. Transcripts of the testimony provided by plaintiff, accused, and witnesses allow us to hear the voices and inflections of the wide variety of people who came before the courts. Some caution is necessary in reading court transcripts, since the voices of the witnesses were recorded through the pens of court officials, who had their own formulas and agendas. Moreover, witnesses undoubtedly tailored their testimony to suit instrumental ends, such as winning a case or mitigating the harshness of a sentence. Nonetheless, these documents are invaluable for helping us understand the experiences of women like our fictional "Oksanka," who occupied a precarious position as the widow of a soldier. Bereft of her husband and his defined position in society, she lacked the fundamental necessities of survival in a world built around rank and affiliation. Without protection, connections, or financial means, a "free person" like Oksanka fell into the suspicious gray zone of masterless and rootless people. When she fell into the hands of an unscrupulous "patron," she found herself in a position where her only defense came in the form of magic.

It is important to note that most of the people accused of witchcraft in Muscovite courts were men. A sizable minority of cases, however, involve women, and the story of our fictional Oksanka draws on those models.

The original trial records are preserved in the Russian State Archive of Ancient Acts in Moscow: RGADA, f. 210, Prikaznyi stol, stlb. 46, ll. 250–57; RGADA, f. 210, Prikaznyi stol, stlb. 186, ll. 984–99. These cases are discussed more fully in Valerie Kivelson, "Coerced Confessions, or If Tituba Had Been Enslaved in Muscovy," in The New Muscovite Cultural History: A Collection in Honor of Daniel

An eighteenth-century lubok depicting Baba Yaga and a dancing old man. Baba Yaga, the archetypal witch of Slavic folklore, lives in a house that sits on chicken legs and she eats little children. Here she wears trousers and carries a wooden spoon and a broom in her belt. According to folklore she uses both to propel the mortar that she uses to fly. The caption reads: "Baba Yaga is dancing with a bald old man; they leap about, dance, and play on the bagpipes, but they know no harmony."

B. Rowland, *ed. Valerie Kivelson, Karen Petrone, Nancy Shields Kollmann, and Michael Flier (Bloomington, IN: Slavica Publishers, 2009), 171–84.*

Oksanka rubbed her chafed wrists and looked back over her shoulder, taking one last look at the office of the town governor, where she had been confined in chains for eight months while her case had dragged on. Released upon the tsar's merciful judgment and decree, she somberly trudged across the square to join her husband, Mitka, who stood waiting for her. She was free to go now, but that prospect filled her with uncertainty and dread. Where would they go? How would they support themselves? Carrying a small bundle with their worldly possessions over his shoulder, Mitka fell in step with her, and together they wound their way through the town streets. With no home to go to and no means of employment, they feared they faced an unenviable future as wanderers and vagrants, drifting from one house to the next, living off the charity of strangers.

Life had not always looked so grim. Oksanka remembered, with a brief smile, an earlier stage of her life, when she had married the first time. Twenty years old, lively and healthy, she had left the home of her father, a soldier in the tsar's foot regiment, and had become the bride of Vaska, Fedor's son. Vaska had been a soldier like her father and had served with him in the same regiment. As her husband had come to the regiment from another town, Oksanka had been fortunate in setting up her own household with her husband. She had counted herself lucky to avoid the situation that so many of her friends described, in which, as the newest daughters-in-law, they found themselves at the bottom of the pecking order in households packed with in-laws and relatives. Unburdened by mother-, father-, or sisters-in-law, Oksanka had proudly become a soldier's wife. Without complaint, she took on the responsibilities of keeping the house and taking care of her husband, so that he could be set and ready in time of war and could tend their stall in the marketplace to earn a living during peacetime. Their small house was located in the soldiers' quarter of town, on land held by the unit as a whole, and they farmed their own small kitchen plot and worked together to produce the pottery that Vaska sold on market days.

Then, the sad times had begun. Vaska, in the prime of life, had fallen ill with the black sickness and languished near death, not leaving his bed, for more than a year. Oksanka had struggled to bear the new burdens, to care for her dying husband while straining to earn a living and support them both. Mercifully, his suffering ended at last, and he departed this life on the eve of the Great Fast in the year 7149 (or 1641 by Western reckoning).

In that same year, just as she was confronting the dire straits in which her husband's death had left her, opportunity came her way. At the time, it seemed like a blessing. A prosperous townsman, Ivan, son of Petr Kirillov, invited her to come live in his house and to work as his housekeeper. Relieved at the chance to find security and protection, the widow quickly moved into the Kirillov household and took up her new responsibilities: cooking, cleaning, and endlessly drawing heavy buckets of water from the well for her washing. At first, all seemed to go well, and she adjusted easily to life in the household with Ivan and his wife. The endless trips to the well allowed her to stay in touch with her friends, the townswomen and soldiers' wives she had known before, and to keep up with the village gossip. On Sundays or market days, she often found a chance to spend time talking with acquaintances at church or in the dusty paths of the market rows.

Soon, however, things again took a turn for the worse. Ivan decided that it was time for his serving woman to remarry, and without the slightest consultation, he announced to her that she was to marry the fellow of his choice, the poor, stooped, homeless Mitka. Mitka was, like Oksanka, a free townsperson who had fallen on hard times. Ivan signed Mitka up to work for him for seven years. As part of the deal, Mitka agreed to marry Oksanka and to work with her in the Kirillov household, in return for support and shelter during those seven years and a payment of ten rubles at the completion of the term. Much older than Oksanka, Mitka might not have been her first choice, but Oksanka saw little option. Perhaps that was her mistake, for Ivan had no business forcing a free woman, a soldier's widow, to marry at his will like a serf or a slave. Hastily married, the two labored side by side in the Kirillov household for seven long years, and to their delight, they were blessed with three healthy children, two sturdy boys and an infant girl. The growing family worked hard and honestly, anticipating the day when the seven years would be over; and, with ten rubles in their purse, they could set up a household of their own.

The seven years passed in due course, but, sadly, the troubles did not end there. For when Mitka approached their master and requested his payment and his release documents, Ivan only laughed. "Slaves!" he taunted. "You have labored in my kitchen and done my bidding, and now you belong to me. You married in bondage, and your children were born in bondage, and I will never let you go."

Mitka returned to his wife and dejectedly reported the conversation. Oksanka, however, was not prepared to take such abuse. She retied her headscarf, collected the few coins that the couple had saved, and stalked off into town, determined to find the one person who could help her. It took some searching, but before too long, she had tracked down her one hope, a woman she had met several times at the well but to whom she had never dared speak: Daritsa, the wise woman and purveyor of spells.

Oksanka found the wise woman at her home, where she sat spinning flax in the still bright light of a late summer evening. The older woman stared at her with sharp, intense eyes and demanded to know her business. After listening grimly to her visitor's plaintive tale, Daritsa asked bluntly, "So what is it you want me to do for you?"

"I want my master and mistress to be kind to me and to soften their hearts toward me. They have some kind of ill will against me, and I just want them to treat me right. If they would soften their hearts and carry through on our agreement, I would even keep working for them of my own free will. But they treat us badly, not according to our station. They treat us like slaves. I am a soldier's daughter and a soldier's widow. I am a townsman's wife! Let them free my children and treat us as free people."

The witch nodded. She bent over and fumbled in a small sack that hung from her belt. With gnarled hands, she drew out a dark, withered root and a folded packet of paper. Placing the items on the table, under the full gaze of the icon of St. Nicholas that hung in the corner, the witch unwrapped the paper packet and exposed a small pile of what looked like ordinary salt. "Is that . . . ?" Oksanka began to ask, but the older woman hushed her with a dark glance. In a low, indistinct voice, she muttered a spell, or a prayer—Oksanka could not quite tell which. As much as Oksanka could make out, it sounded like this: "O St. Nicholas and Most Pure Mother of God! As this root grows in the soil, so let kindness grow in the hearts of this woman's master and mistress. As people crave for salt, so may this woman's cravings be granted. In the sea-ocean stands a rock, burning white and hot, and on that rock grows a tree. Like that tree, may this woman, slave of God, stand firm."

Turning to address her client, Baba Daritsa instructed her: "Take this salt, and sprinkle it in your master and mistress's food. Then crumble this root, and stir it in too. When they have eaten, their hearts will soften toward you and they will treat you kindly. Do as I tell you, and all will be righted." That said, she stretched out her hand and, with a nod, deftly pocketed the coins that Oksanka deposited in it.

Greatly relieved and full of hope, Oksanka ran back through the crowded market rows, past the streets full of wooden houses, to her master's compound. She rushed through the courtyard and into the kitchen, where she hastily hid the ingredients, eagerly anticipating marvelous results on the following day.

The next morning, without a word to Mitka or the children, she busied herself as usual preparing the midday meal for Ivan and his wife. Mitka and Andriushka, the other man who served the household, came in and out of the kitchen as she worked, bringing in loads of firewood for the stove and buckets of mead from the storehouse. Andriushka had sold himself into perpetual slavery with a contractual agreement with the master and did his work uncomplainingly. Oksanka bore him no ill will; there was nothing shameful in his condition. He had entered it knowingly, driven there by desperation, and he carried out his obligations honorably. But his situation had nothing in common with hers. She had been wrongfully forced and swindled into servitude by her master. Forgetting the fear of God and the tsar, he had enslaved her and her children, through his endless greed. Her anger bubbled up again, into boiling hot rage. Yet, she said nothing. The three worked in silence, passing by each other as their tasks took them across each other's paths.

When the time arrived, Oksanka served her master and mistress humbly, with downcast eyes, but she smiled to herself, thinking how well salted the food would be and with what gusto her mistress would swallow it down. The mistress was pregnant again, happily, after losing two infants in the previous two years, and so would eat with good appetite. The root had caused her more anxiety, for she feared that it might show or change the flavor of the soup, but she hoped she had ground it fine enough to pass undetected.

The meal passed without incident, but the afternoon brought rapid results, and not those that Oksanka had hoped to effect. The mistress complained suddenly of cramps and retired to her bed above the stove with loud groans and cries. Within hours the neighbor women had to be called, and the situation looked serious. In the middle of the night, the mistress miscarried, and her cries of pain redoubled, with additional cries of grief at losing the baby that she had so longed to have. The master too looked pale and ill and began to complain of pain in his stomach. Oksanka didn't feel so well herself. Worried about what she had wrought, through no intent of her own, she began to pray fervently to the Mother of God, begging her to intercede on her behalf and for the health of her mistress and master. "I meant them no harm," she prayed. "I only meant for them to treat me kindly. You are a mother, O Most Pure One. You understand how I suffered for my children, how I needed to help them."

It seemed, however, that her unceasing prayers went unanswered, and worse, they called down suspicion on her. When she saw Andriushka, the household slave, whispering in her master's ear, she grew even more alarmed. What had Andriushka observed in the kitchen that morning, as he passed back and forth with the firewood? When her master sent the slave out to summon the bailiff, her blood ran cold. Had he seen? Had he told? Did they suspect? Did they know?

***

The investigation had followed immediately after her arrest. Guards and bailiffs from the town governor's office had marched her off roughly, her hands manacled. As she had feared, Andriushka had seen her crumble the root into the pot and had informed on her. At first she had tried to deny the whole thing, but after being confronted with the instruments of torture, particularly those burning hot pincers, she had confessed everything, or almost everything. "Who taught you to practice witchcraft and whom have you taught?" her interrogators demanded repeatedly, harshly threatening her and then applying the implements to her flesh, "without mercy," as the court had ordered. Even under torture, she had managed to hide the identity of her supplier, the wise woman. If Daritsa had been identified, Oksanka knew, she would have been condemned to die a slow and painful death as a witch. She would have been buried alive with only her head exposed, languishing until she starved to death. Oksanka steeled herself and insisted against all demanding questions and painful ordeals that she had received the salt and the root from a wandering healer who had passed through town, whose name she could no longer recall. Somehow, the interrogators finally accepted her story, perhaps because, at risk of her eternal soul, she had sworn to the truth of her testimony on the Holy Gospels. But the governor had paid no attention to her explanation of her own behavior: that she had meant no harm, had indeed added the magical ingredients simply to make her master and mistress treat her kindly, and that she had never meant to hurt them. The governor reported the court's findings that she was guilty of practicing criminal witchcraft with the intent of killing her master and mistress. A decree arrived from Moscow bearing the tsar's sentence: she was to be buried alive.

Pale but determined to fight this verdict, Oksanka turned to her husband. He had to do something to save her. She implored him to find the scribe who sat in the town square and to pay him a few kopeks to write out an appeal, a petition to the tsar himself, using all the appropriate fancy language to beg for his mercy. Mitka, hesitant and wavering as usual, demurred, terrified at the audacious idea of addressing a petition to the tsar himself, but Oksanka's insistence finally overrode his scruples. Her life, after all, was at stake. Oksanka had heard that the tsar was merciful and just, and she hoped that if the scribe could put her case in just the right words, maybe he would listen. Maybe he would listen to the pleas of his lowly subject and let her go. Returning to the prison house from the square, Mitka reported to her that the petition sounded very official and impressive. It opened with the formula that the scribe had rattled off: "Sovereign, Tsar, and Grand Prince Aleksei Mikhailovich of all Great, Little, and White Russia! I, your orphan Mitka, humble townsman of Kaluga, bow to you and petition you on behalf of my poor little wife, your slave, Oksanka."

The governor did not dare carry out the sentence while her appeal to the tsar was pending. His own career, even his life, might suffer if he were to execute someone against the tsar's will. At last, an ukaz arrived from Moscow ordering the governor to undertake a new investigation. The questioning, the interrogation, and the torture began again, but Oksanka clung to the truth of her story. She had meant her master and mistress no harm. She had wanted them only to acknowledge her legitimate and rightful status as a free woman, the mother of free children, humble subjects of the tsar.

Now, eight months later, after repeated rounds of investigation, the merciful sovereign had responded to her righteous case. He had granted his clemency, and she was free. But what freedom? The children remained the property of her wicked former master, who had held onto them through his sly manipulation of his connections to the governor, and she and Mitka had no roof to shelter them, no hearth to warm them. Slowly, they walked out of the gates of the town, hoping without much hope for a more charitable reception somewhere else.

Suggestions for Further Reading

Kaiser, Daniel H. "'He Said, She Said': Rape and Gender Discourse in Early Modern Russia." *Kritika: Explorations in Russian and Eurasian History* 3, no. 2 (2002): 197–216.

Kivelson, Valerie. "Male Witches and Gendered Categories in Seventeenth-Century Russia." *Comparative Studies in Society and History* 45, no. 3 (2003): 606–31.

———. "Through the Prism of Witchcraft: Gender and Social Change in Seventeenth-Century Muscovy." In *Russia's Women: Accommodation, Resistance, Transformation.* Edited by Barbara Evans Clements, Barbara Alpern Engel, and Christine D. Worobec. Berkeley: University of California Press, 1991, 74–94.

Kollmann, Nancy Shields. "Women's Honor in Early Modern Russia." In *Russia's Women: Accommodation, Resistance, Transformation.* Edited by Barbara Evans Clements, Barbara Alpern Engel, and Christine D. Worobec. Berkeley: University of California Press, 1991, 60–73.

Levin, Eve. "Supplicatory Prayers as a Source for Popular Religious Culture in Muscovite Russia." In *Religion and Culture in Early Modern Russia and Ukraine.* Edited by Samuel H. Baron and Nancy Shields Kollmann. DeKalb: Northern Illinois University Press, 1997, 96–114.

Ryan, W.F. "The Witchcraft Hysteria in Early Modern Europe: Was Russia an Exception?" *Slavonic and East European Review* 76 (1998): 49–84.

———. *The Bathhouse at Midnight: Magic in Russia.* University Park: Pennsylvania State University Press, 1999.

Zguta, Russell. "Witchcraft Trials in Seventeenth-Century Russia." *American Historical Review* 82, no. 5 (1977): 1187–1207.

VII

Siberian Explorer and Trader

19

S.U. Remezov, Cossack Adventurer, and the Opening of Siberia

Christoph Witzenrath

Semen Ulianovich Remezov (1642–after 1720), a Cossack who became a Siberian noble, mapmaker, architect, engineer, and icon painter, succeeded in attaining an up-to-date education in remote Tobolsk decades before Peter the Great even suggested that administrators should master valuable sciences. Not unlike Columbus, who described the New World and its inhabitants using the images and terms that were familiar to him from the Bible, Remezov approached fledgling but unfamiliar Western science with images and terms that were familiar to him; namely, his experience as a Siberian frontline frontier Cossack. As if split between or bridging the continents, as well as the great ages of historical development of the medieval age and the early modern period, he copied maps and tried new instruments, lauding and recommending their usage. Nevertheless, in most cases he stuck to his locally well-established craft of medieval-looking Muscovite mapmaking. He mastered that craft to such a degree and utilized it so meticulously that not just Moscow but the world first learned Siberian topography, history, and ethnography from him.[1] Remezov is an obvious case study in institutional limitation: he had invested heavily in his cognitive and instrumental tools, which had the advantage of mirroring his worldview. Using them, he gained approval and, moreover, took part in empire building in a hands-on way as a Cossack, surveyor. He also functioned in many other roles. He acknowledged in theory that the Western instruments of mapmaking were indeed the best available and advocated scientific methods long before Tsar Peter supposedly "opened the window to the West" and sent young men to study at Western universities. Nevertheless, changing his ingrained habits and tools in fact may not just have been unnecessary from Remezov's vantage point but was

---

[1] The early modern world outside China and Central Asia learned little about Siberia from the knowledge preserved in those areas.

Vision to the Tatars of the Future Site of Tobolsk, from an illustrated edition of the *Brief Siberian Kungur Chronicle* published in St. Petersburg in 1880. In one of the stories of the local Tatars retold by Semen Remezov (the historical figure who is the subject of this chapter), the khan of Sibir and his men have visions of a Christian church on top of the mountain that was to become the site of Siberia's early capital, Tobolsk. They ask shamans and Russian captives whom the khan has brought from beyond the Ural Mountains about the significance of the vision and are foretold of their demise. For Remezov, Tobolsk was a city of liberation whose myth he painted and sketched. He still paid the debts of his father who had ransomed Tatar captives from the Mongol Oirats.

also more than could be asked even from the extraordinary individual he knew he was, "with all my due humility."

The events described below are based on Remezov's writings and on analysis of his maps and drawings. Foreigners who visited him on May 11, 1721, wrote diary entries indicating his attitude. Though there are plenty of records about him, autobiographical notes are almost exclusively service-related and scattered throughout his writings. There are large gaps, especially with regard to the details of everyday life. In some cases, the narrative of his imagined train of thought is informed by Remezov's most glaring omissions. In others, interpretations build on the few available records about his life beyond service, on points of view exposed in his writings, and on the symbolic content of his images.

"Thank you for allowing me a glimpse of your splendid maps," Captain Tabbert said putting the last sheet back on the table, "they truly express the wonders of this land of Siberia." He continued, "May I ask you about the uses of the compass and the circle that you have sketched on some of your maps?" Rising from his drawing table, Remezov answered, "I regret that I am too humble to answer such a wide-ranging question, I am just a modest Siberian mapmaker. Sir, would you be so kind as to consider that I am compelled to return to my work now, since my schedule is very tight. Goodbye."

He accompanied the Swedish prisoner of war to the door and, after closing it tightly behind him, turned thoughtfully. "This was very impolite and shameful, but it is better so. He is an inquisitive individual and a well-trained geographer. If I start to talk to him, I will soon take pleasure and reveal more than is expedient. What might happen, for example, if this Swede finds out about the secret of the Bay of the Ob River, which no map reveals? We narrowly escaped the powerful Western ships due to the quick and decisive reaction of Governor Kurakin during the Time of Troubles,[2] when the foreigners sought a passage beyond the Arctic island of Novaia Zemlia.[3] With God's help we denied them knowledge of the fact that the passage south of the island was navigable when southern winds drove the ice out of the river's mouth. Tobolsk servitors rose as a man when the tsar was weak and set up a fortified place closing the sea-bound way from the White Sea in the west to the once-prospering trade hub of Mangazeia in northern Siberia, which otherwise could have led the foreigners to the estuaries of the Ob and Enisei rivers. It was in Tobolskans' own interest, of course, but Mangazeia's end was near anyway. No Russian forces could have prevented the alliance of the nomads with the Dutch and English weapons. Now we are again in a mortal struggle with the Swedes, and

---

[2] A period of internal convulsions and foreign intervention often referred to as *smuta* in Siberian sources, which according to various definitions lasted from 1598 or 1605 to 1612 or 1619.

[3] Dutch and English ships sought the Northeastern Passage to China in the late sixteenth and early seventeenth centuries.

although our splendid tsar has won at Poltava and elsewhere, it is not all done. If the current severe climatic conditions improve even slightly, they could still seize the opportunity, gaining access to Siberia's riches. Opening a second front, God forbid, they might still wrest the fruits of victory from us."[4]

Remezov fondly remembered how he had told Tabbert and the German scholar Daniel Gottlieb Messerschmidt, sent by the tsar to study Siberia in all its varieties, about the complete skeleton of a mammoth measuring thirty-six ells.[5] He had found it on a service journey and dug it out with thirty Cossacks in the southern Barabinsk steppe between Tara and Tomsk. Standing in the skeleton with his poleax held vertically, he could not reach the spine. On many trips until old age—he was seventy-eight as of now—he had always been curious about the natural world and the bygone one, taking sketches from ancient stone carvings near Kungur to the west of the Stone Mountains (Urals), which equally impressed the scholars. Moreover, he generously imparted his detailed knowledge of the Siberian natives, their legends and languages.

Thoughtful, he rose from his seat and went to the window, returning to the day's meeting: "I imagine what Strahlenberg will think and say about me—I am just an artist despite my maps and my knowledge of the latest improvements in mapmaking.[6] For my fellow countrymen, however, this has always been just fitting and enough, they are awestruck when they glance at Remezov maps, because for the first time they see nomadic hordes in their vicinity that they believed far away, and new lines of communication open before their eyes. My maps generate easily interpreted images of places, depicting houses, homesteads, Tatar yurts, and animals from the perspective of someone standing in the map in a particular place. This has helped them accept my profession. My maps are done the right way, the orthodox way. In writing, I indicate detailed distances from point to point and a plethora of useful observations, from road conditions to the economy, ethnic names, and local resources. I have used earlier maps such as the impressive one authored by Vinius and compared them, checking the available information, and then made my own. I have cut out many nonexistent towns in Central Asia that appear on earlier maps. Khiva is to the east of the Khvalynsk Sea,[7] not to the west as on Vinius's map. The Khvalynsk Sea is elongated, rather than circular, and there is no canal between it and the Aral Sea. My map shows the irrigation canal systems of Central Asia.

---

[4] On Remezov's maps, the ice on the mouth of the river Ob is "eternal." Generally well read about historical events concerning his town, he might have been aware but never mentions the closure of the sea route. His image of "peace" shows some seagoing ships and people in Western dress of whom he warns. The worst-case scenario is not necessarily strategically sound, but such thoughts are close to Remezov's mind.

[5] Remezov may have used his arm with no other measuring rod available.

[6] Strahlenberg (Tabbert) wrote in his diary that Remezov's maps "show that he was no geographer but an artist; nevertheless, he drew the towns, rivers, and lands according to his own ways."

[7] Caspian Sea.

I have also used Chinese sources.[8] In any case, my swift quill and brush's skill pale before the daunting task of collecting all this information. It was scattered in local maps; reports of ambassadors, servitors, and merchants; and in sundry oral testimonies of participants in campaigns, merchant caravans, and diplomatic missions and of the natives of our lands. This was my original legwork, the basis of all the beautiful maps later produced with the aid of my sons. I acquired most of my knowledge about western Siberia when I was a Cossack, accompanying my father, Ulian, on his service trips to bring more natives under the exalted hand of the sovereign. I gained more experience when I was sent with my first son Leontei to record outlying settlements of Russian peasants and natives paying the *iasak* (fur tax) and to levy taxes and, later, to the town of Eniseisk."

The fullness of maps and atlases of Siberia and many parts of the world had come into being when Remezov returned from campaign in the steppe against the raiding Kazakhs in 1696. "How I enjoyed the preparations," he recalled, "from April 1696 to March 1697, according to the decree, I asked people of all ranks, knowledgeable long-time residents, those who lived with the hordes, immigrants and former Russian captives, Bukharan merchants and millers, Tatars and recently baptized natives from Tobolsk town and from other towns about directions and descriptions of the roads from Tobolsk through the steppes and through Siberia. This became my first map, and I sent it off to Moscow immediately. The second was the 'Map of All Heights and Rocks Whence the Rivers Originate,' according to the reports of travelers and settlers, covering mountain ranges from western Siberia to Central Asia and the Caspian. I made a 'Map of All Waterless Lands and Impassable Steppes.' Another is the 'Map of the Lands of the Town of Tobolsk,' which I explained is part of Siberia. It exactly renders the area of Tobolsk, the rivers, lakes, and Russian and *iasak*-paying native settlements and towns within the borders and the troublesome Kazakh horde. It covers a length of 900 and width of 563 versts[9] and 1,600 meters."

The tsar had ordered these maps drawn as part of a program to counter a mounting danger. Increasingly, nomadic raiders captured subjects of the tsar.[10] When Remezov's fellow Tobolsk *syn boiarskii*[11] Andrei Nepripasov mounted an embassy to the Turkmen Tevki-khan in 1692, it was forcibly detained, its members kept in

---

[8] This is the only potential source of the obscure "Lake Tengiz," from which the Irtysh River issues on his map, though European maps placed a Lacus Kitaicus in the same place.

[9] A verst is 1.0668 kilometers.

[10] Russians pressed into the steppe, wresting grazing grounds from nomads, a development that worried Remezov, as it did most contemporary Russians.

[11] *Syn boiarskii*, pl. *deti boiarskie*: rank above Cossack, often assigned to more responsible positions in administration and leading Cossack groups. *Deti boiarskie*, however, frequently took the side of rebels and lived the lives of common Cossacks, as they were treated in most places beyond the Siberian capital only incrementally better.

captivity. Another mission led by Fedor Skibin was sent shortly after and involuntarily roamed the steppes for years. Skibin's adventurous and not entirely voluntary journey led him to Turkestan, Bukhara, Tashkent, Khiva, to the Iaik (Ural) River, and to the Kalmyk khan Aiuka on the lower Volga, whence he returned via Ufa to Tobolsk. By law, the tsar was obliged to ransom captives and slaves sold to faraway countries. Despite a few successes by ambassadors and a trickle of ransomed people returning with the help of merchants, however, the results were patchy.

Remezov recalled that he had sought to warn others of these dangers on the maps the tsar had ordered him to draw: "It is important to spread the conviction that the pious tsar and all Orthodox Christians are obliged to redeem slaves. For redemption is not just a question of the afterlife, but we must act accordingly in this life. The redemptive legend of the True Cross is widely shared in our writings, icons, sculpture, and ritual practice. Symbolically, the narrative connects various redemptive events in the Scriptures in a long, winding story of the wood that was originally the tree in Paradise; it became the wood Moses used to rescue the Israelites, turning bitter water into sweet water in the desert of the Sinai during Exodus from Egyptian slavery; the wooden roof of the wise Tsar Solomon's first temple; and, not least, the wood of Christ's crucifix, redeeming humanity. What a nice, succinct formula of some of Orthodoxy's central ideas is contained in this image of the tree! I have spread it all over Siberia on my maps, filling the blanks with little, beautiful trees. Just beside the sketch of the Cathedral and the House of God's Wisdom, our archbishop's residence in Tobolsk, I have painted Burning Bushes, the sign that obliged Moses to lead the Jews out of slavery. Look in the Holy Scripture. Wisdom divides the waters of the Red Sea, rescuing the Jews from their persecutors and finally drowning Pharaoh and his troops. Even the non-Orthodox live better under the reign of the wise tsar, for captivity is a fate that befalls everyone, sooner or later, the raiders no less than their victims."

Remezov had sought to paint this symbolical legacy of the Orthodox empire in every imaginable way, showing the daughters of Wisdom on the coat of arms of Siberia: Love, Justice, and Hope above the kneeling local Russian "Sibiriak" and the native Ostiak, Samoyed, and Tatar, each offering their tribute. Wisdom, "by which great men rule" according to the Bible, was well known to Tatars and to some of the people who had lived under their rule before the Russians conquered the khanate. It was part of Persian and Ottoman literature. "Love" and payments of cash or grain were owed by the tsar to local nomad rulers further out in the steppe if they lived up to their oath—their "justice," as it was called in the treaties—kept the peace, and delivered all captured subjects of the tsar. Symbolic "trees" grew on icons when nomads settled and captives were released. Muscovite army commanders had the sign of the cross carved into the new, formidable wooden steppe line fortifications of Muscovy beyond the mountains; but such steppe walls were as yet unattainable for Siberia. This was all a worthy task on the maps and in real life. It was adorned with many successes but ultimately, Remezov admitted to himself, at least in his own lifetime, a hopeless case. Many thousands of people from Siberia had been enslaved in the last two decades, and few had returned. All he could do was to remind everyone by his sketches of the peaceful life in the coming imperial paradise and to summon up the formidable natural and built fortifications of his beloved home town of Tobolsk. It was a well-guarded garden of paradise, as the mosque was seen in symbolic terms by Muslims—but this he preferred not to acknowledge openly, as a true Orthodox Christian. "However," he thought, "the Orthodox paradise has the advantage of the tree signifying liberation from slavery and conquest of the Promised Land. Hence the burning bushes I have painted just beyond the symbolic Heavenly Jerusalem, the 'House of Sophia-Wisdom of God,' which is the name of the archbishop's palace on top of Alafi Mountain, the upper town of Tobolsk. Russian slaves and Tatar wise men interpreted the vision of the Church of Sophia in my vividly sketched *History of Siberia*. They presaged the fall of the khanate of Sibir and its ruler, Kuchium, who dissolutely lived with Russian female slaves."[12]

As Cossacks and petty nobles, the Remezovs did their best to bring new foreigners under the exalted hand of the sovereign and did not refrain from brute force if consideration failed. "I suffered with my father, Ulian, in exile in the Siberian town of Tara where I was enlisted as a Cossack. The governor became weary during the years of the Razin rebellion of 1667–71, when the Volga and parts of western Siberia succumbed to the flames of insurrection. Peasants and *iasak* payers leveled charges of embezzlement against Ulian. It did not help that our family was part of the elite of Siberia's capital. In such cases, local rebels often seek to communicate directly with Moscow. Whether they reach their aim or not often depends on the political conditions: which governor of the various towns on the way befriends the Tobolsk governor and arrests or takes advantage of the rebels' delegates for his own feud within the Moscow elite's struggles for power."

"I have drawn my own conclusions. In Siberia, the locals are often a factor in power politics. It can be dangerous to antagonize them, as many deposed governors have discovered. Governors might suffer a period under arrest; some might even die, until the next arrives. The rebels usually send a collective petition, often signed by the whole town—or what they claim is the whole town. Often they submit hundreds of original signatures and proxy signatures representing illiterate signatories. It is important to be literate for a Cossack; and quite a few actually learn to write, whether perfunctorily or with the skill needed to write a petition. It takes months, sometimes years, until the petition arrives in Moscow, where a decree is drawn up and returned. Until that date, the rebels claim to act according to the interests of the tsar. In what ways the governor had contravened this interest they explained in detail in their petition. Partisans of the governor and those who did not accept these measures are banned from the town. Rebels often report collectively during

---

[12] Remezov's view depends on legendary and partly unreliable Russian sources, and Tatar accounts did not survive. Besides, Russians in Siberia were not beyond keeping household slaves.

investigation so that no contradicting statements occur, and group pressure prevents reneging on the petition. Sometimes, as a ruse they imprison themselves in large numbers, showing solidarity with a rebel who had been arrested by investigators either for exemplary reasons or to break his silence. In any case, the new governor is usually well advised to play it safe with them. One of their best arguments is that they cannot serve the sovereign's service if the governor takes as many bribes and taxes as he does."

"What is a bribe, however, and what is not? If a governor is sent on a service assignment—or a *syn boiarskii* and sometimes even a Cossack as head of a subordinated fort—he is entitled to feeding dues, as well as allowances on arrival and leaving and for particular holidays. They differ from place to place and according to the official's dignity and influence and even the leadership he shows locally. Given the sporadic communication, discerning from Moscow or even Tobolsk what is going on locally takes months, if not years. Often not only natives, Russian peasants, and townspeople have to pay the governor but also Cossacks, even *deti boiarskie*. They are not easily checked. There are laws and instructions emanating from Moscow and from Tobolsk, but there are also local customs."

"So," Remezov thought, "the only way of keeping peace in our Siberianess[13] is that the leaders obey not only the laws but also customs as they are locally observed. Taxes must be collected. Meanwhile, insolent behavior must not be tolerated. You cannot just arouse people to rebellion and expect to get away with it. So, it is only just that Ivan Nepripasov lost his position when he tried to incite a rebellion in Tobolsk. My son was recruited in his place, receiving part of Ivan's allowance and that of another, aged *syn boiarskii*. It is true that Cossack custom has always allowed for close cooperation of the ataman with his Cossacks: my *History of Siberia* depicts Ermak's Cossacks as they hold council. We walk for weeks and months with sledges through the most dangerous steppes and forests; we descend rivers and rapids and carry our boats across portages. We suffer famine and eat berries on our journeys through uninhabited lands. Slow-loading and imprecise muskets are not as much help in an ambush in dense woods using silent and quickly reloaded bows and arrows; moreover, in the steppe, against swift nomad horsemen who live their whole lives in the saddle. How can we succeed except by unanimity among the members of the small Cossack group who know one another personally? We stand united, and there is no more economical way of escorting small but valuable loads of furs through the wilderness. More hands mean more greedy eyes and opportunities to siphon off the wealth of the tiny, precious furs. So the tsar is reluctant to send more troops to quell our risings. However, what happens if we turn things upside-down, when the group ceases to obey? So it happened in 1705, when some Cossacks who had been recruited from among the exiles fled and robbed the *iasak* people. I pursued and soon caught them, relieving the natives. Exiles can

---

[13] He calls it "Sibirstvo."

be troublesome, but they are far from the only rabble-rousers. Only determined, wise, and convincing leaders will sway the group and achieve their ends; and that of the Cossacks will be best served by such leaders."

"But how can you make a living in the Sovereign's service? The Remezovs have always taken seriously the obligation to redeem the tsar's subjects, stipulated in the code of laws. During my father's great mission to the descendant of Chinggis Khan, Devlet-Kirei, to Lauzan-taisha, and to the powerful Oirat Ablai-taisha,[14] in 1660, Ulian succeeded in peace negotiations. Returning, he agreed to the request of thirty-one Tatar *iasak* payers from the Barabinsk steppe to ransom them and conveyed them back to Tara on his own camels, buying expensive extra foodstuffs from the Kalmyks. Ulian was memorialized by a street named for him in the upper town, just opposite the governor's palace. He was disappointed, however, when neither the ransomed payers nor the Russian officials paid back the debts he had undertaken to redeem them. More than four decades later, I wrote a complaint: I was still paying off the consequences of this break of trust."

A young Semen had listened excitedly to his father's stories about Ermak. "He received armor from Tsar Ivan IV, in which he drowned when the Tatars assaulted his camp at night. Tatar legend tells us that this armor made its bearer invincible; therefore, it[15] was selected as special gift for Ablai. Russian stories and those of the Tatars, Voguls,[16] and other Siberian natives are so intriguing I had to collect and preserve them for posterity in my writings. I often visited the Tatar yurts. In conversation, the Tatar *murza*[17] Devlet-bey, living on Panin bugr, the hill next to the fortress, told many details about the origins of the Siberian khans. Their capital, Isker, had been located just fifteen versts from Tobolsk until Ermak drove them off. Drawing on all these and many more details, which I meticulously collected and compared, I wrote and illustrated a *History of Siberia* in great detail, authored a description of peoples of Siberia, and drew an ethnographic map of Siberia in 1701. I had never seen such a specimen before it occurred to me."[18] Surely, he omitted the trees on this map as he did on the map of China. Places in which subjects of the tsar were held in slavery did not warrant the sign of redemption. And he would have preferred it if the nomads had indeed stayed within the tightly assigned borders given to each tribe on his ethnic map, rather than roam at will and according to the exigencies of grazing the herds or the hunting season.

Remezov went out for a stroll. From the street in front of his house in the lower town, he had a great view of the fortifications on top of the steep hill. "They look

---

[14] West Mongol prince.
[15] There is no proof that this was indeed the armor of Ermak.
[16] Nenets of the Ob in Old Russian.
[17] Tatar noble.
[18] Thematic maps were invented in the second half of the eighteenth century; however, the first ethnic map was made in Paris in 1700.

marvelous, white against the sky, a veritable New Jerusalem on the hill, with the twelve towers of the archbishop's palace equaling the twelve fruits of the tree in its middle in the Book of Revelation. It is a suitable home for the Siberian New Israel's former slaves returning from captivity in the Egypt of the steppe to the new Promised Land. Cossacks dedicated land ownership rights and precious cult objects to the icon of Sophia after returning safely from the salt fair at Lake Iamysh in the steppe." On the hilltop to the right, the archbishop's House of Sophia and the cathedral glistened, and to the left the governor's palace. In the middle, below the cathedral's cupolas and on top of the narrow incision between the two hills, which provided steep but direct access from the lower town, both fortifications were connected by the Renterei, the tax office whose construction Remezov had overseen.

The security of his beloved hometown had long been uppermost on his mind, so Remezov was pleased when he was assigned a new task in 1697, which gave him the opportunity to improve security. The Siberian Chancellery in Moscow commended him. His maps had been evaluated and found praiseworthy above all others. His reliable and swift work may have convinced the governor and the head of the chancellery to entrust him with a range of building projects, initially at the kremlin and later extending to further sites. The Tobolsk kremlin was to be rebuilt, this time not in wood but in stone. This was to prevent frequent and devastating fires—the town had been reduced to ashes in 1643, and there had been ten blazes since, not counting numerous minor fires. The stone kremlin was the first of its kind in Siberia except for the wall around the archbishop's palace. Even west of the Stone Mountains, in Muscovite Rus,[19] there were by far more wooden than stone fortifications, as well as buildings. That year, Remezov studied the records of Tobolsk town fortifications. He noted that already in 1678, Tobolskans had pleaded to Moscow for "stone construction."

He was invited to Moscow for the second time in 1698. The first occasion had occurred several years earlier, an ordinary service assignment for conveying the fur tax and important documents. "This time, Tsar Peter received me in audience, the grandchild of an exile to Siberia.[20] In his generosity, the tsar allotted five rubles and a piece of cloth. Extra daily allowances supported me while I stayed in the capital. Prince Mikhail Iakovlevich Cherkasskii, the greatest noble serving the tsar and a descendant of the clan of the Circassian princes of the northern Caucasian Kabarda, sheltered me in their Moscow palace. The son of a man born a Muslim in the Caucasus was among the foremost promoting the new tendencies in Moscow. He hired the famous Moldavian adventurer Nikolae Spafarii Milescu to educate

---

[19] Russia west of the Ural Mountains, according to contemporary Siberian usage.

[20] Remezov never mentioned his grandfather in writing. Nonetheless, before exile in 1626 Moisei Remezov had been *syn boiarskii* at Patriarch Filaret's court. Filaret, whose temporal name was Fedor Romanov, was the real power during the reign of his son, Tsar Mikhail Romanov.

his sons. Spafarii had lived in the Latin West for a long time, and borrowed from the writings of Simeon Polotskii, the cleric from western Rus who had brought so many new ideas to Moscow. I met Spafarii already in 1675 in Tobolsk as an ambassador en route to China."[21]

"Andrei Andreevich Vinius, head of the Siberian chancellery and son of a Dutch merchant, the most educated man in Muscovy and an accomplished cartographer, required my personal report. Staying in Moscow, I drafted thirty new maps, drawing on the records and extant maps, which Siberian towns had sent to the capital's chancelleries. Later I united many of these maps in my second large atlas of Siberia. However, the most important assignment during the months in Moscow was to the Armory, where I studied building and fortification according to an Italian manual." Many of Remezov's later projects and ideas originated from this manual. The year 1698 marked the return of Tsar Peter's Great Embassy, which had taken him to London and Manchester, studying building techniques among other things. In London, terraced houses were first built for noble families after the Glorious Revolution of 1688 and the city was rebuilt in brick after the Great Fire of 1666. "I drew detailed plans of two types of terraced and detached houses for Tobolsk shortly after my sojourn in Moscow. One type has a fire-resistant outer stone shell and an internal wooden building, to accommodate the climate in Tobolsk. Average temperatures oscillate between –20 in January and +20 degrees Celsius in summer, a variation that might more than double in extreme conditions. I made them look like a traditional Russian building in Siberia, with a *podklet*, a half-sunken, unheated basement." A few were built; however, mass construction of standardized stone houses was prevented by the burdens the Great Northern War placed on the economy.[22]

"Working and studying in Moscow, I felt obliged to recover arrears owed to fellow Cossacks, but my attempts were not successful. Nevertheless, I used my influence to have a son of prince Gantimur appointed to the position of *syn boiarskii* in Tobolsk. Gantimur was a high-profile defector to the Russians from the Chinese side of the river Amur, whose deliverance the imperial Chinese delegation had unsuccessfully demanded at negotiations for the Treaty of Nerchinsk in 1689.

"Returning in December 1698, my last great enterprise started. I was appointed head of architectural and building works for the new kremlin in Tobolsk. I measured the existing wooden fortifications, drew plans and founded a brickyard in a convenient place near the town, with easy access to clay, wood, and water. The brickworks were operated by Swedish prisoners of war. Initially, discipline, speed,

---

[21] There are no records on this, as generally for the early life of Remezov few survive. Spafarii was detained several months until the ice broke on the river. The Remezovs were part of the Siberian capital's elite.

[22] Nevertheless, Remezov's plans went farther than anything realized at the same time in St. Petersburg or Moscow.

and quality were difficult to maintain. Conflict with the new governor meant that I was temporarily removed from my position. I tried to use my contacts in Moscow. When a decree required immediate delivery of my atlas in 1701, the governor summoned me. However, with the help of a ploy frequently used by rebels, I had already sent it to Moscow with the Cossacks escorting the *iasak* from Iakutsk. I made excuses that I had forgotten to inform the governor. Having received orders directly from Moscow, I felt free to approach the central chancelleries directly. In 1702, Andrei Vinius arrived in Tobolsk to speed up restoration of the artillery lost in the battle of Narva against Sweden. He reinstated me and oversaw building factories that produced war supplies and melted ores at Kungur in 1703. Another project started at this time was the new caravansarai (*gostinyi dvor*) in Tobolsk. Construction of a new palace for the governor was started, too. The plans show a splendid building in the new style, which I had seen in Moscow."[23] Construction on all these projects was slow. In 1709, during an emergency caused by Kazakh incursion, the new walls of the kremlin had not yet been finished and there were unprotected sections.

In 1710, Remezov bought a new homestead in the lower town. In regard to his earlier ideals, some had been overturned. "Or, perhaps," he thought, "it is that wisdom allows foreigners to be enslaved.[24] Some are taken by the sword, others sold by their relatives during famine. In any case, there are those who cannot do without the protection of the strong people while they contribute to the fame of their master's household. Cossack custom allows enslavement of foreigners; imperial law proscribes it." The register couched it in brittle words: "Homestead bought by Semen Ulianov *syn* Remezov. The icon painter declared himself sixty-seven years of age, his wife Efimia daughter of Mitrofanov fifty-seven years, their son Leontei thirty-three years, who was a *syn boiarskii* too; the latter's wife: Varvara daughter of Vasilii, thirty years. Leontei's children: Aleksei was seven, Leontei five, Fedor one year old. Semen's son Semen, also a *syn boiarskii*, 27 years, his wife Uliana daughter of Grigorii twenty-five years, their son Nikifor half a year. Further children of Semen: Ivan, *syn boiarskii*, twenty-six years, lives in a northern Siberian town. Son Petr, fourteen years, daughter Maria, twenty years. Semen's donated concubine of Ostiak origin, Anna Ivanova, thirty years, her daughter Irina, age one year. The Sovereign's annual allowance: For Semen, eleven rubles, five and half quarters[25] and two *chetveriki*[26] rye, three *pud*s of salt, and for his children, Leontei, Semen, Ivan, seven rubles, four quarters rye, oats the same, and two *pud*s[27] of salt per person. Semen pays the Sovereign's dues in the chancellery for this homestead:

---

[23] Remezov is referring here to the Moscow Baroque style, which began to appear in the late seventeenth century.
[24] Wisdom of Solomon 10: 15–20. Laws in Exodus 21.
[25] 905.85 kg.
[26] 52.478 liters.
[27] 36.6 kg per *pud*.

for the steam bath five *altyns*,[28] for smoke[29] eight *den'gas*[30] annually." It was quite possible to live off this, though Semen received only slightly more than a married Cossack. In some years, he was forced to petition for arrears. Since he bought this homestead, the family had not grown much. Nevertheless, they had bought another homestead, where some members of the family lived. His sons were frequently on service assignments far away from Tobolsk. Petr, still living with his father, had married in 1719.

Entering the governor's palace from the side of the upper town, Remezov directed his steps to the room where his son worked. Semen the younger had inherited his father's love for the paintbrush. Under the senior Remezov's more or less nominal supervision, he painted murals for the governor's palace.

Suggestions for Further Reading

Gol'denberg, Leonid Arkad'evich. *Russian Maps and Atlases as Historical Sources*. Translated by James R. Gibson. Toronto: York University, 1971.
———. *Izograf zemli sibirskoi*. Magadan: Magadanskoe knizhnoe izdatel'stvo, 1990.
———. "Russian Cartography to 1700." In *History of Cartography*. Edited by David Woodward and J.B. Harley. Vol. 4. Chicago: University of Chicago Press, forthcoming.
Kivelson, Valerie. *Cartographies of Tsardom*. Ithaca, NY: Cornell University Press, 2006.
Lantzeff, G.V. *Siberia in the Seventeenth Century: A Study of the Colonial Administration*. Berkeley: University of California Press, 1943; New York: Octagon, 1972.
Remezov, Semen Ul'ianovich. *Chertezhnaia kniga Sibiri, sostavlennaia Tobol'skim synom boiarskim Semenom Remezovym v 1701 godu*. Facsimile edition, Moscow: FGUP PKO Kartografiia, 2003. [Not available everywhere. Magnificent edition of the large atlas of Siberia. With helpful contemporary Dutch translations of many terms enlivening the maps.]
———. *Kratkaia sibirskaia letopis' (Kungurskaia). So 154 risunkami*. St. Petersburg: Eleonski, 1880 (also: Berlin, 1888); Found also under different titles: *Remezovskaia letopis'*; *Sluzhebnaia chertezhnaia kniga*, ed. V.M. Guminskii, Tobol'sk: Fond Vozrozhdenie Tobol'ska, 2006; and *Sibirskie letopisi: Kratkaia sibirskaia letopis'*, edited by A. I. Tsepkov. Riazan: Aleksandriia, 2008.
Sibir' XVII veka glazama sovremennika. S.U. Remezov i ego "Istoriia sibirskaia." http://mmedia.nsu.ru/remezov/vbook/obj8/title.htm [scans of sketches from Remezov's *History of Siberia*].
Witzenrath, Christoph. *Cossacks and the Russian Empire, 1598–1725: Manipulation, Rebellion, and Expansion into Siberia*. London: Routledge, 2007.
———. *Slavery, Ransom, and Liberation in Russia and the Steppe Area, 1500–2000*. Farnham, UK: Ashgate, forthcoming.
———. *Holy Russia and Slaving: The Steppe Frontier and Imperial Culture, 1500–1917*. London: Routledge, forthcoming.

---

[28] Three kopeks. A hundred kopeks equaled one ruble.
[29] For the fireplace.
[30] Four kopeks or one twenty-fifth of a ruble.

∞ 20 ∞

A Siberian Trader
Urasko Kaibulin

Erika Monahan

The brief snapshot below imagines an afternoon in the life of Urasko Kaibulin, a Bukharan merchant and servitor who lived in Siberia in the seventeenth century. What follows is a composite of historical events and incidents. Urasko worked in the state customs service. I do not know if he was ever posted at Lake Iamyshev, but other customs servitors were.

Urasko was part of a community of Muslim merchants whose predecessors had emigrated from the Bukharan khanate in Central Asia in probably the late sixteenth or the seventeenth century and settled in the Russian empire. Recognizing that territorial acquisitions in Siberia could not be maintained if the nascent towns and fortresses did not receive adequate supplies, the Muscovite government encouraged such movements of merchants who were connected to the commercial flows of the Silk Roads trade. These immigrant families in the Russian empire formed diaspora communities in the towns of Tobolsk, Tiumen, and Tara. They conducted trade of tremendous regional importance and became an integral part of commercial life in Muscovite Siberia. In addition to pursuing their own commerce, Bukharans were often found serving the Russian state in the customs service, where their linguistic abilities and expertise in valuation of commercial wares proved useful to the Russian state.

In the sketch below, Urasko is stationed at Lake Iamyshev, a salt lake alongside the upper stretches of the Irtysh River, what is now the eastern edge of Kazakhstan. In the last third of the seventeenth century this steppe oasis grew busier than it had ever been, as traders from diverse and distant places converged on this remote salt lake to trade with one another. Ever so gradually, they came in greater numbers with larger caravans as more merchants realized that, by trading here on the desolate Eurasian steppe, they could avoid more sustained border-crossing hassles and other forms of state oversight. Thus state customs regulations, in their absence, had actually contributed to the emergence of a bustling borderlands market in this stateless zone. Of course, the "out-of-the-wayness" was soon noticed, and the Russian state, loath to let revenue escape, established a minor customs post manned by sworn men (tseloval'niki) *from other Siberian towns. In other words, Urasko's posting, the circumstance on which this sketch is built, illustrates in microperspective the Muscovite state's aspirations to extend its reach over Central Asia's commercial potential (which, at this point, mattered more to the Russian state than territory, as the renunciation of territorial claims in the 1689 Treaty of Nerchinsk demonstrated). This sketch also imagines the accommodation and tension that must have accompanied the coexistence and necessary cooperation of Orthodox and Muslim colleagues on the Siberian frontier.*

Most of our information about commerce in seventeenth-century Siberia comes from the records of the Siberian Chancellery (Sibirskii Prikaz, fond 214 in the Russian State Archive of Ancient Acts) and chancery records of provincial Siberian towns, supplemented by occasional ambassadorial and others observers' reports. Several compilations of primary sources by Russian and Soviet scholars also contain invaluable information. A few examples are Istoriia Sibiri *by G.F. Miller (Leningrad, 1937);* Materialy po istorii Uzbekskoi, Tadzhikskoi i Turkmenskoi SSR, *edited by A.N. Samoilovich (Leningrad, 1932); and* Mezhdunarodnye otnosheniia v tsentral'noi Azii XVII–XVIII vv.: dokumenty i materialy, *edited by B.P. Gurevich and G.F. Kim (Moscow, 1989).*

Urasko Kaibulin pulled his kaftan more tightly around him and readjusted his heavy beaver fur to better protect himself from the November steppe wind. His eyes detected no movement besides the undulation of grasses across the tree-dotted plain, but it would be just a matter of time before the thin unhurried line of a caravan appeared in the distance. The rose-colored salt lake was a few versts away, but in the afternoon air the smell—some said of violets—carried to the wooden fort constructed along the bank of the Irtysh River where Urasko stood. Several days travel downstream, the Irtysh meandered past Tobolsk, Urasko's home. From there it continued to flow northward. Gaining strength it joined with the Ob River, flowing as one massive current ever north to meet the icy waters of the Arctic Ocean.

Urasko had never followed the Irtysh so far north. His current posting at Lake Iamyshev was as far from his birthplace as he had ever traveled. Besides that, a trip two springs ago to the town of Verkhoturie, which divided Sibir (Siberia) from Rus (European Russia) was the extent of Urasko's travels so far. As a sworn man in the Tobolsk customs office, he had been sent to secure supplies for the administration of town offices and clerical needs. He had returned with wax for seals, candles for the church, and paper, among other perishables. Urasko was still a young man, so it was only a matter of time before his endeavors sent him farther afield. He was, after all, a Bukharan. His people were merchants; their lifestyle required long, arduous travels. His grandfather, along with his wife, brothers, and their wives and children had, during the turbulent reign of Imomqulikhan (1611–42), left their city of Bukhara and become subjects of the Russian tsar, who had come to rule over what had been the Siberian khanate of Khan Kuchum. Like his grandfather,

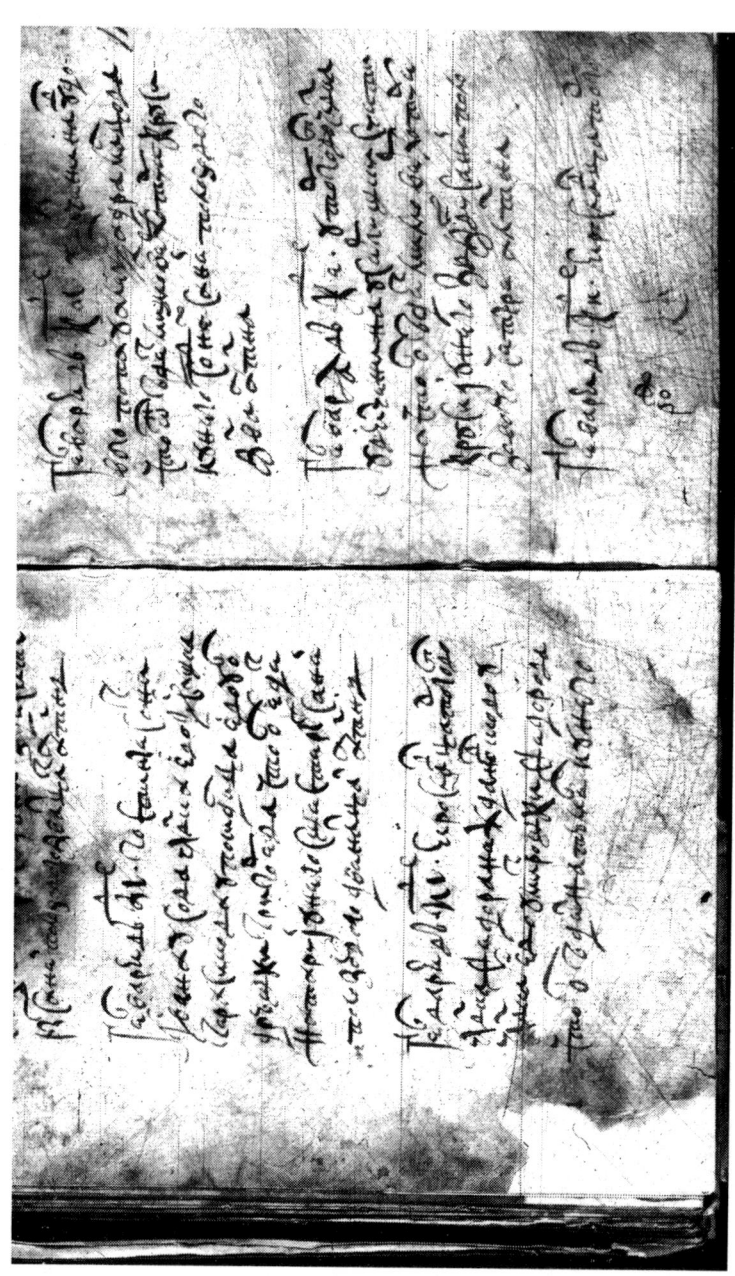

Open pages from a Tobolsk customs book, second half of seventeenth century, from the Russian State Archive of Ancient Acts (RGADA). The four complete and two partial entries visible here date from the second half of January 1653. These pages are from a section that records parties being charged a fee of two *altyn* per sled as they pass through Tobolsk. The entries record the origins of each trader (here, a man working for the merchant Ivan Usov and his market-stall sitter; a man working for a trader from Yaroslavl; a priest; and a trader from Viatka), the destination of each trader (Rus; Tara; Tiumen; Rus; and Rus, respectively), and how many sleds each trader has. The subject of this chapter, Urasko Kaibulin, a Muslim merchant who served as a customs agent for the tsar, would have been tasked with gathering the information for such books.

Urasko's father traveled far; he had been to China with a trade caravan. Urasko's cousin was right now on a trip to Kazan to collect some of his father's debts. While there he would visit the revered Siberian mosque and hear news from acquaintances there of other Bukharans in distant Astrakhan.

When Urasko occasionally reflected on his family's history, it occurred to him that he did not know for certain if they had been inspired or pushed to leave their Muslim homeland for a colder life under a Christian tsar; that is, had they left because of the unrest or for the opportunities that Siberia presented, the privileges—long since curtailed—that the Russian tsar had offered? It did, after all, make sense to have relatives permanently in place to receive and house caravans on their way westward. When his grandfather was a young man and newly arrived in Siberia, it was his cousins and kin that led the caravans. When the caravan arrived, Urasko would translate as necessary and try to help his Russian colleague, Fedor Vakulin, to record the strange-sounding names of arriving merchants in the customs books correctly, but if these soon-to-arrive merchants were his relatives, Urasko did not know them personally. The connections were fading. In 1670, Bukharans in Tobolsk had collectively petitioned the tsar to build a guesthouse so that they would not be burdened with quartering these merchants from afar. Urasko recalled the long serious discussions that preceded the petition. Urasko's own father had resisted revealing such a breach in solidarity among Bukharans before the Russian authorities. Others countered that it was no breach but simply a request to the tsar to maintain the merchant way station, just as the rulers maintained the caravansarai in Persian and Turkic lands.

In Siberia his grandfather and uncles had originally settled near Embaevskii iurt, near the Russian town of Tiumen, but they soon relocated to Tobolsk along the Irtysh. Thus, being from caravan people, Urasko never questioned that long and distant travel would be his lot, and so he paid close attention when the conversation turned to distant lands. All he knew of distant arctic oceans he had gleaned from listening as a youth to conversations his elder relatives had with the mapmaker-scholar Ulian Remezov. The governor Petr Godunov had ordered a map to be drawn, and Remezov had spent long hours questioning the Bukharans to learn details of the routes his relatives traveled with their ware-laden caravans to China or Khiva and Bukhara. It was during these conversations that Remezov shared tales of icy oceans far to the dark and frigid north.

It was not the North that held Urasko's attention today, however. He faced southeast, in the direction from which the Irtysh River came, gathering volume as it descended from its pristine headwaters in the distant Altai Mountains. By the time caravans reached this salt lake along the meandering shores of the Irtysh, he thought to himself, they can almost relax. Marauders were always a threat, and the climate (rain, drought, mud, ice, freezing, locusts) could generate any manner of peril at any time, but at least the desert and mountain passes were behind; the terrain became gentler and the floodplain provided sufficient forage for the horses, camels, and goats.

As usual, the arrival of an advance rider heralding the impending caravan made the final waiting hours all the longer. Not that a caravan was such an unusual event. This early October arrival would be among the first of the autumn season, during which time several caravans would reach this lonely outpost, some of which would carry on along the route northwestward to Siberia—each one unique, yet all variations on a theme. Fabrics made up the bulk in nearly every caravan arriving from the east, but even within them the variety was enormous, from thick, coarse cottons to the finest Chinese silks, in all manner of colors. Livestock, dried fruits (raisins, dates), roots (rhubarb, baidan, and ginseng), slaves, Indian spices, Chinese tea, sometimes precious gems, delicate porcelain ware known as china, paper, and ivory were some of the goods typically transported in the crates, sacks, and leather tarps that protected them on their long journey. On the return journey upstream from Lake Iamyshev, the flat-bottomed riverboats sat low in the water bearing furs, leather hides, frying pans, axes, utensils, mirrors, nails, needles, thread, knit socks, boots, and occasionally clocks or mirrors that Asian merchants had purchased. These would soon be transferred to the backs of camels and horses for the overland portion of the journey. Decades later, the Russians would come to blows with and be forced back by the Djungars after Tsar Peter learned of gold coming from that region. But Urasko knew nothing of those future events. All he knew at present was that, with no discernible movement on the distant horizon in this late afternoon light, the promised caravan would not arrive today.

It would not be fair to paint Lake Iamyshev as too desolate. Since ancient times various peoples of Siberia frequented this salt lake, hauling away the mineral treasure to preserve their fish and game. The Turkic root of the name itself, "Iam," suggested that Lake Iamyshev had probably been a way station on Mongol postal routes centuries ago. The Russians learned of the salt lake early in their Siberian ventures. Regular detachments of the Muscovite army harvested the salt, which supplied all the Siberian towns. The military had hastily constructed a fort, which had become the quarters where Urasko and his two Russian colleagues stayed. In addition to the saltworks, the Russian fort, and the Kalmyk camp on the opposite side of the river, an ad hoc market had been evolving throughout the caravan season. This was precisely why Urasko and his Russian colleagues were here now as a seasonal contingent of customs officials sent from Siberian headquarters in Tobolsk. This marketplace had sprung up to avoid the Muscovite state, but the state followed it here.

Officially, this was not a customs station but a customs outpost. Originally, in theory, the Muscovite state was not here to levy taxes but to monitor against contraband. If one were to ask the caravan merchants, however, they did not see it as a way station without levies. Out on the edge of the steppe, the emerging marketplace and occasional transactions between soldiers on duty hardly obscured the fact that large caravans were the bulk of the business. This was a major difference from the Tobolsk market square, where the majority of transactions were made up by local (or even regional) traders—the odd peasant selling his cow to the local butcher or tanner, a woman selling wool stockings she had knit, a soldier selling an iron pan he had bought on campaign. Of course, having early access to the steppe merchants without the competition of local merchants offered a significant advantage, on which Urasko, too, would capitalize. He would be able to negotiate a purchase of the excellent silks and linens. He planned to arrange to have his colleague Ivan Pestriakov's man carry those goods upstream where they could be stored in a church basement until Urasko could collect them himself. Alternatively, he could arrange for an arriving Bukharan merchant or agent to bring the goods to Urasko's own people in Tobolsk. But the church basement strategy helped avoid any temptation that a better offer down the line would result in the merchant's switching out the highest-quality goods for lesser wares—selling them twice, essentially.

Meanwhile, Urasko's wife, children, fields, herd, and trading stall were all back in Tobolsk. Years ago, some peasants from a village between Tiumen and Tobolsk had prohibited the passage of Bukharan women and children to the lake where they used to fish and water their herds while the men were away. Thoughts that similar hassles might befall his family in his absence every so often nagged at him. Urasko was fortunate to have competent and respected relatives who could attend to his interests while he was away, but this did not erase his misgivings entirely.

All things considered, if it were up to him Urasko would fulfill his service to the Russian tsars near his family and community in Tobolsk. There a veritable town had developed around the town kremlin. The kremlin, governor's office, monasteries, and the Tobolsk market square were surrounded by Russian peasants, native Tatars, and Bukharans whose villages dotted the surroundings up and down the river from whose steep banks Tobolsk rose. Church steeples and the minarets of a mosque defined the town skyline, while homes, buildings, and a bustling market square lined with trading stalls, abutted by warehouses and the customs office, all stretched out beyond the kremlin walls. In Tobolsk, Urasko could go with others to the mosque, and in the evenings they sometimes gathered for readings. Before he departed for Lake Iamyshev on this trip, a friend had obtained a copy of Abul-Gazi's chronicle. Local Tatars would also come, but not Russians. Urasko had been enjoying learning the history that the Khivan khan had written and hoped that the text would still be in his friend's possession when he returned.

Lake Iamyshev, far from Tobolsk, offered little in the way of such edifications and diversions. The arrival of caravans, however, brought the lonely outpost to life. As he surveyed the activity around him, Urasko realized that he was not alone in his anticipation of the approaching caravan. The Kalmyk and Kazakh herds grazing across the river, as well as the increased activity in the Kalmyk camp, advertised the arrival of steppe horse traders. When the caravans arrived, so did others: Russian soldiers, Cossack guards, Tatars, Oiriat women, Vogul and Teleut natives, even a contingent of clerics from the Preobrazhenskii Monastery in Tiumen (they had joined in a brisk horse trade in western Siberia in recent years) were all present. Sometimes even merchants from as far away as the lands of the Ottoman sultan appeared. Dmitrii Konstantinov, a Greek merchant who sometimes worked for one of the wealthiest merchants in Moscow, arrived at Lake Iamyshev that morning. Increasingly, state merchants sent to negotiate trades on behalf of the tsar joined the cast of caravan-awaiting characters. The absence of such a contingent today was an exception. Typically, a member of the Bukharan community, whose expertise in eastern wares was well recognized, was part of any state procurement party, which afforded Urasko an opportunity to visit with a friend or relative.

When it finally did arrive, the caravan, tired as its members inevitably were, brought with it a festival feel. Merchants from Bukhara, Khiva, even India or China, mullahs, porters, security escorts, cooks, the wives that accompanied the leading merchants and lowly help alike, and the young sons and relatives that accompanied their relatives apprenticing to the trades all infused the distant outpost of Lake Iamyshev with new life. They stayed for days, sometimes even weeks, depending on the business that materialized there.

Urasko turned away from the horizon and went back inside to join his Russian colleagues. Fedor Vakulin was a townsman from the Russian town of Velikii Ustiug, and Ivan Pestriakov, a townsman from Tobolsk. They were heating up tea. Tea's novelty had not yet worn off. At seven rubles per *pud* it was a drink that would have been beyond their means had they been shoppers in the Moscow marketplace, but this brick of dried tea leaves had been "donated" by a previous caravan in appreciation for allowing the group to proceed without a painstaking and potentially destructive inspection of the crates they were carrying, tightly packed with two hundred teacups from China. When the caravan arrived, they hoped to receive similar "donations." In particular, paper would be much appreciated; the itinerant customs officials were already writing on the backs of sheets previously used for rough drafts. The thought of paper reminded Urasko to make ready the credit slips he carried on behalf of other Tobolsk Bukharans.

The Bukharan and the Russians sat down and drank tea, something they could do together. There were many things they would not do together. They used separate bathhouses. They did not pray together, for Urasko worshipped in the mosque and they, in a church. None of the men raised the subject of their respective faiths with the other. Although he did not say it, Urasko knew that a young girl from Vakulin's household—he did not know if they were related—had been among those professing faithfulness to the True Orthodox Faith who had burned themselves alive in 1679, protesting, as Urasko had heard it, new changes to the Orthodox liturgy. Pestriakov and Vakulin, in turn, both knew that it was Urasko's uncle, Abazbanei Kulmametev, who had submitted a petition to the Russian tsar in Tobolsk accusing the metropolitan of forcing Tatars to convert to Orthodoxy. The clergy in Tobolsk, for their part, had made a series of complaints that Muslims in the town of Tobolsk were guilty of disrespecting Orthodoxy. It was not just that the cries of their daily prayers poisoned the sanctity of Orthodox services and competed with the ringing of church bells. More egregious, accused the clerics, was that on holy days Bukharans, disrespectfully keeping their hats on, laughed and mocked processions of the Orthodox faithful bearing holy icons through the streets of Tobolsk.

For Urasko Kaibulin, however, practical matters could loom larger than theological allegiances or offenses or alliances. For example, he had complained to authorities about a Tatar neighbor, a co-religionist, whose herd had trampled his barley fields, even as one of his uncles was a community leader in advocating for Muslim Tatars before the Russian authorities. Vakulin and Pestriakov did not know how Urasko felt about his Bukharan uncle petitioning the tsars in Moscow on behalf of Siberian Tatars and they did not care to ask. If any of these conflicts were on the minds of the itinerant customs officials, no one spoke of them. Instead, the men sat together, drinking their Chinese tea and talking of caravans, remembered and anticipated, in the fading light on the shores of the Irtysh River.

Suggestions for Further Reading

Burton, Audrey. *The Bukharans: A Dynastic, Diplomatic, and Commercial History, 1550–1702*. Richmond, UK: Curzon, 1997.

Kotilaine, Jarmo. *Russia's Foreign Trade and Economic Expansion in the Seventeenth Century*, 466–77. Leiden: Brill, 2005.

Lantzeff, George V. *Siberia in the Seventeenth Century: A Study of the Colonial Administration*. Berkeley: University of California Press, 1943.

Monahan, Erika. "Trade and Empire: Merchant Networks, Frontier Commerce, and the State in Western Siberia, 1644–1728." Ph.D. diss., Stanford University, 2007.

———. "Gavril Romanov Nikitin: A Portrait." In *People of Empire: Lives of Culture and Power in Russian Eurasia, 1500–Present*. Edited by Willard Sunderland and Stephen Norris. Bloomington University Press (forthcoming).

Steensgaard, Niels. *Carracks, Caravans, and Companies: The Structural Crisis in European–Asian Trade in the Early Seventeenth Century*. Lund: Studenlitteratur, 1973.

VIII
Peasants, Slaves, Serfs, and Holy Fools

∞ 21 ∞

The Parfiev Family
Northern Free Peasants

Jennifer B. Spock

In the sixteenth and seventeenth centuries in the northern territories of the Muscovite tsar, the bulk of the peasant population was free. This population was surprisingly well off, thanks to the lucrative trades that flourished in the harsh swamp lands and forests of the White Sea littoral and the river systems radiating from it. Salt boiling and salt mining, fishing, trapping (for sustenance and for furs and ivory), or trading (in a variety of natural and handmade products) were employed by most families in some combination. Any of these could bring in significant sums. Many families hired laborers, including boatmen who transported goods along the extensive river systems of the North. It has been estimated, based on grain production and prices, that the approximate value of one Novgorod ruble was necessary to feed a family of five for a year. However, families in this region had many more resources than agriculture, and in addition to paying taxes, they often donated large sums to northern churches and monasteries either to receive prayers in return or as simple gestures of faith. The average donation to the monastery of Solovki from a peasant of the Suma River region or Kargopol was ten to twelve Novgorod rubles, a large sum and an indication of the available wealth in the sixteenth century. In documents of the Solovki Monastery in this period, one ruble equaled 33 altyns at 6 den'gas per altyn'. This meant that a Novgorod ruble was worth 198 den'gas or almost twice the value of the Moscow ruble (100 den'gas).

The following biography is based on information from the following types of sixteenth- and seventeenth-century written sources: monastic financial records of incoming and outgoing monies, books that record gifts for commemorative prayer, land deeds, deeds of sale and debt, deeds of gifts, letters and instructions (to or from the tsar or to and from members of the monastic community), legal documents of complaints or court proceedings, saints' lives that portray a desired ideal, and miracle tales of saints that record peasant and monastic behavior. The following libraries, archives, and special collections contain the materials used for this biography: Manuscript Division of the Russian National Library, St. Petersburg;

This sketch of two peasants in a boat was inspired by a style of image-painting that could be seen in Russia's northern churches in the sixteenth century, and specifically by the "Bogomater Bogoliubskaia" icon (ca. 1545), which included scenes from the life of Zosima and Savvatii of Solovki. Northern peasants spent much of their time engaged in activities other than cultivating fields, such as fishing and handicrafts, as the fictional family, the Parfievs, the subject of this chapter demonstrates. (Sketch by Jennifer B. Spock.)

Archive of the Institute of Russian History, St. Petersburg; Russian State Archive of Ancient Acts, Moscow; Hilandar Research Library/Resource Center for Medieval Slavic Studies, Ohio State University.

The horse stamped on the floor above as howls floated through the frosty night. Matrena and her husband Okat prayed to the Mother of God the wolves would not venture close enough to smell the blood and gave thanks that their newborn son was alive. In the following weeks, the baby's sister, Daria, huddling under a bearskin rug in the family's sleeping loft, wished her new brother would stop howling. Forty days later, Dementii son of Okat[1] was baptized and introduced to the small settlement. His Grandfather Parfii (with whom Okat and Matrena lived) and Uncle Konan, who lived nearby with his wife and son, gave the parents a new ax and a trapping net and toasted the baby with vodka.

In that year of 1550, Dementii's family lived in the northeastern territories of the Muscovite tsar. Their cabin and three others nestled together twenty versts from Sumskii Posad, a town of churches, workshops, and homesteads, built where the Suma River flows into the White Sea.[2] Local families engaged in small-scale farming, but there were surer methods for survival and even success along the White Sea coast. Dementii's family lived by fishing, trapping, trading, and salt production.

Parfii was a well-to-do peasant by northern standards. He owned a large log cabin that had a high airy room for summer living with a smaller room attached for winter where the family stayed around the fire. Parfii also owned two full units of land production rights and two quarter-shares in salt-boiling sites, which were scattered piecemeal along the rivers feeding the White Sea.[3] Shortly after Dementii's birth, Tsar Ivan IV donated one of the salt-boiling sites that Parfii worked to the Solovki Monastery, which was located on an archipelago in the White Sea.

At first, Parfii had not understood the tsar's men from the South, for he only spoke the old language. His people had lived along the White Sea for generations,

---

[1] The Parfiev family was not Russian, but Russian forms were used in documents that survived and have been retained here. Some families acquired a surname that might reflect the trade or name of an ancestor, in this case, the grandfather's name, Parfii.

[2] A verst measures approximately 0.66 miles or 1.067 kilometers. Homestead is a translation of *dvor*, which can also be translated as "court." In a village or town it referred to a house with gardens and other buildings surrounding it, sometimes enclosed by a fence.

[3] At this time, in the North, land was measured by what it could produce, rather than by its dimensions. A *luk* was a theoretical amount of products from trapping, fishing, and salt making that could be extracted from a piece of land in addition to representing the extent of land or water expected to provide that amount of produce. Therefore, a *luk* was not always the same standard measure of territory from one region to another. One could own a portion of a *luk*, a quarter or a half being most common. Often, peasants owned various fractions of production rights that were widely scattered along rivers and lakes of the Northeast. Some salt-boiling or salt-mining sites were considered property apart from the *luk* that surrounded it, and peasants could own shares of the site.

and so the southern interlopers from Moscow called him and his neighbors Karelians.[4] Okat and Konan had picked up some of the southern language from traders, and they interpreted for their father when news of the land transfer arrived. Parfii, a free peasant, was furious. He owned two of the eight cauldrons that hung over the huge fire in the salt-boiling cabin, and he had fully expected either to pass the right to these cauldrons on to his sons or to be able to sell his rights if the family needed money.

Parfii ranted that the tsar had no right to give away his production site and was enraged that now he was obliged to give the monastery a percentage of his income from the salt. He had paid taxes on the proceeds to the tsar previously, but collection would be more regular now, since the monks were almost neighbors. The old man resented paying the monks and insulted the one who came to collect.

Unlike the prince's men, the monk (a Karelian) understood Parfii's rude language perfectly and turned away from the cabin without blessing baby Dementii. Okat exploded and hit his father for jeopardizing the monastery's good will. In contrast to individuals or families, the monastery never died, never moved, and had to buy provisions for five hundred monks and servants. Doing business with Solovki was good for one's purse as well as one's soul. Okat ran after the monk to apologize and pay the sum that Parfii owed.

In a great year, one-quarter share of a salt pan could yield an income close to sixty rubles. Fish might bring in another ten to twenty rubles after it was salted and sold up river in Turchasov. Yet, great years at the salt pan or the fishing grounds were rare and did not necessarily mean a successful year at market: boats foundered, bandits stole, and accidents occurred. Income was never certain.

Parfii's family sold salt to traders who came to Sumskii Posad and used the proceeds to acquire tools: cauldrons, hemp rope, anchors, or canvas. Parfii and Okat acquired forest products such as wax and honey in Sumskii Posad or in isolated villages near their land rights. At market fairs in Turchasov and Kargopol (the only city in that far northern region), Okat traded fish and forest products for rye, oats, leather, and utensils. Trade at the crowded fairs could be lucrative, provided one avoided charlatans. Honesty was at a premium, and Parfii and Okat taught little Dima (Dementii's nickname) to trust only a few.

As the population grew, Parfii and Okat used coins more often. They paid taxes on the homestead, the land rights, and the salt. They paid their wage laborers and the boatmen who hauled their goods. Compensation was required for the services of the tsar's men who dispensed justice and collected taxes and for the priest when he performed church rites.

---

[4] "Karelian," in the Muscovite period, referred to any member of a variety of Finno-Ugric tribes who lived in the region roughly bounded by Lakes Ladoga and Onega to the south, and stretching both to the northwest and to the northeast along the White Sea shore. In sixteenth-century texts, the word emphasizes that an individual was of local origin and not a Slav. The phrase "southern language" refers here to Russian.

Although locals often retained non-Christian names, the younger peasants who lived near a major monastery or along well-traveled routes observed basic Orthodox practices while continuing to honor many old forest customs. The priests and monks traveling on missions or trade tried to teach young Dima his catechism, but their visits were sporadic. One of the most important traditions the boy learned about early on was commemorative prayer.[5] Dima was three when Grandfather Parfii tripped and fell on a stake while setting a snare for game. His wound festered. Okat convinced Parfii to receive baptism on his deathbed and then arranged for Christian burial in Sumskii Posad. He also paid for Parfii's daily commemoration for three years at the Solovki Monastery, where prayer was a primary labor for monks, but they had to eat too. To read long lists of names in church was important but time-consuming and took away from other spiritual and manual labors. Those who desired daily prayers had to help support the monks who could not maintain or supervise their large community without help.

That same year, another accident occurred that eventually exercised a profound influence on the family's fortunes. Not far to the east an English merchant ship ran aground, its crew stranded. Okat's neighbor heard of the large ship from trappers and told the settlement about it. Richard Chancellor's crew was the first trickle of a future stream of English adventurers and merchants who came to Russia to seek their fortunes. Okat actually met one of the strange foreigners in the spring and, using gestures, traded a bag of rye for a squirrel skin: a lousy bargain, but a great story! Soon, the English Muscovy Company received permission from Moscow to conduct business within the realm and Dementii's future became linked to these foreigners.

First, however, young Dementii carried wood. As he grew, he chopped and hauled more wood than he cared to think about to smoke fish, boil salt, cook, and warm the cabin. In time, Dementii learned to repair and make nets and to tend the salt works. The big log cabins where simmering cauldrons reduced seawater to salt were stuffy and hot. Dementii preferred to help Okat set snares for game and repair the wooden fishing weirs. Matrena and his sister Daria cured the catch.

Everyone in the family labored daily in harsh conditions. Matrena's and Daria's responsibilities revolved around the homestead. Food preparation combined rye, barley, and root vegetables with any recent catch. They tended the horse, repaired the linen clothes, wove baskets, shoes, and other necessities out of supple birchbark, spun flax, and closed deals or collected debts whenever Okat was away. In his travels Okat encountered thieves on land and worried about fog, storms, and accidents on water. Dementii often got hurt when an ax or knife slipped, had painful sores from

---

[5] Commemoration in Russia took many forms. Forty-day prayers and reading a name in the liturgy on the anniversary of death were a must if one could afford the modest fees. More expensive options were arranging for an annual feast for a monastic community (one hundred rubles) or being commemorated in a daily service for the dead (one ruble per year).

splinters, and was injured more than once while trapping. Matrena and Daria ached every night from their labors. Backbreaking, monotonous chores made simple diversions welcome, and so the boys from the settlement played chicken with knives while Daria listened to the women tell tales of the saints. Okat and Matrena liked strong drink and dancing. The parish priest deplored all these pastimes except Daria's.

Traveling by boat was both vital and dangerous. Eight-year-old Dementii fell into the icy waters when a storm arose and the dark waves swept him overboard. He was terrified, floundering, gasping, his coarse clothes and squirrel-fur cloak tugging him under, the salt in his mouth and eyes. Throwing a rope overboard, Okat prayed to God and to Saints Zosima and Savvatii (the founders and patron saints of Solovki) to guide the rope to his son. He vowed to donate all the goods in his heavy wooden boat to the monastery if Dementii were saved. Okat's prayer was answered for, like a fish, Dementii caught the line and was hauled aboard, where he promptly threw up. For days after, Dementii preferred to stay home until a painful encounter with Okat's birch rod restored his courage for sea travel.

Okat fulfilled his vow and donated his load of goods to Solovki. Afterwards, Matrena wanted to know: was this a good year (a huge donation to the saints) or a lean year (a major loss of income)? From then on, an image of Saints Zosima and Savatii—protectors and healers of peasants, woodsmen, and traders in the White Sea region—stood on a shelf in the eastern corner of the cabin. The family tried hard to remember to bow and make the sign of the cross in front of the icon in the morning, before meals, and before bedtime. It was a few months before these additional devotions became automatic for Dima and the rest of the family. Okat gave small icons to his partners and his two hired laborers to remind them to pray for protection and prosperity. Dementii grew up aware that the cloister and its saints were ever-present and significant in good times and in bad.

One of the bad years was 1560. Uncle Konan died and left debts, so his wife moved back to her family's house after she sent her son, Ivan (called Vania by his family), to Solovki Monastery. As a servant to the monks, the fatherless boy could learn a trade, his labor would pay for prayers for Konan, and Ivan would be free to stay or leave when he reached adulthood. Dementii missed his playmate, but Ivan's service to the monks tied the Parfiev family more closely to Solovki even while Okat became embroiled in a dispute with the cloister.

Okat had not fished one of his portions along the Keret River for a while, since Konan's death made work harder. Solovki servants had been seen using his fishing weir, and although Okat did not begrudge them the fish, he felt the monks should pay their fair share of taxes for the income they acquired off his land. A local elder negotiated a compromise by which Okat and Solovki would pay taxes for that site proportionate to the amounts of fish each caught.

Dementii was afraid that his father's dispute would anger the saints and the abbot. Okat explained that the monks had to follow the rules like everyone else. People occasionally got away with fishing outside their own waters but had to accept the consequences if discovered, and everyone knew that, including the monks, most of whom were from the North. Written documents showed the owners for each section of the river, each trapping or salt-production site, and each field, so Okat had to sign the back of a deed in the presence of witnesses whenever he bought or transferred rights. The monks kept the papers, so they knew better than anyone where they could and could not fish. Okat and his partners did not read or write well, but they could sound out words to recognize names, landmarks, and amounts. They began to teach Dementii the alphabet.

By the 1570s, Dementii and Daria faced new problems. Daria was five years older and at age twenty, with a dowry of a horse, a dress, and five rubles, she had married a blacksmith, Konstiantin Stefanov *syn*. She left home for Konstiantin's village, but six years after their wedding, in 1571, one day Konstiantin was in the wrong place at the wrong time. A detachment of Ivan IV's troops demanded extra upkeep, and its leader ordered his men to beat the village elders who claimed to have supplied enough provisions and services already.[6] In the resulting mélée, Konstiantin was kicked in the head by a horse and died. Daria and her two-year-old son, Stefan, returned to Okat's homestead.

Death visited again in 1572, when a terrible epidemic swept the North and killed Matrena and Okat. At age twenty-two, Dementii became head of the family with little time to grieve. He sailed to Solovki with a shipment of rye, and while there he arranged commemoration for his parents. He saw his cousin Ivan, who had accepted tonsure and taken a new name, Iosif. Dementii gave Iosif three rubles[7] and rushed to leave, for he was busy supervising new laborers and was rebuilding business partnerships that had been severed by the epidemic.

At twenty-six, the eligible bachelor married Lukeria Vasilieva *doch*, whose dowry was a quarter of fishing rights. They built a cabin on the edge of Sumskii Posad, near the new stone winter church.[8] Daria and Stefan moved with them, and they prospered until the famine hit. Food shortages in 1579 resulted from the wars of Ivan IV, the heavier taxes needed to pay for them, and poor harvests. Dementii's resources diminished as settlements became deserted, and his trading trips to Turchasov and Kargopol became infrequent. He sold some land and water rights to the monastery and his partners but did not sell Lukeria's dowry, for that was her personal property.

---

[6] In Muscovite Russia there had been a long-standing practice called "feeding" (*kormlenie*) by which servitors of the grand princes were entitled to be fed and housed while on the prince's errands. Vestiges of the practice remained in the mid-sixteenth century.

[7] At many monasteries, retention of coins was not allowed, but at Solovki Monastery monks could keep some personal money in their cells and receive gifts from relatives or friends. Although both practices were accepted, they were not necessarily universal at Solovki, nor were large sums generally involved. The reliance on trade in the environment around Solovki probably influenced this more lenient practice.

[8] In northern Russia it was normal for a town to have a summer church that was large with good air flow, and nearby a smaller winter church with a stove, which would provide warmer conditions for worship during cold months.

Daria fell ill that year and sought help from the midwife who had directed Stefan's birth. The old woman's herbal remedies failed. When the ice melted, Daria made a pilgrimage to the shrines of Saints Zosima and Savvatii at Solovki, where women could sit in vigil at the tombs. Daria spent a night alone in prayer; and the next day she was calmer, convinced she would improve. The silence during her vigil, the distant chants of matins, and the icons flickering in the candlelight impressed her deeply.

In the spring, her wracking cough disappeared, but she was weaker. She resumed her chores but insisted that Dementii, Lukeria, and Stefan observe fasts strictly. Daria tried to restrain Dementii from trapping on Sundays—a common practice—since one never knew when the weather might change. After his older sister stressed the evils of Sunday expeditions for two years, however, even Dementii wondered if this explained why he and Lukeria remained childless. He ceased trapping on Sundays, and in 1583 he was rewarded by God when Nikon Dementiev *syn* was born. Nikon was sickly, and coughing in the dirty, damp, smoke-filled cabin.

Lukeria complained of Daria's insistence on family devotions but got little support since the priest upheld Daria's pronouncements. Lukeria was on safer ground when it came to ordering the family's daily affairs. Dementii often left her in charge during his absences and rarely lost his temper over one of her decisions. Lukeria could direct the family's business if Dementii died but if sickly little Nikon passed away, she would have to marry or be without support as she aged. Stefan was almost old enough to be on his own and, without his uncle for a partner, might leave. Dementii knew that the uncertainty caused by his long absences deepened the tension between Lukeria and Daria.

In 1585, a new town, Arkhangelsk, was founded near the mouth of the Northern Dvina River to accommodate the increasing flow of English trade. The English merchants did business with both Moscow and northern contacts, which gave the northerners plenty of opportunities to exchange goods with these foreigners. Dementii discovered that his forest products, especially those used in shipping, could be sold more easily in Arkhangelsk, where both the English and Solovki had warehouses. He decided to stop fishing, trapping, and salt making and to focus on trade, adding tar and hemp to his list of goods. He enjoyed a solid reputation, although in lean times he was sometimes accused of incorrect weights. He hired two permanent boatmen to haul his goods and built a storage barn behind the cabin stuffed with barrels, boxes, and bundles.

Lukeria died in childbirth when their daughter, Olga, was born in 1590. Inheriting his wife's property, Dementii finally sold his remaining fishing and salt rights to Solovki and rented a space in an Arkhangelsk warehouse. The investment was timely. In 1591, Swedes attacked the north. They laid waste the western coast of the White Sea, destroyed villages and saltworks, and killed much of the population. Many peasants fled, including Dementii. He installed the family in a snug cabin in Arkhangelsk near his warehouse, and Daria raised the children while Stefan took on the responsibilities of a full business partner. Some of the villages and forest settlements where Dementii and Stefan traded disappeared due to illness, war, migration, and fire, but the muddy streets of Arkhangelsk, paved with logs and alive with activity, offered new opportunities. Yet travel throughout the North was no less dangerous for Dementii just because he now started his trips from a city, and robbers and drunks made Arkhangelsk's streets hazardous.

War resumed when Tsar Boris Godunov died in 1605 and the succession was endangered. News reached Arkhangelsk that Tsarevich Dmitrii had ascended the throne bringing a Polish retinue. Nikon claimed that was nonsense. The true tsar could not possibly live with heretics, although Nikon had no problem making money off them! He was sure the Muscovite merchant had garbled the information. Months later, more news arrived: Vasilii Shuiskii had been elected tsar. Nikon made rude jokes about stupid Muscovites choosing rulers. By 1609 he was more serious, for only God knew who was ruling in Moscow when Swedes invaded the North again.

Tired and old, Dementii fell sick that year and entered the hospital on Solovki to die.[9] In the summer, lying in the dark hospital with narrow windows, tended by his cousin (the monk Iosif) and sure that death approached, Dementii accepted tonsure and took the name Dionisii.[10] He gave the monastery another ten rubles for his own and his family's memorials.[11]

But Dionisii did not depart to God. He recovered and bought one-quarter of a place in a monastic cell.[12] He learned the daily prayers and worked in the kitchen, which was the labor given to those too infirm to carry out physical tasks. When Nikon arrived in late summer to deliver rye and canvas to the monastery, Dionisii gave him a piece of *prosfora* for Daria, who was ill.[13] He instructed Nikon to place the bread in a bowl near the head of her bed to promote healing. Before leaving, Nikon deposited coins in the pitchers that stood on the tombs of Saints Zosima and Savvatii. He prayed for good sailing and the defeat of the Swedes.

---

[9] Many Russian monasteries had hospitals to care for invalids, and both monks and laymen might be found in these charitable institutions. At Solovki, anyone who died while on the monastery's grounds received three years of daily commemorative prayer for free. Commemoration for all monks, servants, visitors, and invalids was a considerable financial drain.

[10] Deathbed tonsure was common, since it included confession and it was believed that the monastic (angelic) form could help one achieve redemption.

[11] Over his lifetime, Dionisii/Dementii gave seventeen rubles, more than the average for a Suma region inhabitant, for he had become a well-to-do townsman in Arkhangelsk.

[12] It was common for a monk to buy space in a cell shared with two or three people. The monastery used this money to commemorate the former inhabitant.

[13] In Russian Orthodoxy the Eucharist (sacrifice) is performed with pieces cut from leavened loaves that have been blessed by the priest and are called *prosfora*. The entire loaf is blessed before the liturgy, and that part which is not used for the sacrifice (a center portion called the Lamb—*agnets*) is distributed to the congregation as a sign of community and peace after the service. Unused loaves of *prosfora* might also be distributed to the needy or taken to hermit monks.

242 PEASANTS, SLAVES, SERFS, AND HOLY FOOLS

Dionisii passed away at night in 1611 as the ice broke on the rooftops. The wood and dirt monastery of his grandfather's time had become a fortress of God, with stone churches and walls where sentries stood: a community vibrant with trade and work, echoing with prayer and bells. Dementii's family had helped Solovki prosper just as its saints had helped them. Despite fear, violence, disease, and death, he died in holy confession, hoping his son and daughter would carry on the family work and devotions. Dementii's troubles ended, but Russia's Time of Troubles continued, and Nikon's prayers for peace in the North went unanswered until 1618.

Suggestions for Further Reading

Very little has been written in English on the peasants of the Russian North during the sixteenth and seventeenth centuries, but the reader may find the following informative:

Michels, Georg. "The Solovki Uprising: Religion and Revolt in Northern Russia." *Russian Review* 51, no. 1 (1992): 1–15.

The Monastic Rule of Joseph Volotsky. Edited, translated, and introduced by David Goldfrank. Kalamazoo, MI: Cistercian Publications, 1983.

Robson, Roy. *Solovki: The Story of Russia Told Through Its Most Remarkable Islands.* New Haven: Yale University Press, 2004.

Spock, Jennifer. *The Solovki Monastery 1460–1645: Piety and Patronage in the Early Modern Russian North.* Ph.D. diss., Yale University, 1999.

For readers who read Russian, much more is available, of which the following are recommended:

Gadziatskii, S. *Karely i Kareliia v novgorodskoe vremia.* Petrozavodsk: Karelo-Finskii SSR, 1941.

Kopanev, A.I. *Krest'ianstvo Russkogo Severa v XVI v.* Leningrad: Nauka, 1978.

———. *Krest'ianstvo Russkogo Severa v XVII v.* Leningrad: Nauka, 1984.

Savich, A.A. *Solovetskaia votchina XV–XVII vv. Opyt izucheniia khoziaistva i sotsial'nykh otnoshenii na krainem russkom severe v drevnei Rusi.* Perm: Permskii gosudarstvennyi universitet, 1927.

Shapiro, A.L., ed. *Agrarnaia istoriia severo-zapada Rossii XVI veka (Naselenie, zemlevladenie, zemlepol'zovanie).* Leningrad: Nauka, 1989.

———. *Agrarnaia istoriia severo-zapada Rossii XVI veka: Novgorodskie piatiny.* Leningrad: Nauka, 1974.

———. *Agrarnaia istoriia severo-zapada Rossii XVI veka. Sever. Pskov. Obshchie itogi razvitiia severo-zapada.* Leningrad: Nauka, 1978.

———. *Agrarnaia istoriia severo-zapada Rossii: vtoraia polovina XV–nachalo XVI v.* Leningrad: Nauka, 1971.

———. *Agrarnaia istoriia severo-zapada Rossii XVII veka.* Leningrad: Nauka, 1974.

Skopin, V.V. *Arkhitekturno-khudozhestvennyi ansambl' Solovetskogo monastyria.* Moscow: Iskusstvo, 1982.

∞ 22 ∞

Muscovite Lives
A Slave and a Serf

Richard Hellie

Slaves and serfs together made up over 90 percent of the population, perhaps as much as 95 percent. Depending on the locale and the era, slaves in Muscovy comprised 5 to 15 percent of the population. Peasants (later serfs) comprised 85 to 90 percent of the population. Calculating that townsmen accounted for 2 percent of the population, the members of the service classes another 2 percent, and the members of the clergy at most a final 2 percent, then slaves and serfs were the remainder in what was not a very complex society. In this essay the composite imaginary slave is placed in the 1590s, because that is when fundamental changes were made in the institution of slavery. The imaginary serf is placed in the 1640s, because that is when the institution of serfdom was fully established legally by the Law Code (Ulozhenie) of 1649.

The difference between slaves and serfs should be spelled out briefly. Slaves were an ancient category of society present from the beginnings of Russian history. By Muscovite times there were half a dozen categories of slaves, but they were all considered mere objects of the law rather than subjects and the complete property of their owners (with a few limitations: the Church prescribed that their owners had to allow them to marry, and it is doubtful that owners had the right to kill their slaves). Muscovite slaves were primarily of the "household" type, rather than the "production" type. Serfs, on the other hand, did not exist in any fashion in early Russian history. In the Muscovite sense of peasants bound to the land, they began to be created only in the second half of the fifteenth century, and in many respects serfdom was set in place by the 1590s with the introduction of the "temporary" forbidden years, which forbade peasants to move. This prohibition remained in place in one form or another until 1906. There was one "escape": a five-year statute of limitations was decreed for the recovery of fugitive serfs; until this was repealed in 1649, the peasants were not fully enserfed. According to the Law Code of 1649 (chapter 11, articles 1 and 2), all peasants (both seignorial and nonseignorial) were enserfed, bound to the land. Like slaves, after 1649, fugitives could be recovered without any statute of limitations.

Fieldwork miniature from the sixteenth-century *Illuminated Chronicle* (Litsevoi svod). The miniature shows plowing, seeding, and harvesting being done simultaneously, although these were sequential stages of the crop-growing process. It was typical for medieval artists to conflate events occurring at different times into one picture. "The major crop was rye, which was the basis of the peasants' diet.... Their next major crop was oats, which they needed to feed the horses.... The crop yields were extraordinarily low, 3:1—three seeds were harvested for each one sown."

A SLAVE: FOMA SON OF KARP

Foma Karpov *syn* was a hereditary slave registered by his owner Bogdan Posnikovich Sheremetev in the great registration of all slaves required by the Muscovite government in the 1590s. The Sheremetev family had preserved for 150 years the written records of Foma's family's slavery, which commenced when his ancestor Kondrat had sold himself into full slavery to Sheremetev's ancestor for a ruble. The law of those 150 years placed more emphasis on written records documenting slavery than any other form of property, so the Sheremetev family resolved that it would keep all its records as well. The Church insisted that owners had to permit their slaves to marry, and that the marriage was inviolable. Thus each time one of Foma's ancestors married, new documents were generated, either by literate slaves in the Sheremetev household or by independent scribes. The documents were both filed with the government and kept in the Sheremetev archive, which consisted of scrolls for each slave family. Every time a new document was generated, it was glued to the bottom of the ever-lengthening scroll. As Foma's ancestors were married either to other slaves in the Sheremetev household or to new slaves purchased in the market, the new documents were glued on to the scroll of Foma's lineage.[1] Entries were also made in the scroll when children were born, who were also slaves, but those documents were not necessarily filed with the government. The slave family was not inviolable, so that owners could dispose of children apart from their parents if they desired. Foma and his fellow slaves were not aware of the fact that, by world standards, perpetual, hereditary slavery was unusual, because in most other societies almost all slaves initially were outsiders who with the passage of time became "domesticated" and thus became insiders.

Foma lived with his wife Matrona (four years his junior) and their two children, Spiridon and Filip, in slave quarters adjacent to the Sheremetev household. Foma and Matrona had two boys "by accident," but they were very much aware of the fact that people currently selling themselves into limited service contract slavery (which was replacing full slavery as the entry institution), had only boys because they had committed female infanticide, as they tried to hold their families together by reducing the number of mouths that had to be fed before selling themselves into slavery. When Foma's ancestor had sold himself into full slavery, he knew that all of his descendants would be slaves, for at the time Russia did not have a notion that owners should manumit their chattel. Then a new form of slavery, limited service contract slavery, was introduced. It was more complex, for it briefly held out the option that the slave might be freed within a year. In this form of antichresis, the slave "borrowed" money for a year, during which time he worked for the interest and had the right to repay the principle. It turned out that repaying the principle

---

[1] Typically these were persons in need, selling themselves because Russian society offered no other form of welfare, but occasionally by owners selling military captives harvested on the western front or from among the Turkic peoples in the South.

was impossible, so the "borrower" defaulted and thus he, his family, and all their heirs became perpetual, hereditary slaves. This in itself was not an innovation, for throughout all of Russian history defaulting on debt repayment was considered a "crime" punishable by enslavement.

Foma was aware from his fellow slaves that the nature of limited service contract slavery had been changed in the 1590s, at about the same time the government was ordering the universal registration of all slaves. Previously limited service contract slavery had commenced with a loan for a year, which defaulted to perpetual slavery because, it so happened in reality, that no one was ever able to pay off the principal of the loan. In the 1590s, the government was alarmed by the growing number of slaves, who paid no taxes, so it changed the nature of limited service contract slavery. Now the "loan for a year" provision was repealed, as was the possibility of repaying the "loan" at all. The legislation on the new limited service contract slavery stated that fundamentally the slave sold himself to the owner (much as in the older full slavery), but that on the owner's death, the slave had to be manumitted. This expropriated the slaveowner's heirs, without any compensation. Foma sensed that this would not work, that it would not increase the taxpaying population, because once a slave had become dependent upon an owner, he could not lead an independent life and would almost immediately sell himself again either to an heir of the deceased owner or to another person willing to buy him.

Foma's family life in the slave quarters was not burdensome. In fact, it was probably the easiest life in Muscovy. The Sheremetevs did not own slaves for the purposes of producing anything but primarily for the purpose of demonstrating that they were comparatively prosperous members of the Muscovite service class, as a visual demonstration of prestige. The Sheremetevs themselves had to work hard, especially when they were in cavalry service or, rather rarely, in government civil service administering Moscow or the provinces. The Sheremetevs set the tone, and thus all members of the cavalry—most of whom were not prosperous—wanted to have at least one slave.

At times, some of Foma's fellow slaves had to accompany their owner to the military front, where they worked as body servants or drivers of the baggage train. At the front, the slaves risked falling into military captivity at the hands of the Swedes, Poles, or Tatars. Should they flee captivity and return to Muscovy, they were automatically manumitted. Given the dependency created by slavery, however, most manumitted freedmen almost immediately sold themselves back into the relatively easy life of slavery. Also among Foma's fellow chattel were a group of elite slaves, men whom Sheremetev had purchased for the enormous sum of fifteen rubles apiece to accompany him to the front as fellow cavalrymen after the government in 1556 had decreed that all land had to provide military service at the rate of one mounted, fully equipped cavalryman per 230 acres of land. As Sheremetev was a large landowner, he had to provide many armed cavalrymen.

Aside from occasionally accompanying the baggage train to the front, Foma had little work to do. Sometimes he had to drive Sheremetev's coach, deliver messages for him, shop for the Sheremetev family, or even clean the slave quarters and the master's house. Others of Sheremetev's slaves did the cooking, laundry, and sewing of clothing. One of their tasks was going to Sheremetev's estates and collecting their food from Sheremetev's peasants. Foma also had an alcohol allowance, for he, like all Russians (in the famous words of Prince Vladimir, who Christianized Rus in 988), "loved to drink and could not live without it." In general, the slaves ate about the same things the Sheremetev family did—perhaps a little less meat, but otherwise there was no difference. As the Sheremetev family was well-to-do, there was no concern about the heating bill, with the result that neither the owner nor his chattel lived in the smoky huts that peasants inhabited. As a result, they breathed relatively cleaner air than did the peasants. This, combined with a better diet, meant that they lived a little longer, as well as more pleasantly. These facts, along with the security of knowing that food and clothing would be provided and what the daily routine would be, were the major attractions of slavery.

Although unquestionably Foma had one of the best lower-class lives in Muscovy, it was not completely easy. First, he understood full well that he was the complete possession of Sheremetev. He had to live where Sheremetev told him to, had to do whatever Sheremetev told him to whenever the order was given, and was lawfully compelled to submit to whatever discipline or abuse Sheremetev (or one of his slave stewards) desired to mete out to him. Foma believed that the abuse could not extend to killing him but knew that no sanction would be applied should "discipline" result in his death.

Foma also knew that legally he owned nothing. Some of his fellow slaves had tried to flee, and Foma knew that the official documents putting their pursuit in motion had included descriptions of the clothing in which the fugitives had fled. (Most of the other items listed with the fugitives were easy-to-carry things stolen by the slaves from their master's bedroom, such as jewelry.) In his everyday life it made no difference to Foma that he owned nothing, for neither he nor Sheremetev cared what he wore. Foma knew from talking with slaves who belonged to merchants that they traded on their owners' behalf and de facto had considerable assets. This, however, was not the lot of Foma, who possessed only his wife and a relatively comfortable and secure life.

A PEASANT/SERF: IGNATII SON OF IVAN

Ignatii Ivanov *syn* was a peasant living on a service landholding (*pomest'e*) south of Moscow that belonged to the middle service class cavalryman (*pomeshchik*) Danila Ivanovich Miachkov. Ignatii, usually referred to by his diminutive Ignashka, lived in a small village of six peasant households stretched out in a row along the village's "street." He was not a member of a peasant commune, which did not exist in 1649. This village was assigned to Miachkov by the government for his support as a cavalryman. The role of Ignashka in the Muscovite service state was to provide the food and clothing that Miachkov and his family (including one male slave) needed, as well as the fodder for Miachkov's cavalry warhorse. Miachkov purchased the horse, his sword, bows and arrows, and pistol in the market with his annual stipend from the government (which was paid only when combat was anticipated).

It was hard for Ignashka and his fellow serfs to support themselves and Miachkov while also paying taxes. Ignashka lived with his wife and two small children in a log hut he and his neighbors had constructed themselves. The hut was small, the size of the length of the trees they had cut down to build it. The logs were chinked with mud and moss. The roof was covered with shingles the peasants themselves had hewn out of the trees. A good portion of the space inside the hut was occupied by the stove, an elaborate rock and mortar construction with three chambers in it, designed to extract all the heat the wood fire produced. The stove had no chimney, which meant that the stove vented the smoke into the room through a smoke hole in the back of the stove. (Had there been a chimney, 80 percent of the heat would have gone out the chimney.) Ignashka used the stove to heat the hut six months of the year. During the heating season in the ferociously cold winters, the hut was full of smoke all of this time. The smoke was concentrated in the upper part of the hut, with the result that there was a line around the inside of the hut about shoulder-high where the bottom of the smoke was concentrated. Breathing the smoke with its hundreds of harmful particles and carbon monoxide was very hard on everyone's health, and it is not surprising that Ignashka often had very little energy. It was a good fortune that most of the heating season coincided with the time when there was little farm work to do.

Besides the stove, there was little else in Ignashka's hut. There were benches around the walls where people sat during the daytime and on which Ignashka, his wife, and two children slept at night (on cushions filled with straw). There was a trunk in which the family kept its spare and out-of-season clothing. The family's clothing wardrobe was small: male and female blouses, shirts, caftans, caps and hats, winter coats, female dresses, jackets, mittens, pants, stockings, shoes, and boots. In the hut there was also a small table but no chairs or other furniture. There were only three small windows in the hut, with mica panes to conserve heat. There was a dirt floor, which facilitated the cleanup of the slurry of excrement during the winter, when Ignashka's livestock lived inside the hut with the family to keep them from freezing to death outside while generating warmth for everyone.

Ignashka had few livestock: one plow horse, one cow, sometimes a pig or sheep, and a few chickens. The cow gave little milk, and the chickens at best laid one egg a week apiece. Ignashka supplemented the family diet with some fishing in the nearby stream and a little hunting, especially in the winter. Feeding the livestock over the winter was a major problem, and often the animals were so weak that they had to be carried out to pasture in the springtime.

Ignashka's hut was located in a yard (*dvor*), which had a fence around it. Besides the hut, there was a small building to house the livestock except when it was so cold that they had to live with the family inside the hut. There was also an outhouse and a shed where Ignashka's tools were kept, where hay was stored while it lasted, and where the harvest was kept until it became so cold that those things that would perish from freezing were moved inside the hut. Ignashka's inventory consisted of a two-pronged scratch plow (*sokha*), an instrument ideally suited for stirring up the thin (3 inches thick) layer of acidic podzol. He also owned a harrow, a square frame with half a dozen cross pieces from which spikes protruded to break the plowed soil into smaller clumps. The plow and the harrow were pulled by Ignashka's horse. In addition, Ignashka owned an ax for hewing wood, a sickle and a scythe for harvesting grain and cutting hay, and a flail for threshing grain. All these things—his hut, his outbuildings, his furniture, his clothing, his cooking utensils, his livestock, his agricultural implements, his grain stores—belonged to Ignashka. His lord Miachkov had no claim to any of those things. Miachkov really did not even own the land, which was only allotted to him by the state.

Ignashka's major occupation was that of farmer. Miachkov's service landholding contained more land than his peasants could farm. There was also a small forest on it whence came building materials and firewood and a meadow where the peasants grazed their livestock. The meadow was not fenced, so that at least one of the peasants had to act as herdsman while the meadow was open. The land that the peasants had the energy to farm was divided into strips, with each family receiving as many strips as it could plow and cultivate within a three-field system of crop rotation.

The major crop was rye, which was the basis of the peasants' diet. (Miachkov ate what the peasants ate.) Their next major crop was oats, which they needed to feed the horses (especially Miachkov's warhorse). The crop yields were extraordinarily low, 3:1—three seeds were harvested for each one sown. The major explanation for the low yields lay in what Ignashka and his fellow peasants had been doing with their harvest for hundreds of years and would continue to do for centuries: "downward selection." When the harvest was in, they picked out the largest grains and sold them or gave them to their lord to eat (or paid taxes with them), instead of planting the largest ones. Then the peasants themselves ate the medium-sized grains, and planted the smallest ones.

In addition to rye, Ignashka planted a few other grains, primarily barley and wheat. Ignashka and his wife also had a garden, in which they raised cabbage, cucumbers, garlic, and onions. In their yard, they also had a couple of apple trees. This diet kept the peasants alive but not well nourished. When one adds in the smoky hut, one is not surprised to find that the life expectancy was less than thirty years, and that few reached the age of forty. Grandparents rarely lived long enough to see grandchildren.

The climate of Russia provided still other problems for Ignashka. The agricultural year was extremely short. It began around May 15/early June, and frost set in around September 21. At both ends of the agricultural season, during the spring sowing season and during the fall harvest, Ignashka's household was in a frenzy, for they labored as hard as they could to plant their crops and then to harvest them. A major advantage of their winter rye crop was that it could be worked somewhat more leisurely: it was planted in the fall, when there was not so much other work to do, and harvested in the late summer, also at a time when other work was not so pressing.

The short growing season, like the soil, limited the crops that could be grown. Another factor limiting productivity was the absence of fertilizer, for Ignashka's livestock produced meager amounts of manure. Often there was excessive precipitation. As a result, crop failures were frequent, and famines occurred as often as every seven years. Weakened by hunger, Ignashka and his family never knew when they would be attacked by major epidemics, which less frequently afflicted the more well-fed servicemen and their slaves. Unlike the slaves, the peasants had no one looking after them, no safety net. Ignashka tried to store grain reserves. Typically he could survive one season of lower than normal or no yields, but two such seasons in succession threatened the entire family. The lower-class practice was to withhold food first from the girls in the hope that the males would survive, but often they did not.

Ignashka was aware that he was not a free man, that he was a serf. His lord Miachkov had been one of the middle service class provincial cavalry delegates to the Assembly of the Land (*Zemskii sobor*) that met from October 1648 to January 29, 1649, to draft the Law Code (*Ulozhenie*) of 1649. After the meeting of the Assembly of the Land, Miachkov explained to his peasants what had happened. It was part of peasant lore that they had once been free to move on St. George's Day (November 26), but that this freedom had been taken away from them by Boris Godunov in the name of Tsar Fedor in 1592. But along with this decree went a provision that meant that the peasants were not yet fully enserfed: a five-year statute of limitations on the filing of suits for the recovery of fugitive serfs. Thus any fugitive serf who could avoid detection by his "lawful possessor" for five years became a free man, which was relatively easy to do. In the first place, Muscovy was a big country. Second, the country was getting even bigger and recruiters were actively seeking peasants to settle on the expanding frontier south of the Oka, along the Volga River, and in Siberia. Finally, the North (north of the Volga, inhabited largely by Finnic peoples) was becoming a more attractive place to settle with the opening of the White Sea trade, as well as because of the absence of service landholders.

Miachkov and his fellow provincial cavalrymen had discovered from experience that all too often they could not find their fugitive peasants within the five-year time limit. So the servitors initiated what became a petition campaign in 1637 for the repeal of the statute of limitations. The government did not want to agree, because certain other landowners and landholders profited from the limitation to recruit others' serfs and the government wanted the expanding frontiers settled. Therefore, they agreed to extend the statute of limitations only to nine years. Miachkov and his comrades tried again in 1641, and the government extended the statute of limitations to fifteen years. The servicemen petitioned again in 1645, and this time the government agreed to repeal the statute of limitations—after a census had been taken. The census was taken in 1646–47, but nothing was done to repeal the statute of limitations. Tiring of governmental highhandedness and corruption, the people of Moscow and a dozen other towns rebelled in June 1648. The violence and disturbances that resulted forced the government to consent to the compilation of a new law code and to its debate and approval by an Assembly of the Land.

At the Assembly of the Land, Miachkov and his fellow provincial cavalrymen demanded the repeal of the statute of limitations, and that repeal became articles 1 and 2 of chapter 11 of the Law Code of 1649. As a result, any peasant who had fled at any time in the past could be returned to the place where he was registered in official documents.

Miachkov stressed to Ignashka that he, Ignashka, was bound to the land allotted to Miachkov, not to himself (Miachkov) personally. Since Ignashka did not belong to him personally, like a slave, therefore he (Miachkov) was not responsible for him. Ignashka was forbidden to sell himself into slavery. He had to remain a peasant as long as he lived on Miachkov's service landholding—regardless of who owned it.

Ignashka found this situation both confusing and intolerable. He still was the subject of the law, not its object (like a slave). Miachkov was not his owner and was not his personal master. But Ignashka still had to pay taxes (unlike a slave). He still owned his personal property, livestock, inventory, and so on, and Miachkov had no claim to any of it. Yet Ignashka was not a free man, and there was no way he could become a free man. He could not move where he liked, and if he fled, there was a strong likelihood that he would be returned. Miachkov told him that the government had formed a corps of fugitive serf hunters to scour the land looking for runaways and to return them to where they belonged—unlike in former times, when the interested landowner/holder himself had to find the fugitive and sue for his return. Moreover, Ignashka understood that he and his offspring were likely to remain peasants forever, that the chance of becoming anything else, from a slave to a townsman to a soldier, was permanently forbidden. What he did not know was that his descendents would remain serfs until 1861 and would be restricted in their movements within the country until 1906.

Suggestions for Further Reading

Blum, Jerome. *Lord and Peasant in Russia from the Ninth to the Nineteenth Century.* Princeton, NJ: Princeton University Press, 1961.
Hellie, Richard. *The Economy and Material Culture of Russia, 1600–1725.* Chicago: University of Chicago Press, 1999.
———. *Enserfment and Military Change in Muscovy.* Chicago: University of Chicago Press, 1971.
———. "The Russian Smoky Hut and Its Probable Health Consequences." *Russian History* 28, nos. 1–4 (2001): 171–84.
———. *Slavery in Russia, 1450–1725.* Chicago: University of Chicago Press, 1982.
Kivelson, Valerie A. "The Devil Stole His Mind: The Tsar and the 1648 Moscow Uprising." *American Historical Review* 98, no. 3 (1993): 733–56.
The Muscovite Law Code (Ulozhenie) of 1649. Translated by Richard Hellie. Irvine, CA: Charles Schlacks, 1988.
Muscovite Society. Edited and translated by Richard Hellie. Chicago: University of Chicago Syllabus Division, 1967, 1970.
Ostrowski, Donald. "The Assembly of the Land (*Zemskii sobor*) as a Representative Institution." In *Modernization in Seventeenth-Century Russia.* Edited by Jarmo Kotilaine and Marshall T. Poe. London: RoutledgeCurzon, 2004, 117–42.

∞ 23 ∞

Dunia, a Fool for Christ

Hugh M. Olmsted

This is the biographical portrait of an imaginary Russian fool for Christ, Dunia, whose life is set in late sixteenth-century Moscow. In Russia holy fools, traditionally called iurodivye *(singular* iurodivyi, *feminine* iurodivaia), *are persons whose assumed simplicity or insanity puts them outside the normal range of commonplace ethics, discourse, and etiquette. Most typically they behave outrageously, challenge all social norms publicly, shake average people out of their complacency, and reveal deeper truths, generally in the name of difficult Christian ideals. Often the role was assumed purposefully in order to achieve a deeper purpose.*

*This phenomenon of "holy foolery" (*iurodstvo*) was particularly strong in Muscovite Rus, when the growing power of the state and autocracy, not without abuses of power and principle, might leave a major gap between ideal and practice. The* iurodivyi *frequently is portrayed as having fearlessly stood up to the grand prince and tsar. In this role he/she can be imagined as a sort of super whistle-blower, immune from normal retribution because of his or her perceived otherworldliness and sanctity. We have no examples of a female fool in Christ from as early as the sixteenth century, but we can imagine that they existed, if rarely.*

Muscovy had quite a number of male iurodivyi *figures, many of whom became glorified as saints. A special category of sainthood was established for the holy fool: such a saint was called "the Blessed" (Blazhennyi). The perception, behavior, and role of the* iurodivyi *changed over the centuries, especially as it became more and more of an accepted cultural institution, inviting self-conscious manipulation, false* iurodivye's *using the role for personal gain, and the like. Therefore, people of whom the term "*iurodivyi*" is used may differ widely over time, and in later centuries the word could take on a sarcastic or derogatory meaning.*

By necessity, among our major sources for the biographies of this sort of person are hagiographic works—the medieval "vitae," or Lives of saints. These Lives are well known for their embellishment of historical reality, introduced to make the narrative better fit the standard forms and commonplaces of what a saint's Life is supposed to include. The Life is generally written with a definite purpose: to help

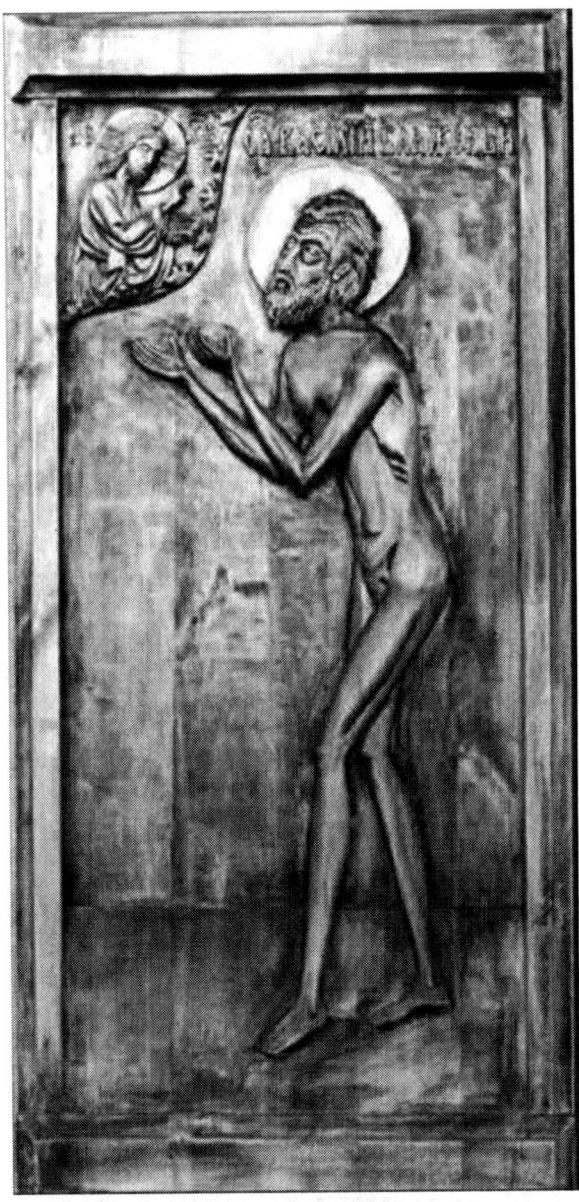

Bas relief icon of Vasilii Blazhennyi (the Blessed) from the Cathedral of Intercession of Theotokos on the Moat in Red Square, now frequently known as St. Basil's Cathedral. The subject of this chapter, a composite character named Dunia, a female fool for Christ, was inspired by the deeds Vasilii Blazhennyi was reported to have done.

the person be glorified in sainthood; and for this to be effective, historical reality is sometimes significantly revised in the name of ideal reality. Posthumous miracles, for example, are generally expected. Frequently it can be shown that stories told of one saint first originated in quite a different saint's Life and migrated to enrich the Life of a second saint. All of this may be effective for devotional purposes, but it can make the task of discerning the historical reality underlying the story very difficult. Though not used as source material here, purely hagiographic stories of one well-known sixteenth-century iurodivyi *(the Blessed Vasilii) are introduced into the narrative as material encountered by the main character, Dunia.*

The fictional life of Dunia as related here is distantly patterned on the life of an historical nineteenth-century iurodivaia, *St. Pelageia Diveevskaia. The narrative is set against a background of real places and cultural realities as best they can be reconstructed. All Moscow streets, churches, and other public structures mentioned are historical. This is an individual story of one person, as all people's stories must be, and should not quite be taken as representing a pattern "typical" for* iurodivye, *for women of her time, or for any other category of person. Our Dunia was a* iurodivaia *for a limited period of time, after which she progressed to quite a different style of life. In some other cases, once a person took up the life of a* iurodivyi *he or she remained in it until death (such was the case with the Blessed Vasilii, for example).*

Among personages in the narrative, Father Antonii Chernoezerskii (of Chernoe ozero, *"Black Lake") is an historical figure, a sixteenth-century Muscovite saint, known to have founded the* Rozhdestva Bogoroditsy pustyn *(the Monastery of the Most Pure Virgin's Birth on the Black Lake (in northern Russia, off the road between Cherepovets and Vologda); he died in the Lord in 1598, and his feast day is celebrated on January 17. In this narrative he is represented as also having founded a women's monastery (convent), the* Chernoezerskaia Sviato-Pokrovskaia pustyn *(the Black Lake Holy Intercession Monastery). Besides Father Antonii and the Blessed Vasilii, Tsar Ivan IV the Terrible is also a known historical figure. All other characters are fictional.*

A fuller version, with greater exploration of the theological and psychological aspects of Dunia's story, can be found online at the website http:/holytrinityorthodox. org/articles_and_talks/Dunia.htm.

In the time of Tsar Ivan IV the Terrible in Moscow's Kitai-Gorod[1] there lived a merchant, Makar Shestov Petrov syn (Makar Sixth-born, Son of Peter). He was hardworking and moderately prosperous and even had his own leather factory. He provided quite adequately for his family—Praskovia, his wife, and three children: Andrei, Ioann, and Avdotia—Dunia for short. Dunia, born in 1573, was the youngest. Andriusha and Vania were, respectively, five and three years older than she.

---

[1] Kitai-Gorod was the merchant section of Moscow—to the east of, adjacent to, and larger than, the Kremlin. Like the Kremlin, it was surrounded by its own imposing brick fortress wall, in its case built in 1534–38, with heavy gates under great guard towers where major thoroughfares passed through.

When Dunia was just two years old, the family was severely shaken by the unexpected death of Makar in a brawl in the new tavern on Varvarka Street.[2] But within the year her mother remarried. The children's new stepfather was also a merchant, Aleksei Mukhomor Nikitin *syn* (Aleksei the toadstool, Nikita's son),[3] himself a widower with six children of his own, who had actually been a competitor of Makar's.

Aleksei Mukhomor's ruddy face was adorned with as many pimples and pockmarks as the flecks on a ruddy-capped *mukhomor* (mushroom),[4] a similarity which was the direct inspiration for his nickname (though there were those who suspected that the connection might also have been suggested by his character). He was short of breath and caustic of tongue and walked with a limp, supporting himself ponderously with a stout walking staff. His uneven footfall and thumping stick resounded over the wooden floors as he made his way through his house on Nikita Lane.[5] And it was here that he and his offspring were joined by Praskovia and her three children. In addition to the promise of regained stability for Makar's family, it was an easy move geographically, just a few streets over from their old house and downhill toward St. Barbara's Gate by the eastern edge of Kitai-Gorod. But in other respects the family merger was not easy.

Mukhomor's children took poorly to the intruders in their domestic space, and the mistrust and distaste was mutual. Family life for the younger generation was little else than fights and squabbles, mostly across original family lines but with shifting alliances for temporary advantage, crafty schemes of retribution, and the general bullying of little ones by big ones. Dunia, youngest of all, had no friends or allies in either brood and received it from all sides.

Nor did she find much protection from the parents. When siblings old and new were after her, they always endeavored to make the disagreement look like Dunia's fault; and the parents, consistently gullible, seemed always to be taken in. Only her mother would sometimes instinctively take pity on her and comfort her, although any thought of overtly challenging a statement or ruling by Mukhomor would never enter Praskovia's mind. That would be far too dangerous.

---

[2] Varvarka Street, "St. Barbara Street," was and is the southernmost of the main west–east streets in Kitai-Gorod. Its western end opened on Red Square (then called Market Square) near St. Basil's Cathedral. From there Varvarka ran along inside Kitai-Gorod's southern wall, on the northern bank of the Moscow River, to the street's eastern end, where it passed through the St. Barbara Gates in the eastern wall. It took its name from the St. Barbara Church, which was and is located on the street.

[3] "Mukhomor" was Aleksei's so-called *klichka,* a person's street nickname (for details see the appendix on personal names).

[4] A poisonous mushroom, the "Amanita muscaria," one of whose traditional folk uses in Russia is in a potion to kill flies. The Russian name *mukhomor* means, literally, "fly-killer." Its use as a nickname in old Russia is well known, and there are Russians today named Mukhomorov, descended from ancestors whose nickname was *Mukhomor.*

[5] In today's Kitai-Gorod section of Moscow the former Nikita Lane is now called Nikitnikov Lane (*Nikitnikov pereulok*).

Her family did provide Dunia with one important service: the church service. They would go to the local Church of the Holy Martyr Nikita the Warrior on the Claypits, a few minutes' walk downhill along their lane.[6] For the rest of the family it was a social occasion, a tradition, a custom. Just something you did because everybody, you included, had always done it, and with the exception of the great church holidays the family regularly attended service once a week.

Dunia went much more often. For her it was a different world. It was reflections of the holy uncreated light; the intense presence here and now of the Lord's time on earth and his sacrifice to redeem poor, fallen humanity; divine services moving through and filling the entire space around and within her, heavenly peace, the holy images, the smell of incense, the colors, the vestments, the sung and chanted word, the music. All the senses rejoiced. For her it was a taste of Heaven, the pure voice of God in His infinite love, and Holy Communion with Him.

She developed into an attractive young woman—somewhat to her own dismay, since her appearance constantly brought unwanted attention from strangers, most typically attempts on the part of burly young men to trick her into flirtatious banter. She maneuvered her way past all this without batting an eyelash and without being drawn into any contact. She somehow had not the slightest interest in all these pursuits.

Praskovia had her own plans for her handsome young daughter. She began to have her eye out for an advantageous marital match: "Now listen to me, my dear. We simply have to find you a suitable young man we can be seen in public with; gotta find somebody who'll do credit to our family, you know!"

"O, Mamochka! Do we really have to?" said Dunia. "Maybe we can live without that?"

Praskovia saw no room for questions. "Don't you worry, my bunny rabbit, my little dove! I know what's best for you!" said Praskovia. And she invited a young man whose family she knew through the St. Nikita parish, and whom she considered a worthy potential catch, to come and make Dunia's acquaintance. The would-be suitor, Mityukha, tall, gangly, self-conscious, busy trying to pull his hands back into sleeves a bit too short, came calling with his mother. Praskovia had gone out of her way and prepared a fine table of mushroom-and-meat pie, savory pickles, fresh vegetables and fruit, and a heavenly concoction of infusion of raspberries and honey on the finest fresh-baked sieve bread,[7] all washed

---

[6] The church's Russian name was *Tserkov' Nikity Voina na Glinishchakh*. The "claypits" referred to the red clay hillside on which the church was built. In Dunia's time the church was wooden; in the seventeenth century it burned down and was rebuilt in stone. That church still stands today, under the name *Khram Zhironachal'noi Troitsy v Nikitnikakh* Church of the Life-Giving Trinity in the Nikitniki Region) with several chapels, including one dedicated to Nikita.

[7] Sieve bread (*sitnyi khleb*) was bread made of flour sifted through a fine sieve, distinguished from the coarser screen bread (*reshetnyi khleb*).

down with *kvass* and *braga*.⁸ Dunia slouched sullenly at the edge of the table, leaned back and stared for some time at the ceiling with her mouth wide open, and then started pouring kvass on each of the flowers in the fabric of her dress and rubbing it in, in careful circles, with her finger. Her mother's eagle eye darted sideways; she tried to prevent this nonsense by quietly ordering Dunia's older stepsister to pinch her.

Dunia overheard this and confronted her mother directly: "Mamochka, what's the matter? Maybe you're specially fond of these flowers? That's all right: these are no flowers of paradise!"

Mityukha's mother later quietly told her son, "Don't make any difference she's got money. Everybody's right: she's just plain stupid. We gotta stay away from her!" Mityukha shrugged his shoulders and looked plaintively at his mother as if he wanted to disagree, but said nothing. They didn't call again or respond to invitations.

After a few more such efforts by Praskovia, all of them neatly turned aside by Dunia, Praskovia and Mukhomor called Dunia in for a family council.

"What is this I hear?" Mukhomor said, "that you're resisting all attempts to find a good husband for you?"

Dunia was silent.

"Come come, Dunechka, are you trying to flout your mother's authority?"

"No, sir."

"Well, then! Are you going to accept your mother's word and marry whom she chooses for you?

"I'm sorry, I'm afraid not, sir."

"What? How can you possibly justify such impudence?"

"I'm very sorry, sir, I mean no impudence. I just can't."

"What do you mean, you can't?"

"I just can't injure my immortal soul that way. It would be wrong before God."

"How dare you talk like that? I'll show you what's right and wrong before God!" So saying, he raised his walking staff, took a full arm's length swing, and with all his might struck her across her back. She staggered and fell, but uttered not a sound. Silently she managed to get up and make her way to her bed, and lay there in misery. She felt she was utterly alone in this world, with only the Lord to turn to, a loneliness made more intense by her conviction that she herself was responsible for drawing her all-too predictable stepfather into his fit of rage. "Put

---

⁸ *Kvass* and *braga* were among the traditional drinks in old Muscovy, before the import of foreign beverages like vodka, tea, and coffee. Both kvass and *braga* are the result of fermentation: the former, from bread, non-alcoholic; the latter, from fruit or grain, mildly intoxicating, like a new raw wine or beer.

not your trust in princes, in sons of men in whom there is no salvation,"[9] she thought to herself. We people are such fragile reeds. Only the Lord is always true. All her trust was in the Lord.

As far as those around could judge, Dunia simply withdrew into herself. When accused of some household atrocity, instead of defending herself she consistently maintained silence. The parents' attempts to control and tame her by arguments and shame and force had no effect whatever.

Out in the city, hanging over the streets and lanes like a great beast always poised to strike, was the constant threat of fire. Especially in winter, when all heated their houses,[10] everyone was at risk. Dunia was haunted by the thought of being caught in the street—or even worse, at home in the middle of the night. Moscow was a well-laid stack of kindling waiting for the torch. The houses and other structures belonging to normal citizens—barns, sheds, stables—were all of wood. Properties were nestled tight against one another along the narrow ways, hidden behind the owners' tall wooden stockade fences. Walking down a street between the unbroken high wood walls was like walking through a narrow corridor with no opening on either side. When an errant spark touched off a blaze, it would spread like wind in the trees. And when all these wooden structures burst on fire, in those streets there was no escape. Great sections of Moscow were destroyed every few decades in catastrophic storms of flame with heavy loss of life, and small fires leveled houses every week. The moment a fire was spotted, the great bell of the local church would burst out in the nervous warning peel used only in dire emergencies. It could wake you at any moment out of the deepest sleep into a mortal panic.

Special supplies of water were kept in strategic locations, and the wooden and thatched roofs would be hastily covered with wet animal skins and ship sails and continually wetted down. But the main defense against the fires was the ax: the fire brigades would mercilessly hack apart and forcefully clear away any structures that were in the path of the fire, in hopes of stopping its spread. In general, of the total number of houses destroyed in a fire, only two-thirds fell victim to the flames themselves; the other third was demolished by the fire brigades.

One night when Dunia was sixteen, in early April just after Easter, when by day the streets were swimming in mud and by night their surface became an icy crust, all were jolted awake by the great bell's baleful fire signal, boom-boom-boom-boom-boom-boom-boom, ominous peals in urgent quick succession. Through the window,

---

[9] From Psalm 145 in the Greek Septuagint and Eastern Orthodox tradition (Ps. 146 in the Latin and western tradition), a passage very familiar to all Orthodox Christians since it is chanted as part of the Second Antiphon near the beginning of every Liturgy service.

[10] Most houses were heated in the "black way," without chimneys, whereby you lived with a careful balance of open windows for fresh air and a blazing stove for heat, and made sure to stay below smoke level in the house. This increased the danger of fire, for loose sparks often issued from the stove, unconstrained by pipes and chimneys, and ignited the roof from inside. At least Dunia's family's house had a chimney.

over the top of their fence along the lane uphill, they could see flames against the sky. The family scrambled to get wet coverings for the roof. A great commotion arose all around; sounds of people yelling and running up and down the lane, the chopping and crashing of properties being cleared, and over it all the terrible roar of flames. Mukhomor stepped out into the yard to peer through the front gate into the lane and came charging back into the house, shouting "Everybody out!"

Even though they were downhill from the flames, prospects looked grave. Properties all round were scorching and exploding into flame, and the heat was nearly unbearable. "No time to grab anything, everybody out! Now!"

All the family rushed out the door—except Dunia, who stood in the icon corner[11] gathering up the holy images in her shawl. "That's right, Dunka!" her brother Andriusha shouted over his shoulder as he bolted out the door. "You stay and look after everything here!"

The cry was taken up by all her siblings: "Dunka stays to look after things! Dunka stays! Dunka stays!"

And they all dashed out into the knee-deep mud, the icy crust long since gone beneath running feet, and headed downhill to St. Nikita's. Dunia did remain, abandoned and resigned. Hugging the icons to herself, she prayed to the Holy Theotokos,[12] Virgin Mother of God, to intercede and save them all from the fire.

The crashing of the fire brigade's devastation continued unabated, but did it seem that the thunder of the flames was just a bit quieter or further off? She suddenly came to her senses and ran to get more water for the roof coverings. As she leaned out of the upper window to splash the water on the roof, she could see that the flames really were racing off uphill, driven faster by a sudden easterly wind. Falling to her knees, Dunia crossed herself, her face streaming with tears, and thanked the Virgin: The Theotokos had heard Dunia's prayers!

When the rest of the family returned to the house, some of them looked at Dunia sheepishly or avoided her gaze, others sullenly stared her full in the face as if in silent challenge, but nothing was said about their having abandoned her to her fate with the flames. For her part, she said nothing about her prayer and the Virgin's intercession. She thought of how the Mother of God protected so many, and remembered the Virgin's great feast on October 14, the Protection or Intercession of the Most Holy Theotokos (*Pokrov Presviatyia Bogoroditsy*), when the Mother of God had descended to the earth amidst a throng of saints and spread out Her protecting veil to save those beneath from catastrophe. This miracle had been revealed in a vision to the Byzantine Orthodox saint, Andrew the Fool for Christ, as he was praying in the Blachernae Church in Constantinople for salvation from

---

[11] The icon corner is a small worship space prepared in the homes of Eastern Orthodox Christians, typically an eastern corner in one of the main rooms of the house. Here is where the icons that the family owns are concentrated, and it is the center of worship in the home.

[12] Theotokos (lit. "God-bearer") is the Greek title of Mary, the mother of Jesus. It is frequently used directly in English; in the Russian church the equivalent is *Bogoroditsa*.

enemy forces attacking the great city. She thirsted to learn more about St. Andrew: what does it mean to be a Fool for Christ? She asked Father Aleksandr, St. Nikita's priest. He said, "Remember the words of the holy Apostle Paul: "God chose what is foolish in the world to shame the wise, God chose what is weak in the world to shame the strong." And: "If any one among you thinks that he is wise in this age, let him become a fool that he may become wise. For the wisdom of this world is folly with God." And again: "We are fools for Christ's sake."[13]

Dunia said, "Yes, Father, I understand the folly of worldly wisdom. But why would one become a fool oneself? Why does that mean becoming wise?"

"Ah, my child. Not just any kind of fool. I think you already understand: it means a fool in the eyes of those who take the ways of the world, and themselves, too seriously. And don't forget the folly of the Cross itself." Then he added, "You know, Dunechka, we in Moscow had the holy gift from God of such a fool among us just recently, the Blessed Vasilii, fool for Christ. He fell asleep in the Lord just thirty-three years back, in the year 65 of the seventh thousand.[14] I, most sinful among men, was given the gift of seeing him with my own eyes. Many wondrous stories are being told of him and of miracles around his grave. He has just recently been glorified in sainthood. You might be interested to learn more of him."

"How could I become worthy to hear some of these stories?" Dunia asked.

"Simplicity itself. You know old Gurii the beggar who hangs around our church—you could ask him. Or down by the St. Barbara Gates. Or better still, at the Church of the Virgin's Intercession on Market Square, the very place where Vasilii of blessed memory is buried.[15] Really, any place where people gather: everybody is talking about him."

Dunia, slightly ashamed not to have gotten wind of these tales before but more grateful to Father Aleksandr than she could say, took her leave of him with thanks and a reverential request for his blessing.

Dunia had no trouble finding people knowledgeable about Vasilii the Fool, and more than willing to tell her about him. She felt that the Lord had prepared her to receive the word, and that now He was bringing the word to her.

The stories told of how young Vasia[16] had been blessed from the start with the Lord's gift of prophesy: he was able to look into men's hearts and read their fates. As a boy Vasia was given by his parents into apprenticeship to a boot

---

[13] The three quotes are, respectively, from 1 Cor. 1:27, 1 Cor 3:18, and 1 Cor. 4:10.

[14] In the year 7065 in the Byzantine and Muscovite way of reckoning—that is, the year 1557 A.D.

[15] Vasilii the Blessed is buried in the Church of the Virgin's Intercession on the Moat (*Khram Pokrova Presviatyia Bogoroditsy na Rvu*), which still stands on Red Square (Market Square)—the church is popularly better known by Vasilii's own name: the Church of Basil the Blessed (*Khram Vasiliia Blazhennago*), or St. Basil's Cathedral, and is now one of the most renowned churches in all of Russia.

[16] Vasia is the normal familiar shortening of the name Vasilii. Vasia and Vasilii are the same person.

maker. His gift of prophecy soon became manifest. One day a prominent boyar appeared, making his condescending way into their workshop, fastidiously avoiding contact with anything in the shop that might brush against his elegant gown. He ordered a pair of special boots custom-made. He gave detailed instructions as to how they were to be measured, cut, and sewn. Young Vasia, who was standing listening, suddenly burst out laughing but then just as abruptly collapsed in tears. After the boyar had completed his order and stridden out, Vasia explained to his master that, for all the fuss, this man would not be able to wear the boots he had ordered, since the very next day he was going to die. And it came to pass just as Vasia said.

Soon thereafter Vasilii left his apprenticeship to seek out a holy man to teach and lead him on the path of silent contemplation and constant prayer. He found such a spiritual father, who taught him the prayer to Jesus—"Lord Jesus Christ, have mercy on me"—which, his teacher told him, had been known since the earliest days of Christianity and should constantly be in his heart and on his tongue.

At the age of sixteen, he began to live as a fool for Christ. He broke all ties with his former life. He tore up his garments and flung them on the ground, and thereafter went about naked. He began creating outrageous scenes, scandalizing unsuspecting citizens by doing improper, offensive, and seemingly senseless things. As thanks for this he was constantly beaten and kicked and spat on. He was dragged by the hair and insulted and scorned and humiliated; mocked, ridiculed, and shunned. By night, after roaming all day as a fool for Christ, he would pray secretly, out of view of witnesses.

In the market stalls on Market Square and in Kitai-Gorod he would sometimes demonstrably destroy perfectly good food and drink being offered for sale—such as kvass and the best sieve bread—and dash them from the merchants' tables into the mud. This caused great outrage, but he only attacked the property of dishonest merchants who tormented their customers with cruelly inflated prices, though he did not call attention to this fact.

Walking the streets of Moscow, sometimes he happened past the dwellings of particularly good and pious people who loved their neighbors and cared about their souls. Vasilii would stop and gather up stones and start throwing them at the corners of those righteous people's houses. He would beat the walls with sticks and make a great commotion. In other cases, if he passed by a house where there was drinking and fighting and cursing within, and all sorts of hatred and blasphemy and violence, he would stop there too, but there he would kiss the corners of the house and seem to be conducting a sweet conversation with invisible gentle companions.

Of course, this behavior caused confusion among the citizenry. But there was hidden reason here as well. At the houses of the righteous, demons would be scrambling outside, trying to get in. And they would hang around the house corners, unable to enter. Vasilii was helping dislodge them and distract them, so they wouldn't interfere with the righteous who might want to come and go. In the houses of the evildoers the demons rejoice and celebrate, while God's guardian angels, set at the moment of holy Baptism as protectors of people's souls, find they have no place within. These angels, weeping despondently outside the house, would be kissed by Vasilii, and it was with them that he would conduct his unintelligible conversations.

The holy man came to the attention of the proud and terrible Tsar Ivan IV himself, who was dreaded for his merciless reprisals against his subjects. Once on an important church feast day the tsar looked forward to seeing Vasilii at the Divine Liturgy in the Uspenskii Cathedral in the Moscow Kremlin. But Vasilii was nowhere to be seen. The tsar managed to find the holy man afterwards, and he asked him why he hadn't been there. "You simply didn't see me," said Vasilii. "I was there. Actually it was you who were absent." Although the church was physically packed, he said, only three people were there: the metropolitan,[17] the God-fearing queen, and Vasilii himself. The tsar was absent, absorbed in thoughts about the opulent new palace which he was having built for himself. Startled by this unexpected criticism, he nonetheless accepted it humbly from Vasilii. "Pray for me, holy one," was all he said.

Vasilii fearlessly castigated Ivan for his repression of his subjects, whom God had put on earth for him to care for and protect. One such encounter occurred during Great Lent, when all Orthodox Christians observe the fast and abstain from meat and other rich fare. Vasilii came to visit the tsar and presented him with a huge piece of raw meat. The tsar marveled, "How do you give me meat during Great Lent, when all know it's quite forbidden?" Vasilii answered "And does little Vania think it wrong to eat the flesh of beasts in Lent, but not worry about devouring so much human flesh as he has already consumed?"

Dunia caught her breath. She bowed her head at Vasilii's exploit.

She knew that he had fallen asleep in the Lord in 1557, fourteen years before she was born, and had been buried in the Church of the Virgin's Intercession on Market Square; and that subsequently his wondrous miracles had begun to rise in a fountain of God's grace. People had been gathering more and more frequently and in greater numbers at Vasilii's grave. Miraculous cures were seen for the lame, the blind, and those most variously afflicted in body or in mind. One monk, Gerasim, whom everybody called "the Bear," for many years had been unable to walk and had had to crawl on his knees, living as a beggar near the Frolov Gate,[18] until suddenly he was healed by Vasilii's posthumous prayers. The miracles continued to

---

[17] The metropolitan was the hierarch in charge of the entire Muscovite Orthodox Church, under the Ecumenical Patriarch of Constantinople. At the end of the sixteenth century the metropolitan's rank was elevated to patriarch of Russia, a sign of the growing strength of Moscow.

[18] The Frolov Gate was the main entrance into the Kremlin from Red Square, in the imposing Frolov Tower, now known as the Spasskii Tower, with its Spasskii Gates.

accumulate, including places far away: as the protector of sailors he saved a ship from a storm in the Caspian Sea.

Dunia pondered all the legends of Vasilii in her heart. She began leaving home more and more frequently at unpredictable times, praying until all hours at night, and initiating peculiar conversations with strangers, with a wild look in her eye—and the gossip made its way back to her mother and stepfather.

Dunia's parents decided they must take serious measures. In hopes of bringing her to her senses, they took her on a chastening many-day pilgrimage far to the north, beyond Vologda, to see Father Antonii Chernoezerskii (Anthony of the Black Lake) in his Monastery of the Most Pure Virgin's Birth. Father Antonii was widely famous for his sanctity of life and his gift of vision and was a figure to whose authority Dunia's parents felt they could appeal.[19] They traveled with a party of other pilgrims. Father Antonii accepted them all graciously, blessed Aleksei and Praskovia and sent them to their local lodging in the village, but talked with Dunia for four hours. Their pilgrim fellow travelers, hanging around the monastery, were most offended by Antonii's paying so much attention to Dunia and said among themselves, "What's he doing spending so much time with her? I mean, we're no poorer than she is; we can make just as good a contribution to his hermitage. How come he's ignoring us?"

Father Antonii, watching them pass the door of his cell, sensed their discontent. Stepping outside, he said to them, "The riches I seek are not of this world but of the spirit." He released them in peace and continued his conversation with Dunia.

Late in the day Dunia's mother lost her patience and hurried back to the monastery with her husband to fetch Dunia. Just as they approached Antonii, she and Mukhomor saw him bow to the ground before Dunia, and say to her, "My dear and respected Avdotia, go now in peace. You are on a difficult path, which you must complete. But we send you home with a request. Some day when you are ready, please return to my other hermitage on the Black Lake, my Convent of the Virgin's Intercession, and help take care of the sisters. When you are ready we will be waiting for you with open arms, to help with the work of the Lord."

Mukhomor was already angry at having been kept waiting so long and at having his stubborn and crazy stepdaughter paid such honor. On hearing the strange declaration from Father Antonii, he said to his wife scoffingly and loudly, "Holy man, hah! He's not even in his right mind!"

For Dunia, her conversation with Father Antonii, on top of what she had understood from the stories of Vasilii the fool for Christ, had a decisive effect on the further course of her life. Back home in Kitai-Gorod she made friends with a merchant's wife, Sofia Ivan's daughter, who was already living the life of a fool for Christ. Under Sofia's tutelage Dunia learned more about the unceasing Jesus prayer, the prayer of the heart, which Vasilii had found so valuable. She herself

---

[19] Father Antonii is a sixteenth-century Muscovite saint, known to have founded the Monastery of the Most Pure Virgin's Birth; he died in the Lord in 1598.

began to practice it and would spend entire nights absorbed in the prayer. It felt clarifying and lightening, a tremendous aid in her struggle for self-purification. As it became more and more habitual it seemed to enter ever more deeply into her heart. It became a constant activity and remained so for the rest of her life.

Side by side with prayer, Dunia began to add exploits of holy foolishness, and with every passing day, as it would appear to any normal respectable person, seemingly lost more and more of her reason. By day, when normal, productive, upstanding citizens were up and about, on the street, in the shops and market stalls, in government offices, going about their daily private, practical, breadwinning, civic lives, absorbed in affairs at hand and of the moment—she would strike. All of a sudden a wraith-like figure—wild-eyed, matted-haired, rag-clad—would rise before them and make some sort of loud demands on their attention that clearly seemed to be patent nonsense—but on the other hand seemed mysteriously to have some haunting connection with their worries or dreams, or perhaps an uneasy conscience. Most would flee, and many would attack her. But some would make a point of approaching and asking for her prayers.

She might, for example, stop a stylish lady in a fine linen shawl and start tugging at it: "Hey Auntie! Let me have my rag back! You swiped it from me just when I had my poor dead pig all wrapped up in it for burial!"

Not surprisingly, all of this pained and saddened her parents, who had no understanding of her behavior. They pleaded and argued for her to return to reason and act like a normal person, but she remained quite indifferent to their wishes.

Praskovia and Mukhomor resolved to beat her back to her senses. Mukhomor thrashed her so mercilessly that her health began to suffer. Dunia made up her mind to get away from that house at any cost. She ran off into the city to one church after another. No matter what people gave her out of pity or whatever else came to hand, she gave all of it away to the poor or spent it on candles to light in church.

Her parents would sometimes catch her and beat her. They would drag her back to the house and lock her up, punish her with cold and hunger, but she would not relent. "Let me go," she would cry. "I've been spoiled by Antonii and Vasilii for any normal life."

Her mother would sometimes try to talk sense to her: "My darling little Dunechka! Why do you fight so fiercely? You know that we only want what is best for you!" But Dunia would not submit to her parents, and she tried by all possible means to avoid having anything to do with them.

Her stepfather pressed ahead. He fastened a stout rope to an iron ring which he welded shut around her ankle with his own hands, and tied her to the wall. Sometimes she managed to break loose and burst out of the house, iron ring clanging, half-dressed, and would run through the streets to the horror of all. Everyone she met was afraid of sheltering her, feeding her, or in any way protecting her from her stepfather's persecution. And so she would again get captured and be subject to new and harsher torments.

Once in the dead of winter, half-naked, she took shelter on the porch of St. Barbara's Church[20] in a coffin, which had been prepared for a soldier who had fallen victim to a current plague. There, half frozen with the cold, she waited for death.

A church guard caught sight of her. At first he took her for a corpse; but then she stirred and groaned. Terrified by this ghostly apparition, he dashed to the bell tower and raised the huge fire-bell alarm. The population through all Kitai-Gorod, across Market Square, and to the Kremlin itself was shocked awake, sure that another fire was upon them.

Praskovia was at the end of her resources and her patience. She had completely run out of ideas for possible solutions and was quite tormented with worry about her daughter. She decided that she herself would pay another visit to the holy man, Antonii, in a desperate search for ideas that might help. She made the trip, met with him, and said, "Father, my daughter Dunia, remember we visited you not long ago? She's gone clean out of her mind! She's completely out of hand. She's just impossible, won't listen to reason, and keeps running wild. We've tried everything, but nothing helps! She makes all kinds of problems for the family: all our other girls want to get married: but poor dears, nobody will come near them because everybody's scared they might turn out like Dunia. No one can talk any sense into her: she doesn't listen. The problem is, is she's so awful strong; there's no way of keeping her under control by any normal means. So the only solution is we've had to tie her up and lock her in."

"What!? How is this possible?" The elder's voice had never sounded so piercing. "How could you have done that? Release her this instant! Let her go! Don't touch her! Of course she's strong. The Lord doesn't call weaklings to pursue her kind of path. For this sort of exploit He chooses only the strongest and most courageous. But don't you even think of keeping her tied up, or else the Lord will wreak a terrible revenge on you."

In terror of the wrath of God, Mukhomor and Praskovia immediately eased up on Dunia. They stopped tying her up and no longer forbade her to leave the house. By day she was again abroad in the streets of Moscow: the picture of a fool for Christ: dressed in rags, challenging people in unexpected ways on points of commonplace behavior and belief. She spent practically every night on the porch of one or another of the churches in Kitai-Gorod, and she would pray to God for nights on end.

And so she spent a year and more, seldom appearing at her stepfather's house. She never ceased visiting her teacher, the fool for Christ Sofia, who had taught

---

[20] This church was built in 1514 by the Italian architect Aloisio Lamberti da Montagna, known in Russia as Aleviz Friazin (Alois "the Italian") or Aleviz Novyi ("the New"). He was responsible for building a number of imposing white stone churches in Moscow, most celebrated among them the Cathedral of the Archangel Michael, which still stands in the kremlin. In 1796–1804 St. Barbara's Church was rebuilt on Aloisio's old foundation: while bearing the same name, the church that now occupies the spot is no longer the original structure.

her the constant repetition of the Jesus prayer. Dunia grew in confidence in her calling. Her zeal for the Lord matured and strengthened—for spreading His truth, for emulating His self-sacrificing and self-emptying example, for challenging the proud and powerful, so mired in this distorted world.

Early one fateful Sunday morning she again visited the white stone Church of St. Barbara. She arrived while it was still dark and few people were on the streets, and as she approached the church she witnessed a strange scene. She was astounded to see the round figure of the church's deacon,[21] Father Feofan, quietly stealing coins from the blind beggar, Pasha, on the steps before the church.

Dunia, in shock, made her way into the church's great central space, the nave. Among the crowds of worshippers she found a place off to the side and near the back. She stood there for some time, still shaken by what she had seen, praying for Deacon Feofan. The Divine Liturgy began. The moment came for the Gospel reading. Deacon Feofan, large and imposing, beautiful in his gleaming vestments, in his golden *stikhar'* with his *orar'* over his shoulder,[22] swayed slowly as he ascended the readers' platform.

"The reading is from the Holy Gospel according to St. Matthew," he chanted in Church Slavonic.[23]

"Glory to You, O Lord, Glory to You," sang the chorus, and from inside the altar came the answering Slavonic intonation from the priest, "Let us attend."

The deacon began chanting the Gospel passage in a booming, didactic, condescending voice, the nails on his plump manicured fingers gleaming as he stroked his well-groomed beard: "Do not lay up for yourselves treasures on earth, where moth and rust consume and where thieves break in and steal, but lay up for yourselves treasures in heaven, where neither moth nor rust consumes and where thieves do not break in and steal. For where your treasure is, there will your heart be also."[24]

He looked around disdainfully at the parishioners. He seemed convinced that those preoccupied with laying up treasures for themselves on earth were precisely those who were milling around him in the church. But Dunia thought, "Poor, poor

---

[21] Deacon is a special rank within the Orthodox clergy, ordained in the sacrament of holy orders, as are priests and bishops. Serving under the priest, a deacon is responsible for helping celebrate the Divine Liturgy and other services. He leads the congregation in prayer, reads from Scripture, and sometimes participates in distributing the Eucharist to the faithful. In the Eastern Orthodox tradition, both deacons and priests may be married.

[22] The *stikhar'* is the deacon's specialized robe or gown; the *orar'* is a stole, an ornate strip of cloth carried, worn, and used by the deacon in the service.

[23] Church Slavonic, the liturgical language of the Holy Scriptures and the entire church service, is like an ornate, old-fashioned relative of the spoken Russian everyone used and uses in daily life. It is still the language of Russian Orthodox church services. The entire service is chanted and sung, without the use of any musical instruments. Only the priest's sermon is spoken, not chanted; and it is delivered not in Church Slavonic but in normal, everyday speech.

[24] Matt 6:19–21.

Father Deacon Feofan. May the Lord help him realize where his own treasure is." And she crossed herself and soon had lost herself in the service.

But the next day she saw the Deacon in the street. On a sudden impulse she confronted him: "*Let us attend!* Do you lay up for yourself treasures on earth? Just who is the thief that breaks in and steals?"

He screamed, "Why, you raving *bitch!* Who are you to challenge *me?*" and rushed at her, knocking her to the ground. But he immediately came to his senses and disappeared as quickly and inconspicuously as possible.

Dunia immediately felt great waves of remorse and fell to her knees, tears streaming down her face, thinking: "Who am I to pass such judgment on my brother?—And besides, to lead him into the sin of such fury?" And she pondered her own sinfulness, and her entire calling as a fool for Christ.

It was not long before word of Dunia's shocking encounter with the widely admired Deacon Feofan reached Praskovia's ears. Such scandalous disrespect for the universally respected Father Deacon Feofan, from one of the most important churches in all Kitai-Gorod! How much can a long-suffering mother bear? You devote yourself to your children completely and selflessly, and this is how they repay you? It reflected so shamefully on her, Dunia's poor self-sacrificing mother! Why would her little Dunechka want to do this to *her?* She racked her brain for some explanation or for some solution that she hadn't tried before.

Suddenly she remembered Dunia's desire to go live in the Black Lake Convent. Maybe she should let Dunia go to a monastery after all, only better not such a shabby, inconvenient one as that.

One day not long afterwards, there happened to be in Moscow on monastery business, a small party of nuns from that very convent. It was led by Sister Uliana, a resident of the convent and a protégée of Father Antonii. As they were riding through the city, Dunia came running up to them out of nowhere, slipped into their carriage, discovered who they were, and invited them to her house. "Please come have a visit at my house. My stepfather is alien to me and has no love for me, but he's well off and has plenty of everything. I will welcome you. Let's go! Please! I need you to come!"

The nuns accepted her invitation, and as they sat at the table drinking kvass and eating fresh-baked bread Sister Uliana recounted to Dunia's family how they had met. Then she said, "You should let her come with us to the Black Lake. What is there for her here?"

Praskovia's unwillingness to send her there faded in the face of this concrete invitation, and she said, "Why, I suppose I'd actually be relieved for you to take her with you. It would be a real solution to my problems. Because we're fed up, the Mother of God knows how we're at the end of our rope, it's just terrible. So take her!"

To which Uliana said, "Why then it's decided. We'll be happy and honored to take her with us."

At these last words the whole family saw the wild and crazy Dunia jump up and bow before Uliana's feet like a normal well-bred lady, and they heard her say, "I am ready to go, although I am completely unworthy. If you think I can be of service, I will be eternally grateful to be taken under your care."

Everyone was amazed. Mukhomor said, "My God! Look at this *lady!* But I gotta warn you! You better be ready: she'll just run off wild again."

Dunia's family was even more astonished when, at these words from her stepfather, Dunia turned and bowed humbly before his feet and answered, addressing the entire family, in a quiet voice, "Please forgive me, for the sake of Christ, for all I've put you through. I know I have not made your lives easy. But now you are free of me. Please pray for me." She realized that all her life she had set herself apart from and above her family, and that this had been a kind of fierce and sinful pride. Now she felt at one with all sinful humanity, including her stupid, coarse, selfish, violent family. So what if they were sinful? Who was without sin? Certainly not she, the first of sinners.

The time had come for Dunia to move on. She had made her peace with her family and herself and was ready to serve her Lord humbly and peacefully in whatever way He should require. So she left Kitai-Gorod with the three nuns, and they made their way to the Convent at Black Lake. There she entered a completely new existence as Sister Anna. But if anything, she continued to ponder the true calling of a fool for Christ more intently than ever.

Suggestions for Further Reading

Much fuller bibliography will be found cited in some of the works listed below. I have included a few titles in Russian because of their importance in studying the subject.

Blazhennaia Pelageia Ivanovna Serebrennikova: skazaniia o Khrista radi iurodivoi podvizhnitse Serafimo-Diveevskogo monastyria. Moscow: Pravoslavnyi Sviato-Tikhonovskii bogoslovskii institut, 2003, p. 158. The hagiographic work that suggested the life of Dunia, the subject of this portrait—although Dunia's story turned out to be very different.

Fedotov, G.P. *Sviatye Drevnei Rusi.* Rostov-on-Don: Feniks, 1999. *(Istoricheskie siluety)* Earlier editions, with various publishers: 1931, 1959, 1985, 1990, 1991, 1997, and others. Chap. 13, "Iurodivye," is a classic introduction to the subject, including an analysis of the principles driving the exploit of *iurodstvo*.

Ilarion (Alfeev), Episkop. *Sviashchennaia taina tserkvi: vvedenie v istoriiu i problematiku imiaslavskikh sporov.* 2 vols. St. Petersburg: Aleteiia, 2002. For those able to read Russian, this is a detailed and clear elucidation of many of the central church-historical and theological issues in Eastern Orthodox asceticism, mysticism, and such particular points as the Jesus Prayer, hesychasm, silence, and name worshipping.

Ivanov, Sergei A. *Holy Fools in Byzantium and Beyond.* Translated by Simon Franklin. New York: Oxford University Press, 2006. A translation with major additions and revisions of the author's *Vizantiiskoe iurodstvo* (Moscow: Mezhdunarodnye otnosheniia, 1994). The most detailed history and study of *iurodstvo* in English, with new source material and analysis; represents an analytic social-scientific approach.

Kovalevskii, Ioann. *Iurodstvo o Khriste i Khrista radi iurodivye Vostochnoi Russkoi Tserkvi: istoricheskii ocherk i zhitiia sikh podvizhnikov blagochestiia.* Moscow: Donskoi monastyr', 1992. Originally published: Moscow: Izd. A.D. Stupina, 1902. A study rich in detail, with Scriptural foundations and many excerpts and summaries from Lives of *iurodivye*, told from a traditional pietistic Orthodox perspective as of ca. 1900.

Murav, Harriet. *Holy Foolishness: Dostoevsky's Novels and the Poetics of Cultural Critique*. Stanford, CA: Stanford University Press, 1992.

Preobrazhenskii, A.S. "Vasilii Blazhennyi." In *Pravoslavnaia entsiklopediia*. Vol. 7. Moscow: Tserkovno-nauchnyi tsentr "Pravoslavnaia entsiklopediia," 2004, 123–28. Followed directly by companion article, "Ikonografiia," on the iconography of Vasilii Blazhennyi by K.Iu. Erusalimskii, 128–31. An authoritative recent summary of what is known concerning Vasilii Blazhennyi (St. Basil the Blessed).

The Way of a Pilgrim and the Pilgrim Continues His Way. Trans. R.M. French. New York: Seabury Press, [1974], other editions: 1954, 1965, etc. An autobiographical account of the life of an unknown nineteenth-century Russian pilgrim and wanderer, in whose life the "Jesus Prayer" plays a dominant role. Not directly representative of *iurodstvo* as such, this is still an absorbing and convincing introduction to the spirituality of the culture close around.

Glossary

Hugh M. Olmsted

Below are listed terms whose definitions may be useful in reading the articles in this volume. Most of them are Russian words, although some are technical English terms that may be unfamiliar. Less familiar English terms are printed with an acute accent to show the stressed syllable (as for Russian terms). Some of the terms are words with broader meanings, which are used in a more narrow sense in this volume. In such cases, the relevant narrower meaning is the only one glossed.

Like all Russian words and names met in this volume, the Russian terms in this list are transcribed from the original Cyrillic into the Latin alphabet. For more detail about transcription and pronunciation, see the Transcription and Pronunciation Guide for Names; the same conventions are followed here, with pronunciation of Russian words given in parentheses.

ádres (A-dryes)—a military or civil title.

agnéts (ag-NYETS)—"lamb"—a center portion of the *prosfóra* not used in the service.

altár' (al-TAR')—in an Eastern Orthodox church the altar is the entire space at the Eastern end of the nave, behind the iconostasis. It contains the altar table, on which the Holy Mysteries are celebrated.

altýn (al-TYN)—a monetary unit equal to three kopecks (*kopéiki*).

amunítsiia (a-mu-NI-tsy-ya)—ammunition.

analói (a-na-LOY)—a raised and angled pedestal used to hold icons in churches.

ántiphons—three sets of Psalm verses sung near the beginning of the Divine Liturgy; called antiphons because they were originally, and sometimes still are, sung by two choirs, each responding antiphonally to the other.

arshín (ar-SHYN)—.71 meters or 2.3 feet.

belóvka, pl. belóvki (bye-LOF-ka, bye-LOF-ki)—final copy of a document.

bezchést'e (beschést'e) (bi-SHCHEST'-ye)—dishonor, a legal category of insult or injury to honor.

blazhénnyi (bla-ZHEN-nyi)—blessed, a category of sanctity reserved for holy fools (in addition to the two Western saints Jerome and Augustine).

Bogoróditsa (bo-go-RO-di-tsa or ba-ga-RO-di-tsa)—(lit. God-bearer) is the title of Mary, the mother of Jesus. It is the Russian equivalent of the Greek *Theotókos*.

Bol'shoi dvoréts (bal'-SHOY dva-RYETS)—"great household office," the central office for administration of palace lands and their population.

boyár (ba-YAR)—highest rank among the service elite and members of the Boyar Duma.

Boyár Dúma—the council of state in Muscovy.

bróga (BRA-ga)—a traditional drink in old Muscovy. *Bróga* was the result of fermentation from fruit or grain, mildly intoxicating, like a new raw wine or beer.

cadáster—a public record of land ownership, kept as a basis for taxation.

chámbul (CHAM-bul)—Tatar raiding party.

chasoslóv (cha-sa-SLOF or chi-sa-SLOF)—book of prayers containing texts of fixed prayers for various times of the day in the daily cycle, and also a few of the most used changing prayers.

chétvert' (CHET-vyert')—a taxation unit equal to 1.35 acres, also used as a dry measure, as for grain; sometimes shortened to *chet'*.

chin (CHIN)—rank.

den'gá, pl. *dén'gi* (dyin'-GA, DYEN'-gi)—a monetary unit equal to one-half kopeck (kopeika).

déti boiárskie (DYE-ti ba-YAR-ski-ye)—plural of *syn boiárskii*.

d'iak (D'YAK)—scribe, government clerk, or state secretary.

dozórnye knígi (da-ZOR-ny-ye KNI-gi)—recording books.

dvor (DVOR)—court or household.

dvoriánstvo (dva-RYAN-stva)—mid-ranked servitors, lit. courtiers.

efímok, pl. *efímki* (ye-FI-mak, ye-FIM-ki))—seventeenth-century silver coin, the Joachimsthaler, minted in Joachimsthal, Bohemia.

eikón—image (Gr.).

Entrance, Little or Great—Procession of the clergy, deacons, and subdeacons from within the *altar* out into the *nave* through the congregation, proceeding back into the altar. In the Little Entrance the Gospels are carried aloft by the deacon; in the Great Entrance the sanctified Gifts of bread and wine are carried, to be transferred to the altar table.

famíliia (fa-MI-li-ya)—usually refers to family (last) name, but can be used to refer to "family" itself.

frunt (FRUNT)—military front.

gosudár' (ga-su-DAR')—sovereign, lord. Could be used by a serf or slave toward his lord or by a servitor toward the ruler.

gróznyi (GROZ-nyi)—terrifying, formidable, awe-inspiring; as a princely sobriquet it is often translated as "terrible" or "dread."

gubnói stárosta (gub-NOY STA-ra-sta)—an elder elected by a local community to perform the role of criminal judge for the district.

hegúmen (Rus. igúmen [i-GU-myen])—the head of an Orthodox men's monastery, similar to an abbot in Western Christian monasticism.

hegúmenia (Rus. igúmen'ia [i-GU-myen'-ya])—the Mother Superior of an Orthodox women's monastery.

iarlýk (yir-LYK)—a document issued by a khan granting privileges, immunities from taxation or other duties, or authority to rule over an area.

iasák (yi-SAK)—a fur tax paid by non-Christians.

iazýk, pl. *iazýki* (yi-ZYK, yi-ZY-ki)—tongue, language, faith. In seventeenth-century military slang, it referred to informers (lit. tongues).

iconostásis—(also known as an icon screen) a large screen or wall of icons, typically with multiple tiers, that separates the *altar* of the church from the *nave*, where the congregation stands during services.

ierodiiákon (i-yer-a-di-YA-kan)—hierodeacon, a monk ordained as a deacon.

igúmen (i-GU-myen)—see *hegumen*.

igúmen'ia (i-GU-myen'-ya)—see *hegúmenia*.

iuft', pl. *iúfti* (YUFT', YUF-ti)—a processed oxhide, often called Russian leather.

iuródivyi, pl. *iuródivye*, fem. *iuródivaia* (yu-RO-di-vyi, yu-RO-di-vy-ye, yu-RO-di-va-ya)—holy fool, fool for Christ.

klíchka (KLICH-ka)—nickname based on personal characteristics, street name; equivalent to *prózvishche*.

kholóp (kha-LOP)—slave.

kopeck—(Rus. *kopéika* [ka-PYEY-ka])—a monetary unit equal to two den'gi; from 1704, equal to one-hundredth of a ruble.

kormlénie (karm-LYE-ni-ye)—lit. feeding; prescribed payments in kind or in cash from the inhabitants in lieu of a salary, by which grand-princely administrators in local districts maintained ("fed") themselves.

kuiák (ku-YAK)—a leather jacket sewn with thin iron strips and worn by cavalryman.

kvas (KFAS)—a traditional drink in old Muscovy. Kvas was the result of fermentation from bread, nonalcoholic.

litany—a series of requests to the Lord during the church service, typically chanted by the deacon, for such mercies as peace, salvation, and well-being, with the congregation each time responding, "Lord, have mercy."

luk (LUK)—the amount of output a piece of land could produce from trapping, fishing, and salt making.

mántiia or *mántiya* (MAN-ti-ya)—a long, sleeveless black robe or cloak that is worn by monks and nuns as an outer garment. At times a bishop could don a mantiia. The absence of sleeves symbolizes that fleshy appendages are dead to the world. The bishop's mantiia can be a color other than black, usually red (or blue for Russian metropolitans).

máslenitsa (MA-slye-ni-tsa)—the week before Lent (i.e., the Great Fast of Forty Days).

médnyi bunt (MYED-nyi BUNT)—Copper coin riot of July 25, 1662.

méstnichestvo (MYEST-ni-chi-stva)—system of precedence by which each member of the aristocracy was assigned a place (*mésto*) according to the status of his clan and his status within his clan. Appointments were made according to an individual's *mestnichestvo* ranking.

nave—the central worship space in a church; the eastern end of the nave, typically behind the iconostasis, is the *altar*, where the altar table is located and the church services are centered; typically the largest part of nave is open, without pews, and here the congregation stands and much of the service is celebrated.

nemchín (nyem-CHIN)—"Westerner," primarily natives of the Germanic nations traveling or resident in Russia; sometimes used to denote also a type of military officer who was born of a Russian mother and West European mercenary father and raised in Russia.

némtsy, sing. *némets* (NYEM-tsy, NYE-myets)—"Westerners," primarily the Germanic speakers (German, Dutch, Scandinavian, et al.); used primarily in the plural to designate the areas and nations referred to. Original meaning: those who cannot speak [Russian]; in modern Russian the meaning has narrowed to refer specifically to Germans.

nemétskaia slobodá (nye-MYETS-ka-ya sla-ba-DA)—a town's quarter of settlement for West Europeans.

novík (na-VIK)—in military terms, a novice eligible for being assigned to a service category.

óbrok (OB-rak)—a tax or rent payable in cash or in kind.

odnodvórets (ad-na-DVO-ryets)—homesteader; yeoman farmer.

ofitséry, pl. (a-fi-TSE-ry)—military officers.

oklád (a-KLAT)—entitlement to compensation for service.

okládchik (a-KLAT-chik)—elected distributor of compensation paid by the government.

okól'nichii, pl. *okól'nichie* (a-KOL'-ni-chiy, a-KOL'ni-chi-ye)—lit. a person near or around (*ókolo*) the ruler. They were members of the boyar council and ranked immediately below the boyars in status.

opríchnina (a-PRICH-ni-na)—a division of the government Ivan IV personally commanded from 1565 to 1572 infamous for a reign of terror during which many thousands of people perished; the term is derived from the adjective *opríchnyi* "separate," "special," originally from the adverb *opríchʹ* ("apart," "outside of," "separate from").

orárʹ (a-RAR')—stole, an ornate strip of cloth carried or worn by the deacon for use in the church services.

otéchestvo (a-TYE-chi-stva)—"patrimony"; rights and claims based on hereditary status.

panikhída (pa-ni-KHI-da)—a longer version of the Trisagion Service.

perepísnye knígi (pi-ri-PIS-ny-ye KNI-gi)—census books.

pistsóvye knígi (pis-TSO-vy-ye KNI-gi)—cadaster books (tax rolls).

póchestʹ (PO-chist')—a gift given before a deal is made as a good-will gesture or token of good will.

podʹiáchii (pa-D'YA-chiy)—government clerk. The position was divided into three ranks: *stárshii* (senior), *srédnii* (middle), and *mládshii* (junior). A *podʹiáchii s prípisʹiu* was a designated signatory clerk who was allowed to sign documents.

polkováia slúzhba (pal-ka-VA-ya SLUZH-ba)—campaign duty.

pomést'e, pl. *pomést'ia* (pa-MYEST'-ye, pa-MYEST'-ya)—a military land grant from the ruler. From it a cavalryman could derive maintenance for his horses, equipment, weapons, and himself and his family. He could also collect taxes and pass them on to the central authority. In return, he provided administrative and judicial functions to the peasants on the estate.

poméshchik (pa-MYE-shchik)—the holder of a *pomest'e*.

poméstnyi prikáz (pa-MYEST-nyi pri-KAS)—Service Land Chancellery.

pomínok (pa-MI-nak)—a church service for memory of the dead; also, in civilian life, a gift given once a deal has been made (bribe).

póprishche (PO-pri-shche)—a unit of distance calculated by the church for the purposes of travel per diem, equivalent to 20 *versty* or 13 miles.

posád (pa-SAT)—urban settlement that surrounded a town's kremlin or central fortress.

posádskie liúdi (pa-SAT-ski-ye LYU-di)—townsmen (legally defined social stratum).

posúl (pa-SUL)—a monetary bribe (or promise of a bribe) given to an official.

prikáz (pri-KAS)—lit. order, command; a temporary administrative responsibility assigned to a boyar by the Grand Prince, hence the administrative department responsible for implementing the order: eventually, the primary term for government chancellery, office, agency, or bureau.

prikaznáia izbá (pri-kaz-NA-ya iz-BA)—office of the provincial governor.

prosforá or *prosfóra* (pra-sfa-RA, pra-SFO-ra)—In the Russian Orthodox Church service, the Host, which is a leavened loaf blessed by a priest.

prosveshchénie (pra-sfye-SHCHE-ni-ye)—"Enlightenment"—the Russian Church program of reform in the second half of the seventeenth century to enlighten and uplift society spiritually.

prózvishche (PRO-zvi-shche)—nickname based on personal characteristics, street name; equivalent to *klíchka*.

pýtochnyi dvor (PY-tach-nyi DVOR)—torture chamber.

Razbóinyi prikáz (raz-BOY-nyi pri-KAS)—Felony Chancellery.

razriádnaia kníga—military register or deployment book; contains lists or registers of servitors.

Razriádnyi prikáz (raz-RYAD-nyi pri-KAS)—Military Chancellery.

Ríurikovich, pl. *Riurikovichi* (RYU-ri-ka-vich, RYU-ri-ka-vi-chi)—a descendant of the presumed archiprogenitor of the first clan of Russian princes, Riurik.

ruble (Rus. *rubl'*)—a monetary unit equal to one hundred kopecks (from 1704).

sákos, sákkos—a liturgical vestment similar to the Roman Catholic dalmatic. It has wide slit sleeves and was often tied with small bells. It was initially worn only by the patriarch, but after 1453 began to be worn by other prelates as well.

sázhen' (SA-zhyn')—7 feet or 2.133 meters, equivalent to 3 *arshiny*.

sbórnik (ZBOR-nik)—collection or miscellany; here in the sense of a personal manuscript owned and/or used by a monk containing copies of edifying texts.

schema (rus. skhíma)—The spirtually and ascetically most advanced degree of monkhood. After tonsuring, if the hegumen feels a monk has reached a sufficient degree of spirituality, then that monk may be allowed to take the Little *Schema*. After further spiritual development and again with the approval of the hegumen, a monk may take the Great *Schema*. Corresponding garb accompanies each degree of monkhood.

shatër (sha-TYOR)—tent. Used to describe the campaign chancellery that kept the ruler's official itinerary as well as records of appointments.

shirínka (shy-RIN-ka)—a square cloth.

skhíma (SKHI-ma)—see under *schema*.

siábr (SYABR)—lit. neighbor; household head and member of a homesteader village commune.

slúzhba (SLUZH-ba)—service, particularly to the ruler. Also could mean the servitors collectively.

sobórnyi stárets (sa-BOR-nyi STA-ryets)—monk who was on the council (*sobor*) for the monastery.

sokhá (sa-KHA)—a wooden scratch plow; also an arable land taxation unit.

stárets (STA-ryets)—elder monk, usually one with special spiritual authority.

stikhár' (sti-KHAR')—the deacon's specialized robe or gown.

stikhíry (sti-KHI-ry)—short verses sung at Vespers and Mattins interspersed with Psalm verses; as a collection they may be thought of as a sort of hymnal.

stól'nik (STOL'-nik)—lit. tableman, one who served at the ruler's table. By the mid-seventeenth century, according to Grigorii Kotoshikhin, the holders of this rank numbered approximately five hundred men who served the tsar in various civil, diplomatic, and military capacities. They ranked just below Duma members in status.

syn boiárskii, pl. *déti boiárskie* (SYN ba-YAR-skiy, DYE-ti ba-YAR-ski-ye)—lit. boyar's son (pl. "boyars' sons"), but most of them were not biological sons of boyars. Instead they were lower-ranked servitors, who were clients of boyars.

Theotókos—lit. God-bearer; the Greek title of Mary, the mother of Jesus. It is frequently used directly in English; in the Russian church the equivalent is *Bogoróditsa*.

tiáglye liúdi (TYAG-ly-ye LYU-di)—unfree men who were subject to being drafted for particular work details as part of their obligation.

Triságion—lit. Thrice-Holy; the "Thrice Holy" hymn, "Holy God, Holy Mighty, Holy Immortal, have mercy on us," met in the Divine Liturgy between the Little Entrance and the Epistle reading.

Triságion Service—an abbreviated memorial service for the dead, including the "Thrice Holy" hymn. A longer version of the same service is called a "Panikhida." Both of these contain selected hymns and prayers met also in the Rite of Burial, or Funeral Service.

tselovál'nik (tsy-la-VAL'-nik)—sworn man; from *tselovát'* (to kiss; as in kissing the cross when taking an oath).

ubrúsets (u-BRU-syets)—an oblong towel, often of a decorative nature.

Ulozhénie (u-la-ZHE-ni-ye)—Law Code of 1649.

ushkúinniki (ush-KUYN-ni-ki)—marauding boat raiders from Novgorod.

vakántsiia (va-KAN-tsy-ya)—furlough.

verstánie, verstán'e (vir-STA-ni-ye, vir-STAN'-ye)—assigned service category.

voevóda (va-ye-VO-da)—a military governor.

vótchina, pl. *vótchiny* (VOT-chi-na, VOT-chi-ny)—an estate that was "in the family." A *vótchina* could be bought and sold, mortgaged, or donated to a church or monastery. Such transactions were not allowed for *pomést'ia*.

vótchinnik (VOT-chin-nik)—holder of a *vótchina*.

vskórmlenniki (FSKORM-lyen-ni-ki)—fosterlings. Sometimes used by subordinates to refer to their position vis-à-vis their superior.

Zémskii sobór (ZYEM-skiy sa-BOR)—Assembly of the Land, which was made up of all the church prelates, the entire Boyar Duma, and representatives from the gentry, as well as leading townsmen.

zhálovanie (ZHA-la-va-ni-ye)—grant or reward for service.

zhitié, pl. *zhitiiá* (zhy-ti-YE, zhy-ti-YA)—written life of a saint; *vita*.

On the Use and History of Personal Names in Muscovy

Hugh M. Olmsted

This volume is populated with quite a variety of characters, and the names they bear are just as various. Most of their names consist of several parts: sometimes these look like our familiar pattern of first name plus last name, but frequently the situation is more complicated. Failure to understand how the names work can interfere with understanding the characters themselves and their historical context. The present section is intended to introduce and explain some features of these names and to give a summary of some of the relevant historical developments.

FIRST (CHRISTIAN, BAPTISMAL) NAME

Some of the characters in the biographical portraits are identified by just a simple first name—generally some version of their Christian given name, their baptismal name. In Muscovy these names were drawn from a limited list of saints' names in the Eastern Orthodox church calendar and given to the infant by the priest at the moment of baptism. In the essays in this volume, use of just the first name is typical of unpretentious country folk, children, people in the context of friends or family, or humble monks and nuns. People we meet with this simple sort of identification in this volume include women and girls named *Praskóv'ia, Ul'iána,* and *Dária*; and the men and boys *Geórgii, Matvéi,* and *Nikíta*. For these people in these contexts, just their first name is all we hear, and generally it is all we need to know.

We must also note certain variants that can appear in addition to or even take the place of the given first name itself: especially the *diminutive* and the *nickname* (two separate things).

Diminutives

Almost all Russian personal names have informal *diminutive* (affectionate, familiar) forms. These existed in the Muscovite period and continue to exist in rich diversity in Russia today. They can be automatically used by family and friends, as we might call somebody named Margaret "Maggie" or "Peggy"; Robert "Bob," "Rob," or "Bobby"; or William "Will," "Bill," "Billy," or "Willy." In Russian these diminutives frequently end in *-a* or *-sha*. In the texts we meet girls and women called *Oksánka* (diminutive for *Oksána*), *Nádia* (for *Nadézhda*), and *Dúnia* (for *Avdot'ia*) and men and boys called *Vásia* (for *Vasílii*), *Sásha* (for *Aleksándr*), *Ignásha* or *Ignáshka* (for *Ignátii*), and *Lár'ka* (for *Ilarión*). In Muscovy, diminutives like these might at times be used by their bearers publicly or officially (for instance, in petitions to higher authorities or in court cases), especially to stress their modesty, dependence on their masters, or the like. Sometimes the diminutives are reserved for private use among the near and dear, and sometimes they are so routinely used for a particular person that they lose their special meaning and become as neutral as any name.

The range of variant forms and the use of diminutives in Russian was then, as it is now, rich and complex. It allowed and allows for the expression of many different degrees of closeness, affection, irony, condescension, and so on. Typically the diminutives occur in series of increasing "diminutivization." For example, the most basic diminutives of the names *Andréi*, *Iván*, and *Avdótia* are *Andriúsha*, *Vánia*, and *Dúnia*, respectively—the form that you would expect to use for a child or for any person with whom you were on familiar terms. Further steps of endearment or closeness can be expressed by more diminutivized forms of the name, such as *Andriúshka* or *Andriúshen'ka*, *Ván'ka* or *Vánechka*, or *Dún'ka* or *Dúnechka*. Many other variants exist as well, each with its own shade of affective meaning. Any of these forms could be selected for use with a given individual at the appropriate moment, and all may occur in historical documents in place of the full, official, baptismal name.

Nicknames

The nickname (called in Russian the klíchka or prózvishche), extremely common, was a sort of informal personal epithet, sometimes used together with the baptismal name, sometimes used instead of it. It was frequently jocular, sometimes derogatory, and could reflect anything from which child you were in your family's birth sequence to your geographical origin, a bad habit, a character trait, or a physical defect. It could spring from a praiseworthy term used ironically or a derogatory term used lovingly. It could be an affectionate childhood name, a matter-of-fact description, or a demeaning insult that you were unfortunate enough to get stuck with. Such nicknames were widely and seriously used—not at all limited to informal contexts or simple common folk. In sixteenth-century Muscovy, for example, there were prominent people who were publicly and officially known by such names as "Horned Louse" (Rogátaia vosh'), "Dog" (Sobáka), and "Gooseberry" (Bersén')—the name of a famously prickly fruit, applied to an irascible, "prickly" nobleman. You could be known as Tolstiák (Fatso), Khudiák (Scrawny or Skinny), Zubák (Toothy), Reviáka (Crybaby), Khrushch (June Bug), Gorbách (Humpback), Usách (Whiskers), Guzýnia (Fat Ass), Púshka (Cannon), Medvéd' (Bear), Záiats (Bunny Rabbit), or Tretiák (Third-Born). The possibilities for nicknames like these are limited only by people's creativity and imagination.

For some people in this volume of portraits we are given both their baptismal names and their nicknames, as in *Makár Shesták* (Makar Sixth-Born), or *Alekséi Mukhomór* (Aleksei the Toadstool).

PATRONYMIC

In traditional Old Russia an important part of your identity, crucial in identifying to the outside world who you were, was the connection with your father. Accordingly, one of the most important and distinctive parts of Muscovite name lore is the *patronymic*, which explicitly shows that connection. The patronymic consisted of your father's name with a special added suffix that means "son of" or "daughter of." This part of a person's name also revealed his or her social class, specifically whether the individual belonged among the nobility or the common folk:

1. The **nobility** is identifiable by a name in which the patronymic has the father's name plus the patronymic suffix *-ovich / -evich* (for males) or *-ovna / -evna* (for females). Commoners were actually not allowed to use such forms.

Russian form	*English translation*
Fëdor Alekséevich	Fëdor, son of Alekséi
Il'iá Danílovich	Il'iá, son of Daniíl or Danílo
Borís Fëdorovich	Borís, son of Fëdor
Mikháilo Ivánovich	Mikháilo, son of Iván
Dmítrei Mikháilovich	Dmítrei, son of Mikhaíl
Borís Petróvich	Borís, son of Pëtr
Bogdán Póstnikovich	Bogdán, son of Póstnik
Semën Ul'iánovich	Semën, son of Ul'ián
Aleksándr Vasíl'evich	Aleksándr, son of Vasílii
Vasílii Vasíl'evich	Vasílii, son of Vasílii
Matvéi Vladímirovich	Matvéi, son of Vladímir
Sóf'ia Alekséevna	Sóf'ia, daughter of Alekséi
María Vladímirovna	María, daughter of Vladímir

For fathers' names that end in *-a* (such as *Fomá, Il'iá, Nikíta,* or *Ióna*), the nobility's patronymic is formed not by *-ovich / -ovna*, but by *-inich* or *-ich* (for male children) and *-inichna* or *-ichna* (for female children). Such forms do not happen to occur in this volume, but they were standard in Muscovy. They, too, were used only by the nobility.

Iván Fomích	Iván, son of Fomá
Margaríta Fomínichna	Margaríta, daughter of Fomá
Pëtr Nikítich	Pëtr, son of Nikíta
Véra Nikítichna	Véra, daughter of Nikíta

This upper-class patronymic, distinctive in form, always retained its use strictly as a patronymic. With the passage of time, its social use broadened to include more and more of the lower classes—to the point where since the nineteenth century it has been used by just about anyone. But it has always remained a patronymic, never sliding over into use as a family name (unlike the common-folk patronym, discussed below).

2. **Common folk**, whose patronymics in Muscovite usage are father's name plus *-ov* / *-ev* (for males) or *-ova* / *-eva* for females. The patronymic is typically accompanied by the word *syn* (son) or *doch'* (daughter). The *-ov(a)* / *-ëv(a)* suffix is equivalent to the English possessive ending "'s," so *Aleksándr Ivánov syn* simply means "Aleksándr, Iván's son" (Aleksándr, son of Iván); *María Petróva doch'* means "Maria, Pëtr's daughter."

The father's personal name that figures in these combinations may be either his Christian baptismal name or a diminutive form or a more colorful individual nickname. So we may see combinations like "Matvei, son of Fatso" (*Matvéi Tolstiakóv syn*), "Dmitrii, son of the Bear" (*Dmítrii Medvédev syn*), "Mikhail, son of the Hunchback" (*Mikhaíl Gorbachëv syn*), or Nikita, son of the June Bug (*Nikita Khrushchëv syn*. The social distinction between kinds of patronymics, *-ov(a)* / *-ev(a)* for commoners and *-ovich* / *-evich* / *-ovna* / *-evna* for the nobility, is well represented in this volume; and by paying attention to the form of people's patronymics, you get an important clue to their social status. Some of our authors mention people using the English form (Foma son of Karp), some use the Russian (*Fomá Kárpov syn*)—these are completely equivalent in meaning. The table of selected examples below shows which language is used for some of the specific individuals met in the volume. The form with the asterisk is the form that the author has chosen to use:

Russian	*English*
Deméntii Okátov syn	*Deméntii, Okát's son (or son of Okát)
*Fomá Kárpov syn	Fomá, Karp's son (or son of Karp)
*Grigórii Filátov syn	Grigórii, Filát's son (or son of Filát)
*Ignátii Ivánov syn	Ignátii, Iván's son (or son of Iván)
Ilarión Póstnikov syn	*Ilarión, Póstnik's son (or son of Póstnik)
*Ovdokím Vasíliev syn	Ovdokím, Vasílii's son (or son of Vasilii)

ON THE USE AND HISTORY OF PERSONAL NAMES IN MUSCOVY

Iván Petróv syn	*Iván, Pëtr's son (or son of Pëtr)
*Rodión Afanásiev syn	Rodión, Afanásii's son (or son of Afanasii)
*Tomílo Ivánov syn	Tomílo, Iván's son (or son of Iván)
*Lukéria Vasílieva doch'	Lukéria, Vasílii's daughter (or daughter of Vasílii)
Nádia Alekséeva doch'	*Nádia, Alekséi's daughter (or daughter of Alekséi)

For fathers' names that end in -a (such as *Fomá, Il'iá, Nikíta,* or *Ióna*), the commoners' patronymic is formed not by -ov / -ova, but by -in (for male children) and -ina (for female children). They are less common than the patronymics in -ov or -ova but perfectly standard.

Iván Fomín syn	Iván, son of Fomá
Margaríta Fominá doch'	Margaríta, daughter of Fomá
Pëtr Nikítin syn	Pëtr, son of Nikíta
Véra Nikítina doch'	Véra, daughter of Nikíta

As suggested above, the patronymic was often based on the father's nickname instead of his formal baptismal name (both were common). Given the list of nicknames above, the corresponding patronymics would be:

Nickname	*Patronymic*
Vosh' (Louse)	Vshin
Sobáka (Dog)	Sobákin
Bersén' (Gooseberry)	Bersénev
Tolstiák (Fatso)	Tolstiakóv
Khudiák (Scrawny)	Khudiakóv
Zubák (Toothy)	Zubakóv
Reviáka (Crybaby)	Reviákin
Usách (Whiskers)	Usachóv
Guzýnia (Fat Ass)	Guzýnin
Púshka (Cannon)	Púshkin
Záiats (Bunny Rabbit)	Záitsev
Tret'iák (Third-Born)	Tret'iakóv

EXTENDED MULTI-PART NAMES: FATHER'S PATRONYMIC, SLIDING INTO FAMILY NAMES

Sometimes instead of first name and patronymic, a more extended name was used. It traced your family connection another generation back by adding your father's own patronymic. For example, assuming we are dealing with a brother and a sister, Aleksandr and Maria, children of Ivan son of Vasilii (*Iván Vasíl'ev syn*), their names could take the form:

1. *Aleksándr Ivánov syn Vasíl'eva* (meaning "Aleksandr, son of Ivan-son-of-Vasilii" or "Aleksandr, Ivan-son-of-Vasilii's son")
2. *María Ivánova doch' Vasíl'eva* (meaning "Maria, daughter of Ivan-son-of-Vasilii" or "Maria, Ivan-son-of-Vasilii's daughter")

This would in effect incorporate into your name both your father's and your grandfather's name.

For those who know Russian, the father's patronym is given in the possessive (genitive case) form "Vasíl'eva," since it is linked to the father's name, which is being used in a possessive sense. Particularly during the sixteenth century, this complex pattern began to break down, as society seemed to tire of the constant generational switching of first name plus patronymic plus father's patronymic. The father's patronymic began increasingly to be kept for more than one generation, starting to function as a family name, not just as the grandfather's name. This change was visible in the formal switch of the father's patronymic from the possessive (genitive case) form to the basic (nominative case) form.

Earlier form (with father's patronymic)	*Later form (with father's old patronymic used as family name)*
Aleksándr Ivánov syn Vasíl'eva Aleksandr, Ivan-son-of-Vasilii's son Aleksandr (son of Ivan) Vasiliev or	Aleksandr, son of Ivan-son-of-Vasílii, or *Aleksándr Ivánov syn Vasíl'ev* Aleksandr Vasiliev, son of Ivan

The names on which the patronymics were based had standard types of origins. We have mentioned the nicknames, diminutives, and baptismal names above. Altogether, depending on what the name or nickname of your grandfather had been, the patronymic-becoming-family name could be based on:

1. baptismal names (e.g., *Dmítrii, Iván, Pëtr*, leading to patronymics and thence family names *Dmítriev, Ivánov, Petróv*);
2. nicknames (see the examples listed above, such as *Medvédev, Gorbachëv, Khrushchëv, Záitsev, Púshkin, Tret'iakóv,* or *Tolstiakóv*);
3. diminutives based on the baptismal names (e.g., if we take the diminutives of the same three names as in no. 1, we have *Mítia, Vánia, Pétia* leading to *Mítin, Vánin, Pétin*);
4. terms for occupations (e.g., *kuznéts* [blacksmith], *pop* [priest], *trubách* [horn player], leading to *Kuznetsóv, Popóv, Trubachóv*); or
5. geographical and ethnographic names (e.g., *Vólga* [Volga River], *nemchín* [German], *sibiriák* [Siberian], *chekh* [Czech], leading to *Vólgin, Nemchínov, Sibiriakóv, Chékhov*).

FAMILY NAME

The process described above resulted in the widescale development of family names. For both social groups—nobility and commoners—a last name in *-ov(a)* / *-ev(a)* or *-in(a)* is common.

Family names tended to appear earlier historically among the nobility, whose families had more prominence, proud heritage, and self-consciousness, than among commoners. Here are some examples from this volume:

Bogdán Pósnikovich *Sheremétev*
Borís Fëdorovich *Godunóv*
Borís Petróvich *Sheremétev*
Daníla Ivánovich *Miachkóv*
Iván Vasílievich *Bírkin*
Mikháilo Ivánovich *Speshnëv*
Pëtr Alekséevich *Shubálov*
Semën Uliánovich *Rémezov*
Vasílii Vasílievich *Golítsyn*

But we meet some family names among commoners as well:

Andréi Nikíta's son *Beklénshev*
Colonel Afanásii Nikítin *Nelídov*
Deméntii Okátov syn *Párfiev*
Grigórii Filátov syn *Zótov*
Ilarión Póstnikov syn *Sharápov*
Nádia daughter of Alekséi *Beklénsheva*
Ovdokím Vasíliev syn *Skvortsóv*
Iván Petróv syn *Kiríllov*
Rodión Afanásiev syn *Vorypáev*
Stepán (Stëpych) Aleksándrov syn *Pálkin*
Tomílo Ivánov syn *Ukólov*

This process we have described, of the development of stable family names from the various categories of former frozen or fossilized patronymics, was altogether the most common source of Russian family names.

However, other types of sources also played important roles in the history of family names. Starting at the end of the Muscovite period in the late seventeenth century, one of the most productive and colorful methods was the wholesale creation of last names for students in church schools. These students came to school without family names but were supplied with arbitrary, ready-made ones just to meet the requirement that every student must have a family name. The sources for invention were many. Among the most common:

1. saints' names and epithets (Petropávlovskii, Areopagítskii, Zlatoústovskii);
2. names of Eastern Orthodox Church holidays or feasts (Blagovéshchenskii, Tróitskii, Preobrazhénskii, Uspénskii, Pokróvskii);
3. names newly coined consisting of Church Slavonic elements (Dobroliúbov, Blagonrávov, Potselúevskii);
4. names of plants (Giatsíntov, Nartsíssov, Rózov);
5. names of animals (Orlóvskii, Panteróvskii, Golubínskii, Lebedínskii);
6. names of minerals (Brilliántov, Ametístov, Korállov, Kristalévskii);
7. names of natural and geographical origin (Vostókov, Gorizóntov, Kliuchévskii, Zefírov);
8. names of people and mythological beings from classical antiquity (Aristótelev, Orféev, Afrodítin, Satúrnov); and
9. other names based on Latin and Greek elements (Velosipédov, Gloriózov, Speránskii, Preferánsov, Amfiteátrov).

As a result, side by side with the typical patronymic-based names surveyed above, Russian family names also include a striking—even at times bizarre-seeming—variety of quite un-Russian-looking allusions and forms.

SUMMARY

The most typical type of name in Muscovite Russia consisted of one or more of the following parts:

1. personal name (full or diminutive form);
2. nickname;
3. patronymic (either noble or common, as appropriate); and
4. father's patronymic (sliding into use as family name from the sixteenth century on).

Other sources for family names also existed, leading to still greater variety.

ENGLISH PARALLELS

It may be interesting to notice how very similar the sources for family names in certain other countries are to the types of frozen patronymics we have described for Russian. English family names, for example, have strikingly similar kinds of sources (with strikingly different-looking results, of course). They, too, typically developed from:

ON THE USE AND HISTORY OF PERSONAL NAMES IN MUSCOVY

1. baptismal names in old patronymics that became frozen and stayed from generation to generation, instead of changing with each father and son (*Peters, Peterson* [from *Peter's* (son), with the apostrophe and/or the "son" left out]; *Andrews, Anderson* [from *Andrew's* son]; *Jones, Johnson* [from *John's* son]);
2. nicknames (*Armstrong, Merriweather, Shakespeare, Lightfoot*);
3. diminutives of baptismal names (*Tompkins* [a double diminutive, from *Tomkin* from *Tom* from *Thomas*], *Simpkins* [similarly, from *Simkin* from *Sim* from *Simon*]);
4. occupational terms (*Smith, Carpenter, Taylor, Wainwright* [wagon maker], or *Harvard* [alt. *Hereward*, "army guard"]); or
5. place names of family location or residence (*Newton* [from New Town], *Oxford* [the place where oxen cross the river by fording it], *Akeley* [Oak-lea, oak glade or clearing], or *Brigham* [bridge-home, homestead by the bridge]).

OTHER TYPES OF NAMES

Alongside the typical forms of Russian names described above, other sorts of names could also be found in Muscovy and are represented in this volume as well. They include:

1. First name plus descriptive identifier

Certain categories of people had names that fell outside of the descriptions above. Most typical is the use of first name plus descriptive identifier. Such a form was commonly used for:

a. Foreigners, ethnic minorities

Foreigners or representatives of non-Russian ethnic groups—Greeks, Tatars, Jews, West Europeans, Gypsies, or Central Asians. Foreigners resident in Muscovy, or members of ethnic minorities, were often known simply by their first name and their nationality or place of origin.

Feófan Grek	Feofan (Theophanes) the Greek
Maksím Grek	Maksim the Greek
Nikolái Nemchín	Nikolai the German
Alevíz Friázin	Alois the Italian
Isaák Zhidóvin	Isaak the Jew

b. Historic figures

Those renowned for exploits connected with specific places, respected religious figures, the founders of movements or monasteries. These, too, were often known by their first name and the name of the geographical location they were associated with (typically expressed with an adjective in *-skii* or *-skoi*):

Sergei Rádonezhskii	Sergei of Radonezh
Kirill Belozérskii	Kirill of Belozersk (Beloe ozero, "White Lake")
Antónii Chernoezérskii	Anthony of Chernoezersk (Chernoe ozero, "Black Lake")
Aleksándr Névskii	Aleksandr of the Neva River
Dmítrii Donskói	Dmitrii of the Don River
Tikhon Zadónskii	Tikhon of zadon'e (the area beyond the Don)
Dmitrii Rostóvskii	Dmitrii of Rostov

2. Purely foreign names

Visitors' or immigrants' names which were maintained in their original form by their bearers, such as Ukrainians, Belorussians, other Slavs; Greeks; Arabs or Persians; Tatars and representatives of other Turkic nationalities; German, Dutch, English; Italians or French.

In this volume we meet the names of several such people. They include the Tatars *Ismail ibn Ahmed, Mehmed Emin, Melik-Tagir, Ulug Mehmed, Mengli Girey*, and *Abazbanei Kulmametev*; the Greeks *Chatzēkyriakēs Vourliōtēs* and *Melétios*, and the Englishman *Col. William Allen*. We also encounter several names of people who are known both by their original, native names and by Russified variants: the Italian architect *Aloisio Lamberti da Montagna*, known in Russia as *Alevíz Friázin* (Aloís "the Italian"), the Dutch merchant *Georg Janszoon*, known in Russia as *Iúrii Ivanóv*, and the foreigners Baldwin Edwards and Michael Crowe, serving in the Russian army under partially Russified names: *Bóldvin Édvart* and *Mikhaíl Kro*.

CONCLUSION

Altogether, the names of the characters met in these portraits provide a window onto the variety, dynamism, and international contacts of Russian society in the premodern age. Understanding something of their structure and their development over time can give valuable insight into understanding that society and its representation in the portraits offered here.

ON THE USE AND HISTORY OF PERSONAL NAMES IN MUSCOVY

For further reading on this subject, see Unbegaun, Boris O. *Russian Surnames*. Oxford: Clarendon Press, 1972. A lucid and thorough introduction, written in English.

A further amplified and enriched version is available in Russian: Unbegaun, Boris O. *Russkie familii*. Translated from English under the general editorship of B.A. Uspenskii. Moscow: Progress, 1989. The major single source for the historical information presented here.

Transcription and Pronunciation Guide for Russian Names

Hugh M. Olmsted

Russian is normally written in the Cyrillic alphabet. For those who don't know Cyrillic, Russian words and names throughout this volume are transliterated into the Latin alphabet. The list below gives a summary of the names met in the chapters, with a guide to their pronunciation. Each word is first *transliterated* into the Latin alphabet, followed by an approximate *phonetic transcription in parentheses*.

The following conventions are followed.

1. TRANSLITERATION (LETTER-FOR-LETTER)

In the List *words are first given in letter-for-letter transliteration* (following the "so-called" modified Library of Congress system). The systematic use of the LC transliteration makes it possible to look up words or names in standard reference sources such as library catalogues. An acute accent mark (as in á or ó) is added to show which syllable is stressed.

Basic letters and sounds

The five basic vowels are to be pronounced with their traditional European values. Thus, in transliterated words:

"a" is to be read like the "a" in *father* (never as in *jazz* or *Jason*);
"e" is to be read like the "e" in *red* (never as in *he* or *the*), generally with the consonant sound "y" supplied before it, as in *yes;*
"i" is to be read like the "i" in *ski* or *antique* (never as in *strip* or *stripe*);
"o" is to be read approximately like the vowel in *code* or *cawed* (never as in *cod*);

291

"u" is to be read like the "u" in *Luke* (never as in *putt* or *put*);

the diphthong "ai" is to be read as in the first syllable of *Saigon*, so as to rhyme with *eye* (never as in *saint* or *said*); and

the diphthong "ei" is to be read as in the first syllable of *reindeer*, so as to rhyme with *hey* (never as in *seize* or *feisty*).

In the phonetic transcription, the letter "y" has both vowel and consonant uses, depending on its position in the word:

Between two consonants it sounds somewhat like the "i" in *lip*. (Ex.: an-TSY-far)
Next to a vowel it sounds like the "y" in *yes* (Ex: a-ZYOR-na-ya, SHUY-skiy).
Exception: in the few words ending in "-yi" the "y" has the vowel sound.

Other specific letters and letter-combinations are pronounced as follows:

"ch" is to be read as in *church;*
"sh" is to be read as in *shop* or *posh;*
"zh" is to be read like the "zh"-sound in *vision* or *treasure;*
"shch" is to be read like the "sh ch" in combinations like *rash choice* or *ticklish child*. It is a single letter in the Russian Cyrillic alphabet; and
"kh"—like "k" except continuous—like the "ch" in German *Bach* or *ach*, or in Scottish *loch*.

Notice that in one Greek name, *Chatzekyriakes*, the consonant combination "ch" is used for this same sound as "kh" in Russian words. This has been the practice for representing Greek words in Latin letters for centuries (the "ch" in old Greek borrowings in English such as *choral, chrome, Christ,* and *charisma* all go back to this pronunciation, although by now it has been simplified to a simple "k" sound).

"ë"—initially and after most consonants, sounds like "YO," but after the consonants "sh" "zh" "ch" or "shch", sounds like O.

Use of stress-mark

To pronounce a Russian word, you need to know which syllable of the word is stressed (pronounced with more emphasis). Stress changes affect meaning, as they do in English: cf. the difference we see in pairs of English words such as PER-fect (adjective) vs. per-FECT (verb). An acute accent mark (´) is added in the spelling transliteration to show which syllable is stressed.

TRANSCRIPTION AND PRONUNCIATION GUIDE FOR RUSSIAN NAMES

"Soft sign vs. "hard sign"

A single quote mark ('), which can look similar to the acute accent, has a different meaning. It is used not over a vowel, but directly after consonants, as in *Rus_'*, *Pústyn'*, or *Praskóv'ia*. This represents the so-called soft sign in the Cyrillic alphabet. It does affect the pronunciation, but for people unfamiliar with Russian it is easiest just to ignore it. The soft sign is a letter of the alphabet, and to eliminate it entirely would be to misspell a word as well as misrepresent the pronunciation.

In a few cases the so-called hard sign (represented as a double quotation mark ["]) is also met, used only as a separator between certain prefixes and the rest of the word. In older Russian orthography—until the Bolshevik Revolution of 1917—all words phonetically ending in a consonant, if not followed by a soft sign, were automatically spelled with an added hard sign. For transcriptions into the Latin alphabet, such as ours, it has long been standard practice to omit and ignore this redundant final hard sign, and this practice is followed here.

"Phonetic" spelling and exceptions

In general, Russian spelling is "phonetic," in that the spelling of a word is a fairly good guide to the pronunciation, but there are some *exceptions*.

Spelled "o" in unstressed position is pronounced as though it were an "a." Similar reductions happen with other sounds but are not systematically represented here.

Voiced consonants—b, v, d, z, zh, and g—when they appear at the end of a word or before an unvoiced consonant (p, f, t, s, k, kh, sh, ch, shch) are pronounced as their voiceless counterparts.

Voiceless consonants—p, f, t, s, k, kh, sh, ch, shch—when they appear before a voiced consonant (b, v, d, z, zh, or g) are pronounced as their voiced counterparts.

Some syllables containing a stressed "e" (written in transliteration as "ë") are pronounced "YO."

It is for reasons like these that the rough phonetic transcription is also given.

2. PHONETIC TRANSCRIPTION

An approximate *phonetic transcription* is given in parentheses after the letter-for-letter transliteration, to help with pronunciation as you read the texts. The stressed syllable is capitalized, and a broad idea of the pronunciation is suggested. For a more precise idea of how these Russian words are actually pronounced, it would be best to get the help of a native speaker.

The individual sounds are represented with the same letters and equivalencies as those listed above for the letter-for-letter transliteration.

294   TRANSCRIPTION AND PRONUNCIATION GUIDE FOR RUSSIAN NAMES

Abazbánei (a-baz-BA-nyei)
Afanás′ev (a-fa-NAS-yef)
Afanásii (a-fa-NA-siy)
Afonásii (a-fa-NA-siy)
Agáf′ia (a-GAF′-ya)
Agáfiia (a-GA-fi-ya)
Aglítskii dvor (a-GLITS-kiy DVOR)
Aidárov (ay-DA-raf)
Aigústov (ay-GU-staf)
Akákii (a-KA-kiy)
Aleksándr (a-lyek-SANDR)
Aleksándrov (a-lyek-SAN-draf)
Aleksándrova Slobodá (a-lyek-SAN-dra-va sla-ba-DA)
Alekséevich (a-lyek-SYE-ye-vich)
Alekséevna (a-lyek-SYE-yev-na)
Alekséi (a-lek-SYEI)
Alevíz Friázin (a-lye-VIS FRIA-zin—from Aloísio or Aloís, pron. in Russian a-le-VIS)
Anastasía (a-na-sta-SI-ya)
Andréevich (an-DRE-ye-vich)
Andréi (an-DREY)
Andriúsha (an-DRYU-sha)
Andriúshka (an-DRYUSH-ka)
Ánna (AN-na)
Antonieva chernoezerskaia v chest′ Rozhdestva Bogoroditsy Pustyn′ (an-TO-ni-ye-va cher-na-ye-ZYER-ska-ya fchest′ razh-dye-STVA ba-ga-RO-di-tsy PU-styn′)
Antónii (an-TO-niy)
Apráksia (a-PRAK-si-ya)
Arkádii (ar-KA-diy)
Arkhangél′sk (ar-KHAN-gyel′sk)
Arsénii (ar-SYE-niy)
Artëm (ar-TYOM)
Artémii (ar-TYE-miy)
Arzamás (Ar-za-MAS)
Ástrakhan′ (A-stra-khan′)
Avderíkhin (av-dye-RI-khin)
Avdót′ia (av-DOT′-ya)
Avraám (a-vra-AM)
Avrám (a-VRAM)
Avvakúm (av-va-KUM)
Azéev (a-ZYE-yev)
Ázov (A-zaf)
Balándin (ba-LAN-din)
Barabínsk (ba-ra-BINSK)
Batúrin (ba-TU-rin)
Beklénshev (bye-KLYEN-shyf)
Beklénsheva (bye-KLYEN-shyva)
Bélgorod (BYEL-ga-rat)
Beloózero (bye-la-O-zye-ra)
Belozérsk (bye-la-ZYERSK)
Belozérskii (bye-la-ZYER-skiy)
Bersén′ (byer-SYEN′)
Bezzúbtsov (byez-ZUP-tsaf)
Bírkin (BIR-kin)
Boborýkin (ba-ba-RY-kin)
Bobróvsk (ba-BROFSK)
Bogdán (bag-DAN)
Bogoróditsa (ba-ga-RO-di-tsa)
Bóldvin [Baldwin] (BOL-dvin)
Borís (ba-RIS)
Borísovich (ba-RI-sa-vich)
Bóshchev [monastery] (BO-shchef)
Bukhará (bu-kha-RA)
Býkov (BY-kaf)
Chatzēkyriákēs [Grk] (kha-tsi-ki-ri-A-kis)
Chelnováia [river] (chel-na-VA-ya)
Cherepovéts (che-re-pa-VYETS)
Cherkásskii (chir-KAS-skiy)
Cherkásy (chir-KA-sy)
Chërnoe ózero (CHOR-na-ya O-ze-ra—"Black Lake")
Chernoezérskaia (cher-na-ye-ZYER-ska-ya—"Black Lake" [adj., fem.])
Chernoezérskii (cher-na-ye-ZYER-skiy—"Black Lake" [adj., masc.])
Chúdov (CHU-daf)
Daniíl (da-ni-IL)
Daníla (da-NIL-a)
Danílov (da-NIL-af)

TRANSCRIPTION AND PRONUNCIATION GUIDE FOR RUSSIAN NAMES

Danílovich, Daniilovich (da-NIL-a-vich)
Dankóv (dan-KOF)
Dária (DAR-ya)
Dáriia (DA-ri-ya)
Dáritsa (DA-ri-tsa)
Davídovich (da-VI-da-vich)
Dedílov (dye-DI-laf)
Dem'iánov (dyem-YA-naf)
Deméntiev (dye-MYEN-tyef)
Deméntii (dye-MYEN-tiy)
Dëmka (DYOM-ka)
Denísko (de-NIS-ka)
Denísov (de-NI-saf)
Derévianitsy (dye-RYE-vya-ni-tsy)
Detínets (dye-TI-nyets)
Dimítrii (di-MI-triy)
Divéevskaia (di-VYE-yef-ska-ya)
Dmitrei (D'MI-triy)
Dmítrievich (D'MI-tri-ye-vich)
Dmítrii (D'MI-triy)
Dnepr [river] (DNYEPR)
Dómna (DOM-na)
Dosiféi (da-si-FYEI)
Dubonós (du-ba-NOS)
Dúnechka (DU-nyech-ka)
Dúnia (DU-nya)
Dvína (DVI-na)
Édvarts [Edwards] (ED-varts)
Efím (ye-FIM)
Efím'ia (ye-FIM-ya)
Efrosín (yef-ra-SIN)
Eléna (ye-LYE-na)
Éléts (ye-LYETS)
Eliazárov Monastery (ye-li-a-ZA-raf)
Embáevsky [iurt] (em-BA-yef-skiy)
Eniséi (ye-ni-SYEI)
Eniséisk (ye-ni-SEISK)
Epifán' (ye-pi-FAN)
Epifánii (ye-pi-FA-niy)
Erázm (ye-RAZM)
Ermák (yer-MAK)
Eroféi (ye-ra-FYEI)
Evdokíia (yev-da-KI-ya)
Evfímiia (yef-FI-mi-ya)
Féd'ka (FYET'-ka)
Fëdor (FYO-dar)
Fëdorovich (FYO-da-ra-vich)
Fedótov (fe-DO-taf)
Feódor (fe-O-dar)
Feófan (fe-O-fan) in Muscovy until 17th century; thereafter Feofán (fe-a-FAN).
Feógnost (fe-OG-nast) in Muscovy until 17th century; thereafter Feognóst (fe-ag-NOST).
Fétin'ia (FYE-tin-ya)
Filarét (fi-la-RYET)
Filátov (fi-LA-taf)
Filípp, Filíp (fi-LIP)
Filoféi (fi-la-FYEI)
Fomá (fa-MA)
Frolóv (fra-LOF)
Frolóvskie voróta (fra-LOF-ski-ye va-RO-ta)
Gagárin (ga-GA-rin)
Gálich (GA-lich)
Gantimúr (gan-ti-MUR)
Gavril (ga-VRIL)
Gelásii (ge-LA-siy)
Gennádii (gen-NA-diy)
Gerásimov (ge-RA-si-maf)
Gérman (GYER-man)
Gleb (GLYEB)
Glébov (GLYE-baf)
Gliníshchakh (gli-NI-shchakh)
Godunóv (ga-du-NOF)
Golítsyn (ga-LI-tsyn)
Gorétovo (ga-RYE-ta-va)
Gorodéts (ga-ra-DYETS)
Gorodísche (ga-ra-DI-shche)
grek (GRYEK)
Grigór'ev (gri-GOR-yef)
Grigór'evich (gri-GOR-ye-vich)
Grigórii (gri-GO-riy)
Grísha (GRI-sha)

Gródno (GROD-na)
Gusílov (gu-SI-laf)
Iáblonov (YA-bla-naf)
Iákov (YA-kaf)
Iákovlevich (YA-ka-vle-vich)
Iarosláv (ia-ra-SLAF)
Iaroslávl' (ia-ra-SLAVL')
Ignáshka (i-GNASH-ka)
Ignátii (i-GNA-tiy)
Il'iá (il-YA)
Íl'men' (IL'-myen')
Ilarión (i-la-ri-ON)
Ilováiskii (i-la-VAI-skiy)
Innokéntii (in-na-KEN-tiy)
Ioákim (i-o-A-kim)
Ioánn (i-o-AN)
Ióna (i-YO-na)
Iósif (i-YO-sif)
Iósifov-Volokolámskii (i-YO-si-fav va-la-ka-LAM-skiy)
Irinárkh (i-ri-NARKH)
Irtýsh [river] (ir-TYSH)
Isáia (i-SA-ya)
Ismaíl (i-sma-IL)
Ístra (I-stra)
Iúl'ia (YUL'-ya)
Iúr'ev (YUR-yef)
Iúr'eva (YUR-ye-va)
Iúrii (YU-riy)
Iván (i-VAN)
Ivánov, Ivanóv (i-VAN-af, i-va-NOF)
Ivánovich (i-VAN-a-vich)
Iváshka (i-VASH-ka)
Izhóra (i-ZHO-ra)
Kaibúlin (kay-BU-lin)
Kalíka (ka-LI-ka)
Kalitá (ka-li-TA)
Kalúga (ka-LU-ga)
Káma (KA-ma)
Karélia (ka-RE-li-ya)
Kárgopol' (KAR-ga-pal')
Karp (KARP)
Kárpov (KAR-paf)
Kartávtsov (kar-TAF-tsev)
Kashíra (ka-SHY-ra)
Kasímov (ka-SI-maf)
Kassián (ka-si-YAN)
Kazákh (ka-ZAKH)
Kazán' (ka-ZAN')
Kazí-kérman (ka-ZI - KYER-man)
Kerét' [river] (kye-RYET')
Khíva (KHI-va)
Khóbotets [forests] (KHO-ba-tits)
Khólmov (KHOL-maf)
Khomutéts (kha-mu-TYETS)
Khram Zhivonachál'noi Tróitsy v Nikítnikakh (KHRAM zhy-va-na-CHAL'-nay TRO-i-tsy vni-KIT-ni-kakh)
Khristofór (khri-sta-FOR)
Khvalýnsk [Caspian Sea] (khfa-LYNSK)
Kipriánov (ki-pri-YA-naf)
Kiríll (ki-RIL)
Kiríllo-Belozérskii monastýr' (ki-RI-la-bye-la-ZYER-skiy ma-na-STYR')
Kiríllov (ki-RIL-laf)
Kiríllovich (ki-RIL-la-vich)
Kitái-Górod (ki-TAI GO-rat)
Klíment (KLI-myent)
Kliméntii (kli-MYEN-tiy)
Klópskii (KLOP-skiy)
Kolómna (ka-LOM-na)
Koltóvskaia (kal-TOF-ska-ya)
Koltóvskii (kal-TOF-skiy)
Kólychev (KO-ly-chef)
Kónan (KO-nan)
Kondrát (kan-DRAT)
Konstantín (kan-stan-TIN)
Konstantínov (kan-stan-TI-naf)
Konstantínovich (kan-stan-TI-na-vich)
Konstiantín (kan-styan-TIN)
Koréla (ka-RYE-la)
Kornílii (kar-NI-liy)

TRANSCRIPTION AND PRONUNCIATION GUIDE FOR RUSSIAN NAMES

Kóshelev (KO-shy-lyef)
Kostiantín (ka-styan-TIN)
Kostromá (ka-stra-MA)
Kótorosl' (KO-ta-rasl')
Kozlóv (ka-ZLOF)
Krásnikov (KRAS-ni-kaf)
Kro [Crowe] (KRO)
Krongórt (kran-GORT)
Krutítskii (kru-TIT-skiy)
Kubénskii (ku-BYEN-skiy)
Kulikóvo (ku-li-KO-va)
Kulmamétev (kul-ma-MYE-tyef)
Kungúr (kun-GUR)
Kurákin (ku-RA-kin)
Kúritsyn (KU-ri-tsyn)
Kyriakēs [Grk] (ki-ri-A-kis)
Lýsye Góry (LY-sye GO-ry)
L'vítskii (L'VITS-kiy)
Ládoga (LA-da-ga)
Lavréntii (la-VRYEN-tiy)
Lebedían' (li-bye-DYAN')
Leoníd (li-a-NIT)
Lesnói Vorónezh [river] (lis-NOY va-RO-nesh)
Levítskii (li-VITS-kiy)
Lífland (LIF-lant)
Likharëv (li-kha-RYOF)
Likharëva (li-kha-RYO-va)
Lipóvka (li-POF-ka)
Lúga (LU-ga)
Luká (lu-KA)
Lukín (lu-KIN)
Lukínich (lu-KI-nich)
Lykóv (ly-KOF)
Makár (ma-KAR)
Makárii (ma-KA-riy)
Mangazéia (man-ga-ZYE-ya)
Márfa (MAR-fa)
Már'ia (MAR-ya)
Maríia (ma-RI-ya)
Markéll (mar-KYEL)
Martírii (mar-TI-riy)
Matrëna (ma-TRYO-na)

Matróna (ma-TRO-na)
Matvéi (mat-VYEI)
Mazépa (ma-ZYE-pa)
Melétios [Greek] (me-LE-ti-os)
Ménshikov (MYEN-shy-kaf)
Meshchérinov (mi-SHCHE-ri-naf)
Miachkóv (mich-KOF)
Mikhaíl (mi-kha-IL)
Mikháilo (mi-KHAY-la)
Mikháilov (mi-KHAY-laf)
Mikháilovich (mi-KHAY-la-vich)
Míkífor (mi-KI-far)
Miloslávskaia (mi-la-SLAF-ska-ya)
Miloslávskii (mi-la-SLAF-skiy)
Mísha (MI-sha)
Mit'ka (MIT'-ka)
Mítrofán (mi-tra-FAN)
Moiséi (mo-i-SYEI)
Mológa (ma-LO-ga)
monastýr' (ma-na-STYR')
Mstislávskii (msti-SLAF-skiy)
Mtsensk (MTSENSK)
Mukhomór (mu-kha-MOR)
Músa (MU-sa)
Nádia (NA-dya)
Nagói (na-GOY)
Narýshkin (na-RYSH-kin)
Narýshkina (na-RYSH-kina)
Nárva (NAR-va)
Natál'ia (na-TAL'-ya)
Nelídov (nye-LI-daf)
Nepripásov (nye-pri-PA-saf)
Nérev (NYE-ryef)
Nerónov (nye-RO-naf)
Nével' (NYE-vyel')
Nikífor (ni-KI-far)
Nikíta (ni-KI-ta)
Nikítin (ni-KI-tin)
Nikítniki, Nikitnikakh (ni-KIT-ni-ki, ni-KIT-ni-kakh)
Nikítnikov pereúlok (ni-KIT-ni-kaf pi-rye-U-lak)
Nikíty Vóina (ni-KI-ty VO-i-na)

Níkon (NI-kan)
Nízhnii (NIZH-niy)
Nízhyn (NI-zhyn)
Nóvaia Zemliá (NO-va-ya zye-MLYA)
Nóvgorod (NOV-ga-rat)
Novospásskii monastýr' (na-va-SPAS-skiy ma-na-STYR')
Ob' [river] (OP')
Oká [river] (a-KA)
Okát (a-KAT)
Oksánka (ak-SAN-ka)
Oléshenka [creek] (a-LYE-shen-ka)
Oléshenskii [bailliage] (a-LYE-shen-skii)
Oléshka (a-LYE-shka)
Ólgerd [Algerdas] (OL-gyert)
Ondréshko (an-DRYE-shka)
Ontsífor (an-TSY-far)
Opóka (a-PO-ka)
Orékhov (a-RYE-khaf)
Oshevénskii (a-she-VYEN-skiy)
Ósip (O-sip)
Ostaféi (a-sta-FYEI)
Ótnia (OT-nya)
Ovdokím (a-vda-KIM)
Ozërnoe (a-ZYOR-na-ya)
P'iána [river] (P'YA-na)
Pálkin (PAL-kin)
Paraskéva (pa-ra-SKYE-va)
Parfënovna (par-FYO-nav-na)
Párfiev (PAR-fi-yef)
Párfii (PAR-fiy)
Pável [Paul] (PA-vyel)
Pávlov (PAV-laf)
Pelagéia (pye-la-GYE-ya)
Pereiaslávl' (Pe-re-ya-SLAVL')
Pestriakóv (pe-strya-KOF)
Pëtr (PYOTR)
Petróv (pye-TROF)
Petróvich (pye-TRO-vich)
Piterbúrg [St. Petersburg] (pi-tyer-BURK)
Piterbúrkh [St. Petersburg] (pi-tyer-BURKH)
Pitirím (pi-ti-RIM)
Podól'nyi (pa-DOL'-nyi)
Pokróvskaia tsérkov' (pa-KROF-ska-ya TSER-kaf')
Pokróvskii Chernoezérskii zhénskii monastýr' (pa-KROF-skiy chir-na-ye-ZYER-skiy ZHEN-skiy ma-na-STYR')
Pokróvskoe (pa-KROF-skaya)
Pol'nói Vorónezh [river] (pal'-NOI va-RON-yezh)
Pólotsk (PO-latsk)
Pólotskii (PO-lats-kiy)
Poltáva (pal-TA-va)
Pórkhov (POR-khaf)
Pósnikovich (POS-ni-ka-vich)
Póstnik (POST-nik)
Póstnikovich (POST-ni-ka-vich)
Pozhárskoi (pa-ZHAR-skay)
Praskóv'ia (pra-SKOV'-ya)
Prókhor (PRO-khar)
Prokóf'ev (pra-KOF-yef)
Proshchénik (pra-SHCHE-nik)
Prózorovskii (PRO-za-raf-skiy)
Prútskii (PRUT-skiy)
Pushéchnikov [clan in Ruza] (pu-SHECH-ni-kaf)
Púshkin (PUSH-kin)
Pústyn' (PU-styn')
Putíla (pu-TI-la)
Putílov (pu-TI-laf)
Putívl' (pu-TIVL')
Rádonezh (RA-da-nyesh)
Rádonezhskii (RA-da-nyesh-skiy)
Rázin (RA-zin)
Rémezov (RYE-mye-zaf)
Repnín (re-PNIN)
Réval (RYE-val)
Riazán' (rya-ZAN')
Riazhsk (RYASHSK)
Ríga (RI-ga)

TRANSCRIPTION AND PRONUNCIATION GUIDE FOR RUSSIAN NAMES

Rodión (ra-di-ON)
Rogataia Vosh' (ra-GA-ta-ya VOSH)
Román (ra-MAN)
Románov (ra-MA-naf)
Rostóv (ra-STOF)
Rozhdestvá Bogoróditsy, Pústyn' (ra-zhdye-STVA ba-ga-RO-di-tsy, PU-styn')
Rozhdéstvenskii (razh-DYE-stven-skiy)
Rozhdestvó (razh-dye-STVO)
Rúkin (RU-kin)
Rumiántsev (ru-MYAN-tsyf)
Rúza (RU-za)
Sabúrov (sa-BU-raf)
Sagaidáchnyi (sa-gay-DACH-nyi)
Sarái (sa-RAY)
Savínov (sa-VI-naf)
Sávva (SAV-va)
Savvátii (sav-VA-tiy)
Semën (sye-MYON)
Serébrianyi (sye-RYE-brya-nyi)
Sergéi (syer-GEY)
Sergíi (syer-GIY)
Serpukhóv (ser-pu-KHOF)
Sharápov (sha-RA-paf)
Shavtsóv (shaf-TSOF)
Shchelkálov (shchel-KA-laf)
Shelón [river] (shy-LON)
Shemiáchin (shy-MYA-chin)
Shemiáka (shy-MYA-ka)
Sheremétev (shy-rye-MYE-tyef)
Shesták (shy-STAK)
Shubálov (shu-BA-laf)
Shúiskii (SHUY-skiy)
Shushérin (shu-SHE-rin)
Sibír' (si-BIR')
Sigismúnd (si-gis-MUNT)
Sil'véstr (sil'-VESTR)
Simeón (si-mye-ON)
Sitskói (sits-KOY)
Skíbin (SKI-bin)
Skvortsóv (skvar-TSOF)
Slavinétskii (sla-vi-NYETS-kiy)
Smolénsk (sma-LYENSK)
Snetogórsk (snye-ta-GORSK)
Snévins (SNYE-vins)
Sobáka (sa-BA-ka)
Sobákina (sa-BA-ki-na)
Sóf'ia (SOF-ya)
Sofía (sa-FI-ya)
Sofónii (sa-FO-niy)
Solovétskii (sa-la-VYETS-kiy)
Solovkí (sa-laf-KI)
Sophía (sa-FI-ya)
Sórskii (SOR-skiy)
Spaso-Kámennyi (SPA-sa-KA-men-nyi)
Spásskie voróta (SPAS-ski-ye va-RO-ta)
Spásskii (SPAS-skiy)
Spéshnev (SPYESH-nyef)
Spiridón (spi-ri-DON)
Stáeva Poliána (STA-ye-va pa-LYA-na)
Starodúb (sta-ra-DUB)
Stefán (stye-FAN)
Stefánov (stye-FA-naf)
Stepán (stye-PAN)
Stëpych (STYO-pych)
Stréshneva (STRYESH-nye-va)
Sukhóna (su-KHO-na)
Súma [river] (SU-ma)
Súmskii Posád (SUM-skiy pa-SAT)
Súra (SU-ra)
Súzdal' (SU-zdal')
Taganróg (ta-gan-ROK)
Tamára (ta-MA-ra)
Tára (TA-ra)
Tashlykóv (tash-ly-KOF)
Tátar (TA-tar)
Temriúkovna (tyem-RYU-kav-na)
Tíkhon (TI-khan)
Tíkhvin (TIKH-vin)
Tiumén' (tyu-MYEN')
Toból'sk (ta-BOL'SK)

Tomílo (ta-MI-la)
Torzhók (tar-ZHOK)
Tret′iák (trit′-YAK)
Trífon (TRI-fan)
Tróitskoe (TRO-its-ka-ya)
Tsérkov′ Pokrová prechístyia Bogoróditsy (TSER-kaf′ pa-kra-VA pre-CHI-sty-ya ba-ga-RO-di-tsy)
Tsérkov′ Pokrová Presviat′yia Bogoróditsy (TSER-kaf′ pa-kra-VA pre-svya-TY-ya ba-ga-RO-di-tsy)
Tsérkov′ sviatágo múchenika Nikíty Vóina na Gliníshchakh (TSER-kaf′ svya-TA-go MU-che-ni-ka ni-KI-ty VO-i-na na gli-NI-shchakh)
Tsérkov′ velikomúchenitsy Varváry (TSER-kaf′ vye-li-ka-MU-che-ni-tsy var-VA-ry)
Túla (TU-la)
Tulúpov (tu-LU-paf)
Turchásov (tur-CHA-saf)
Úglich (U-glich)
Ukólov (u-KO-laf)
Ul′ián (ul′-YAN)
Ul′iána (ul′-YA-na)
Ul′iánovich (ul′-YA-na-vich)
Úmnoi-Kolychëv (UM-nay ka-ly-CHOF)
Urásko (u-RA-ska)
Urliápovo (a ford) (ur-LYA-pa-va)
Úza [river] (U-za)
Vakúlin (va-KU-lin)
Vánechka (VA-nyech-ka)
Vánia (VA-nya)
Varlaám (var-la-AM)
Varvára (var-VA-ra)
Varvárka (var-VAR-ka)
Varvárskie voróta (var-VAR-ski-ye va-RO-ta)
Vás′ka (VAS′-ka)
Vásia (VA-sya)
Vasíl′ev (va-SIL′-yef)
Vasíl′eva (va-SIL′-ye-va)
Vasíl′evich (va-SIL′-ye-vich)
Vasílieva (va-SI-li-ye-va)
Vasílii (va-SI-liy)
Velíkie Lúki (vye-LI-ki-e LU-ki)
Véra (VYE-ra)
Verkhotúr′e (vyer-kha-TUR-ye)
Viátka (VYAT-ka)
Viazheozérskaia (vya-zhe-a-ZYER-ska-ya)
Viáz′ma (VYAZ′-ma)
Víl′no (VIL′-na)
Vladímir (vla-DI-mir)
Vladímirovich (vla-DI-mi-ra-vich)
Vladímirovna (vla-DI-mi-rav-na)
Vol′ynia (va-LY-nya)
Volkónskii (val-KON-skiy)
Vólkov (VOL-kaf)
Vólogda (VO-lag-da)
Vólotovo (VO-la-ta-va)
Vólotskii (VO-lat-skiy)
Vorónezh (va-RO-nyesh)
Vorypáev (va-ra-PA-yef)
Vourliōtēs [Grk] (vur-li-O-tis)
Vsévolod (FSYE-va-lat)
Zakhárov (za-KHA-raf)
Zaslávskii (za-SLAF-skiy)
Zinóvii (zi-NO-viy)
Zosíma (za-SI-ma)
Zótov (ZO-taf)
Zvérin (ZVYE-rin)

About the Editors and Contributors

Sergei Bogatyrev is senior lecturer in early Russian history at the School of Slavonic and East European Studies, University College London. He has published extensively on Russian history and culture in the sixteenth century. He is the author of *The Sovereign and His Counsellors: Ritualised Consultations in Muscovite Political Culture, 1350s–1570s* (2000), and the editor and coauthor of *Russia Takes Shape: Patterns of Integration from the Middle Ages to the Present* (2004). He is currently working on a book about the Russian dynasty in the sixteenth century.

Peter B. Brown is professor of history at Rhode Island College. He has edited *Studies and Essays on the Soviet and Eastern European Economies* by Arcadius Kahan, 2 vols. (1991–94) as well as a *Festschrift for Aleksandr Aleksandrovich Zimin (1920–1980)* (1998) and coedited a *Festschrift in Honor of Richard Hellie*, 3 vols. (2007–9). His main areas of research interest are the administration of Muscovy and the command and control structure of the Muscovite army, on both of which he has written a number of articles and reviews.

Nikolaos Chrissidis is associate professor of history at Southern Connecticut State University. He has published articles on the cultural and religious history of Russia and on Greek–Russian contacts. He is currently preparing a monograph on education in seventeenth-century Russia.

Brian L. Davies is professor of history at the University of Texas, San Antonio. His publications include *State Power and Community in Early Modern Russia: The Case of Kozlov 1635–1649* (2004) and *Warfare, State, and Society on the Black Sea Steppe, 1500–1700* (2007).

Michael S. Flier is the Oleksandr Potebnja Professor of Ukrainian Philology at Harvard University. He has edited *Ukrainian Philology and Linguistics* (1996) and co-edited *Medieval Russian Culture*, 2 vols. (1984–94), *Architecture and the Expression of Group Identity: The Russian Empire and the Soviet Union, 1500–Present* (2003), and *Aspects of Nominal Determination in Old Church Slavic* (1974). He has also published a number of articles on East Slavic linguistics and Muscovite ritual and artistic culture.

David M. Goldfrank is finishing, as of spring 2011, his forty-first year on the Georgetown University history faculty. He did a stint as director of Russian Area Studies there (1976–80) and organized and directed a Georgetown M.A. program at the U.S. Army Russian Institute in Garmisch-Partenkirchen, Bavaria (operated 1983–85). He has dabbled in diplomatic history, producing the multicountry archive-based *Origin of the Crimean War* (1994), and he contributed the first eight chapters (to 1613) of the Houghton-Mifflin *A History of Russia* textbook (with Catherine Evtuhov, Lindsey Hughes, and Richard Stites, 2003). But his chief work has been his trilogy of translations, with analysis and source identification, of Russia's first major treatises and related writings: *The Monastic Rule of Iosif Volotsky* (1983; revised 2000); *Nil Sorsky. The Authentic Writings* (2008—the 500th anniversary of his death); and Iosif's *Prosvetitel'* (projected by 2015, likewise the 500th anniversary of Iosif's death).

Richard Hellie was Thomas E. Donnelly Professor of History and chairman of the College Russian Civilization Program at the University of Chicago. He was the author of three major studies: *Enserfment and Military Change in Muscovy* (1971), which won the 1972 Herbert Baxter Adams Prize of the American Historical Association; *Slavery in Russia, 1450–1725* (1982); and *The Economy and Material Culture of Russia, 1600–1725* (1999). His many articles ranged over a wide variety of topics from studies of the Russian law code, *Ulozhenie*, to analyses of social groups from the elite to townsmen, peasants, and slaves; to efforts to understand the impact of violence and living conditions on the Russian populace; and to examinations of what he believed to be the fundamental structures of Russian history.

Valerie Kivelson is professor of history at the University of Michigan. Her interests include early modern Russia, witchcraft, cultural history, gender, religion, history of cartography, and empire. Her books include *Cartographies of Tsardom: The Land and Its Meanings in Seventeenth-Century Russia* (2006) and *Autocracy in the Provinces: Russian Political Culture and the Gentry in the Seventeenth Century* (1997). She has also coedited *Orthodox Russia: Studies in Belief and Practice* (2003) and *Picturing Russia: Essays on Visual Evidence* (2008).

Nancy S. Kollmann is William H. Bonsall Professor in History at Stanford University. Her interests include politics and society in early modern Russia. Her books include *Kinship and Politics: The Making of the Muscovite Political System*,

1344–1547 (1987) and *By Honor Bound: State and Society in Early Modern Russia* (1999). She is currently working on the practice of the criminal law in seventeenth- and early eighteenth-century Russia.

J.T. Kotilaine is chief economist of NCB Capital, a Riyadh-headquartered investment bank. He received his Ph.D. in Russian history from Harvard University and has published *Russia's Foreign Trade and Economic Expansion in the Seventeenth Century: Windows on the World* (2005). He coedited *Modernizing Muscovy: Reform and Social Change in Seventeenth-Century Russia* (2004) and co-wrote *Stuarts and Romanovs: The Rise and Fall of a Special Relationship* (2009).

Lawrence N. Langer is associate professor emeritus at the University of Connecticut. He served as director of the Slavic and East European Program at the University of Connecticut and is currently editor in chief of the journal *Russian History*. He has written on the social and economic history of Rus in the Mongol era. He is also an associate at the Davis Center for Russian and Eurasian Studies at Harvard University.

Russell E. Martin is professor of history at Westminster College, in New Wilmington, Pennsylvania. His recent publications include "Ritual and Religion in the Foreign Marriages of Three Muscovite Princesses," *Russian History* 35, nos. 3/4 (2008): 357–81; "Gifts for Kith and Kin: Gift Exchange and Social Solidarity in Muscovite Royal Weddings, 1495–1671," in *The Rude and Barbarous Kingdom Revisited: Essays in Russian History and Culture in Honor of Robert O. Crummey*, ed. Chester Dunning, Russell E. Martin, and Daniel Rowland (2008), 89–108; "Gifts for the Bride: Dowries, Diplomacy, and Marriage Politics in Muscovy," *Journal of Medieval and Early Modern Studies* 38, no. 1 (2008): 119–45; and "Muscovite Royal Weddings: A Descriptive Inventory of Manuscript Holdings in the Treasure Room of the Russian State Archive of Ancient Acts, Moscow," *Manuscripta* 50, no. 1 (2006): 77–189. He is currently completing a book on bride shows in Muscovy.

Erika Monahan is assistant professor of Russian history at the University of New Mexico. She received her Ph.D. from Stanford University, where she wrote her dissertation, "Trade and Empire: Merchant Networks, Frontier Commerce, and the State in Western Siberia, 1644–1728" (2007). Her research interests include early modern commerce; merchant cultures; political economy of early modern empires; the Russian empire; history of corruption; environmental history; and Central Asia.

Hugh M. Olmsted is former head of the Slavic Division of Widener Library at Harvard University. He is the compiler of *Translations and Translating: A Selected Bibliography of Bibliographies, Indexes, and Guides* (1975), and *Russia, Soviet,* and East European Studies: A Selected Bibliography of Bibliographies and Other Primary Reference Sources* (1993). He received his Ph.D. from Harvard University, where he wrote a dissertation titled "Studies in the Early Manuscript Tradition of Maksim Grek's Collected Works" (1977), a topic on which he has published a number of articles. He and his wife Maria run Russian Studies Publications.

Donald Ostrowski is research advisor in the social sciences and lecturer at Harvard University's Extension School, where he teaches world history. His publications include *Muscovy and the Mongols: Cross-Cultural Influences on the Steppe Frontier, 1304–1589* (1998) and *The Povest' vremennykh let: An Interlinear Collation and Paradosis* (2003). He also chairs the Davis Center for Russian and Eurasian Studies' Early Slavists Seminars at Harvard University.

Michael C. Paul earned a bachelor's degree in political science from the University of Kansas in Lawrence in 1993 and master's degrees in political science and Russian and East European studies in 1996, also from Kansas. He completed his Ph.D. in Russian history in 2003 at the University of Miami, in Coral Gables, where he studied under the direction of Janet Martin. In 2006–7, Dr. Paul was a Fulbright scholar in St. Petersburg, Russia. His articles have appeared in *Orientalia Christiana Periodica, Russian Review, Jahrbücher für Geschichte Osteuropas, Kritika, Russian History,* and *Church History.* Dr. Paul is currently an independent scholar in North Carolina.

Marshall T. Poe teaches history at the University of Iowa. He is the author of *"A People Born to Slavery": Russia in Early Modern European Ethnography, 1476–1748* (2000), *The Russian Elite in the Seventeenth Century* (2004), *The Russian Moment in World History* (2006), and *Communications and Humanity: The History of Media from the Evolution of Speech to the Internet* (2010). He co-founded and for several years co-edited the journal *Kritika: Explorations in Russian and Eurasian History.* He founded and hosts the podcast "New Books in History." His current research focuses on human history in the very long term.

Cathy J. Potter taught Russian, Soviet, and European history at the Chinese University of Hong Kong. She published articles on the Russian Church and on law and society in early Russian culture, as well as articles on women and gender in nineteenth- and early twentieth-century Russia. She retired in 2005, returned to the United States, and entered law school. She is currently practicing immigration law in the Rio Grande Valley and remains an avid student of, and active participant in, the continually unfolding human comedy/tragedy.

W.M. Reger IV is instructional assistant professor in the Department of History, Illinois State University. He is the author of "European Mercenary Officers and the Reception of Military Reform in the Seventeenth-Century Russian Army," in

Modernizing Muscovy: Reform and Social Change in Seventeenth-Century Russia, ed. Jarmo Kotilaine and Marshall Poe (2004) and "Baptizing Mars: The Conversion to Russian Orthodoxy of European Mercenaries during the Mid-Seventeenth Century," in *The Military and Society in Russia, 1450–1917,* ed. Eric Lohr and Marshall Poe (2002).

Robert Romanchuk is associate professor in the Department of Modern Languages and Linguistics at Florida State University. He has published *Byzantine Hermeneutics and Pedagogy in the Russian North: Monks and Masters at the Kirillo-Belozerskii Monastery, 1397–1501* (2007).

Jennifer B. Spock is associate professor of history at Eastern Kentucky University. She received her Ph.D. from Yale University, where she wrote her dissertation, "The Solovki Monastery, 1460–1645: Piety and Patronage in the Early Modern Russian North" (1999). She has published articles on donations to Solovki and on its instructive literature, coedited *Culture and Identity in Eastern Christian History* (2009), and is president of the Association for the Study of Eastern Christian History and Culture.

Carol B. Stevens is associate professor of history at Colgate University, specializing in early modern Russia. She is the author of *Soldiers of the Steppe* (1996) and *Russia's Wars of Emergence, 1460–1730* (2007), has been published in numerous journals, and is now co-editor of the journal *Russian History*.

Christoph Witzenrath has a Ph.D. from the University of Aberdeen in Scotland and has published *Cossacks and the Russian Empire, 1598–1725* (2007) and edited *Eurasian Slavery, Ransom, and Abolition in World History, 1500–1860* (forthcoming). His research interests include medieval and early modern Europe, as well as Russian and Soviet history.

Index

Key: This is an index of personal names, placenames, institutions, and titles. All individuals who are of the fourteenth to eighteenth centuries have their names listed alphabetically according to their first name rather than family name. Listing them this way represents how they were known at the time and how present-day Russian indexes of, say, chronicles are done. Names of fictional characters are given in bold.

Abazbanei Kulmametev, 228, 288
Abdullatif, 16, 17
Aberdeen, University, xxvi
Aberdeenshire, 82
Ablai-taisha, 217
Abraham, 134
Abul-Gazi, 227
Adam, 30, 119
Advent, 194
Aegean Sea, 156
Afanasii Demianov, 44
Afanasii Nagoi, 52
Afanasii Nikitin Nelidov, colonel, 74, 285
Afanasii Prokofiev, 188–197
Afonasii, 9
Agafia Borisovna Lykova, 9
Agafia Parfenovna, 100
Aiuka, Kalmyk khan, 214
Akakii, elder of Solovki Monastery, 165
Akakii Balandin, xxvi, xvii, 165–176
Alafi Mountain, 215
Alda, Alan, xxiv
Aleksandr, Bishop of Kolomna, 111
Aleksandr, Bishop of Viatka, 109
Aleksandr (formerly Aleksei) Oshevenskii, saint, 139, 144–148
Aleksandr Daniilovich Menshikov, field marshal, 79
Aleksandr Mikhailovich, prince of Pskov, 120
Aleksandr Mikhailovich, prince of Tver, 27
Aleksandr Vasilievich Kolychev, 9, 281
Aleksandr Vasilievich Volkonskii, 54
Aleksandr, monk, *see* Andrei Putilov
Aleksandr, Nevskii, 288
Aleksandr, Prince of Pskov, 118
Aleksandr, priest, 260
Aleksandrovskaia Sloboda, 54, 116
Aleksei Koltovskii, 6, 8, 9
Aleksei Leonteev *syn*, Remezov, 220
Aleksei Mikhailovich Romanov, Tsar, xxv, 39, 81, 110, 155, 156, 162, 164, 181, 189, 196, 204
Aleksei Mukhomor Nikitin *syn*, 255, 257, 259, 262, 265, 268, 281
Aleksei Petrovich Shubalov, xxvi, 179–187
Aleviz Friazin, *see* Aloisio Lamberti da Montagna
Aleviz Novyi, *see* Aloisio Lamberti da Montagna
Allen, Colonel William (Vilim Alin), 81–91, 288
Aloisio Lamberti da Montagna, 265, 287, 288
Altai Mountains, 225
Amanita muscaria, 255
Amsterdam, 190, 197
Amur River, 219
Anastasia Iurieva, 7
Anastasia Nikiforovna Pushechnikova, 50, 52
Andrei Vasilievich Sitskoi, boyar, 61
Andrei Alekseev *syn* **Shubalov**, 179–187
Andrei (Andriusha) Makarov *syn*, 254, 259

Andrei Nikitin *syn* **Beklenshev**, xxv, 71–80, 285
Andrei Nepripasov, *syn boiarskii*, 213
Andrei Putilov, xxv, 44–55
Andrei Rublev, iconographer, 131, 134
Andrei Shchelkalov, 44, 53, 54
Andrew the Fool for Christ, saint, 259, 260
Andriushka, worker, 202, 203
Anna Alekseevna Koltovskaia, tsaritsa, xxiv, xxvii, 3–13
Anna Ivanova, concubine, 220
Anna, Sister, *see* **Avdotia (Dunia) Makarova** *doch*
Annunciation Cathedral, Moscow, 131
Annunciation, Church of the, Gorodishche, 122
Anthony, saint, 172
Anton (name of Akakii Balandin in this world), 170
Anton Alekseevich, 73, 76
Antonii, Archbishop of Novgorod, 124
Antonii Chernoezerskii, Father (*otets*), 254, 263, 264, 267, 288
Anya Antonova *doch*, 73
Ancient Rome on 5 Denarii a Day, xxiv
Andrei Makarov *syn*, 254
Apocalypse, the, 135, 136
Apocalypse of Baruch, 30
Apophthegmata partum (*Sayings of the Desert Fathers*), 145, 148
Apothecary Chancellery, 87
Arab-Shah, Tatar prince, 31
Arab, Arabic, Arabs, 16, 119, 288
Archangel Michael Cathedral, 65, 111, 113, 131, 265
Arctic, 211
Arctic Ocean, 223
Aral Sea, 212
Aristotelian philosophy, 143
Arkadii, leather dresser, 196
Arkhangelsk, 191, 192, 195, 240, 241
Arsenii, hieromonk, 121
Arslan-Ordek, 74
Artemii Afanasiev, clerk, 99
Artemii Lukin, 182, 183, 184
Arzamas, 179, 181, 183
Asian merchants, 226

Assembly of the Land (*Zemskii sobor*), 63, 250, 251, 277
Astrakhan, 18, 49, 225
Auchleuchries, 83
Augustine, saint, 271
Augustus II, King of Poland, 77
Avdotia (Dunia) Makarova *doch*, xxvii, 252–269
Avraam, *tysiatskii*, 121, 123
Avvakum, Archpriest, 105, 109, 112, 115
Azeev, 183
Azika, prince, 14
Azov, 73

Baba Yaga, 199
Balkans, 156, 164
Baltic lands, 71, 72, 189
Barabinsk steppe, 212, 217
Basil of Caesarea, 134 (icon of), 171
Baturin, 77
Baumann, General, 88
Bayezid, Sultan, 14
Belarus, Belarusian, 110, 162, 189, 288
Belev, 16
Belgorod, 39, 74, 79
Beloozero, 29, 31, 139, 142, 145
Berdibeg, khan, 29
Bezobrazovs, 73
Bible, 66, 108, 110, 209, 214
  Genesis, 119
  Gospels, 12, 130, 134, 169, 203, 272
  Gospel of Matthew, 142, 266
  Old Testament, 29, 134
  Psalms, Psalter, 47, 136, 141, 154, 165, 167, 169, 171, 270, 276
  Revelation, 135, 218
Bilibin, Ivan, 45
Blachernae Church, Constantinople, 259
Black Sea, 160
Boborykin, Roman Fedorovich, governor, 101
Bobrovsk, 83
Bogatyrev, Sergei, xxv
Bogdan Posnikovich Sheremetev, slave owner, 245, 285
Bogoliubskaia Mother of God (*Bogomater*) icon, 234

Bohemia, 272
Boris Alekseevich, prince, 40, 41
Boris Fedorovich Godunov, tsar, 12, 56, 241, 250, 285
Boris Godunov, opera, 45
Boris Godunov, play, 45
Boris Ivanovich Lykov, prince, 9
Boris Petrovich Sheremetev, boyar, General, field marshal, 73-77, 79, 285
Boris Vasilievich Kolychev, 9
Borshchev Monastery, 93
Boyar Duma, 272, 277
Brackett, William, 87
Brief Siberian Kungur Chronicle, 210
British, Britons, 91
Brown, Peter B., xxv
Bukhara, Bukharan, Bukhrans, xxvi, 213, 214, 222, 225, 228
Bulgaria, Bulgarian, Bulgarians, 139, 142, 156, 157
Bulgars, Volga, 30
Busurman, *see* Muslims
Bykov, Captain, 97
Byzantine, Byzantines, 32, 125, 129, 136, 139, 141, 144, 145, 146, 147, 151, 160, 259, 260
Byzantine empire, xxviii, 141, 149

Caesargrad, *see* Constantinople
Calvinists, 159
Captain from Castile, xxiii
Carmichael, Mungo, 87
Casimir, King of Poland, 121
Caspian Sea, 212, 213, 263
Cathedral Square, Moscow, 12
Caucasus, Caucasian, 218
Central Asia, Central Asians, 209, 212, 213, 222, 223, 287
Chancellor, Richard, 237
Charles XII, King of Sweden, 74, 77, 86
Chatzekyriakes Vourliotes, xxvi, 154-164, 288
Chelnovaia River, 97
Cherkassy, 83, 93, 101
Chernigov, 121
Chernoezerskaia Sviato-Pokrovskaia pustyn, 254
Chicago, University of, xxvi

China, Chinese, 209, 211, 213, 217, 218, 225, 226, 228, 229
Chinggis Khan, 18, 19, 217
Chinggisid, xxiv
Chios, 156, 157
Chrissidis, Nikolaos A., xxvi
Christ the Savior icon, 132
Christian, Christianity, Christians, 16, 17, 18, 19, 20, 21, 22, 78, 87, 108, 111, 112, 121, 129, 136, 142, 169, 252, 261, 273, 279
Christmas, 194
Chudov (Miracle) Monastery, 50, 109, 113
Church Slavonic, 47, 108, 110, 141, 266
Circassians, 83, 218
Colgate University, xxv
Columbus, Christopher, 209
Conley, Thomas, 141
Connecticut, University of, xxiv
Constantinople, 121, 122, 131, 157, 262
Copenhagen, 79
Copper Riot (*Mednti bunt*), 193
Cosmas Indicopleustes, 29
Cossack, Cossacks, 75, 77, 85, 92, 93, 95, 96, 97, 99, 157, 160, 209, 212, 213, 215, 216, 218, 220, 221, 227
Covent of the Intercession of the Mother of God, Suzdal, 12
Crawford, Colonel, 86
Crete, 156, 160
Crimea, Crimean, xxv, 16, 17, 19, 20, 52, 53, 73, 78, 95, 96
Criminal Articles of 1669, 184, 186
Cronkite, Walter, xxiii
Crummey, Robert, 37

Danes, 79
Daniel, 134
Daniil, hegumen, 151
Daniil Grigorievich Gagarin, Prince, 5-6, 12, 13
Danila Ivanovich Miachkov, *pomeshchik*, 247-251, 285
Dankov, 93, 95
Dar al-Islam, see Islam, Abode of
Daria Okatieva *doch*, 235, 237, 238, 239, 240, 241
Daria, nun, *see* Anna Koltovskaia

310 INDEX

Daritsa, purveyor of spells, 201, 203
David, 134
David Fedorovich, prince of Yaroslavl, 26, 34
David, Archbishop of Novgorod, 124
David, Yaroslavl miracleworker, 50
Davies, Brian, xxv
Davis Center for Russian and Eurasian Studies, xxvii
Day of the Assumption of the Mother of God (August 15), 120
Dead Souls, 151
de Bruyn, Cornelius, 190
de Gron, Jean, 83, 85
Dedilov, 93
Deësis, 134
Dementii (Dima) Okatiev *syn* Parfiev/Dionisii, monk, 235–242, 282
Demin, 79
Demka Ivanov *syn* Tashlykov, 101
Denisko Rukin, 95
Denisov, Colonel, 79
Derevianitskii Monastery, 125
Derpt, 75, 76
Detinets, 120, 122, 123
Devlet-Kirei, 217
Diaghilev, Sergei, 45
Dialectica (or *Philosophical Chapters*) of John Damascene, 141, 142, 143, 150, 152
Dionisii, monk, *see* **Dementii Okatiev *syn***
Dionysios, hegumen, 142, 146
Dionysios of Fourna, 131
Dionysios Iverites, 163
Djungars, 226
Dmitrii, Tsarevich, 241
Dmitrii, governor of Pskov, 40
Dmitrii, prince, 42
Dmitrii Aidarov, 182, 184, 186
Dmitrii (Erasmus) Gerasimov, 20
Dmitrii Ivanovich (Donskoi), Grand Prince of Rus, 27, 30, 288
Dmitrii Konstantinov, merchant, 227
Dmitrii Konstantinovich, Prince of Suzdal and Nizhnii Novgorod, 30, 31
Dmitrii Mikhailovich Pozharskii, prince, 62

Dmitrii Rostovskii, 288
Dmitrii Shemiaka, prince, 149
Dmitrii Vasilievich Kolychev, 9
Dmitrii Vasilievich Tulupov, 9, 53
Dnieper River, 74
Domna Tomilova *doch* Ukolova, 96, 101
Don River, 96, 99
Dormition Cathedral, 65
Dosifei, elder, 173
Dukes, Paul, 90
Duma, 61
Dunia, *see* **Avdotia (Dunia) Makarov *doch***
Dunning, Chester, 90, 91
Dutch, 88, 89, 97, 107, 188, 190–197, 211, 221, 274, 288
Dvina River, 192

East Slavic, xxviii
Easter, 136, 258
Eastern Kentucky, University of, xxvi
Eco, Umberto, xxiii, xxviii
Edigei, 16
Edvart, Boldvin (Baldwin Edwards), Captain, 81–91, 288
Efim, archimandrite, 123
Efimia, Mitrofanova *doch*, wife of S. U. Remezov, 220
Efrem Trebes, 140
Efrosin, monk, 139, 140, 148, 149–152
Egypt, Egyptian, Egyptians, 28, 29, 152, 214, 218
Eight Parts of Speech, 141, 142, 143, 153
Elena Likhareva, 53
Elets, 96, 99
Elijah, 130
Elijah Street, Novgorod, 131, 135
Embaevskii yurt, 225
Enisei River, 211
Eniseisk, 213
England, 83, 87
English, xxvii, xxviii, 86, 87, 114, 188, 211, 237, 240, 286–287, 288
Entrance into Jerusalem, Church of the, 116, 119, 123
Ephraim, 171
Ephrosinius, saint, 120

Epifan, 93
Epifanii the Most Wise (*Premudryi*), 131
Epifanii Slavinetskii, 106, 107, 108, 110, 112, 113, 114
Epiphany, 123, 193
Ermak, 216
Ermolai/Erazm, of Pskov (fl. 1540s–1560s), priest-writer, then elder monk, 171
Erofei Meshcherinov, 182
Esif, archimandrite, 124
Estonia, 124
Eucharist, 162
Europe, European, 37, 71, 80, 85, 86, 88-91, 141, 149, 164, 189, 191, 209, 212-3, 219, 274, 287
Evdokia, 109
Evdokia Dmitrievovna Tulupova, 9
Evdokia Dmitrievovna (wife of Dmitrii Donskoi), 30
Evdokia Ivanovna (daughter of Ivan III), 19
Evdokia Ivanovna (daughter of Ivan I), 24, 27, 34
Evdokia Streshneva, 13
Evfimia Romanovna Glebova, 9
Exodus, the, 214
Ezekial, 134

Fahrensbachs, 89
Fast, Howard, xxiii, xxviii
Fatima, 17
Feast of the Annunciation of the Holy Mother of God (March 25), 152
Feast of St. Nicholas, 9
Fedka (Fedor) Vasiliev *syn* Zotov, 99, 101
Fedor, Lithuanian prince, 121
Fedor Aleksandrovich, 27
Fedor Alekseevich, tsar, Romanov, 39, 40, 196, 250, 281
Fedor *Chernyi* (the Black), prince, 32
Fedor Daniilovich, mayor of Novgorod, 121, 123
Fedor Glebovich, prince, 24, 34
Fedor Ivanovich, tsar, 12
Fedor Leonteev *syn*, Remezov, 220
Fedor Mikhailovich, prince, 34

Fedor Rostislavich, Prince of Smolensk and Mozhaisk, 34
Fedor Skibin, 214
Fedor Vakulin, 225, 228, 229
Fedor Vasiliev *syn* Glebov, 179–187
Fedor, son of Melik-Tagir, 14
Fedor, Yaroslavl miracleworker, 50
Fedor Grigoriev *syn* Zotov, 93
Felony Chancellery (*Razboinyi prikaz*), 53, 183, 186, 276
Feodor, Bishop of Tver, 119
Feodor, Kuritsyn, 149
Feodosii, hegumen of Oshevenskii Monastery, 145
Feofan, deacon, 266, 267
Feofan Grek, xxv, 130–136, 165, 287
Feognost, Metropolitan of Rus, 29, 120, 121
Fetinia Vasilievna Kolycheva, 9
Filaret, Patriarch, (Fedor Romanov) 12, 218
Filip Fomin *syn*, 245
Filipp, Metropolitan of Moscow (r. 1566–1569), 174
Filofei, monk of Pskov Eliazarov Monatsery, 171
Finland, 119
Finland, Gulf of, 124
Finnic peoples, 250
Finno-Ugric, 236
Flier, Michael S., xxv
Florida State University, xxvi
Foma, deacon, 169
Foma Karpov *syn*, xxvi, 245–247, 282
Foreign Affairs Chancellery (*Posol´skii prikaz*), 157, 158, 160
Foreign Suburb, 83, 91
Franklin, Miles, 71
Frederick III, Duke of Holstein, 38, 57, 180
French, 84, 288
Frolov Gate, Moscow, 262

Gabriel, icon of Archangel, 134
Galich, 31
Gantimur, prince, 219
Gavril Burfa, colonel, 73
Gdansk, 79
Gebler, Ernst, xxiii, xxviii

Gedeminas, Grand Prince of Lithuania, 120
Gelasii of Volotovo, 169, 170, 171, 172, 173, 174, 175
Genesis, *see* Bible, Genesis
Gennadii, hegumen, 142
Geographica, 141
Georgetown University, xxvi
Georgi, monk, 116, 119
Georgian, 146
Gerasim "the Bear," monk, 262
German, Germans, 42, 86, 87, 91, 97, 101, 121, 188, 192, 274, 288
German, monk, 166
German Podolnyi, monk, 150, 151
Germany, 71, 84
Gireys, 18, 21
Gleb Ivanov *syn*, 131–136
Gleb Vasilievich, prince, xxiv, 24–34
Glorious Revolution of 1688, 219
Gogol, Nikolai, 151
Golden Horde, *see* Qipchaq (Kipchak) Khanate
Goldfrank, David M., xxvi
Golitsyns, princes, 49, 73
Golk, 77
Golovinskoe, 28
Gordon, General Patrick, 82, 83, 84, 90, 91
Gorelik, M. V., 15
Goretovo, 99
Gorodishche, 123
Gorokhovskaia, Tatiana, 4
Gospels, *see* Bible, Gospels
Grammatica, 141
Granberg, Jonas, 118
Graves, Robert, xxiii, xxviii
Great Fast, *see* Lent
Great Household Office (*Bol´shoi dvorets*), 47, 48, 99
Great (London) Fire of 1666, 219
Great Northern War, 219
Greek Church, 88
Greek, Greeks, xxvi, 28, 108, 109, 110, 111, 112, 114, 116, 118, 120, 122, 129, 136, 141, 142, 144, 145, 146, 154, 156, 157, 158, 159, 161, 162, 164, 227, 258, 259, 277, 287, 288
Gregorian calendar, xxviii

Gregory Nazianzenus, 141
Gregory the Sinaite, 171
Grigorii Filatov *syn* Zotov, 93, 282, 285
Grigorii Kotoshikin, 277
Grigorii Vasilievich Kolychev, 9, 12
Grigorii Volkov, 62
Grigorii (Grisha) Vasiliev *syn* Zotov, 99, 101
Grim Reaper, 188
Grimmelshausen, Hans Jakob Christoph von, German novelist, 91
Grisha, 132
Grodno, 77
Gurii the beggar, 260
Gypsies, 287

Habsburg, 41
Halil, Khan, 16
Halperin, Charles J., 33
Hamburg, 191, 194, 195, 197
Harvard University, xxv, xxvii
Hasan ibn Ismail, 14
Heaven, 256
Hellie, Richard, xxvi, 90
Hexaemeron, 29
Hilandar Monastery, 116, 119
History of Siberia, 215, 216, 217
Holy Angels Monastery, Novgorod, 120
Holy Communion, 256
Holy Land, 161
Holy Martyr Nikita the Warrior on the Claypits, Church of, 256, 259
Holy Roman Empire, 73
Holy Sepulcher, 161
Holy Theotokos, 259
Holy Writings/Scriptures, 112, 145, 147, 148, 171, 214
Homilies of Gregory Nazianzenus, 141
Horde, the, *see* Qipchaq Khanate

I, Claudius, xxiii
Ioann (Vania) Makarov *syn*, 254
Iablonov, 101
Iaik River, *see* Ural River
Iakov Moislavov *syn*, the merchant, 119
Iakutsk, 220
Iamyshev, Lake, 222, 223, 226, 227, 228

INDEX   313

Ianin, Valentin Lavrent'evich, 118
Iaroslav's Charter, 123
Iaroslav's Court, 124
Ibn Battuta, 14
Ibrahim, Khan, 16
Idel, *see* Volga river
Iev Balandin, of Iosifov Monastery, elder, 165
Ignatii, elder, 172
Ignatii (Ignashka) Ivanov *syn*, xxvi, 247–251, 282
Igor Tale, 152
Ilarion, Metropolitan of Rostov, 109, 112
Ilarion, Metropolitan of Suzdal, 109
Ilarion Postnikov *syn* Sharapov, 59, 60, 285
Ilham, khan, 16, 17
Ilia Danilovich Miloslavskii, *stol'nik*, 99, 100, 281
Ilia Street, Yaroslavl, 188, 192, 193, 195
Illinois State University, xxv
Illuminated Chronicle (Litsevoi svod), 244
Ilmen, Lake, 118
Ilovaiskii bailliage, 98
Imaginary Portraits, xxiii
Imomqulikhan, ruler of Bukhara, 223
India, 228
Intercession of Theotokos on the Moat, Cathedral of, *see* St. Basil's Cathedral
Ioakim, Patriarch, 110, 111, 114, 115, 163
Ioan, exarch of Bulgaria, 29
Iona Sisoevich, Metropolitan of Rostov, 109
Iona, archimandrite, 46
Iona, archbishop, 171
Iona, patriarch, 112
Iosif, Archbishop of Kolomna, 110, 111
Iosif, monk, *see* **Ivan/Iosif**
Iosifov-Volokolamskii Monastery, 165
Iowa, University of, xxv
Irina, daughter of Anna Ivanova, 220
Irinarkh, hieromonk, 173, 174
Irtysh River, 213, 222, 223, 225, 229
Irwin, Julie, xxiii, xxviii
Isaac, 134

Isaac the Syrian (7th c.), saint, monastic church father 171, 174
Isaak, nephew of Aleksandr Oshevenskii, 145
Isaia Grek, iconographer, 116, 119, 123, 125
Isaiah, 134
Iskander, 22
Islam, 17, 21, 22
Isocrates, 142
Israelites, 214
Ismail ibn Ahmed, Tatar prince, xxvii, 14–23, 288
Istra River, 50
Italian, Italians, 28, 134, 219, 288
Itil, *see* Volga River
Iulia Ivanovna Saburova, 9
Iuriev, 31
Iuriev Monastery, 123, 173
Iurievs, 53
Iurii Borisovich, boyar, 37–43
Iurii Daniilovich, grand prince, 119, 122
Iurii Ivanov (Georg Janszoon), 191, 192, 194, 195, 196, 288
Iurii Mikhailovich Koshelev, 41
Ivan I Daniilovich (Kalita), grand prince, 24, 26, 27, 123
Ivan II Ivanovich, grand prince, 29
Ivan III Vasilievich, grand prince, 16, 17, 19, 33, 40, 46, 47, 56
Ivan IV (the Terrible), Vasilievich, tsar, xxiv, 3, 4, 6, 7, 8, 11, 12, 20, 21, 33, 49, 51, 52, 53, 54, 116, 156, 165, 172, 217, 235, 239, 254, 262, 275
Ivan Dmitrievich, prince, 31
Ivan Dmitrievich Shemiachin, prince, 149
Ivan Fedorovich Mstislavskii, prince, 22, 50, 53
Ivan Glebovich, prince, 24, 34
Ivan Ivanovich, boyar, 41
Ivan Ivanovich Bezzubtsov, *okol'nichii*, 8, 9
Ivan Ivanovich Kubenskii, prince, 47, 48, 49
Ivan Ivanovich Saburov, 9
Ivan Petrov *syn* **Kirillov, townsman**, 200–204, 283, 285

Ivan Kirillovich, prince, 42
Ivan Mikhailovich, prince, 32, 34
Ivan Neronov, 109, 112
Ivan Nepripasov, 216
Ivan Pestriakov, 227, 228, 229
Ivan Petrovich Zaslavskii, prince, 181–186
Ivan Semenov *syn* Remezov, *syn boiarskii*, 220
Ivan Semenovich, prince, 29
Ivan Semenovich Kubenskii, prince, 47
Ivan (Tretiak) Vasiliev *syn* Glebov, 179–187
Ivan Usov, merchant, 224
Ivan (Vania)/Iosif, monk, 238, 239, 241
Ivan Vasilievich Birkin, *voevoda*, 92, 95, 96, 97, 285
Ivan Vasilievich Kolychev, 9
Ivanov, Sergei Vasil′evich, 94
Izhora, 121

Jacob, 134
James (son of Zebedee), apostle, 130
Janibeg, khan, 27, 29
Jerome, saint, 271
Jerusalem, 119, 150, 156, 161, 163, 215
  Patriarch of, 161, 162
Jesuits, 111, 160
Jesus Christ, 111, 119, 130, 135, 136, 141, 146, 150, 173, 214, 252, 253, 259, 261, 272, 277
Jewish temples, 78
Jews, 214, 287
Joachimsthaler, 272
Job, OT figure, 169
Jochid princes, 19, 20
Jochid ulus, *see* Qipchaq (Kipchak) Khanate
John, apostle, 130, 135
John Chrysostom, archbishop of Constantinople, saint, 119, 134, 150, 171
John Climacus (7th c.), saint, monastic Church Father, 167, 169
John Damascene (of Damascus), (8th c.), hieromonk, saint, 114, 141, 142, 144, 150, 152

Judgments of Solomon, 151
Julian calendar, xxviii, 136
Justinian, Emperor, 147

Kabarda, 218
Kalil ibn Ismail, 14
Kalmyks, 217, 226, 227
Kaluga, 59, 160, 204
Kama River, 30
Kanbar, *mirza*, 14
Karelians, 122, 236
Kargopol, 233, 236, 239
Kartavtsovs, 99
Kashira, 50
Kasimov, 18, 22
Kasimov Crossing, 97
Kassian, *starets* of Solovki Monastery, 165
Kassian, hieromonk, 165
Kassian Gusilov, *starets*, 165, 167, 169, 172
Kassian Rumiantsev, monk, 141, 142, 147
Kazakhs, 213, 220, 227
Kazakhstan, 222
Kazan, xxiv, 14, 16, 17, 18, 19, 20, 21, 22, 23, 48, 49, 165, 169, 171, 174, 225
Kazi-kerman, 74
Keret River, 238
Khiva, 212, 214, 225, 227, 228
Khobotets forest, 99
Kholmov Monastery, 120
Khomutets, 100
Khristofor, hegumen, 142, 143
Khvalynsk Sea, *see* Caspian Sea
Kiev, Kievan, 121, 139, 155
Kiev Infantry regiment, 78
Kiprian, Metropolitan, 32
Kirill, Metropolitan, 7
Kirill, archimandrite, 131
Kirill Belozerskii, 288
Kirill, hegumen, 139, 146
Kirillo-Belozersk Monastery, xxvi, 29, 139–153
Kitai-Gorod, 65, 254, 255, 261, 263, 265, 267, 268
Kitaicus, Lake, 213
Kivelson, Valerie, xxvi

Kliment, Archbishop of Novgorod, 124
Klimentii Fedotov *syn* Avderikhin, 93
Kol Sharif, 20
Kollmann, Nancy S., xxvi
Kolomna, 6, 8, 9, 10, 30, 48, 110, 111, 113, 132
Koltovskiis, 7, 9
Konan Parfiev *syn*, 235, 236, 238
Kondrat, 245
Kondratii Bulavin, 77
Konstantin Fedorovich, 9
Konstantin Glebovich, prince, 24, 34
Konstantin Vasilievich, prince of Rostov, 30
Konstantin Vsevolodovich, prince, 34
Konstantin, Yaroslavl miracleworker, 50
Konstiatin Stefanov *syn*, 239
Koporie, 122, 124
Kopys, 88
Korela, 122
Kornilii, monk, 171, 172
Kornilii-Kirill, 145
Koshelevs, 41
Kosmas, bishop of Masuma, 142
Kostroma, 31
Kotilaine, Jarmo T., xxvi
Kotorosl River, 26
Kozlov, xxv, 92, 94, 95, 96, 98, 99, 100, 101
Krasnikov, captain, 97
Krasnikovs, 99
Kreits, general, 77
Kro, Mikhail (Michael Crowe), 81, 87, 88, 288
Krongort, general, 75
Krutitskii, 107, 109
Kuchum, Khan of Sibir, 215, 223
Kudai Kul/Petr Ibramovich, 17, 18, 19, 20, 21, 23
Kulikovo field, battle of, 15, 24, 25, 26, 31–32
Kumans, 28
Kungur, 212, 220
Kurakin, governor, 211
Kursk, 73, 75, 76, 78, 79

Ladder of Divine Ascent (*Lestvitsa*), 167, 170, 171
Ladoga, 122
Ladoga, Lake, 119, 236
Langer, Lawrence N., xxiv
Larion, *see* Ilarion
Larka Lvitskii, (Illarion Savinov Lvitskii/Levitskii), xxv, 56–67
Last Judgment, 135–136, 152
Latin, 20, 108, 109, 110, 114, 121, 158, 159, 162, 219
Lauzen-taisha, 217
Lavrentii, archimandrite, 121, 123
Law Code (*ulozhenie*) of 1649, 64, 179, 186, 243, 250, 251, 277
Lebedian, 92
Lent, 123, 136, 200, 262, 274
Leonid-Leontii, 145
Leontei Leonteev *syn*, Remezov, 220
Leontei Semenov *syn* Remezov, *syn boiarskii*, 220
Leslie, Alexander (Avram), 89
Lev Mikhailovich, 34
Lexicon of Slavic archaisms, 141
Life of Aleksandr Oshevenskii, 145
Life of Aleksandr Svirskii, 145
Life of Bishop Nikita, 171
Life of Martinian of White Lake, 141, 145
Life of Theodore Stoudite, 145
Life-Giving Trinity in the Nikitniki Region, Church of, Moscow, 256
Lifland, Livland (Latvia), 77, 79, 169
Lipovka, 95, 96, 98, 100
Lithuania, Lithuanian, Lithuanians, 30, 46, 51, 79, 96, 121, 122, 169, 189, 193
Litsevoi svod, see *Illuminated Chronicle*
Little Russia, *see* Ukraine
Little Russian Chancellery, 64
Litvak, *see* Lithuanian
Livonia, 50, 89
Livonian War, 50, 51
London, 90, 219
Luga, 121
Luka, 124, 133
Lukeria Vasilieva *doch*, 239, 240, 283
Lutheran, 159
Lwów, 158
Lysye Gory, 97

Macarius the Great, 120
Magnus Erickson, King of Sweden, 116, 121
Makar Shestov Petrov *syn*, 254, 255, 281
Makarii, metropolitan, xxvii
Maksim Grek, xxvii, 287
Mamai, 31
Manchester, 219
Mangezeia, 211
Marfa, nun, 12
Marfa, wife of Anton, 169
Marfa Sobakina, 6, 7, 10
Margeret, Jacques, 91
Maria Andreevovna Putilova, 50, 54
Maria Miloslavskaia, 39
Maria Temriukovna, 7
Maria Vasilievna, princess, 34
Maria Vladimirovna, tsaritsa, 5–6, 281
Markell, hagiographer, 171
Market Square, Moscow, 255, 261, 265
Marshall, Edison, xxiii
Martin, Russell E., xxiv
Martirii, archbishop, 124
Mary, 259, 272, 277
Maslenitsa, 136
Matrena, 235, 237, 238, 239
Matrona, 245
Matvei, 133
Matvei (nephew of Vasilii Kalika), xxv, 116–126
Matvei Treiden, 75
Matyra steppe, 97
Matyszak, Philip, xxiv
Mazepa, Ivan Stepanovych, hetman, 74, 77
Mecklenburg, 79
Mehmed Emin, 16, 17, 288
Mehmed Girey, 18, 19, 20
Meletios, hierodeacon, xxvi, 154–164, 288
Melik-Tagir, prince, 14, 17, 288
Menezius, Paul, 91
Mengli Girey, khan, 16, 17, 288
Messerschmidt, Daniel Gottlieb, German scholar, 212
Michael, Archangel, 50, 113, 114, 134 (icon of), 135
Michael the Archangel, Monastery of, 116, 118, 120
Michigan, University of
Mikhail Davidovich, prince of Mologa, 26, 28, 34
Mikhail Fedorovich Romanov, Tsar, 5–6, 13, 38, 57, 63, 95, 99, 218
Mikhail Iakovlevich Cherkasskii, prince, 218
Mikhail Putilov, 46
Mikhail of Klopskii, saint, shrine of, 172
Mikhail, son of Prince Aleksandr of Pskov, 118
Mikhailo Ivanovich Speshnev, *dvorianin*, 92, 93, 95, 96, 97, 285
Mikifor, archimandrite, 120
Milescu, Nikolae Spafarii, 218, 219
Miloslavskiis, 39, 40
Military Chancellery (formerly Office) (*Razriadnyi prikaz*), xxv, 48, 49, 50, 51, 53, 54, 92, 97, 101, 276
Misha, nephew of Afanasii Prokofiev, 192
Mitka, second husband of Oksana, 200–204
Mityukha, 256, 257
Moisei, Archbishop of Novgorod, 120, 125
Moisei Remezov, *syn boiarskii*, 218
Moislav, Novgorodian merchant, 119
Moldavian, Moldavians, 78, 156, 157, 160, 164, 218
Monahan, Erika, xxvi
Mongol, Mongols, 24, 26, 27, 28, 31, 32, 33, 109, 121, 124, 210
Mortimer, Ian, xxiv
Moscow, xxviii, 3, 5, 8, 9, 10, 12, 18, 20, 24, 27, 28, 30, 31, 32, 33, 39, 40, 41, 46, 47, 50, 52, 53, 59, 60, 61, 62, 63, 64, 65, 83, 84, 87, 92, 96, 97, 100, 107, 108, 109, 110, 119, 124, 132, 154, 156, 157, 158, 159, 160, 162, 163, 172, 179, 182, 184, 186, 190, 195, 196, 203, 213, 215, 216, 218, 219, 219, 220, 228, 229, 233, 236, 237, 241, 247, 250, 254, 258, 260, 261, 265, 267
Moscow River, 107, 255

Moses, 130, 214
Most Pure Virgin's Birth Monastery, 263
Mother of God, 235
Mother of God (*Bogomater*) Church, Snetogorsk Monastery, 120
Mother of God (*Bogomater*) Church, Zverin Monastery, 122
Mount Athos, 116, 119, 121, 139, 142
Mount Sinai, 155, 156, 158, 161, 162, 163
Mount Tabor, 130
Mozhaisk, 139, 142
Muhammed Yar, 16, 21
Mtsensk, 59
Mubaret-kerman, 74
Murom, 21
Musa, prince, 14, 18
Muscovy, Muscovite, Muscovites, xxiii, xxiv, xxv, xxvi, xxviii, 3, 6, 7, 11, 14, 16, 17, 18, 19, 20, 21, 22, 23, 24, 27, 29, 32, 33, 37, 38, 44, 48, 50, 52, 53, 54, 55, 58, 60, 61, 63, 64, 66, 67, 83, 87, 89, 91, 92, 97, 98, 100, 108, 129, 131, 139, 141, 149, 154, 156, 157, 158, 159, 161, 184, 189, 192, 194, 196, 197, 198, 209, 214, 218, 219, 222, 223, 226, 239, 240, 241, 243, 245, 247, 250, 252, 257, 260, 262, 272, 273, 279, 280, 286, 287
Muscovy Company, 237
Muslim, Muslims, 14, 21, 95, 96, 215, 218, 222, 223, 224, 225, 228, 229, 233, 235
Mussorgsky, Modest, 45
Mustreb-kerman, 74
My Brilliant Career, 71

Nadia Alekseeva *doch* Beklensheva, xxv, 73, 74, 75, 76, 78, 283, 285
Name of the Rose, The, xxiii
Narva, 74, 75, 76, 165, 169, 175, 220
Naryshkins, 39
Natalia Andreeva *doch* Beklensheva, 75
Natalia Naryshkina, Tsaritsa, 39
Nefimonovo, 50, 52
Nenets, *see* Voguls

Nerchinsk, Treaty of, 219, 223
Netherlands, 191
Neva River, 119, 121
Nevel, 89
New Commercial Code, 195, 196
New Israel, 218
New Jerusalem, 135, 218
New Mexico, University of, xxvi
New Savior (*Novospasskii*) Monastery, Krutitskii, 107
Nicholas, saint, 169, 202 (icon of)
Nikifor, 145
Nikifor Semenov *syn* Remezov, 220
Nikifor Vasiliev *syn* Pushechnikov, 50
Nikita, apprentice, 131–136
Nikita, librarian, 174
Nikita Andreevich Putilov, 50, 53, 54
Nikita (Nikitnikov) Lane, Moscow, 255
Nikita, saint, 256
Nikolskii, Nikolai, 149
Nikon, Patriarch, xxv, 105–115, 154, 155, 159, 161, 162, 163
Nikon Dementiev *syn*, 240, 241, 242
Nil Sinai, 171
Nil Sorskii, 145, 148
Nizhnii Novgorod, 24, 30, 31
Nizhyn, 158
Nogai, Nogais, 16, 17, 19, 95
Nogai Road, 92
Northeastern Passage, 211
Northern Dvina River, 240
Northern Sea, *see* White Sea
Noteburg, *see* Schlusselburg
Novaia Zemlia, 211
Novgorod, xxv, 11, 30, 31, 75, 76, 108, 116–126, 131, 141, 165, 167, 168, 169, 171, 172, 173, 174, 195, 233
Novgorod First Chronicle, 116, 126
Novgorod III Chronicle, 131
Nur Sultan, 16, 17
Nyenskans, 76

Ob River, 211, 212, 217, 223
Ochakov, 74
Oirats, 210, 227
Oka River, 250
Okat Parfiev *syn*, 235, 236, 237, 238, 239
Oksana, townswoman, xxvi, 198–205

Old Belief, Old Believers, 42, 114
Olearius, Adam, 38, 57, 180
Oleshenka Creek, 99
Oleshenskii bailliage, 98
Oleshka (Aleksander) Palkin, 139, 141–144, 145, 147, 148, 149, 153
Olga Dementieva *doch*, 240
Olgerd (Algerdas), Grand Prince of Lithuania, 121
Olmsted, Hugh M., xxvi, xxviii, 165
Ondreshko, 124
Onega, 145
Onega, Lake, 236
Ontsifor Lukinich, mayor, 124
Opoka, 121
Oprichnina, 7, 53, 54, 165, 174, 275
Orekhov, 119, 122
Orsha, 46
Orthodox Church, Orthodox Christian, xxvi, 7, 66, 78, 113, 131, 152, 154, 155, 156, 157, 158, 159, 160, 162, 164, 193, 214, 215, 223, 225, 228, 243, 245, 258, 259, 262, 266, 268, 273, 279
  Greek, 161
  Western, 273
Orthodox monasteries, 144
Orthodox Slavs, 141, 236, 288
Oshevenskii Monastery, 145
Ostafei Dvorianets, mayor of Novgorod, 121
Ostiak, 214, 220
Otnia Hermitage, 165, 171, 172
Ottoman, 18, 214
Ottoman empire, 73, 78, 106, 156, 157, 159, 160, 164, 227
Ottoman Turks, 39, 42, 72, 78, 101, 119, 156, 157
Ovdokim Vasiliev *syn* Skvortsov, 95, 282, 285

Pacific Ocean, xxviii
Panin bugr, 217
Pantocrator, 135
Papacy, 73
Papists, *see* Roman Catholics
Paradise, 214
Parfievs, xxvi, 233–242
Parfii, 235, 236, 237

Paris, 217
Pasha, blind beggar, 266
Pater, Walter, xxiii
Patericon, 174
Paul, apostle, 134 (icon of), 260
Pavel, Metropolitan of Sarai and the Don, xxv, 105–115
Pavel, Bishop of Kolomna, 111
Paul, Michael C., xxv
Pereiaslavl, 31, 123
Persia, Persian, Persians, 22, 214, 225, 288
Peter, apostle, 130, 134 (icon of)
Peter I, Alekseevich Romanov, Tsar, xxiii, xxviii, 39, 56, 73, 76, 77, 78, 79, 80, 81, 82, 196, 209, 218, 219, 226
Petr Alekseev *syn* **Shubalov**, 179–187, 285
Petr Goduov, governor, 225
Petr Ivanov *syn* Remezov, 220, 221
Petr Ivanovich Khovanskii, prince, 77
Petr Petrovich, tsarevich, 79
Philosophical Chapters, see *Dialectica*
Piana River, 31
Pilgrimage of Hegumen Daniil, 151
Pimin, Archbishop of Novgorod, 172
Piterburkh, *see* St. Petersburg
Pitirim, Partriarch, 113
Platonic, 143
Pleskau, *see* Pskov
Plymouth Adventure, xxiii
Poe, Marshall T., xxv, xxvii
Pokrovskoe, 93, 95
Poland, xxv, 39, 42, 51, 61, 79, 162
Poles, Polish 12, 42, 52, 77, 101, 108, 114, 157, 158, 160, 179, 191, 194, 241, 247
Polish-Lithuanian Commonwealth, 61, 73, 80, 87, 164, 189
Polotsk, 51, 52, 110
Poltava, battle of, 72, 77, 212
Pomerania, 79
Porkhov, 121
Potter, Cathy J., xxv, 105
Pouncy, Carolyn, xxvii
Pozharskii, Prince Dmitrii, 99
Praskovia, 254, 255, 256, 257, 263, 264, 265, 267

Preobrazhenskii Monastery, Tiumen, 227
Printing Office, 113, 156, 162
Prokhor of Gorodets, iconographer, 131, 134
Prokofievs, xxvi, 188–197
Prokofii, 188
Promised Land, 215, 218
Proshchenik, 118
Protection of the Most Holy Mother of God (*Pokrov presviatoi Bogoroditsy*) church, 97
Protestant, Protestants, 66, 88, 89, 168
Pruth River, 72, 78
Prutskii (also Prutskoi), Osip, clerk, 92, 95
Pskov, 29, 40, 74, 75, 76, 83, 116, 118, 119, 120, 121, 123, 165, 167, 171, 175, 195
Pskov-Eliazarov Monastery, 171
Pskov Caves Monastery, 171
Pushechnikovs, 50
Pushkin, Alexander, 45
Pushkin, Governor, 100, 101
Putivl, 156
Putilov Mikhailov, 44
Putilovs, 46

Qipchaq (Kipchak) khanate, 14, 24, 29, 30, 31, 33, 118, 123
Qur'an, 16, 20, 21

Rakoczy, 87
Reception of the Blessed Virgin's Icon, Church of the, 109
Red Sea, 214
Red Square, Moscow, 253, 255, 260
Reger, W.M. IV, xxv
Remezov, Semen Ulianovich, xxvi, xvii, 209–221, 281, 285
Renaissance, 66, 81
Repnin, Prince, 75
Resurrection, the, 135
Reval, 78
Revelation, Book of, *see* Bible, Revelation
Rhenish wine, 42
Rhode Island College, xxv
Riazan, 31, 48, 92, 95

Riazhsk, 92, 93, 97
Riga, 78, 79, 196
Rihla, 14
Riurik, 26
Riurikid dynasty, 26, 47
Rodion Afansiev *syn* Vorypaev, 97, 283, 285
Roman Dmitreevich Glebov, 9
Roman Fedorovich, 101
Roman Vasilievich, prince of Yaroslavl, 26, 28, 31, 34
Roman Catholics, Catholicism, 42, 78, 121, 125, 159, 189, 276
Roman empire, 40, 129
Romanchuk, Robert, xxv
Romania, 72
Romanovs, Romanov Dynasty, 162, 189
Rome, 159
Rostov, 26, 27, 30, 31, 139, 142
Royal Gates, 134
Rozhdestva Bogoroditsy pustyn, 254
Rus, xxv, xxviii, 15, 24, 25, 26, 29, 30, 31, 32, 33, 97, 98, 101, 105, 120, 123, 129, 131, 136, 139, 218, 219, 223, 252
Russe, Russes, 84, 85, 86, 87, 88, 89, 90
Russia, Russian, Russians, xxiii, xxiv, xxv, xxvi, xxvii, xxviii, 3, 7, 26, 28, 30, 31, 32, 33, 37, 44, 52, 53, 61, 64, 66, 67, 71, 72, 73, 74, 77, 78, 80, 81, 84, 85, 91, 94, 108, 109, 111, 112, 114, 115, 118, 125, 134, 139, 154, 155, 157, 158, 159, 160, 161, 162, 163, 164, 168, 169, 175, 179, 182, 188, 189, 191, 193–196, 211, 213, 215, 222, 223, 225, 226, 227, 228, 233, 235, 236, 239, 241, 242, 243, 245, 246, 249, 252, 255, 259, 260, 274, 276, 279, 280, 285–287
Russian empire, 105
Russian Orthodoxy, 16, 58, 66, 71, 74, 78, 87, 88, 89, 90, 91, 105, 117, 119, 120, 122, 125, 129, 133, 158, 166, 169, 171, 172, 174, 237, 241, 266, 276
Ruza, 49, 50, 52

Sagaidachnyi, Petro Konashevich, Hetman, 93
Sahib Girey, 18, 20
Said Mehmed, 14
Saif-i Sarai, 22
Samarkand, 33
Samoyed, 214
Sarai, 27, 28, 29, 31
Satan, 42, 135
Savior, Church of the, Novgorod, 131, 135
Savior, Church of the, Yaroslavl, 27, 28, 32
Savior on the Rock (Spaso-Kamennyi) Monastery, 139, 143
Savior Transfiguration Cathedral, Pereiaslavl-Zalesskii, 130
Savior Transfiguration Monastery, Yaroslavl, 26, 47, 54, 142
Savva Vasilievich Aigustov, Colonel, 74
Savvatii, saint, 166, 168, 172, 173, 234, 238, 240, 241
Saxony, 77
Scandinavian, 274
Schlusselburg, 75, 76
Scot, Scotsman, 82, 84
Semen Ivanovich, Grand Prince, 27, 28, 29, 122
Semen Likharev, 53
Semen Semenovich, prince, 29
Semen Semenov *syn* Remezov, *syn boiarskii*, 220, 221
Semen Vasilievich Prozorovskii, *okol'nichii*, 59
Serb, Serbian, Serbs, 116, 139, 141, 142, 156
Sergii (Sergius) of Radonezh, saint, 32, 139, 288
Serpukhov, 31, 48
Septuagint, 258
Service Land Chancellery (*Pomestnyi prikaz*), 56, 58, 59, 60, 61, 62, 63, 65, 275
Shah Ali (Shigalei), Khan, 18, 22
Shagin-kerman, 74
Shakh-kerman, 74
Shatsk, 92, 97
Shavtsov, Frol, 99

Sheikh Ahmed, 14
Shellabarger, Samuel, xxiii, xxviii
Shelon River, 116, 118
Sheremetev, Field marshal, *see* Boris Petrovich Sheremetev
Sheremetevs,
boyars, 49, 53
family, 245, 247, 248
Shirin clan, 18
Short Chronograph, 141
Shrovetide, 95
Shuiskiis, 53
Shuserin, Ivan Kornilievich, 1–8
Siberia, Siberian, xxvi, xxviii, 88, 159, 209–229, 250
Siberian Chancellery (*Sibirskii prikaz*), 218, 219, 223
Sibir, 18, 215, 223
Sigismund II, King of Poland, 50
Silk Roads, 222
Silvestr, 171
Simeon the Receiver of God church, 50
Simeon Polotskii, 110, 111, 113, 114, 115, 219
Simonov Monastery, 139
Simplicissimus, 91
Sign or Praying Virgin, icon of the, 168
Skomorakhov, 28
Slave Street, Novgorod, 120
Slavic, 146, 159
Slavonic, *see* Church Slavonic
Smith, Andrew, 81–91
Smolensk, 39
Smolensk War, 61, 97
Snevins, officer, 85
Sofia First Chronicle, 116, 139
Sofia Ivanova, fool for Christ, 263, 265
Sofonii of Riazan, 149
Solomon, OT king, 134, 150, 214
Solovki (Solovetskii) Monastery, xxvi, 164–176, 233–242
Sophia (Wisdom), 214, 215, 218
Icon of, 218
Sophia Alekseevna, Tsarevna, 39, 73, 281
Southern Connecticut, University of, xxvi
Soviet scholars, 223

INDEX   321

Spassky Gates, 65, 262
Spiridon Fomin *syn*, 245
Spock, Jennifer B., xxvi, 165
Spartacus, xxiii
St. Barbara's Church, Moscow, 255, 264–265, 266
St. Barbara's Gate, Moscow, 255, 260
St. Basil's Cathedral, 253, 255, 260
St. Catherine's Monastery, 154, 155, 156, 158, 161, 162, 163, 164
St. George's Day (November 26), 250
St. John the Evangelist, Church of, 120
St. Makarii of the Yellow Waters Monastery, 112
St. Nicholas, Church of, Arzamas, 181, 185
St. Nicholas on the Market, Church of, 123
St. Nicholas on the Nerev End, Church of, 124
St. Nicholas Monastery, 154, 160, 161
St. Nicholas's Day, 51
St. Nikita parish, 256
St. Paraskeva, Church of, 123
St. Pelageia Diveevskaia, 254
St. Petersburg, 76, 210, 219
Sts. Cosmas and Damian Church, 118, 120
Sancta Sophia Cathedral, Constantinople, 28
Sancta Sophia Cathedral, Novgorod, 120, 124
Sinai Desert, 214
Staeva Poliana, 99
Stanford University, xxvi
Starodub, 29
Stefan, Archbishop of Suzdal, 113
Stefan Konstiantinov *syn*, 239, 240, 241–2
Stepan (Stepych) Aleksandrov *syn* Palkin, 141, 285
Stettin, 72, 79
Stevens, Carol B., xxv, 90
Stoic philosophy, 143
Stone Mountains, *see* Ural Mountains
Stranger Office, 87
Stranger suburb, *see* Foreign Suburb
Stroev, Pavel M., 105
Stuart, 84

Sukhona River, 192
Suleiman, Sultan, 18, 22
Suma River, 233, 235
Sumskii Posad, 235, 236, 237, 239
Sura River, 31
Susanna, 83
Suzdal, 12, 24, 27, 29, 30, 31
Sweden, 61, 78, 189, 196, 220
Swedes, 12, 42, 72, 75, 77, 79, 119, 121, 211, 240, 241, 247
Swedish, 74, 75, 76, 77, 79, 119, 122, 125, 160, 175, 211, 219
Sweet Liberty, xxiv
Symeon the New Theologian, 171
Syrians, 28

Tabbert (later Strahlenberg), Philip, Captain, 211, 212
Taganrog, 74
Tale of Dracula, 149
Tamara Prokofieva, 188
Tamerlane, *see* Timur
Tara, 212, 215, 217, 222, 224
Tashkent, 214
Tashlykov, Ivan, 100
Tatar, Tatars, xxiv, xxv, xvii, 14, 15, 23, 25, 27, 39, 48, 51, 73, 76, 78, 84, 92, 94, 95, 97, 98, 101, 157, 160, 182, 210, 212, 213, 214, 215, 217, 227, 228, 229, 247, 272, 287, 288
Teleut, 227
Tengiz, lake, 213
Terem, 10, 11, 12
Texas, University of, at San Antonio, xxv
Theophanes the Greek, *see* Feofan Grek
Thessalonika, 119
Thirteen Years War, xxv, 61, 81, 91
Tikhon Afanasiev, 195, 196
Tikhon Zadonskii, 288
Tikhvin Convent of the Presentation of the Virgin in the Temple, 3, 12, 13
Tikhvin Mother of God (*Bogomater*) icon, 5–6
Time of Troubles (*smuta*), 12, 40, 43, 56, 59, 108, 154, 211, 242
Time Traveler's Guide to Medieval England, The, xxiv
Timur, 33, 109

Tiumen, 222, 224, 225, 227
Tobolsk, 209–221, 222, 223, 224, 225, 226, 227, 228
Tomilo Ivanov syn Ukolov, 96, 99, 283, 285
Tomsk, 212
Torzhok, 27, 123
Transfiguration, Church of the, Krutitskii, 107
Transfiguration, Church of the, Solovki, 170
Transfiguration of Christ, 130
Traurnikhts, 89
Tretyakov Gallery, Moscow, 130
Trifon, hegumen, 139, 141, 142, 143, 144, 145, 146, 147, 148, 152
Trinity, the, 124
Trinity Cathedral, Pskov, 120
Trinity Chronicle, 131
Trinity Monastery, Novgorod, 172
Trinity-St. Sergius Monastery, 32
Troitskoe, 182, 183
Trostenka Creek, 98
True Cross, 214
Tula, 95
Tulupovs, 9
Turchasov, 236, 239
Turkestan, 214
Turkic, Turkish, 74, 78, 225, 226, 245, 288
Turkish-Venetian War, 156
Turks, *see* Ottoman Turks
Turkey, 158
Tver, 24, 27, 30, 31, 131

Ufa, 214
Uglich, 31
Ukraine, Ukrainian, 72, 73, 74, 100, 162, 189, 288
Ulan, *mirza*
Ulian Moiseevich Remezov, 213, 215, 217, 225
Uliana, Sister, 267, 268
Uliana Grigorieva *doch* Remezova, 220
Ulozhenie, *see* Law Code of 1649
Ulug Mehmed, 16, 18, 288
Uniate, 78
Urasko Kaibulin, xxvi, 222–229
   ¬l Mountains, 210, 211, 218

Ural River, 214
Urliapovo Ford, 97
Uspenie (Resurrection) Church on Volotovo Field, 117
Uspenskii Cathedral, Moscow, 262
Uza River, 116, 118

Valley Forge, xxiii
van Kerkhoven, Colonel Justus, 90
van Rodenburg, Jan Cornelius, 97
Varlaam, hegumen, 173, 174
Varvara, Vasilieva *doch*, Remezova
Vazheozerskaia, 145, 147
Varvarka Street, Moscow, 255
Vasia, *see* Vasilii
Vassian Gusilov, scribe, 165
Vassian Toporkov, xxvii
Vasilii I, Dmitrievich, Grand Prince, 131
Vasilii II, Vasilievich, Grand Prince, 149
Vasilii III, Ivanovich, Grand Prince, 17, 19, 20, 21, 46
Vasilii, son of Melik-Tagir 14
Vasilii the Blessed (*Blazhennyi*), saint, 252, 253, 254, 260–263, 264, 269
Vasilii (Vasia) Afanasiev syn Prokofiev, 188–197
Vasilii Davidovich (the Dread), prince of Yaroslavl, 24, 26, 27, 34
Vasilii Grigoriev syn Zotov, xxv, 92–102
Vasilii Grigorievich Zakharov, 49, 51
Vasilii Ivanovich, boyar, 37–43
Vasilii Ivanovich Kolychev, 9
Vasilii Ivanovich Umnoi-Kolychev, 53
Vasilii Kalika, Archbishop, xxv, 116–126
Vasilii Kiprianov, councilar secretary, 186
Vasilii Semenovich Serebrianyi, prince, 51, 53
Vasilii Shchelkalov, 44, 53, 54
Vasilii Shuiskii, Tsar, 241
Vasilii Vasilievich, prince of Yaroslavl, 26, 31, 34, 281
Vasilii Vasilievich Glebov, xxvi, 179–187, 281
Vasilii Vasilievich Golitsyn, 73, 281, 285
Vasilii Vladimirovich Dolgorukii, prince, 77

INDEX   323

Vasilii Volotskii, 182, 183, 185, 186
Vasilii Vsevolodivich, prince, 34
Vasilii Gates, Novgorod, 116, 124
Vaska Fedorov *syn*, **first husband of Oksana**, 200
Vazheozerskaia, 145, 147
Velikie Luki, 51
Velikii Ustiug, 228
Venetians, 156, 160, 152
Venice, 73, 159, 163
Vera Afanasieva *doch* **Prokofieva**, 189
Verkhoturie, 223
Viatka, 111, 112, 224
Viazma, 50, 79
Vienna, 84, 87
Viking, The, xxiii
Vilno, 51
Vinius, Andrei Andreevich, 219, 220
Vinius, Andrei D., 212
Virgin's Intercession Convent, Black Lake, 263, 267, 268
Virgin's Intercession on Market Square, Church of, Moscow, 260, 262
Vladimir Andreevich, prince of Serpukov, 31, 32
Vladimir Sviatoslavich, Prince of Kiev, 33, 247
Vladimir-in-Volynia, 119, 120
Vladimir-on-the-Kliazma, 24, 26, 27, 29, 31, 40, 109
Vladimir Mother of God (*Bogomater*) icon, 168, 170
Vod, 121
Vodskaia Fifth (*piatina*), 122
Voguls, 217, 227
Volga Bulgars, *see* Bulgars, Volga
Volga River, 17, 26, 28, 30, 31, 189, 190, 191, 214, 215, 250, 283

Volkhov River, 123, 125
Volkonskiis, 54
Vologda, 192, 195, 263
Volok, 20
Volotovo Monastery, 165, 166, 171, 172, 173, 174, 175
Volotovo Dormition Cloister, 168
Volynia, 118, 121
Von Shonbek, Adam, General, 76
Voronezh, 96, 97
Voronezh Forest, 99
Voronezh River, 95, 99
 Lesnoi, 92
 Polnoi, 92, 97
Vsevolod Konstantinovich, prince, 34
Vyborg, 78

Wallachia, Wallachian, 78, 156, 157, 158, 160, 164
War College, 79
Washington, George, xxiii
Westminster College, xxiv
White Russia, *see* Belarus
White Sea, 119, 159, 192, 211, 233, 235, 236, 238, 240, 250
Wisdom, *see* Sophia
Witzenrath, Christoph, xxvi

Yaroslavl, xxiv, 24–34, 46, 47, 49, 50, 188–197, 224
You Are There, xxiii
Young Elizabeth, The, xxiii

Zadonshchina, 139, 149, 151
Zinovii (Otenskii), 171, 172
Zosima, (d. 1478), saint, 166, 168, 172, 173, 234, 238, 240